Morality and the Market
Consumer Pressure for Corporate
Accountability

Can businesses abandon the axiom that the customer is always right when consumers start questioning the ethics of business practices? The current debate about business ethics and the role of business in society has focused attention on corporate moral and commercial obligations. As a consequence, consumer sovereignty, and its use to determine ethical business practice, has become an important issue. In this stimulating review of the relationship between business and society, Professor Craig Smith examines the theory and practice of ethical purchase behaviour, a crucial mechanism for ensuring social responsibility in business. He explains how and why consumers, often in conjunction with pressure groups, have used their purchasing power to influence corporate policies and practices. He argues the case for the social control of business, drawing on perspectives from marketing, economics, politics, sociology, and business policy. In asking 'What decisions do consumers make in markets?', he concludes that the market may act as an arbiter of 'good' and 'bad' business practice.

Dr Smith considers the practical aspects of ethical purchase behaviour, focusing on consumer boycotts as a specific form of this consumer behaviour, and explaining how boycotted businesses should respond. Many supporting examples are provided, together with detailed case studies such as Barclays and South Africa, the California Grape Boycott, and Nestlé and the marketing of baby milk in Third World countries.

The author: N. Craig Smith is Lecturer in Marketing at Cranfield School of Management and Visiting Assistant Professor at Harvard Business School. He is the author of more than twenty publications on marketing management and business policy issues and has acted as a consultant for several large and medium-sized companies.

Consumer Research and Policy Series
Edited by Gordon Foxall

Also in the series
Consumer Psychology in Behavioural Perspective
Gordon Foxall

Morality and the Market

Consumer Pressure for Corporate Accountability

N. Craig Smith

London and New York

First published 1990
by Routledge
11 New Fetter Lane, London EC4P 4EE

Published simultaneously in the USA and Canada by
Routledge
a division of Routledge, Chapman and Hall, Inc.
29 West 35th Street, New York, NY 10001

New in paperback 1990

Typeset by LaserScript Ltd, Mitcham, Surrey.
Printed in Great Britain

British Library Cataloguing in Publication Data

Smith, N. Craig, 1958- .
    Morality and the Market : consumer pressure for corporate accountability
    1. Business firms. Policies of influence on consumers.
    I. Title II. Series
    658.4'012
ISBN 0-415-00437-3
        0-415-05821-X (Pbk)

Library of Congress Cataloging-in-Publication Data
applied for

TO MY MOTHER AND FATHER

Contents

Contents

Preface

I am sure as a consumer you have many stories you could relate about bad service or buying shoddy products. Our basic response to these problems – assuming they are not created for us by monopoly suppliers – is that we will go elsewhere next time and similarly advise others. Conversely, good experiences of products and service will promote loyalty and favourable recommendations. Marketing, as an area of study and practice, recognises this. Indeed, the essence of good marketing can be very simply expressed: it is to keep customers happy within the constraints of the organisation's resources and so as to realise its objectives.

The imperative of customer satisfaction is central to marketing thought and activity. I am hardly the first to acknowledge this; however, there has been little recognition to date of an interesting way in which this sovereignty of the consumer is being exercised. Friends of mine refuse to buy South African products, such as wine, Cape fruit, or clothing, unless there is no other alternative available. On the other hand, a Jewish friend will, where possible, buy Israeli products in preference to those of other countries – and she does not, of course, care for bacon! I am sure that, again, you know of other similar examples of this sort of behaviour, as practised by your friends and acquaintances and perhaps yourself. Ethical purchase behaviour even extends to the Royal Family. Prince Charles received considerable press coverage for his comment earlier this year that aerosols are banned from the Royal household. He is concerned about the damage to the ozone layer caused by the chlorofluorocarbons (CFCs) in aerosols.

Ethical purchase behaviour, as this study shows, amounts to consumer pressure for corporate accountability. It is the social control of business via the market. Prince Charles's comments about aerosols were made within a speech to the Royal Society urging companies to pay more attention to the environment. Companies involved in South Africa have found that their business suffers as a consequence. And these are just two examples.

There are long-standing historical precedents for ethical purchase behaviour; it is not a new phenomenon. However, within the growing concern about business practices it must be seen as one mechanism for ensuring social responsibility in business. In employing market forces it is particularly appropriate to what, in Britain at least, may best be described as a post-socialist society. Recent events have highlighted a lack of ethics in business, financial scandals involving Ivan Boesky and others, in the United States and in the United Kingdom. This current concern about business ethics extends beyond the City of London. Disasters involving substantial loss of life, the Zeebrugge ferry sinking, the King's Cross Underground fire, and the Bhopal gas explosion are partly, if not largely, attributable to poor management and a failure by the managers concerned adequately to look after the welfare of those for whom they were responsible, as various inquiries have indicated. Yet these disasters are only the more manifest symptoms of a much larger problem, that of the relationship between business and society and how society can ensure that business delivers what is in society's best interests. This study points to the actual and potential role of consumer sovereignty within this control process.

Morality and the Market is the outcome of more than six years research and reflection. During this time many people have helped me and I am grateful to them. I would, in particular, like to mention Professor Gordon Foxall, an excellent doctoral supervisor and now a good friend. I have also received a lot of support from Professor Martin Christopher and my other colleagues at Cranfield. I am especially grateful to Martin for not dismissing this work as unimportant within a business school context – a reaction I found when presenting some of my research at another major UK business school, whose faculty seem only able to understand business problems in terms of their impact on net present value. Finally, a big thank you is due to Derry Young and to Tracey Bolton for the production of the book and for being patient with both me and the script!

Craig Smith
Cranfield School of Management
Cranfield
Bedford
England

Introduction

Preview

You'll have to get off the land. The ploughs'll go through the dooryard.

And now the squatting men stood up angrily. Grampa took up the land, and he had to kill the Indians and drive them away. And Pa was born here, and he killed weeds and snakes. Then a bad year came and he had to borrow a little money. An' we was born here. There in the door – our children born here. And Pa had to borrow money. The bank owned the land then, but we stayed and we got a little bit of what we raised.

We know that – all that. It's not us, it's the bank. A bank isn't like a man. Or an owner with fifty thousand acres, he isn't like a man either. That's the monster.

Sure, cried the tenant men, but it's our land. We measured it and broke it up. We were born on it, and we got killed on it, died on it. Even if it's no good, it's still ours. That's what makes it ours – being born on it, working it, dying on it. That makes ownership, not a paper with numbers on it.

We're sorry. It's not us. It's the monster. The bank isn't like a man.

Yes, but the bank is only made of men.

No, you're wrong there – quite wrong there. The bank is something else than men. It happens that every man in the bank hates what the bank does, and yet the bank does it. The bank is something more than men. I tell you. It's the monster. Men made it, but they can't control it.

John Steinbeck
The Grapes of Wrath

Are companies monsters? Are they creations of people, but beyond our control? Steinbeck's concern with the ravages of capitalism, particularly its dehumanising effects, is well expressed in *The Grapes of Wrath*. Yet capitalism has brought much good to Western society. As the West re-embraces capitalism and moves into what might, in the UK at least, be described as a post-socialist society, questions about the role and effects of business become increasingly pertinent. This study considers the social control of business and examines ethical purchase behaviour as a mechanism employed to achieve this end. Consumer sovereignty, a central feature of capitalism, is the key to this mechanism and to the study. This introduction points to the role and dimensions of consumer sovereignty within consumer pressure for corporate accountability. It discusses the possibilities for the use of such pressure – ethical purchase behaviour – on the specific issue of sex-role stereotypes in advertising, the starting-point for this study. An overview of the book concludes the introduction.

Consumer pressure for corporate accountability

Ethical purchase behaviour

What decisions do consumers make in markets? In command economies decisions on the allocation of resources are centralised and made by the state. In market economies these decisions are decentralised and made by 'the people'. Consumers under capitalism are, according to the ideology, the decision-makers on the allocation of society's resources. This study considers this notion by looking at some of the ethical decisions consumers make – or could make – in markets. It is a study therefore of ethical purchase behaviour, a form of behaviour with profound implications for the relationship between business and society.

Ethical purchase behaviour abounds! It can be seen everywhere. It can be found in industrial markets as well as consumer markets. It is practised by people of all ages, classes and nationalities. Yet it is largely unrecognised in the literature. Ethical purchase behaviour can mean people not buying a certain product. There are one million vegetarians in Britain, all choosing not to buy meat for ethical reasons.[1] During the Falklands crisis many people chose not to buy Argentinian products, such as corned beef and wine. Ethical purchase behaviour can also mean a deliberate restriction of choice in purchase behaviour. People often prefer to buy domestically produced goods. Many private and fleet car buyers will still only buy British cars. However, ethical purchase behaviour is not always as straightforward and clear-cut as this. While in some cases ethical concerns will dictate that a specific product (meat) must not be bought, or that a specific product must be bought (British cars), in other cases ethical concerns are one influence among a number in the purchase decision. This is neatly illustrated in the following quotation: 'Times are surely hard for the consumer with a conscience. That Chilean wine may have a military bouquet, but can we afford the alternative?'[2]

Of course, it has long been recognised in the marketing literature that there may be many influences on purchase behaviour, buyer characteristics in particular. Ethical concerns do not, however, appear to have been specifically identified, at least not in the broad sense intended here. Some forms of ethical purchase behaviour, such as ecologically concerned consumption, have been examined. (This very limited work is considered in Chapter 6.)

The less straightforward type of ethical purchase behaviour, where purchases are influenced by ethical concerns but these concerns are not so strong as to override all other concerns, suggests the product is a bundle of considerations, concerns, or attributes in the eye of the consumer. Such a conception of the product is not new, but as is shown in Chapter 6, there may be negative product attributes as well as the conventionally identified positive ones. In other words, the product is more accurately conceived as a package of costs as well as benefits for the consumer, with ethical considerations being possible costs or benefits. One way of acknowledging that products may have undesirable characteristics in addition to desirable ones is to use the term 'offering' instead of 'product'. Hence, one could say, *some* offerings will for *some* people have ethical dimensions. The outcome in such cases is ethical purchase behaviour. However, the use of the term 'product' will predominate, meaning both products and services, to conform with common usage.

Ethical purchase behaviour is all-pervasive. But it is not always readily identifiable. After having presented the argument for ethical purchase behaviour therefore – and to delimit the investigation appropriately – this study examines one specific form of ethical purchase behaviour. This form is clearly identifiable and readily accessible, and the most manifest and deliberate form of ethical purchase behaviour: pressure group organised consumer boycotts. These boycotts of business are where people choose not to buy certain offerings as part of an organised boycott action.

Consumer sovereignty is the key to this study. It is the basis for the argument. It is, moreover, the rationale for capitalism, the political-economic system in the West. The legitimacy of such a system rests on whether and what decisions are made in markets. Hence the argument for ethical purchase behaviour becomes an argument for capitalism. A vital point which this study will emphasise is simply the significance of asking questions about the extent of consumer sovereignty, such as the question above about the decisions made by consumers in markets; questions which generally attempt to assess consumer authority in the market-place. By referring to how much competition there is, such questions are usually considered to be answered. Here, in contrast, the concern is not so much with the amount of authority the buyer has *vis-à-vis* the seller, though that is important, but with the domain of that authority. Put otherwise, it is not the degree of consumer sovereignty, how much influence the buyer has, but the issues over which the buyer may have influence.

Consider a simple example. Consumers may choose to buy Israeli oranges in preference to South African oranges because they taste better or are cheaper. They may, alternatively, choose to buy Israeli oranges in preference because they do not wish to support apartheid. In either case there must be consumer choice, there must be competition to provide some degree of consumer sovereignty. The domain of consumer sovereignty, however, refers to whether consumers can only express concern about such features as the price, colour, or taste of the product, or whether they can express concern about much wider issues. Country of origin, dubious activities of the firm in some remote sphere of its operations, and many other ethical considerations can feature in purchase behaviour. Whether they do – or whether they could – depends on the domain of consumer sovereignty.

Ethical purchase behaviour is identified here. Such behaviour prompts this novel perspective on consumer sovereignty. Why and how this behaviour should occur, and its implications, are explored in the study. The importance of this topic relates to the relationship between business and society and specifically the social *control* of business, for ethical purchase behaviour amounts to consumer pressure for corporate accountability.

Sex-role stereotypes in advertising – the starting-point

The starting-point for this study was an investigation of the issue of sex-role stereotypes in advertising. A brief overview of the issue and the conclusions reached will quite adequately serve as an explanation of the study origins and their part in formulating the questions addressed here.

Criticism of sex-role stereotypes in the media stems largely from the influence these stereotypes are claimed to have on society. Such criticism is frequently polemic, with one writer, for example, claiming 'the mass media moulds everyone'.[3] Feminist critics are of the opinion that the meanings reflected and reinforced within advertising portraying or directed to women are distinctly undesirable. They see advertising as yet another determinant of a sexist status quo.[4] More reasoned or, at least, less overtly angry criticism, comes from those working in the area of sex-role formation. Current theories on sex-role formation largely attribute the sex-role to social rather than biological determinants,[5] and advertising plays a part in this process.[6] These arguments about the influence of advertising are widely accepted. Research on the content of advertising confirms that traditional sex-role stereotypes prevail;[7] while socialisation theories and research on sex-role formation and sex-role stereotypes support the idea that such stereotypes have an effect.[8] Even some advertisers are prepared to acknowledge this.[9] However, they suggest advertising has to reflect majority attitudes, that it must be congruent with the market segment with which it is intended to communicate.[10]

What is at issue here? If one accepts that traditional sex-role stereotypes in advertising are socially undesirable, one would conclude that advertisers are not behaving in a socially responsible manner, that they are not acting in society's best interests. The issue is concerned with social responsibility in business. What remedies does society have? Advertisers could be coerced by legislation. This seems extremely unlikely, not least because of the difficulties of legislating, short of banning all advertising. Could advertisers then be persuaded to adjust their advertising voluntarily? Advertising is more heavily criticised than the rest of the media for the use of traditional sex-role stereotypes. This may be because advertising is the worst offender or because the critics of sex-role stereotypes have a more general dislike for advertising. But it is at least partly due to the concern that advertising is selling sexism as well as the product featured. The irony is that consumers seem to buy it. So advertising is not likely to change through advertisers voluntarily meeting the wishes of their critics, unless, of course, traditional portrayals were found to be detrimental to advertising effectiveness.

This interrelationship between the audience and the media, and advertising in particular, is acknowledged in a report for UNESCO by Gallagher. She concludes that women should be more concerned with changes in the political and economic structure – matters of far greater importance – than in the media. But at the same time, it should, if possible, be ensured that the media does not lag behind the broader social system: 'For even if the media cannot be expected to initiate change, they can certainly be expected to reflect it.' She asks whether (and which) mechanisms can be developed to ensure the currency of the media.[11] Her questions reflect a concern for the social control of business. But as far as advertising is concerned, it would seem that an appropriate mechanism already exists. Jane Reed, as editor in chief of *Woman*, says that she is not greatly worried about 'the mildly sexist ads that do appear now – using female stereotypes and traditional female concepts'. This is because 'advertising is about selling things, and if the advertisement misses the mark – through adopting the wrong sell-line, image or target – then it is the manufacturer who should worry'.[12] Moreover, if advertisers carry on regardless, the market can be employed deliberately to put the matter to rights by using the consumer boycott. As Beasley and Silver write, 'Pressure has been applied on advertisers through demonstrations, mail and telephone complaints, and, in some cases, boycotting of a product marketed via a sexist ad. Advertisers have yielded to the pressure, knowing that women spend more dollars in the American marketplace than men or teenagers.'[13]

So this author concluded that the problem – if one sees it as such – of sex-role stereotypes in advertising could not be directly resolved. Furthermore, advertisers, if doing their job properly, could not be criticised for not being socially responsible, because of the self-regulating role of the market. The market ensures social control of business (in this case, advertisers). As Baroness Lockwood, former Chairman (*sic*) of the Equal Opportunities Commission, suggests in a research report on *Adman and Eve:* 'there need be no conflict of interests between those whose job it is to sell, and those who seek to further equality of opportunity in our society.'[14] With wider adoption of feminist thinking or perhaps simply changes in the roles of women, the traditional sex-role stereotypes in advertising will, of necessity, largely disappear.[15] The issue is not so much resolved as dismissed. However, this is only so long as one accepts the market as an effective mechanism for the social control of business. Put otherwise, it assumes consumer sovereignty can ensure social responsibility in business.

Many, if not most, would accept this is the case. With advertisers in particular, the concern for effective communication must make the interests of the consumer of overriding importance. Given a marketing orientation, one could argue that such an observation surely applies with equal force to all elements of the marketing mix. After all, this is what capitalism and free competitive markets are all about. This is expressed in the following quotation from Thomas A. Murphy, as Chairman of General Motors:

> competitive markets and free consumer choice could be relied on
> to set an economic course which would maximise human welfare
> ... The individual citizen has great capacity to modify his
> consumption patterns through free markets. If he does not like one
> product, he can choose any of several other possibilities – or none
> at all ...[16]

This idea of 'purchase votes' (as Gist[17] and others put it) for expressing preferences in product markets as conveyed above is what is explored in this study. In particular, the interest is with the expression – and realisation – of preferences on what may be referred to as issues of social responsibility in business. As is apparent, such an expression of preferences is described here as ethical purchase behaviour. However, the focus of the study is on the more deliberate attempts to realise these preferences in markets, in consumer boycotts. As this discussion of such an approach to the issue of sex-role stereotypes in advertising shows, one is a part of the other; consumer boycotts are a form of ethical purchase behaviour.

The idea of purchase votes on social responsibility issues is not in principle new, in practice or in theory. It has, however, not been conceptualised as here. Neither has it been subjected to much objective criticism. A major reason for this is that the view of the market expressed is ideological. The market philosophy – belief in the market and all that goes with it – is, moreover, probably the most dominant ideology in the West. The conclusion above on sex-role stereotypes in advertising makes certain assumptions about how the market operates: advertising which lacks congruity with its audience may not only fail to communicate the intended message, but may also communicate something entirely unintended – the sexism in the advertising may be seen as part of the offering and the offering as well as the communication is rejected. The advertising expenditure then gives no return or possibly a negative return; it is at least less effective than it might be. The result is competitive disadvantage. The requirement to maximise competitive advantage is in accord with the survival of the fittest notion and affects all the company's activities. So those competing in the market, to ensure their survival, would seek to maximise their competitive advantage by adjusting their advertising in line with social change, or changing any other activity that likewise influences competitiveness. Pursued to its logical conclusion, such an argument suggests that the market mechanism, in demanding efficiency, may also as a consequence pass judgement on social practices of firms – be an arbiter of 'good' and 'bad'. But does the market 'really' operate in this way? What evidence, if such may be obtained, is there for these claims?

Advertising effectiveness, like the effectiveness of most of the promotional elements of the marketing mix, is notoriously difficult to measure. As Wight wryly observes, 'if sales go up, it's because of the advertising; if they go down it's because of something else'.[18] Indeed, advertisers, with support from marketing academics, like to distance themselves from measures of the sales effectiveness of advertising, preferring awareness or some other proxy variable. This is justifiable. Advertising must be assessed against the objectives set, even if the long-term overall objective is to sell the product. However, this does illustrate one difficulty in suggesting advertisers are accountable to the market. Understanding the way advertising is produced casts further doubts on claims about market pressure for effectiveness.[19]

There are more important and generalisable factors. Probably most important is the degree of consumer sovereignty, that is, the amount of competition. Some markets are highly competitive, many less so, and some not at all. There is also the requirement for consumer information, not only of competitive offerings but about the alleged grievance, the social practices of concern. Consumers do not all have an equal vote and not all are enfranchised on all issues. They may not even wish to use their vote when it is contrary to their economic self-interest. To some, the idea of the market as an arbiter of good and bad is sacrilege, if not dangerous, for the market is assumed to be at its most efficient where decisions are guided solely by self-interest. But, of course, self-interest need not be so narrowly defined as to exclude non-economic considerations;[20] though it might still be argued that if consumers are prepared to define their self-interest quite widely – perhaps as enlightened self-interest – then this distorts the market mechanism, entailing inefficiency. Another factor is that competitive advantage is the outcome of an aggregate of company efforts; some inefficiencies – such as ineffective advertising – may continue either because they are counterbalanced by greater efficiency in other areas or because they are hidden or unknown. Further factors include company accountability to other constituencies such as employees and/or unions (an influence even if the consumer takes precedence); government intervention and consumer dependence on and expectation of government action on misdemeanours; and the conflicts in the consumer choice process.

So there are many weaknesses to the proposition that the way the market operates will ensure changes in advertising portrayals of women in line with social change. They cannot all be considered here. What this study attempts to do is to show how the market *can* operate in this way, by providing an argument in justification and part explanation of ethical purchase behaviour, and some evidence. For this author, having come to the conclusions stated on the issue of sex-role stereotypes in advertising, then looked for evidence that consumer sovereignty could ensure social responsibility in business – and on issues more remote from the consumer's purchase behaviour than advertising content. In so doing, the concept of ethical purchase behaviour was developed and a role for pressure groups identified in the marketing system.

An overview of the book

Ethical purchase behaviour occurs where people are influenced in purchase by ethical concerns. This may mean a specific product must be bought, or must not be bought, or involve ethical concerns as one factor in the purchase decision. The study is delimited by concentrating on the most clearly identifiable, accessible, and deliberate form of ethical purchase behaviour: pressure group organised consumer boycotts. This is where people do not buy a specific product as part of an organised boycott action. Although fairly commonplace, ethical purchase behaviour is not really recognised in the relevant literature. Yet it is important not simply as a form of consumer behaviour, but, in its implications, in three other quite major ways which constitute the dominant themes within the study. First, a role for pressure groups is indicated in the provision of information for the awareness and understanding which is necessary for ethical purchase behaviour (though it is acknowledged that this information may come from other sources). Second, ethical purchase behaviour constitutes an attempt at the social control of business via the market. Finally, it suggests a novel perspective on consumer sovereignty, drawing attention to the domain of consumer authority in the market-place. In so doing, it raises questions on what decisions consumers make or could make in markets and thereby, in its absence, may challenge consumer sovereignty as the rationale for capitalism.

Accordingly, three major questions are addressed here. First, at the practical level: How may pressure groups most effectively employ the consumer boycott tactic and how should boycotted businesses respond? Guidelines for action are suggested on the basis of previous studies of pressure group tactics, descriptions of consumer boycott actions given in the literature, and empirical work. The empirical work consists of survey research on boycotts of business and five case studies of consumer boycotting based on primary and secondary data. Second, and at a more conceptual level of abstraction, there is the concern with describing and to some extent explaining ethical purchase behaviour. This is expressed in the question: Can consumer sovereignty ensure social responsibility in business and in what way? The answer lies largely in the argument which follows in Part One of the book. Finally, at the highest, philosophical level of abstraction: How far does consumer sovereignty extend? This question is about whether and what decisions consumers make in markets.

The study is presented in two parts. Following a general introduction, Part One provides an analysis of the case for ethical purchase behaviour and the social control of business. Part Two looks at consumer boycotts, a specific form of ethical purchase behaviour, providing evidence for the argument given. The book ends with some general conclusions.

Ethical purchase behaviour and the social control of business

Chapter one

Capitalism and consumer sovereignty

Preview

> What is the difference between capitalism and communism?
> Capitalism is the exploitation of man by man; communism is the
> reverse.
>
> Polish joke[1]

> every individual ... neither intends to promote the public interest ...
> he intends only his own gain, and he is in this, as in many other
> cases, led by an invisible hand to promote an end which was no
> part of his intention.
>
> Adam Smith[2]

This chapter looks briefly at the form of political-economic systems and
then examines capitalism, the form predominant in the West. It is
concluded that the rationale for capitalism is consumer sovereignty.
This is demonstrated by exploring the origins of capitalism and, more
importantly, the competitive model of capitalism, the dominant
interpretation of capitalism. However, there are other interpretations
and these are briefly considered. According to the competitive model of
capitalism, the individual's pursuit of self-interest results in the welfare
of the community, as indicated in the famous quote above from Adam
Smith. Capitalism provides material progress, but also economic and
political freedom. This is both achieved by and expressed in consumer
sovereignty. Consumer sovereignty as the rationale for capitalism and
the degree to which it exists is the theme of this chapter.

While this feature of consumer sovereignty is shown to underlie
classical economic thought, it is found to be questioned in later
economic thought which emphasises the concept as a technical term;
whereas in marketing, it is found that consumer sovereignty is central to
the marketing concept. This rigid and theoretically suspect application

of consumer sovereignty to marketing is shown to be a consequence of the ideological basis of marketing thought. Consumerism is briefly considered in illustration of this. Not surprisingly, this whole area is clouded by ideology. The conclusion is that despite the impact of one's ideological position in assessing consumer sovereignty, it may at least be presumed that it is both the rationale for capitalist systems and does exist in some form and to varying degrees in different markets.

So this chapter demonstrates the significance of consumer sovereignty in capitalist societies, but raises doubts as to its substance. The scene is then set for the examination of the social control of business and the consumer's role in this, the theme of Chapters 2 and 3. Equally important though is the identification in this chapter of a philosophical basis for ethical purchase behaviour, including consumer boycotts. Consumer sovereignty is here examined from a quite radical perspective and shown to be about the decisions made in markets. As explained in the Introduction, the degree of consumer sovereignty refers to whether decisions are made by consumers in markets – to who makes those decisions. The domain of consumer sovereignty refers to the issues involved – to what those decisions are or encompass. If this latter notion is accepted, then there is recognition given to the possibility of ethical decisions in purchase behaviour.

Political-economic systems

The role of the market in a society is the major distinguishing feature in identifying the form of the political-economic system. Western society is characterised by the extent to which the market predominates. This system is then justified in terms of efficiency and the freedom of the individual. Central to markets, and a necessary feature for the achievement of these benefits, is consumer sovereignty. Capitalism, consumer sovereignty, and the benefits which accrue are then inextricably linked.

In the Preface to his treatise on the world's political-economic systems, Lindblom writes: 'Aside from the difference between despotic and libertarian governments, the greatest distinction between one government and another is in the degree to which market replaces government or government replaces market. Both Adam Smith and Karl Marx knew this.'[3] The role of the market is then a major political and economic issue. Economics texts, while tending not to be concerned with the political aspects, observe that the form of an economy will tend toward one or the other of the two possible extremes of the free-market economy and the centrally controlled or command economy. Neither of these two extremes has ever existed, at least in recent history, and in practice all economies are mixed economies with some decisions taken by firms and households and some by central authorities.[4]

Accepting Mills's definition of power as 'to do with whatever decisions men make about the arrangements under which they live, and about the events which make up the history of their period',[5] this observation on decision-making indicates the political significance of the form of the economy. This is because the form of the economy determines the locus of power within society. Hence the distinction between politics and economics is in this way arbitrary; a distinction which did not exist when economics was political economy. Although simplistic (and in accord with Western ideology), it can be claimed that decisions are decentralised and in the hands of 'the people' in a free-market form of economy, and centralised and in the hands of the state in a command form of economy.[6] Western economists claim that the mixed economy in the West, which has a tendency toward the free-market extreme and is known as capitalism, is more efficient. Western politicians, not surprisingly, tend to agree with them, and claim that capitalism also means greater freedom. As Galbraith puts it: 'Its solution of the problem of efficiency was what commended the competitive model to the economist ... For the businessman and the political philosopher, by contrast, the appeal of the competitive model was its solution of the problem of power'.[7]

Decentralised decision-making expressed in markets means consumer sovereignty. This book is fundamentally concerned with whether and what decisions are made in markets. A major question it asks is: How far does this sovereignty extend? Consumer sovereignty as the rationale for capitalism is implied above and is argued in more detail in what follows. This chapter then considers the degree of consumer sovereignty; though, of course, the whole issue is plagued by ideology. Subsequent chapters then, in essence, examine the domain of consumer sovereignty. The importance of establishing the extent of consumer sovereignty is self-evident. It strikes not only at the core of economic and marketing thought, but also, as this section has shown, at the legitimacy of market society.

The origins of capitalism

Capitalism, progress, and freedom

The development of capitalism has brought two fundamental features to Western society: progress, in the form of continual improvements in the standard of living for much of the population; and economic and political freedom. This, at least, is the claim by Western economists; though some might question the human costs of these features and dispute the claim that capitalism entails political freedom. These two features are briefly examined below and then shown to be a consequence of the development of capitalism.

It is difficult to dispute the claim that material progress is a consequence of capitalism. Mises describes his *Human Action* as a treatise on economics, but it is perhaps more accurately described as an eloquent argument for capitalism. Yet one cannot but agree with his observations on the material progress benefits of capitalism:

> The system of market economy has never been fully and purely tried. But there prevailed in the orbit of Western civilization since the Middle Ages by and large a general tendency toward the abolition of institutions hindering the operation of the market economy. With the successive progress of this tendency, population figures multiplied and the masses' standard of living was raised to an unprecedented and hitherto undreamed of level. The average American worker enjoys amenities for which Croesus, Crassus, the Medici, and Louis XIV would have envied him.[8]

Heilbroner and Thurow's description of the origins of capitalism further confirms this, as will be seen. Freedom, however, is altogether a more complicated feature to establish. As Mises observes, 'Freedom and liberty always refers to interhuman relations',[9] but are they, as he claims, only obtainable within a market society?

> There is no kind of freedom and liberty other than the kind which the market economy brings about. In a totalitarian hegemonic society the only freedom that is left to the individual, because it cannot be denied to him, is the freedom to commit suicide.[10]

For Mises, there is no distinction between the economic sphere and the non-economic sphere. Freedom means economic freedom – which invites the Marxist criticism that one's personal worth amounts only to one's exchange value, a point considered later. Friedman is more circumspect, permitting economic and political freedom: 'Economic freedom is an essential requisite for political freedom. By enabling people to co-operate with one another without coercion or central direction, it reduces the area over which political power is exercised.'[11] This amounts to the same argument, however. As Mises explains, 'Government means always coercion and compulsion and is by necessity the opposite of liberty. Government is a guarantor of liberty and is compatible with liberty only if its range is adequately restricted to the preservation of economic freedom.'[12] This is an extreme perspective. But this, perhaps in a more diluted form, is the argument of all advocates of capitalism; for it is posited on the recognition, expressed above, that societies can best be distinguished on the degree to which the market replaces government, or vice versa, and on the assumption that freedom is determined by this. Mises describes how freedom is a consequence of the market and the form which it takes:

> The freedom of man under capitalism is an effect of competition. The worker does not depend on the good graces of an employer. The consumer is not at the mercy of the shopkeeper. He is free to patronize another shop if he likes. Nobody must kiss other people's hands or fear their disfavour. Interpersonal relations are businesslike. The exchange of goods and services is mutual; it is not a favour to sell or to buy, it is a transaction dictated by selfishness on either side.[13]

While acknowledging that every person is, as a producer, ultimately dependent on the demands of consumers – because of consumer sovereignty – he or she is, even in this, 'free to choose'. However, 'He may have to pay a price for conviction.'[14] (Ethical purchase behaviour may therefore come at a price!)

But freedom can have many other meanings. Hayek argues that socialism's promise of freedom from necessity, another meaning of freedom, was only another name for the old demand for an equal distribution of wealth.[15] He elaborates, in a manner similar to Mises:

> The economic freedom which is the prerequisite of any other freedom cannot be the freedom from economic care which the socialists promise us and which can be obtained only by relieving the individual at the same time of the necessity and of the power of choice; it must be the freedom of our economic activity which, with the right of choice, inevitably also carries the risk and responsibility of that right.[16]

The Austrian and Chicago schools of economists do not have a monopoly on the definition of freedom. However, this view of freedom is basic to what shall later be described as the competitive model of capitalism. This model is dominant within business and probably society as a whole. Therefore, accepting the limitations and simplicity of this position, it will be assumed that the concept of freedom is as Mises, Friedman and Hayek claim: the freedom to choose in the market. This is thought to be in keeping with the dominant ideology, but is also a satisfactory position for this study, as will become apparent.

The road from serfdom

Given this all too brief examination of freedom (though it is to be considered further), it is possible to trace the origins of capitalism and sensibly assess these features of progress and freedom, with the past as a standard for comparison. A perspective on the past offers a standard for comparison that is different to and supportive of comparisons with other possible political-economic systems but perhaps less ideologically tainted than comparisons with current and competing political-economic systems, such as communism. Heilbroner and Thurow's description of the origins of capitalism is used here.[17] It is not sophisticated; Polanyi, for example, is far more detailed and analytical.[18] However, they do convey the basic features, as follows.

Capitalism is not 'as old as the hills', as some claim. Societies prior to the sixteenth century lacked two special characteristics of capitalism: the institution of private property and a market system. Non-capitalist societies recognised the right of some individuals to own wealth, but the idea that a person's property was inviolate was not acknowledged and none of these societies accorded the right of ownership to all persons. Slaves were a common, if not predominant feature of most precapitalist systems. Markets did exist prior to capitalism, but most production and distribution took place according to the dictates of tradition or the orders of a lord: 'Markets were the ornaments of society, tradition and command its iron structure.'[19] Freedom, in the sense earlier described, was not a relevant concept. Peasants were subject to the commands of their lords; the right to withhold one's labour could not be conceived. Money-making was close to sin and society's wealth was owned by the powerful, not the rich. Indeed, riches flowed from power, not power from riches. Economic life was stable for economic positions were fixed, and a comparison of Greek technology to that of the fifteenth century shows how little material progress took place over a thousand years, which ensured these fixed economic positions, but was perhaps a consequence too. So the revolutions which produced capitalism brought a phenomenal change to the world. The gradual and often violent dismantling of the feudal way of life under the 'ancien regime' gave rise to economic freedom. But this was a two-edged sword:

> For the up-and-coming bourgeois merchants, it was the passport to
> a new status in life. Even for some of the poorest classes, the
> freedom of economic contract was a chance to rise from a station
> in life from which, in earlier times, there had been almost no exit.
> But economic freedom also had a harsher side. This was the
> necessity to stay afloat by one's own efforts in rough waters where
> all were struggling to survive.[20]

The material progress which came as a consequence of capitalism was realised through the unleashing of technology. There was no incentive to innovate in precapitalist society. The technology of the time, while lavished on the needs of the ruling class – in the building of the Egyptian pyramids, for example – did not touch common, everyday (productive) work. It was competition in the free-for-all of the market that brought the incentive to innovate – so as to maximise competitive advantage. Capitalism gave rise to a gradual but sustained increase in the standard of living, particularly with the industrial revolution and the recognition of the efficiency advantages of the division of labour. Heilbroner and Thurow warn against arguments, such as those by Mises and Friedman above, that capitalism either guarantees or is necessary for political freedom. While they would not claim that political freedom is a consequence of capitalism, they do concede that 'Along with the emergence of the market system we find a parallel and supporting emergence of more open, libertarian political ways of life.'[21]

In short, then, capitalism supplanted feudalism or similar systems of oppression (as they would be described from current perspectives), providing the benefits (and costs) of material progress and freedom. Vital to this is the role of consumer sovereignty. And it is this historical perspective, the understanding of this as expressed in the theory of classical capitalism, and the comparison of contemporary capitalism with socialist/communist systems, that leads *laissez-faire* advocates to criticise the government intervention in the market which (they claim) threatens consumer sovereignty. Such intervention is, as Hayek puts it, *The Road to Serfdom*. Accordingly, Heilbroner and Thurow conclude: 'from the beginning, capitalism has been characterised by a tension between *laissez-faire* and intervention ... that tension continues today.'[22] However, before considering the theory of classical capitalism as expressed in the competitive model of capitalism, it is useful to consider some of the other interpretations of capitalism. These other views, although they do not dispute the material progress of capitalism, do question this view of freedom and the supposed benefits of capitalism. There are also, despite the rosy impression given above, drawbacks to the competitive model, acknowledged by its advocates and others. The main drawbacks need also to be considered. So consumer sovereignty as the rationale for capitalism has been proposed and found plausible. To what extent does this stand up to closer analysis?

Models of capitalism

Economics and the real world

The competitive model of capitalism prevails. Those that understand capitalism in this way are believers in the market, advocates of the market philosophy, one of the most dominant ideologies in Western society. The thesis expressed in this book is largely conceived within such a framework. Yet this does not permit ignorance of other interpretations of capitalism. Although the following sections are cursory, they illustrate the possibility for other views. Moreover, the argument proposed does attempt to operate within the real world and some of the inaccuracies of the competitive model are remedied by other models.

Kamarck has analysed the failure of economics to deal with the real world.[23] Much of this failure he attributes to an excessive concern for precision. He argues that loose concepts and rough approximations might make economics more realistic and useful. He observes, for example, that the organisational nature of the firm makes it unlikely to be a profit maximiser and that the consumer is more likely to be a satisficer than an optimiser. Yet such considerations rarely figure within economic models. While recognising the danger in generalisation, it would seem that one feature of this failure of economics to deal with the real world is the assumption of the competitive model of capitalism. The firm as profit maximiser and the consumer as optimiser are two major features of this model. This tendency to assume the competitive model of capitalism is certainly evident within economics texts, for example. Some, such as Gill[24] and Samuelson,[25] refer to the ideas of those that have interpreted capitalism in a different way, but for the most part, they assume the competitive model. This is not to suggest that the other models do not incorporate competition to some degree, a point considered shortly, merely that they recognise that the form of an economy cannot be and is not divorced from political considerations. The only concession to this in most economics texts is the acknowledgement of the mixed economy. They do not then consider the economic consequences of this, but continue to describe economic phenomena within the sterile notion of the free-market economy.

A description of other interpretations follows on the basis of four models identified by Honour and Mainwaring: the competitive model, the crisis model, the compromise model, and the corporatist model.[26] A categorisation, they accept, is neither exhaustive nor exclusive. Each model could be said to be a description of capitalism in contemporary Western society and also an expression of how it could or should be. While it is recognised that there are differences in the economies of the different countries in the West, these differences do not detract from the applicability of the models other than in degree.

The competitive model

This, as already indicated, is the traditional model of capitalism. The development of capitalism, described above, was given some semblance of order by Adam Smith, who 'glimpsed in the social world of economics what Isaac Newton (1642-1727) had recognised in the physical world of the heavens: self-regulating natural order'.[27] Classical political economy provides the origins for the competitive model, but the model also features the criticisms of the centralising and equalising tendencies of democracy as expressed by Alexis de Tocqueville. It is founded on the belief in economic individualism as expressed in nineteenth-century liberalism. Its prime contemporary exponents are Hayek and Friedman. 'Economically, they justify market society on the grounds that it promotes efficiency and prosperity and permits choice; politically on the grounds that it does so with a minimum of state intervention.'[28] As the more detailed examination reveals later, it is more than the free-market economy model of mainstream economists, for it includes political elements. (The distinction here is between an economic system (the free-market economy) and a political-economic system (the competitive model of capitalism).) Terming it the competitive model is perhaps a misnomer, possibly inspired by the desire to have all four models beginning with the same letter. All of the models involve competition to some extent. What distinguishes this model is the emphasis on letting the market work, the market philosophy. It might be better described as the *laissez-faire* or classical model of capitalism.

The crisis model

The crisis model of capitalism assumes there are inherent tendencies within capitalism towards recurrent crises. It rejects the Smithian notion of self-regulating natural order, mentioned above. Its prime exponents are Marx and Schumpeter, although, of course, their interpretations are from different ideological and historical perspectives. As Honour and Mainwaring explain:

> Both emphasise the periodic crises that convulse capitalism and restructure its economy, although Marx interprets this as the failure of capitalism whilst Schumpeter interprets this as its success; both emphasise the importance of class and class conflict, although for Marx it is the proletariat and for Schumpeter the bourgeoisie that is crucial; both direct attention to the role of ideology, though for Marx its function is to protect capitalism while for Schumpeter its effect is to undermine capitalism; both call for purposive action, although for Marx this involves working with historical developments to transcend capitalism, whilst for Schumpeter it involves working against such developments to defend capitalism; both believe that the end result of capitalist development is likely to be socialism, though they attach very different meanings to the term.[29]

The emphasis in Marx's analysis of capitalism is criticism, of the costs incurred and in rejection of the notion of freedom under capitalism. In considering his central themes of alienation, exploitation, and domination, Honour and Mainwaring show how Marx came to view capitalism as inherently unstable, creating the conditions which make possible its own transformation. Alienation, according to Marx, results from the worker selling himself, in the selling of his labour – therein giving rise to the claim that 'capitalism denies man's essential humanity, and that it must be and can be transformed by purposive collective action'.[30] Exploitation results because it is argued that the worker is the source of all value, but does not receive all value for his efforts. Domination is required to maintain such a system. This is performed by the state, which Marx viewed as class based, noting: 'The executive of the modern state is but a committee for managing the common affairs of the whole bourgeoisie.' More importantly, and part of this, is the role of ideology; for as Marx and Engels wrote, 'The ideas of the ruling class are in every epoch the ruling ideas.' But while capitalism increases the size of the proletariat, it also increases its awareness of its class interests and organisation in pursuit of those interests. It is through this class consciousness that Marx saw the means for transforming capitalism.

Schumpeter also anticipates a transformation of capitalism, but sees this as a consequence of the success of capitalism, not its failure. The instability, he suggests, is a result of 'waves of creative destruction'; necessary for innovation, and which are disruptive and destabilising in the short run but the motive force behind capitalist development in the long run. Schumpeter defends oligopolies in contrast with the neoclassical economists, by arguing that they are essential for large-scale innovation and therefore the success of capitalism. However, this success has destructive consequences in three ways:

(1) Large-scale, bureaucratised enterprises entail a quantitative and a qualitative loss – in the reduction of the number of entrepreneurs and in the creation of a growing body of managers imbued with 'the employee mentality' and thereby lacking entrepreneurial flair.

(2) The destruction by capitalism of non-bourgeois groups who performed important political functions for which the bourgeoisie is ill-equipped, leaves the bourgeoisie politically vulnerable.

(3) The critical rationing tendencies encouraged by capitalism turn ultimately against capitalism itself. As Schumpeter puts its: 'the bourgeois finds to his amazement that the rationalist attitude does not stop at the credentials of kings and popes but goes on to attack private property and the whole scheme of bourgeois values'.

This latter problem Schumpeter attributes to the failure of the masses to appreciate the long-term success of capitalism and defend it, allowing a disillusioned intelligentsia to vocalise their criticisms but thereby fostering a climate of opinion critical to capitalism. So as with the competitive model of capitalism, there is a problem of reconciling liberalism and democracy. Schumpeter's solution is a highly elitist form of democracy: 'The democratic method is that institutional arrangement for arriving at political decisions in which individuals acquire the power to decide by means of a competitive struggle for the people's vote.'

Habermas also posits a crisis model of capitalism. He suggests, though, that capitalism has a great capacity to adapt and survive, achieved through state intervention. In such a way, the economy becomes increasingly politicised and no longer the consequence of the unchangeable laws of the market. This suggests the third model.

The compromise model

This Honour and Mainwaring describe as an 'attempt to graft some of the elements of socialism onto capitalism, with the aim of both reforming it and strengthening it'.[31] Its prime exponents are J. S. Mill and J. M. Keynes, 'representatives of an educated and enlightened bourgeoisie who were fearful of the threat posed to liberalism by the failure of an unreformed capitalism'.[32] Both were concerned about the injustice entailed by *laissez-faire* capitalism. For Mill, the solution lay in the socialisation of production through its communal ownership and operation. For Keynes, the solution lay in demand management.

The impact of Keynes's ideas on economic policy – and, therefore, state intervention in the market-place – has been considerable; though, as he to some extent foretold, his ideas did not have a substantial impact until after his death (in 1946). He rejected state socialism because he thought it irrelevant, in its emphasis on supply rather than demand; inefficient, on the basis of his Soviet experiences; and illiberal because of his belief in individualism. He did, however, remark that 'the battle of socialism against unlimited private profit is being won in detail hour by hour'. This he saw to be the consequence of big enterprise socialising itself, by management being more concerned with the general stability and reputation of the institution than with maximising returns to shareholders. Keynes favoured a market system, but subject to state intervention as he viewed *laissez-faire* capitalism unworkable and unjust, 'indeed, it was unworkable because it was unjust'.[33] He argued that there was no reason why savings and investment should be in equilibrium at a level necessary to maintain full employment; that the injustice of the system lay in its failure to provide full employment and in the arbitrary and inequitable distribution of wealth and income; and

23

that the two are linked by the economic argument that excessive savings were responsible for the depression. Hence there was an argument in support of the redistribution of wealth and income in favour of the poor – because the poor spent proportionately more than the rich – both on economic and moral grounds. Keynes's solution 'involved the state doing what the market could not do, namely managing the aggregate level of demand to ensure full employment'.[34] But in practice there were two major assumptions that presented problems: insulating the management of the economy from political pressures and preventing detailed state interference with market forces.

The corporatist model

The corporatist model 'is a rejection of the competitive market economy in favour of the concentration of productive resources in predominantly private hands, and their extensive regulation by the state'.[35] Honour and Mainwaring identify three forms of corporatism: an economic system, a state form, and a system of interest intermediation. They refer to Winkler, Middlemas, and Schmitter, respectively. Winkler's definition of corporatism is 'an economic system in which the state directs and controls predominantly privately owned business according to four principles: unity, order, nationalism and success'. Winkler has noted that corporatism has become 'a term of political abuse not economic analysis', through its association with fascism, and therefore has few supporters in post-war Britain. If, however, one considers the Schmitter perspective on corporatism, it can be argued that there are elements of this model in evidence. He views corporatism as a system of interest representation, similar in many respects to pluralism. However, whereas pluralists suggest 'spontaneous formation, numerical proliferation, horizontal extension and competitive interaction', corporatists advocate 'controlled emergence, quantitative limitation, vertical stratification and complementary interdependence', Schmitter argues. (The meaning of these terms will become clearer below.) But he then claims that this is an 'ideal type' definition and the distinction is found to be less precise in the real world. He finds that there is both 'state corporatism', where the system is imposed and controlled by the state, and also 'societal corporatism', a system that has evolved gradually and spontaneously with some independence from the state, and which seems very close to the notion of pluralism. Elsewhere, Schmitter has written that pluralism means 'all with interests will get a democratic chance to play in the game, none, however, will be capable of controlling its course or rigging its outcome'. He then goes on to suggest that corporatism is the system that operates, whereas pluralism is the way in which the system operates in an equitable manner.[36]

Hernes and Selvik have quite succinctly explained the distinction between the corporatist model and the competitive model:

a corporate system would partly supplement and partly replace the market as the automatic regulator of decentralised economic decisions ... By joint action between the effected interests and political authorities, the free determination of prices could be modified (for example, by public guarantees of minimum prices), free entry into the market could be limited (so as to prevent overcapacity or price wars), free establishment of firms could be confined (so as to secure balanced growth), and free access to commercial activities could be regulated (so as to reduce wide fluctuations in income). In this perspective, corporatism can be considered a way of systematically modifying the free operation of the market by incorporating into the public decision-making apparatus those groups that are affected by the unhampered operation of the market.[37]

Much more could be said about corporatism and the other models of capitalism. The brief sketches above consider only basic features from each model. It is not the concern here to demonstrate that one model is a more accurate interpretation of contemporary capitalism, or more desirable. The 'correctness' of each model either individually or in combination and both as a description of contemporary capitalism and as an objective for capitalism, must at least be partly determined by one's ideological position. However, this section has considered some of the alternative interpretations of capitalism rarely encountered in marketing thought, which assumes the competitive model. They add a sophistication to the analysis which will become apparent, particularly in looking at the relationship between business and society and the problem – as implied within the last three models – of the social control of business. Of most importance at this point is that the models have shown that freedom and the supposed benefits of capitalism are not its inevitable consequences when one considers some of its complexities.

The competitive model of capitalism

Its philosophical basis of individualism

A full description of the competitive model of capitalism would be lengthy and unnecessary. Discussed here are those features that demonstrate the role of consumer sovereignty in such a model and consumer sovereignty as the rationale for capitalism. A comprehensive description would be redundant: the workings of capitalism according to the competitive model are described in every economics textbook, for economically, it is the free-market model. There is, however, the political dimension. The emphasis here will be on the latter, in so far as the two can be considered independently. Again, though, a full exposition is not possible, but can be obtained from Friedman, Hayek, and others.[38] As will be seen, the model is founded on the philosophy of individualism and that an expression, if not the supreme expression of individualism, is consumer sovereignty. The main economic and political features of the model and the main criticisms are then briefly considered.

The term individualism is used in a number of ways and can create some confusion. Here the term is used to express, as Hayek puts it, the idea of 'the respect for the individual man *qua* man, that is the recognition of his own views and tastes as supreme in his own sphere, however narrowly that may be circumscribed, and the belief that it is desirable that men should develop their own gifts and bents'.[39] Individualism does not in this sense mean being individualistic or the individual approach (although this can be a consequence of individualism), but it is sometimes used in this way. Schumpeter also identifies different uses of the term individualism. Again the terms are connected, but there is a distinction between them. Political individualism is 'a *laissez-faire* attitude in matters of economic policy'. Sociological individualism is a perspective on social processes where 'the self-governing individual constitutes the ultimate unit of the social sciences'. Methodological individualism, while not claiming that the latter perspective is a tenable theory of social processes, recognises that it can be a useful perspective for a particular set of investigations.[40] Methodological individualism (a distinguishing feature of Austrian economics) is not so greatly removed from political individualism. It recognises the difficulty of knowing others' needs, other than in analysing each individual. Hence in policy terms, should it not be left to each individual to express his or her preferences? Can a state presume to know all or even some of the preferences of individuals that comprise collectives over which it may have jurisdiction? Consequently, Hayek writes:

> Individuals should be allowed, within defined limits, to follow their own values and preferences rather than somebody else's ... within these spheres the individual's system of ends should be supreme and not subject to any dictation by others. It is this recognition of the individual as the ultimate judge of his ends, the belief that as far as possible his own views ought to govern his actions, that forms the essence of the individualist position.[41]

Does such a position not point to *laissez-faire* policies? Certainly it is the basis for Hayek's rejection of socialism: 'Although we have been warned by some of the greatest political thinkers of the nineteenth century, by de Tocqueville and Lord Acton, that socialism means slavery, we have steadily moved in the direction of socialism.'[42] This he attributes to a decline in individualism, suggesting this philosophy has been basic to Western civilisation. This claim that individualism dates back to the earliest Western societies seems to conflict with the perspective on the historical development of capitalism described earlier. However, the conflict may be resolved if it is noted that the idea of individualism has a lengthy heritage but not the application of this idea, at least as far as the masses were concerned.

Steiner and Steiner note: 'Individualism to the Romans, for example, meant the importance of individuals of only certain classes.'[43] But surely to claim that it is applicable to one group of individuals but not another contradicts the basic doctrine? To claim individualism dates back to precapitalist societies, other than as an idea of idealistic thinkers, seems suspect, for it is not possible to reconcile individualism with the slavery prevalent in these societies. Yet one can accept that individualism has found an expression in later, capitalist societies, agreeing with Steiner and Steiner that 'the operation of the individual enterprise system and political democracy is predicated on the theory of individualism'; perhaps also with their observation that individualism's 'comparatively widespread acceptance in the eighteenth century altered the economic and political history of the world in the most profound sense – and for the better'. However, before examining how individualism is expressed in the market, it is worth considering further this link beween capitalism and freedom that occurs via individualism.

Individualism is, at one and the same time, both the means by which liberty is realised and liberty itself, or, at least, liberty as envisaged by Friedman, Hayek, Mill, and many others. Steiner and Steiner observe that individualism: 'is the idea of the supreme importance of the individual in society, the idea of the inherent decency of people, and a belief in their rationality'; concepts which 'led to the conclusion that authority over people should be held to a minimum'. This suggests the distinction crucial to this view of liberty: are you forbidden to do anything which is not specifically allowed? Or are you allowed to do anything which is not specifically forbidden? As Robbins puts it: 'The authoritarian wishes to issue from the centre ... positive instructions about what shall be done ... the Classical Liberal ... proposes ... the state shall prescribe what citizens shall *not* do.' (original emphasis)[44]

However, liberty may have another form. Lindblom, in contrasting communism and liberal democracy, recognises that liberty as conceived under liberal democracy is of course repressed under communism. 'Communist systems, everyone knows, largely refuse to their citizens the civil liberties: freedom of thought, speech, religion, assembly, and movement, as well as privacy ... Nor do communist systems maintain due process.'[45] Yet he recognises that liberty may have the form of freedom from indoctrination, for under liberal democracy people are not really free, they only think they are:

> A communist intellectual asks: 'What are people free from in the Soviet Union? They are free from exploitation, from all moral oppression, and consequently their thinking and deeds are free from the age-old shackles created by the economic, political and moral rule of the exploiters.' It is not a ridiculous argument ... in polyarchy not only are people indoctrinated – as inevitably in all societies – but they are heavily indoctrinated by leadership and a favored class.[46]

Marx's ideas about the role of ideology, referred to earlier, are central to this perspective. They are an important source of criticism of individualism and the idea of freedom as a feature of capitalism. The flaws in the competitive model of capitalism are considered later; suffice to note here that liberty can have more than one form and individualism may be questioned in this regard (or, at least, the application of individualism, rather than the idea).

Given this perspective, one is then better equipped to deal with Mill's statement on liberty, as quoted by the Friedmans and fundamental to their market philosophy: 'the only purpose for which power can be rightfully exercised over any member of a civilized community, against his will, is to prevent harm to others. His own good, either physical or moral, is not a sufficient warrant ... Over himself ... the individual is sovereign.'[47] A review of *Free to Choose* describes the Friedmans as disciples, their god as the market, and their bible as Adam Smith's *Wealth of Nations*[48] – a comment the Friedmans would likely endorse. In the Introduction, they trace their philosophy back to two documents, both published in 1776. One, of course, is *The Wealth of Nations*, and inevitably they quote the passage given at the outset of this chapter about how the individual, in intending only his own gain, promotes an end which was no part of his intention. The other document is the Declaration of Independence drafted by Thomas Jefferson, which embodies 'certain unalienable Rights'. (The quotation above by John Stuart Mill is, the Friedmans claim, a better expression of these rights.) Their argument, of course, is that this individual sovereignty should be allowed to be freely expressed in the market, i.e. as consumer sovereignty. Steiner and Steiner also recognise the Declaration of Independence as embodying individualism, for it represented a freedom for people to 'improve their economic position as they saw fit, to enjoy freely the results of their labors, and to manage their own affairs with a minimum of government regulation'.[49] This, quite obviously, finds its expression in *laissez-faire* policies.

Accordingly, the device for expressing and realising individualism is the free market. The market mechanism assures that 'so long as co-operation is strictly voluntary, no exchange will take place unless both parties do benefit' – Adam Smith's key insight.[50] In consumption decisions this beneficial facet of exchange ensures the individual sovereignty described by Mill and central to individualism, resulting in what is referred to as consumer sovereignty. So given the minimum of government intervention, each individual is 'free to choose'. Thus the free market brings not only prosperity, but human freedom.

This view of individualism and the market is basic to what Steiner and Steiner describe as the classical ideology and which predominates in business.[51] This is illustrated in the comment below by Thomas A. Murphy as Chairman of General Motors:

> This sensitive tailoring of productive resources to the complex and diverse preferences of people, expressed through free markets, is a fundamental though often under-appreciated characteristic of our system. Each consumer, given his free choice, can purchase those products which he feels most suit his own special needs and resources. Unlike the political system, every person can win in an economic 'election'.[52]

So consumer sovereignty prevails. This view is found throughout Silk and Vogel's *Ethics and Profits* (from which the above quotation was taken), which is based on their observation of meetings of The Conference Board 1974-1975, and captured contemporary business thinking. The book is both evidence of the predominance of the classical ideology and a description of the form it takes and how it relates to the problems of social responsibility in business. The claim that the competitive model of capitalism is the dominant interpretation seems justified.

Honour and Mainwaring acknowledge the renewed interest in the competitive model of capitalism. Currently, both Britain and the USA have premiers with policies of minimising state intervention in the market, in accordance with the competitive model. In Britain, the Thatcher government has sought greater scope for letting the market work – as in privatisation policies, the encouragement of private refuse collection services, and the subcontracting of laundry, catering, and cleaning in the health service. In the 1983 election, a Tory party slogan was 'Every man and woman a capitalist'.[53] Underlying this, as this section must show, is the more fundamental belief in individualism. It is undoubtedly Mrs Thatcher's attachment to this belief which is expressed not only in her attempts to 'let the market work' but throughout her policies. She advocates: 'a society where there is both more power and finance in the hands of the people than in the hands of the government. That means a society where you have people willing to exercise responsibility as a condition of freedom.'[54] Individualism underlies her philosophy and her policies. The competitive model of capitalism is her interpretation of capitalism, and this, of course, is seen as expressing individualism. The form of this expression is consumer sovereignty. Capitalism brings the benefits of material progress and freedom, or freedom as envisaged in individualism. Consumer sovereignty therefore becomes the rationale for capitalism.

The model's main features and criticisms

The model works according to the 'game' of the market. This has been described in every economics text since Adam Smith's *Wealth of Nations*. As he observed: 'It is not from the benevolence of the butcher, the brewer or the baker, that we expect our dinner, but from their regard to their own interest.'[55] This is not a zero-sum game, but one of mutually beneficial exchange. However, one must consider whether and in what ways, the game benefits the rest of society, as Smith claims. And does it necessarily benefit the consumer?

The purpose of economic systems is to allocate scarce resources. Le Grand and Robinson identify four objectives specified by society: efficiency, equity, freedom or civil liberty, and altruism.[56] Efficiency refers to the excess of benefits over cost. Equity refers to how fair or just is the resultant allocation. Freedom refers not only to the freedom of choice in markets but also to political freedom. Altruism refers to the acting in the interests of others without any expectation of personal gain. These are the criteria against which the competitive model needs to be assessed. Both advocates and critics rate the efficiency of the market as being very high. This is because of its ability to deal with the countless decisions necessary in a decentralised manner. They do, however, acknowledge certain failings. These failings are a consequence of monopolies (including those that result from public goods), externalities, imperfect information, and other market imperfections. Adam Smith, of course, observed that monopolies would limit the efficiency of the market because, as Galbraith has more recently noted, of the theory of capitalism's 'pivotal dependence on competition' – a dependence which Galbraith viewed in 1952 as unrealistic, recognising that much of American industry is oligopolistic.[57] This view was endorsed by Berle, in 1954, and many others subsequently.[58] Concern about externalities centres on (but is not restricted to) pollution, an early observation on the consequences of which was Rachel Carson's *Silent Spring*, in 1962. The problem of imperfect information has been recognised for some time but did not seem to receive much attention until Ralph Nader became active, particularly with the publication of his

Unsafe at Any Speed in 1965. These failings are, again, considered in the basic economics texts.[59] The point is that the market will not answer all things, even on its own terms. However, relative to alternatives, it might still be the most efficient system despite these problems.

The competitive model of capitalism rates highly on the criterion of efficiency. Its proponents argue that it would rate even higher if it were given the opportunity. On the basis of the discussion above, it would also seem to rate highly on the criterion of freedom or civil liberty, the debate about what this means notwithstanding. It is on the criteria of equity and altruism that the competitive model falls down. It is these failures, more than the failures regarding efficiency and freedom, that give the greatest justification for government intervention.

Individualism holds that each individual should be the best judge of his or her own interests. This places the burden of responsibility on the individual. The injustice results because some are less able or even unable to help themselves. The question arises: 'Should one help them, and who is to help them?' Heilbroner and Thurow observe that while the market is efficient and dynamic, it is blind to any claim on society's output other than for those with wealth or income. Consequently, 'To abide just by the market system of distribution, we would have to be willing to tolerate individuals starving on the street.'[60] Hence, the state must provide. But 'state help kills self help', Friedman observes.[61] As Spencer so eloquently puts it: 'The ultimate result of shielding men from the effects of folly is to fill the world with fools.'[62] Hayek argues that individualism has a bad name because of its association with egotism and selfishness.[63] Yet this seems inevitable. As Honour and Mainwaring write, in reference to the game of the market: 'Plainly the justification for the game is not to be found in ideals of social justice but quite simply in its success in raising the general level of prosperity and in maximising individual freedom from state controls.'[64]

The issue is acknowledged by both Hayek and Friedman. Hayek recognises the injustice but is swayed by the benefits in terms of output and individual freedom. Friedman argues likewise, suggesting that capitalism is the best means by which injustice may be minimised,[65] but also claiming that equality is not possible because life is not fair. He argues that there is no difference between the inheritance of wealth and the inheritance of talent and, indeed, goes on to claim that this unfairness is both desirable and a necessary benefit. He asks: 'What kind of a world would it be if everyone were a duplicate of everyone else?' He then explains that it is this unfairness that motivates participation in the game of the market.[66] In other words, the success of the market would be 'threatened if the game were fairer and the stakes were lower'.[67] Hence, it is claimed that the criteria of efficiency and equity are inevitably in conflict. Adam Smith's claim that the welfare of the general community

31

would be an epiphenomenal consequence of the pursuit of individual self-interest assumed welfare to be material progress. This was undoubtedly the case in his day. It is, however, less appropriate today. As Friedman recognises in the quotation above, inequities will be perpetuated. Is this acceptable in an affluent society? Can they be minimised without impairing the efficiency of the market system?

The competitive model of capitalism also falls down on the criterion of altruism. Again this seems to be in conflict with efficiency. Economic injustice is not the only criticism of the game of the market. More profound, less quantifiable, and more contentious is the recognition by Marx that the market 'resolved personal worth into exchange value', that it 'has left no other bond between man and man than naked self-interest, than callous "cash payment" '. As Lindblom explains:

> A hypothetical pure unmodified market system would be extraordinary – and intolerable – in that it would strip the individual of all but one claim on other members of the society. He could not ask for their help in distress ... In a pure market system his claim on others would be established if and only if he had something to offer in exchange.

Of course, he concludes that such a pure market system has never existed and that the 'world market systems are intertwined in varying degrees with other methods of organisation to soften the severity of market systems alone'.[68] And as Gill notes, John Stuart Mill was also critical of the idea of mankind in a constant struggle for riches, as this quotation illustrates:

> I confess I am not charmed with an ideal of life held out by those that think that the normal state of human beings is that of struggling to get on; that the trampling, crushing, elbowing and treading on each others' heels, which form the existing type of social life, are the most desirable lot of human kind, or anything but the disagreeable symptoms of one of the phases of industrial progress.[69]

Would Mill agree with Friedman now quoting him in approbation?

Lipsey defines individualism as where the household is the best judge of its own interests. Somewhat disparagingly, he defines the alternative as being paternalism, where authorities are viewed as the better judge of the household's self-interest than the household itself.[70] The issue is not as clear-cut as he would imply, for individualism not only has consequences for freedom but inevitably has consequences for equity and altruism. Yet if these criteria are to be accepted as important, it follows that state intervention is inevitable. Where, then, does this leave consumer sovereignty?

Consumer sovereignty in economics

In the competitive model of capitalism

There is an intuitive appeal to the competitive model of capitalism in its efficiency and promise of freedom. However, as the previous section showed, there can be market failure, it can be inequitable (perhaps inevitably so), and it is contrary to any community or caring ethos as evinced under collectivism. It should also be noted that one's vote in the market, as a consequence of consumer sovereignty, is in proportion to one's wealth. There is a limited franchise. It is because of these problems that the game is threatened by representative democracy. As Honour and Mainwaring observe: 'true to the tradition of Tocqueville, there is an underlying fear of the "tyranny of the majority" in that the masses may not share Hayek and Friedman's appreciation of the game, may use their political power to amend it, or more passively, may not use their power to defend it.'[71]

However, despite this, and obvious extensive intervention by the state, belief in consumer sovereignty prevails. The centrality of consumer sovereignty to the competitive model is illustrated in Adam Smith's observation that consumption is the sole purpose of production. Yet consumer sovereignty must inevitably be limited and this claim of production being entirely driven by consumption somewhat suspect, in view of what has been noted. Steiner and Steiner observe that the belief in consumer sovereignty is basic to the classical ideology, yet they conclude that reality and ideology need not be that similar: 'The significance of the ideology is lost if it is not understood that, fundamentally, it is not meant to be a description of what is going on today but rather is a prescription of what ought to be.'[72] The competitive model of capitalism as part of this classical ideology should be seen in the same way. A good expression of this ideological view of consumer sovereignty is given by Mises:

> The direction of all economic affairs is in the market society a task of the entrepreneurs. Theirs is the control of production. They are at the helm and steer the ship. A superficial observer would believe that they are supreme. But they are not. They are bound to obey unconditionally the captain's orders. The captain is the consumer.[73]

It is an attractive analogy, but one shown to be incorrect and, even if viewed as prescriptive, likely to be unattainable. This can be demonstrated by looking at mixed markets.

In mixed markets

Baumol and Blinder define consumer sovereignty in terms of purchase votes:

> In a market economy, consumers, by registering their dollar votes,
> determine which goods and services shall be provided and in what
> quantities. Items that are not wanted, or that are overproduced, will
> suffer a fall in price, while items that are in short supply will rise in
> price. These price movements act as signals to profit-seeking firms,
> which then produce larger amounts of the goods whose prices rise
> and less of the goods whose prices fall. This mechanism is what we
> call consumer sovereignty.[74]

They are, in contrast with Mises, more reserved about consumer
authority in the market, identifying consumer sovereignty as a
mechanism within the price system. They also go on to make certain
qualifications, in line with the comments made earlier about government
intervention and externalities, for 'the doctrine of consumer sovereignty
must be qualified in several ways when we deal with the real (as
opposed to the ideal) world'.

Other economists also recognise that there may be a degree of
producer sovereignty. A number refer to Galbraith's *The New Industrial
State*. After having noted that in 'virtually all economic analysis and
instruction, the initiative is assumed to lie with the consumer', Galbraith
suggests this 'uni-directional flow of instruction from consumer to
market to producer may be denoted the Accepted Sequence'. This he
rejects and argues that there is a Revised Sequence, whereby, 'the
producing arm reaches forward to control its markets and on beyond to
manage the market behaviour and shape the social attitudes of those,
ostensibly, that it serves'.[75] The Revised Sequence, claims Galbraith, is
achieved by advertising moulding consumers' preferences to conform
with the wishes of suppliers. This is generally held to be exaggerated.
Kirzner soundly illustrates the confusion in this perspective by pointing
out that, contrary to neoclassical economics, the demand curve cannot
be taken as given in the real world, and production decisions are in
anticipation of patterns of demands. There is, then, neither an Accepted
Sequence, nor a Revised Sequence: 'The entrepreneurial competitive
process consists ... of selecting by trial and error opportunities to be
placed before consumers.'[76] For Kirzner and other Austrians, there is not
a sequence, but an entrepreneurial process. Yet this permits a form of
consumer sovereignty.[77] In the second edition of *The New Industrial
State*, Galbraith is prepared to concede a little ground:

> while my case may hold for the world of the very big corporations,
> there still remains a world of the market. Farmers, lawyers,
> cleaners and cobblers, bookstores, musicians and houses of casual
> pleasure still survive. Here the market still rules; here consumer
> sovereignty is still inviolate ... [but] with increasing size and
> corporate power the market gives way to planning.[78]

Fulop suggests that there are degrees of consumer sovereignty in the real world: 'Broadly the more competitive the market the stronger the power of the consumer; the larger the element of monopoly, the more he is at the mercy of the producer.'[79] This accords with Galbraith, although she disputes the extent to which the producer, in Galbraith's analysis, predominates in the real world. As with Baumol and Blinder, she makes certain qualifications. Consumer sovereignty is limited by information, income, and state restrictions on certain goods such as drugs, or drink before driving. She concludes that the degree of sovereignty will be determined by information and, above all, choice: 'the consumer must have the authority to exert his sovereignty over the producer by exercising the strongest sanction of all – the ability to take his custom elsewhere. Information, advice and guidance are valueless unless the customer has a choice between alternatives.'[80] This seems a fair conclusion. It is worth mentioning her reply to arguments such as those by Galbraith that producers dominate consumer choice through advertising. Employing Galbraith's concept of countervailing power, she observes that the power of retailers curtails monopoly practices and, in effect, enhances consumer sovereignty.[81] Further, retailers reduce the problem of decision-making in choice by acting as preliminary assessor for the consumer, particularly valuable when the product requires technical knowledge for adequate assessment.

In short, consumers are not sovereign but one can refer to a degree of sovereignty, enhanced by choice, information, and possibly (though not necessarily in all cases) retailer assessment; but restricted by limitations on competition, actions by the state, and individual wealth. Lindblom describes consumer sovereignty as being a technical term and not accurately descriptive.[82] Before concluding, it is necessary, for reasons that will become apparent, to describe the conditions under which consumer sovereignty, as an accurately descriptive term, would occur. Consumer sovereignty, in this sense, can only occur in conditions of perfect competition. The misunderstandings consequent on the use of the term stem from, as Galbraith observes above, economic analyses. This is due to the failing of economics to deal with the real world and to only deal in ideal, free markets. Heilbroner and Thurow observe that real world markets are characterised by imperfect, not perfect competition. They explain the importance of this for consumer sovereignty. Under perfect competition, the consumer is king, allocating resources by virtue of his or her demand and enjoying goods sold as cheaply and abundantly as possible. There are no profits (the firm is a price taker) and each firm produces the goods consumers want in the largest quantity and at the lowest cost possible. Under imperfect competition, the consumer loses much of this sovereignty as firms have strategies, including the strategy of influencing consumer demand, and

35

profits are not competed away, so consumers' surplus is transferred to firms and output is not maximised but reduced by whatever amount results from higher-than-competitive prices.[83]

Consumer sovereignty in marketing

Consumer sovereignty and the marketing concept

Marketing is the application of the competitive model of capitalism. Definitions of marketing emphasise the consumer: 'the "marketing view" looks at the business as directed toward the satisfaction of a customer want and as a purveyor of a customer utility';[84] 'Marketing is the performance of business activities which direct the flow of goods and services from producer to consumer or user in order to satisfy customers and accomplish the company's objectives';[85] 'Marketing is the way in which an organisation matches its own human, financial and physical resources with the wants of its customers.'[86] The marketing discipline and a marketing orientation in practice are predicated upon a belief in consumer sovereignty. This is implicit in all definitions of marketing. Kotler makes it explicit:

> The marketing concept expresses the company's commitment to the time-honored concept in economic theory known as consumer sovereignty. The determination of what is to be produced should not be in the hands of the companies or in the hands of government but in the hands of consumers. The companies produce what the consumers want and in this way maximise consumer welfare and earn their profits.[87]

However, as revealed above, this is erroneous in two ways. First, this concept of consumer sovereignty in economic theory is only found in perfectly competitive markets. Second, perfect competition would not permit marketing activities because firms cannot have strategies; they are price takers and can only compete in this sense. Hence, not only is consumer sovereignty unlikely to be found in practice, but it is incompatible in theory with the notion of marketing strategies. So if markets in the real world were characterised by perfect competition then one could not have marketing. The notion of marketing and of consumer sovereignty are not, at least in a pure sense, complementary; they are contradictory. This seemingly irreconcilable connection between marketing and consumer sovereignty is dominant within the marketing discipline. Indeed, without this connection, there could not be marketing as it is currently understood and practised. It seems that it is because marketing is the application of the competitive model of capitalism that this connection is made. Given the observations above about the ideological nature of this model, it would follow that the unlikely combination of consumer sovereignty and marketing is the consequence of the ideological underpinnings of the discipline.

Marketing, ideology, and consumer sovereignty

It could be countered in reply to the observation that marketing and consumer sovereignty are incompatible, that this is only in some pure, abstract sense. This is correct. However, it does not deny that consumer sovereignty is employed as the central concept of marketing and in the way described earlier in the quotation by Mises where 'the captain is the consumer'. If consumer sovereignty and marketing are not incompatible, then consumer sovereignty is at least a suspect basis for the discipline, given the reservations expressed above. The competitive model of capitalism as the interpretation dominant in marketing and, therefore, marketing as the application of this model, points to the ideological basis to marketing thought. For these reasons marketing may be more of an ideology than a science.

Baker, after having pointed to the problems in the definition of marketing, concludes:

> From a negative point of view, then, marketing is just a
> hotch-potch of ideas 'borrowed' from other disciplines. More
> positively it rests on the simple principle that supply must be a
> function of demand. In the opinion of marketing men this offers the
> best approach to the solution of the central economic problem – the
> allocation of scarce resources so as to maximise satisfaction.[88]

If one also acknowledges that marketing has developed some unique concepts and techniques, this seems a reasonable position to adopt. Although Baker probably did not see it in these terms, marketing as a discipline may best be described as: 'The study of the application of the ideology of the competitive model of capitalism, central to which is the notion of consumer sovereignty, by drawing on the social science disciplines and by developing unique concepts and techniques so as to enable producers to most effectively realise mutually beneficial exchanges with consumers in markets.' This position on marketing will be considered further. Of importance here is the degree of consumer sovereignty in real world markets. The purpose of this section is to show that marketing expressions of consumer sovereignty may be somewhat suspect, by revealing the ideological basis to marketing thought.

After having shown that marketing rests on the notion of consumer sovereignty – 'a truism which has been in currency since Adam Smith wrote his *Wealth of Nations*'[89] – Baker goes on to explain the relative recency of the marketing concept. This he attributes to the affluence of contemporary society where there is 'excess' supply and therefore 'large numbers of producers are competing for the privilege of supplying the consumer'.[90] Of course, as has been suggested elsewhere,[91] this happy situation may only be a phase. However, Baker is confident that technology will ensure the continuation of an excess of supply over demand. This explanation for the relative recency of marketing offers the best support for the claim that there is consumer sovereignty. Yet it is not a new argument; it merely points to the importance of competition for consumer sovereignty. While Baker's later claim that marketing is 'one of man's oldest activities'[92] seems questionable in view of the version of the origins of capitalism given earlier in this chapter, it would seem that consumer sovereignty has always been a feature of capitalist societies according to the degree of competition. This must always be the case. Marketing simply recognises that competition in contemporary society is acute, in some markets.

Baker suggests in his later book that society has merely come full circle, back to a position where consumer sovereignty predominates.[93] It is more likely that consumer sovereignty exists, and always will exist, but only to a degree and according to how much competition there is within the market in question. However, this is not the consumer sovereignty envisaged in marketing or by Mises. The consumer is not king. The consumer may be king in certain markets, at certain times, and the producer is then required to meet the consumers' needs to remain competitive. There are then degrees of sovereignty in different markets. The domain of this sovereignty is yet another consideration – can the consumer express concern about matters not related to the product and expect remedy? This, of course, is a key question within this study. Both the degree and domain of consumer sovereignty are a function of competition. Yet as the rationale for capitalism, there must surely be the absolute consumer sovereignty described by Mises. The role of the ideology is to suggest this is the case.

Ideologies serve two purposes: they provide explanation for and the justification of interests. The ideology of the competitive model of capitalism both explains capitalism and justifies the interests of capitalists (producers). A cynic might be tempted to observe that the activities and power of business are made acceptable to society by an ideology that proclaims business is not powerful at all, but under the control of consumers. This is the latent function of marketing. To twist the quotation from Lindblom employed earlier, consumers are not really sovereign under capitalism, they only think they are. Marketing fosters this belief. The connection between consumer sovereignty and marketing is, from the economics perspective, erroneous. However, it is not erroneous from the marketing perspective because it is the dominant view. It is, then, ideological. As the previous section showed, marketing is predicated upon a *belief* in consumer sovereignty. This in itself is 'correct', even though there may be no legitimate theoretical or empirical foundation for this.

Ideology both serves as an idea structure for understanding, and also for legitimising one's interests. Founding the marketing concept on consumer sovereignty might be seen as highly convenient. At the base level it permits corporate power – expressed in strategies and other ways – while claiming the corporation has no power and is merely acting in accord with the wishes of the consumer. Of course, this is not the way the corporation would see it – or, perhaps, the marketing academics speaking on their behalf. The corporate executives believe in the power of the consumer because this is how ideologies work. Any guilt they may have, about dubious practices that are a consequence of corporate power or merely the recognition of that power, is allayed in the process. Bartels has shown that marketing's origins lie in the separation of economics and marketing, with the practitioners falling into the latter camp.[94] Is it surprising that they should build a body of knowledge legitimising their activities, and on the most convenient grounds of all, that they are merely serving the best interests of the consumer and are tools at his or her command?

Andreski, in *Social Sciences as Sorcery*, claims that the social sciences frequently act to serve the interests of the wielders of power, putting a pseudo-scientific gloss on the crude realities of power and giving their blessing to the status quo. This is more of a latent than a manifest function, but marketing as a discipline may well be a prime exponent of this.[95] However, what matters is the degree to which ideology conforms with reality. While many marketing academics and practitioners genuinely believe that consumer sovereignty is the basis for marketing thought and action, what evidence is there for this? Surely if practitioners and academics alike believe in consumer sovereignty, then their actions will reflect this?

Consumerism – the antithesis of marketing

The advent of consumerism provides some evidence that consumer sovereignty is the basis for marketing thought, but not necessarily marketing action. It also questions whether belief in consumer sovereignty will be reflected in action. Baker observes that 'the nature of marketing and consumerism reflect a fundamental paradox for while they are invariably seen as being in conflict both activities possess the same objective – customer satisfaction'.[96] That such a paradox should arise, he attributes to the changes in society's expectations of business and some firms being less responsive. This is acceptable, but not if one claims some sort of absolute consumer sovereignty, as he implies in observing that:

> free market economics largely permit the evolution of consumer sovereignty by allowing consumers to express their preferences as between goods and services through the daily casting of their money 'votes' ... marketing economies and the marketing philosophy rest upon the same fundamental proposition that consumer preferences will determine the allocation of available inputs to the creation of the most desired outputs.[97]

Consumer sovereignty is not in this sense reconcilable with consumerism. Perhaps it was the ideology of the competitive model of capitalism, expressing consumer sovereignty, that led to consumerist demands; the ideology and the reality were too far out of step. However, the reply to consumerism as advocated by Baker, Christopher *et al.*, Kotler, and others,[98] is that it should be seen as an opportunity. Somewhat reluctantly, it seems, this idea was adopted by business. Consequently business now claims to practise consumerism! Consumerism has been incorporated within the ideology and become consumer sovereignty, as a marketing dictionary indicates in defining consumer sovereignty: 'Power of consumer to influence production, presentation and distribution of goods and services in a competitive market, thus expressing demand, and emerging more recently as consumerism'[99] – a remarkable example of doublethink. And so consumerism results in the reaffirmation of consumer sovereignty in marketing thought but not, necessarily, in action. The ideology is upheld. Consumer sovereignty in marketing action will still be but a consequence of the degree of competition within the market. The response to consumerism is then a demonstration of the ideological basis of marketing thought.

Consumer sovereignty: a myth?

This chapter has shown that consumer sovereignty is the rationale for capitalism. However, it has also shown that consumer sovereignty may not be as prevalent in practice as supposed. It emerges that there are two forms of consumer sovereignty. One, which may be described as absolute consumer sovereignty, is the form as expressed within the competitive model of capitalism and underpinning marketing thought. The other form is consumer sovereignty as a technical term, which recognises degrees of consumer authority in markets. The former seems to be grounded in ideology, the latter seems to be grounded in fact.

Yet it may be that there is a greater degree of consumer sovereignty today than there has ever been. For Adam Smith, consumer sovereignty was an idea, perhaps even an ideal. As Hughes observes, 'Economics still bears the marks of the Smithean morality of attempting to reconcile and derive the good of the collective out of the individual pursuit of self-interest.'[100] While Galbraithian critiques suggest that oligopolistic competition limits consumer sovereignty, it may be, as Austrian economists claim, that this form of competition provides the greatest degree of sovereignty. It can, of course, be more efficient because of the economies of scale achieved through not having an innumerable quantity of small producers as would be the case under perfect competition. And, as Lindblom observes, despite Galbraith's claims in *The New Industrial State*, the market is not dead,[101] and 'big corporations are clearly not generally co-ordinated by a government plan or any other overarching governmental direction, but through market exchanges'.[102]

But if there is a greater degree of consumer sovereignty today, why is there so much criticism of business? Why, if consumer sovereignty is at its height, is there so much complaining about the limits to consumer sovereignty? There seem to be two immediate possible answers to this. First, as Fisk puts it, 'the more consumer sovereignty the greater the opportunities for its abuse'.[103] Second, and this is related, greater affluence might mean greater discontent. As Fulop explains:

> it may seem an odd paradox that higher incomes and more discretionary spending power should lead shoppers to be more, rather than less, critical about their purchases, it is only variety and choice that encourage criticism and make rejection possible. While any washing machine would probably be welcome to a housewife accustomed to scrubbing clothes at the nearest river bank, she would no longer be satisfied easily when there is a choice of automated washing machines, laundries and launderettes.[104]

Choice itself leads to greater criticism. This is a feature of the 'phenomenon of rising expectations'.[105] The point is that greater consumer sovereignty may mean greater demands for more consumer sovereignty, because the amount of abuses will increase and those abuses will be perceived as being more detrimental.

It seems safe to conclude that absolute consumer sovereignty is a myth. However, one can accept that there are degrees, perhaps quite considerable, of consumer sovereignty in certain markets as they are today. Yet where does this leave marketing? It may be that marketing is more of an ideology than a science and the search for that elusive paradigm for the discipline is meaningless. One might alternatively suggest that consumer sovereignty is the paradigm for marketing. But of course it cannot be seen as such for this would mean, if given any serious thought, acknowledging the ideological basis to the discipline. (Marketing's ideological basis is discussed further in Appendix A.)

Chapter two

Social control of business : corporate social responsibility

Preview

> The consumer is, so to speak, the king ... each is a voter who uses his votes to get things done that he wants done.
>
> Paul A. Samuelson[1]

> But the Emperor has nothing on at all! cried a little child.
>
> Hans Christian Anderson
> *The Emperor's New Clothes*

What is left of consumer sovereignty when stripped of the ideology of the competitive model of capitalism? If, as the previous chapter concluded, the market will not or cannot answer all things because the consumer is not sovereign, how may the social control of business be realised and what will the market answer? This is the theme of this and the following chapter.

A claim, which is endorsed here, is that this problem of the social control of business is at the core of the business and society discipline. Earlier business and society writing is preoccupied with the social responsibilities of business. More recently, there seems to be an emphasis on the social control of business with social responsibility viewed as an aim of social control mechanisms. In examining the social role of business, this chapter looks at the meaning of social responsibility in business in theory and in practice, and the arguments for and against it. In effect, the view is taken that if business has a social role, it therefore has social responsibilities. But what are these responsibilities? For what issues and to what degree is business responsible? Is profit maximisation sufficient or even necessary? These questions are addressed in looking at the meaning of social responsibility in business. A model is proposed which identifies four different levels of social responsibility; so in theory at least, the extent of social responsibility can be identified. However, while both the stakeholder and social cost approaches offer some scope in identifying social responsibility issues, it is difficult to see how management should decide between conflicting social issues and determine issue priority. This assumes, of course, that one favours or even acknowledges managerial discretion on social issues.

Social responsibility in practice can be considered in terms of managerial creeds. Contributions are considered which identify different creeds or, if one prefers, ideologies. Importantly, it is recognised that managers do not, regardless of creed, view themselves as not having social responsibilities. Some, if not the majority, however, view profit maximisation as fulfilling their social responsibilities. Although this position may seem rather unsophisticated, there are sound philosophical arguments for supporting it – whether managers are aware of them or not – as Friedman has shown. So the conclusion to this chapter examines the arguments for and against social responsibility in business ('against' in the sense of against going beyond profit maximisation). These philosophical arguments against social responsibility in business are shown to be based on the competitive model of capitalism. Yet, in keeping with the previous chapter, it is recognised that this model of capitalism lacks verisimilitude. This in itself provides a strong counter-argument to the arguments against social responsibility. There are also the arguments for social responsibility of the 'moral minimum', of enlightened self-interest, and the long-term profitability and survival of the firm, and arguments which recognise the extent of corporate power. It is acknowledged that in practice managers will to some degree be responsible for social issues because they have discretion and because of human nature.

The extent of corporate power provides an argument for social responsibility because it is suggested that this power needs to be tempered by self-regulation. If this is not achieved then governments may step in and take away corporate power and perhaps also threaten the market economy system. So social responsibility is partly achieved by self-regulation: indeed, many practitioners view social responsibility as being about their voluntary (and perhaps arbitrary) efforts to be good corporate citizens. But the extent of corporate power also points to the requirement for the social control of business. Chapter 3, therefore, takes the analysis from responsibility and philanthropy to accountability, and examines the mechanisms for the social control of business, including legislation, self-regulation, and the market. The latter mechanism, of course, involves consumer sovereignty, with ethical purchase behaviour (and consumer boycotts in particular) being an interesting attempt at the social control of business – or at least making business aware of its social responsibilities. First, however, it is necessary to consider the social role of business, the basis for identifying the social responsibilities of business.

Business and society

Academic perspectives on business and society

The previous chapter showed that the competitive model of capitalism is suspect. This raises an important question about the role of business in society: What is, and what should be, the relationship of business to society if it is not determined by the market? Jones suggests business and society is 'an emerging discipline'. He notes that there is a clearly identifiable body of literature about business and society – going back at least as far as 1952, to Galbraith's *American Capitalism* – as well as courses with this title.[2] Yet despite a rapid growth in the study of business and society and the consequent proliferation of publications in the area, there is no ready answer to this key question. Consensus within the literature about the role of business in society is limited. There are a number of reasons for this – principally, a dominant anti-business attitude, the undue influence of values, and the scope of the issue.

First, there is the problem of 'where one is coming from' in writing about business and society. The academic perspective on the relationship between business and society seems notably partial. Business and society as an academic field does not concern itself with the benefits to society of business, but, in the main, with the criticism of the role of business in society. Perhaps in view of the managerial bias in the other business disciplines, as cited by Honour and Mainwaring and others,[3] this to some extent redresses the balance. However, the anti-business attitude evident in many writers' work in this field does seem to cloud the issues. There is the persistent assumption that there is something gravely wrong with the position of business in society. For example, Sethi, in the Preface to the second edition of *Up Against the Corporate Wall*, writes in reply to the criticism that he omitted success stories in business and society controversies: 'The instances of business failure to handle social controversies have been far greater in number and magnitude than the instances of success.'[4] This ignores the fact that every day, every business is making decisions which are potentially controversial in that they involve the allocation of resources in one particular way rather than in a number of other possible ways. One must at least presume that as there is only controversy over a small proportion of the numerous business decisions made, these non-controversial decisions are at least accepted, if not successful. But the business and society literature is characterised by observations on the failures of business. This seems a partial perspective unless one is ideologically opposed to capitalism. Recognising this partiality, one can at least understand the observation made by Silk and Vogel: 'There seems to be a widespread feeling among businessmen that the university system has had its loyalties captured by forces hostile to the business system and that this accounts for much of the public's misunderstanding of business.'[5] Criticisms of business predominate in the business and society literature and there is a consequent tendency towards polemics rather than analytical thought. Description of what is and what could be seems confused with what might be and what should be.

A second reason for the lack of consensus on the role of business in society is the muddiness of the issue. This muddiness is a result of the different values and different ideological perspectives which writers in the area permit to play too great a part in their work. One outstanding exception to this is Milton Friedman, as Heilbroner comments: 'In an area in which syrup flows freely, there is something astringent and bracing about Friedman's position.'[6] In terms of clarity, Friedman's renowned position on the role of business in society is far superior to the well-meaning rhetoric which abounds elsewhere. So, for example, two key officers of the American National Council of Churches write: 'corporate decision-makers should begin to consider the social implications of their decisions as carefully and with as much weight as they do the economic ... life and death are more important than profit and loss.'[7] Similarly, Sadler, a British writer in the area, notes: 'A trade-off has been made between economic efficiency and the quality of life, in favour of the latter... society has the right to require industry (which is part of itself) to pursue social objectives.'[8] Although well-meaning, such forthright expressions of what business should do – and they are not uncommon – add little to the analysis of the role of business in society. And as Ackerman observes, they give no practical guidance to the manager to whom one imagines they are addressed.[9]

But perhaps the main reason for the lack of consensus on the role of business is the scope of the issue. The question above on the role of business is a big question indeed. Because of the scope of the issue, there are many different approaches to its analysis. For example, what should the writer's position be on the nature of the state in society? Sturdivant identifies five perspectives: libertarian, Marxist, pluralist, welfare state, and cynical.[10] Alternatively, what should the writer's position be on the function of business organisations in society? There is the Friedman view of the firm which defines its function in economic terms alone, while at the other extreme there is Bell's view of the corporation as a sociological institution: 'Corporations are institutions for economising; but they are also ways of life for their members.'[11] Analysis of the role of business in society involves a great many different issues, positions, and perspectives. So there are different approaches to the analysis. Yet a perspective can be taken without undue compromise between brevity and depth, and with minimum interference by anti-business attitudes and value or ideological bias.

Social control of business – an adequate perspective

The more analytical work in the business and society field tends to be that which, while still concerned with the role of business in society, adopts a focus on the problem of the social control of business. Indeed, there may even be a trend towards this focus. The earlier writings of the late 1960s and early 1970s seem primarily concerned with what business should do (the social responsibilities of business), while the later and current writings seem more concerned with how society can ensure business does as is required (the social control of business). Steiner and Steiner observe on business and society, 'that there is no underlying theory integrating the entire field, nor is there likely to be one in the foreseeable future. The field is extremely diverse, complex, and fluid, and there is no consensus about its precise boundaries.'[12] Writing in a similar vein, Jones suggests that while it may be some time before the elusive paradigm can be identified, it is, however, possible to postulate an integrating framework. He then writes:

> The central focus of the field can be refined further by introducing the notion of 'social control of business', defined as the means by which society directs business activity to useful ends. In essence, the social control of business is the core of the business and society field.[13]

His framework will be considered later. Suffice to note here that the perspective of the social control of business does seem to be a meaningful focus. And other writers have indicated this. For example, Beesley and Evans write about corporate social responsibility 'as one element in a strategy for the control of power and for stable progress'.[14] This perspective is also appropriate to the concern here with ethical purchase behaviour. As Jones notes, the field deals with two general questions relating to the social control of business:

(1) How compatible are the outputs and processes of the economic system with the values of the cultural and political systems? (How appropriate are existing social control mechanisms?)
(2) How can the outputs and processes of the economic system be made more compatible with the values of the cultural and political systems? (How can social control mechanisms be improved?)

47

This study addresses these questions in examining the role of consumer sovereignty as a social control mechanism and the potential for ethical purchase behaviour. The rest of this chapter considers why social control of business is considered necessary and the notion of social responsibility in business. The following chapter then examines the forms of social control of business and the potential for ensuring social responsibility in business through consumer sovereignty.

The requirement for social control of business

Digressions

Business digressions, instances where business behaviour is widely acknowledged as having been undesirable, provide an argument for the social control of business. In *The Consumer and Corporate Accountability*, Nader proposes federal chartering of businesses to ensure social control. Elsewhere in the book, business digressions are cited which would seem to support the need for this. They include the advertising of cigarettes, the sale of flammable children's sleepwear, safety defects in automobiles, strip-mining, and claims without substance in advertising.[15] Others refer to ITT's abortive coup attempts in Chile, the illegal corporate contributions to the campaign to re-elect President Nixon as revealed in Watergate, the manufacture of napalm, investments in South Africa, and General Motors' 'investigation' of Ralph Nader following the publication of *Unsafe at Any Speed*.

However, identifying digressions requires considerable caution. While the interference in the democratic process revealed in Watergate might be widely acknowledged as a business digression, there is less agreement about, say, the advertising of cigarettes or the manufacture of napalm. Indeed, on the latter issue, Vogel observes that during the boycott of Dow Chemical's Saran Wrap, in protest at Dow's manufacture of napalm, the purchase of Saran Wrap became, in effect, a referendum on the war.[16] Similarly, there might be less agreement on safety defects in automobiles than Nader supposes, because of the additional cost that safety features can entail. Moreover, as Simon *et al.* observe, requests received by institutions to invest ethically may come not only from those concerned about shareholdings in companies that make DDT, pollute, or fail to employ minorities but also from those concerned about shareholdings in companies that trade with Eastern Europe or manufacture the Pill.[17] In other words, while digressions do point to the requirement for the social control of business, there will be differences of opinion as to whether behaviour on a particular issue constitutes a digression.

There will, though, be less disagreement about digressions that are widely viewed as atrocities. As Heilbroner notes, efforts to realise the social control of business are often a consequence of such digressions: 'Atrocities are not, of course, the only, or perhaps even the central issue with regard to the problem of corporate responsibility. But they serve to give life to questions that otherwise tend to become too abstract to command the thoughtful attention they require.'[18] So as Hay *et al*. note, the Thalidomide case opened the door for quite stringent regulations of drugs.[19] *In the Name of Profit*, by Heilbroner and others, is largely a catalogue of business digressions. In his contribution, 'Controlling the Corporation', Heilbroner suggests that the digressions described bore similarities to the recent My Lai massacre in Vietnam: 'For like My Lai, the incidents in this book are atrocities. Moreover, in one case as in the other, the atrocities are not merely hideous exceptions but, rather, discovered cases of a continuing pattern of misbehaviour.'[20] Referring to Libby's sale of cyclamate-sweetened fruit overseas following a United States ban on cyclamates, he writes: 'What we have here is a business version of the principle behind the Vietnam War – the imposition of casualties on other peoples in the name of some tenet, such as freedom or profits as the case may be. Not that Libby is the only adherent to this principle.'[21] Digressions provide one argument for the social control of business. But as Heilbroner observes, they may not be the central issue. Digressions point to the underlying problem, power without accountability.

Power and accountability

Sethi writes: 'The twentieth-century corporation has replaced the church as the dominant social institution in the lives of citizens of the industrialised nations. Like the white man's religions of a bygone era, the white man's economic institutions cast a long shadow on the rest of the world.'[22] Digressions by business merely illustrate the extent of corporate power and why this is undesirable. As Bell observes:

> Corporate power, clearly, is the predominant power in the society, and the problem is how to limit it. The concern for public policy, summed up in the phrase 'social responsibility', derives from the growing conception of a communal society and the controls which a polity may have to impose on economic ventures that generate unforeseen consequences far beyond the intentions, or powers of control, of the initiating parties.[23]

Heilbroner makes the point even more forcefully. He observes that if people are asked what is bad about corporations, they will refer to the rape of the environment or the abuse of the consumer: 'The chances are the answer will have something to do with smoke or sludge, or with faulty brakes or poisonous vichyssoise.'[24] Yet although such digressions are often cited in answer to questions about what is bad about corporations, the issue is about power:

> Thus when corporations rape the environment or abuse us as guinea pigs, suddenly we awaken to the realities of our individual powerlessness *and of our dependence on their smooth and presumably benign functioning*. Then our frustrations and resentments surface with a rush, in the demand that corporate power be brought to heel and that corporate officials be made accountable. (Heilbroner's emphasis)[25]

Heilbroner then notes that the problem is about how this power may be controlled, and solutions to this problem, from Heilbroner and others, are considered later. Yet this problem is not so much a matter of corporate power *per se*, but the legitimacy of that power. This is even recognised by practitioners. Sir Frederick Catherwood, as Managing Director of John Laing and Son Ltd., observed at a British Institute of Management (BIM) conference on social responsibility 'that alone of the great social institutions in our Western democracies, the company manager has no democratic base for his authority',[26] Vogel interprets the American counter-corporate movement as an 'effort on the part of citizens to expand their definition of political conduct to include the policies and decision-making processes of the large business corporations'.[27] In so doing, they demand the public scrutiny and accountability of business, to the same extent as government institutions. The basis for this demand is what Vogel terms 'the crisis of corporate legitimacy'. Berger also sees the criticism of business as a problem of corporate legitimacy: 'if the American people no longer believe in the rightness of business, the private sector faces a crisis of legitimacy.'[28] This is fundamental to understanding the social control of business and contemporary concern with this, for legitimacy, as 'the social justification of power',[29] is precisely what the methods for the social control of business attempt to achieve. It is when these methods or forms of control are perceived to be inadequate that corporate legitimacy is questioned.

As will be seen later, solutions to the problem of corporate power do not necessarily involve an end to the corporation in its current form. Vogel (with Silk) in a later publication observes that 'talk of the business corporation as facing a "crisis of legitimacy" does not imply that there exists any significant controversy as to whether it should exist'. They continue by suggesting that this crisis of legitimacy means corporate leaders are faced with two basic questions: 'By what right do you who manage these huge corporations exercise your power? And what means do we have to ensure that corporate power will be exercised in accord with some generally accepted notion of the public interest?'[30] Answers to these questions are a prerequisite for legitimate corporate action. Yet they are not always evident.

In describing the concept of legitimacy, Berger writes that it is the acceptance of power which is important:

> Legitimacy ... concerns neither ethics or legality. A tyrant may exercise power in a manner both technically unlawful and ethically scandalous; but his power is nonetheless legitimate as long as the people over whom it is exercised accept it as rightful. It is their acceptance, not value judgements imposed from the outside, that matters.[31]

The grounds for corporate legitimacy have changed: corporate power has grown while, partly as a consequence, its basis in property rights has been eroded. The scope of corporate power, as noted earlier in this section, is considerable. As Heilbroner observes, many corporations have incomes larger than the gross national products of some respectable nations.[32] This growth in size and power has brought with it the separation of ownership and control and, as a consequence, doubts about the legitimacy of corporate action based on property rights alone. Most writers generally attribute the first recognition of this to the Berle and Means classic 1932 study,[33] though Silk and Vogel suggest the creation of US Steel as early as 1901 marked the beginning of a trend toward the replacement of owners by professional managers. They go on to quote Berle and Means's observation that 'The dissolution of the atom of property (the separation of formal ownership and effective control) destroys the very foundation on which the economic order of the past three centuries has rested.'[34]

In a later work, Berle shows that much of American industry is oligopolistic and, echoing Galbraith's earlier claim in *American Capitalism*, suggests in contrast to the competitive model of capitalism that competition is only a partial check on corporate power. Indeed, he suggests that corporations are primarily checked by the requirement for legitimacy rather than competition and the more commonly acknowledged constraints.[35] A more recent empirical study by Blumberg confirmed this view of the scope of corporate power. He also concludes that this growth in power has led to a questioning of corporate legitimacy:

> The ideological foundations of the business society are being severely shaken. Business is no longer able to articulate its objectives in a way that will command support. Many businessmen are no longer willing to assert profit

maximisation as the overriding goal of the corporation. Business is in search of an ideology that will embrace not only the drive for profit but the social responsibilities business has increasingly assumed. With the erosion of confidence in the ideological foundations of the business society the legitimacy of the corporation as an institution has been challenged.[36]

Yet again the argument can be seen to turn on the legitimacy of corporate action. Corporate power can be demonstrated by referring to the structural importance of business in the economy – the resources business commands – and this becomes all the more evident and disturbing when these resources are seen to be misused or some atrocity or digression forces a reluctant public to examine the issue. The demand is then that this power should only be exercised with adequate accountability. Only with assurances of accountability will corporate action then be able to claim legitimacy.

If business can claim the right to identify its social responsibilities, an issue Blumberg dodges in the quotation given above, it must then administer them in accord with some sense of priority. This again is an incredibly difficult issue. As an alternative to further discussion of this in abstract terms, consider Medawar's practical example. He asks whether it is more 'responsible' for a company to introduce improved pollution control equipment and pass on the cost in the form of higher prices to consumers, or to allow more pollution and keep prices down.[37] If, for argument's sake, this was a privately owned power utility, would one then wish that it could establish such a priority, or, for that matter, should even be able to address the question? Medawar's position on the problem of corporate power is that while what is important is what an organisation actually does with its power, there should, as far as possible, be full accountability for the use of that power: 'those within corporate bodies with decision-making powers should propose, explain and justify the use of those powers to those without.' He claims abuse will occur if the powers of an organisation are not checked and advocates social audits: 'The main reason – self-evident as a democratic ideal – is to ensure that power of all kinds is exercised to the greatest possible extent with the understanding and consent of the public.'[38] In other words, power requires accountability.

So, in sum, the extent of corporate power has been demonstrated and it has been shown that the exercise of this power lacks legitimacy and a sufficient basis for identifying priorities. Resolution of the problem would seem to demand greater accountability, social audits being one suggested mechanism. Corporate accountability is achieved through the social control of business, the forms of which are examined in the next chapter. Before considering them, it is necessary to examine the intention behind these attempts; that is, social responsibility in business. Moreover, social responsibility in business through the voluntary assumption of 'responsibilities' is seen by many practitioners as an adequate solution to the problem of corporate power. Social responsibility, as both a practitioner doctrine and as a goal for corporate accountability measures, is considered next.

The meaning of social responsibility in business

A diversity of views

The meaning of social responsibility in business is not as straightforward as it might appear. Indeed, in considering it, one is presented with a similar conundrum to that experienced by Alice in *Alice in Wonderland*, to whom Humpty Dumpty said: 'When *I* use a word, it means just what I choose it to mean – neither more nor less.' Dow Votaw illustrates the ambiguity surrounding social responsibility, suggesting the term is a brilliant one:

> it means something, but not always the same thing, to everybody. To some it conveys the idea of legal responsibility or liability; to others it means socially responsible behaviour in an ethical sense; to still others the meaning transmitted is that of 'responsible for', in a causal mode; many simply equate it with 'charitable contributions'; some take it to mean socially 'conscious' or 'aware'; many of those who embrace it most fervently see it as a mere synonym for 'legitimacy', in the context of 'belonging' or being proper or valid; a few see it as a sort of fiduciary duty imposing higher standards of behavior on businessmen at large.[39]

As Sethi observes, because of the positive connotations of the term it has been co-opted by many different groups such that it has come to mean all things to all people and 'language so debased becomes meaningless and simply breeds contempt'.[40] So Silk and Vogel suggest that 'The doctrine of "corporate social responsibility" emerged in the United States, precisely because it is seen by many businessmen as a way of reducing the role of government in their affairs.'[41] Of course, it then comes as little surprise to learn that corporations believe they act responsibly. Indeed, some go to great lengths to publicise this.[42] Yet as Medawar notes, 'virtually any government, trade union, political party or other major organisation will have the same perceived view of its own propriety – and can always be counted on to provide such evidence of its activities as will support these claims'.[43] He then suggests that because the claim to be acting responsibly is 'natural', it should also be as natural to be suspicious of such claims, not least because they are so universally made and there is little to distinguish them in content. One might then conclude that responsibilities, so professed, should go hand in hand with accountability.

While corporate social responsibility may be seen to have a number of different meanings, they are, as Beesley and Evans note, based on the recognition of the growth of corporate power and the consequent 'perception of a relative shift from government to companies as the source of social improvement and the means to promote specific items of social welfare'.[44] So Farmer and Hogue define corporate social responsibility in terms of 'actions that, when judged by society in the future, are seen to have been of maximum help in providing necessary amounts of desired goods and services at minimum financial and social costs, distributed as equitably as possible'.[45] Unfortunately, unless one is endowed with foresight, this definition offers little guidance to practitioners. However, it does indicate the usefulness of the social costs concept in identifying social responsibilities.

Social costs and stakeholder approaches to defining responsibilities

In explaining an economic solution to pollution, Hoskins observes that 'most of the costs and benefits associated with resource use are concentrated upon the person doing the producing or consuming'. However, he adds, 'market prices do not always accurately reflect the total costs of production and consumption in society ... As a result, the private cost associated with his use of resources differs from the social cost.'[46] These social costs, or externalities, can, if thought of in such economic terms, provide a criterion for corporate decision-making. But while pollution might be something to which costs can be ascribed – albeit with great difficulty, as Hoskins, Marlin, and others acknowledge[47] – it is far more difficult to ascribe a cost to the human suffering that results from, say, the manufacture of napalm. Furthermore, social costs are not always immediately apparent or willingly recognised. Despite these problems, this concept of social costs is of value in determining social responsibilities. It also features in the argument for ethical purchase behaviour, as later discussed, for social costs may be at least partially converted into private costs via ethical purchase behaviour.

In *The Social Costs and Benefits of Business*, Klein points to the importance of identifying who bears the costs of externalities.[48] Hence the meaning of social responsibility can involve the responsibilities of the corporation to the various constituencies which may benefit and suffer from its effects. These constituencies are also known as stakeholders. This, for Ansoff *et al.*, means 'an interest group which has expectations of the firm and which attempts to influence the firm's objectives, the way these objectives are achieved or the conditions under which the firm operates'.[49] More comprehensive (and less managerially partisan) is the definition by Sturdivant:

> The stakeholder concept suggests that stockholders are by no means the only corporate constituents who have a vested interest in the conduct and performance of a given firm. Stakeholder groups consist of people who are affected by corporate policies and practices and who see themselves as having a stake in the business.[50]

Typically four major constituencies are identified. One practitioner observes: 'Our corporate statement of philosophy identifies the four major publics that we serve: our customers, our employees, our shareholders, and the communities in which we do business.' He continues by suggesting that there is no conflict in serving all four constituencies because their interests are mutually entwined. This philosophy is justified in terms of enlightened self-interest.[51] Yet while the stakeholder concept may help to identify who bears social costs, what criteria are available when there is a conflict between the interests of two constituencies?

Jones defines corporate social responsibility as 'the notion that corporations have an obligation to constituent groups in society other than stockholders and beyond that prescribed by law or union contract'.[52] But he then asks 'How can corporate managers decide what behaviour is socially responsible?' Jones rejects the use of public policy decisions as a basis for corporate decision-making, as suggested by Beesley and Evans,[53] for example. He suggests social responsibility should be viewed as a process, with full consideration given to the social impact of corporate decisions. Although he is not clear about the criteria for decision-making, his example would suggest that the company should formally incorporate the views of the constituency most directly affected. But identifying this constituency is likely to be less than straightforward. It is also close to the practitioner doctrine of social responsibility: for such a doctrine, as Jones notes, is 'a form of self-control'. Indeed, Beesley and Evans advocate such a doctrine as a solution to the problem of corporate power, in addition to external controls (regulation and the market). However, as discussed later, this does not resolve the problem of power without accountability. And if social responsibility is viewed as a doctrine, there is still little indication as to what issues business should be responsible for, and with what priorities. There is still a further complication of how far such a responsibility should extend. An executive from Marks and Spencer neatly reveals the difficulties faced by management in dealing with

55

these three problems of determining which issues to respond to, with what priority, and the extent of the efforts made:

> What are we expected to do? Improve product safety, employ school leavers, introduce pension schemes, prevent redundancies, increase productive investment, recycle waste products, engage ethnic minorities, improve welfare facilities, conserve energy, repackage, depackage, open up the board room to the unions as well as to consumer representatives (something the Co-op has been doing for ages!) or cut prices? And if we are socially responsible and try to satisfy all these demands as far as honour, compassion and the cash flow will allow, then customers have a perfect right to ask – who the hell's minding the shop?[54]

The extent of corporate social responsibility

Rockefeller observes: 'Put quite simply, the difficult question inherent in the challenge of corporate responsibility is: How far should business go in helping to resolve the problems of our society?'[55] Farmer and Hogue propose a continuum with four principal degrees of responsibility: profit maximisation, where social goals are incidental; profit growth, where social goals are also important; social goals, with a break-even on money; and social goals, with money losses acceptable.[56] While this is clear in itself, it does not define corporate responsibilities, but merely identifies possible corporate goals. Beyond profit maximisation, defining corporate responsibilities is extremely difficult. Heilbroner asks:

> Should a business be held responsible for the social consequences of its profitable products? Are antipersonnel weapons, fast cars, electronic surveillance equipment, detergents, pesticides, and the like, just 'economic commodities'? Is business responsible for the human consequences of arranging work in boring and monotonous ways in order to achieve its lawful profit? Is business supposed always to support the policies of its national government by producing goods that the government orders, even if it disapproves of these policies? May business legitimately seek to alter government policies in ways that will enhance its profits?[57]

Such questions point to the difficulty in putting boundaries around corporate power. However, some resolution of the problem is possible by distinguishing between negative injunctions – a moral minimum requirement – and affirmative action. Simon *et al.*, in considering the responsibilities of the individual, show that the choice portrayed by Friedman, Levitt, and others between profit maximisation and creating munificence for all is artificial, because there is always the moral minimum of making profits in such a way as to minimise social injury: 'The negative injunction to avoid and correct social injury threads its way through all morality. We call it a "moral minimum", implying that however one may choose to limit the concept of social responsibility, one cannot exclude this negative injunction.'[58] Competing obligations can override this, but they do not deny the basic obligation to avoid harming others. However, Simon *et al.* do concede that there may be disagreement over what constitutes affirmative action for public good, and disagreement over what constitutes social injury. So, for example, some might see positive discrimination in the recruitment of minorities as an affirmative action, while others might see it as the correction of social injury caused by years of institutionalised racism. Furthermore, by referring to individual social responsibility, Simon *et al.* show that there may be a responsibility for correcting or averting injury even if one may or may not appear to have caused or helped to cause the social injury: 'Life is fraught with emergency situations in which a failure to respond is a special form of violation of the negative injunction against causing social injury: a sin of omission becomes a sin of commission.'[59]

Here they invoke what they term the 'Kew Gardens Principle'. This is based on a tragic and disturbing emergency situation: the stabbing and agonisingly slow death of Kitty Genovese in the Kew Gardens part of New York while 38 people watched or heard and did nothing. On analysis of this, they conclude that critical need, proximity, capability, and being a last resort determine the responsibilities of the individual in such situations. Moreover, because of the danger of assuming someone else will act when others are present, or because one is trying to find out who is the last resort, or because of the possibility of pluralistic ignorance (not acting because no one else is and the situation therefore seeming less serious), there may be a situation where no one acts at all. This suggests that the criterion of last resort is less useful, particularly in an organisational context, and there should be a presumption in favour of taking action when the first three criteria are present.

Their particular purpose in delineating individual responsibility in this way is to point to the responsibilities of investors and the role of ethical investment. So, for example, they might argue that investing in companies operating in South Africa becomes a special form of the violation of the negative injunction against causing social injury, through inaction (whereby omission becomes commission), and by employing the above criteria of critical need, proximity, capability, and last resort. Such an analysis would suggest that investors in such companies should press for changes in company policy.[60] However, such a perspective is equally useful in determining the responsibilities of managers. One can conclude that corporate social responsibility does at least extend to the 'moral minimum':

From the conclusion that all citizens, individual and institutional, are equally subject to the negative injunction against social injury, it follows that there is a prima facie obligation on the part of business corporations to regulate their activities so that they do not injure others and so that they correct what injury they do cause.[61]

Simon *et al.* then continue by identifying four different categories or meanings of corporate responsibility. These are:

(1) Self-regulation in the avoidance of social injury (the negative injunction).
(2) The championing of political and moral causes unrelated to the corporation's business activities, perhaps including some gifts of charity.
(3) Affirmative action extending beyond self-regulation but falling short of the championing of causes, such as co-operation with government in the training of the hard-core unemployed.
(4) Internal reforms and changes in corporate structure affecting the voting rights of shareholders, or the prerogatives of management, or increased disclosure.

The last category relates more to corporate accountability than to responsibility, although a great deal of the British writing on social responsibility is concerned with such issues of accountability as employee participation on boards, the 'fifth directive', or responsibilities to shareholders.[62] Putting this category aside, however, one is left with a continuum describing three different degrees of corporate social responsibility, from self-regulation, to affirmative action, to the championing of political and moral causes. Of course, a fourth category could be added where the negative injunction is ignored and one has corporate irresponsibility.

Yet this model is not easy to combine with that by Farmer and Hogue, described above. A composite model relating goals (Farmer and Hogue) and responsibilities (Simon *et al.*) would be useful, as the Farmer and Hogue model falls down in its inadequate definition of responsibilities, while the Simon *et al.* model suffers from too little consideration of corporate goals. The problem is the uncertainty about the role of profit: Is profit a prerequisite for corporate social responsibility or is social responsibility necessary for profit?

Vogel, Beesley and Evans, Chamberlain, and many others[63] argue that profitability and responsibility are on the opposite sides of a cost equation. Vogel writes, 'the more profitable a company or the more secure its market position, the more able are its managers to consider the impact of the company on the welfare of its various constituencies. From this perspective, profitability can be regarded as a necessary condition of responsible social performance.' But, he adds, 'some firms have compiled records of outstanding economic performance while remaining insensitive to social concerns'.[64] As a practitioner at the Conference Board meetings on corporate social responsibility put it: 'It is true of companies as it is true of man that it is easier to be moral when you are successful than when your back is to the wall.'[65] While Drucker observes: 'The first "social responsibility" of business is then to make enough profit to cover the costs of the future. If this "social responsibility" is not met, no other "social responsibility" can be met.'[66]

Others, however, take a different view.[67] As Henry Ford put it: 'There is no longer anything to reconcile, if there ever was, between the social conscience and the profit motive ... Improving the quality of society ... is nothing more than another step in the evolutionary process of taking a more far-sighted view of return on investment.'[68] Marlin's study of the US iron and steel industry, paper industry, and petroleum-refining industry showed that the best pollution-control performance was achieved by the more profitable companies. This she claims is because 'Good managements are likely both to earn higher profits and to be more careful in protecting the environment.'[69] But although this shows that profitability and responsibility are not mutually exclusive, it may be that this is merely support for Vogel's argument that profitability is a prerequisite for responsibility. The view that responsibility comes first is based on enlightened self-interest, a longer-term perspective. It is summed up in Sethi's claim that 'It is a fallacy that business can prosper – or, indeed, even exist – without regard to broader social concerns.'[70] And as Haas argues, there are three rationales for corporate social responsibility: moral obligation, long-term self-interest, and the necessity to preserve the private sector – longer-term self-interest.[71] Put otherwise, adequate profitability is necessary for long-term survival, not profit maximisation.

Perhaps the issue can best be resolved by accepting that social responsibility up to some minimum level is in the best long-term interests of business, but beyond this, while it might be desirable, it can only be possible given adequate profitability. This would then suggest four positions on the extent of corporate social responsibility:

(1) Profit maximisation and social irresponsibility.
(2) Profit maximisation tempered by the 'moral minimum' through self-regulation.
(3) Profit as a necessary but not sufficient goal, with affirmative action extending beyond self-regulation.
(4) Profit as a necessary but not sufficient goal, with social responsibility extending beyond self-regulation and affirmative action to include the championing of political and moral causes

unrelated to the corporation's business activities, perhaps even including gifts of charity but only as long as profitability permits.

The notion of social irresponsibility will be explained in the subsequent discussion of the Friedman position on social responsibility. Suffice to note here, anything less than the 'moral minimum' is viewed as social irresponsibility. It is also worth noting that profit need be interpreted broadly. It refers not so much to the declared profit in the annual report but to the true 'bottom line' of financial success. As the discussion at the BIM conference on social responsibility indicates, it is not so much the loss of profits *per se* that constitutes the threat from socially responsible actions, but ultimately the risk of takeover. In other words, in Britain at least, the City of London calls the tune.[72]

Yet despite this model, a problem for the practitioner remains:

> Every manager faces an area, everyone of us in the whole series of decisions, between the strict letter of the law, which of course we all comply with, and on the other hand the maximum possible profit for this year's balance sheet. We are inclined to the latter because we are afraid of being taken over if we don't. Somewhere in this area we make an ethical judgement ... Are we entitled to put in some margin as responsible citizens as well as managers?[73]

This area of discretion is discussed in looking at the 'Friedman Misconception'.

The 'Friedman Misconception'

Sir Frederick Catherwood's affirmative reply to this question of discretion would not have the support of Milton Friedman, nor Hayek. There is little confusion in the competitive model of capitalism on the issues of which business has a social responsibility or the extent of this responsibility. Hayek writes:

> If we want effectively to limit the powers of corporations to where they are beneficial, we shall have to confine them much more than we have yet done to one specific goal, that of the profitable use of the capital entrusted to the management by the stockholders ... the fashionable doctrine that their policy should be guided by 'social considerations' is likely to produce most undesirable results.[74]

Social responsibility is here viewed as a fundamentally subversive doctrine. Friedman argues that to suggest corporations should have a social responsibility is to fail to understand the way in which the game of the market is and must be played: 'there is one and only one social responsibility of business – to use its resources and engage in activities designed to increase its profits so long as it stays within the rules of the game, which is to say, engages in open and free competition, without deception or fraud.'[75]

Friedman is concerned about how a corporate official is to know how to act if not guided by profit maximisation – as a surrogate for the self-interest of the entrepreneur of Adam Smith's day. He asks, although these questions are overlooked by many of his critics, 'if businessmen do have a social responsibility other than making maximum profits for shareholders, how are they to know what it is? Can self-selected private individuals decide what the social interest is?'[76] So Friedman's position is more than the blind self-interest many of his critics argue against; it includes the recognition of corporate power and the need for it to be appropriately limited. His position is attractive in both its clarity, simplicity, and elegance, and also in its solution of the problem of the social control of business. Given such a position, profit maximisation within the rules of the game would give little discretion to managers. There would be no need for the confusing and potentially dangerous – as well as possibly illegitimate – ethical judgement referred to above. Yet social policies would not necessarily be precluded, for they may well contribute to long-term profitability. So, for example, one could, within the Friedman position, justify when building a new plant the fitting of pollution-control equipment that exceeds the minimum legal requirement, but is in anticipation of changes in legislation and recognition of the higher costs of fitting retrospectively.

Heilbroner admires Friedman's position, without being reconciled to it. He asks: Should not stockholders be allowed to do with their money as they see fit? But, more importantly: Should corporations be allowed to 'play God'?

> When the Dow Chemical Company announces that it is making
> Napalm not for profit but for patriotism, I am sure that its directors
> swell with feelings of social responsibility; and when it
> discontinues the manufacture of Napalm in response to public
> protest, I have no doubt that its officers again experience the flow
> of social benefaction. But I am not sure that such motives provide
> the best grounds on which social decisions should be made. For,
> indeed, when Friedman asks on what basis the businessman is
> qualified to make good social decisions, he is asking a question
> that is not easy to answer. Why should we entrust the disposition of
> large sums to men whose sympathies and prejudices, not to say
> 'philosophy', are different from mine, or from yours? How far does
> the philanthropic impulse properly go? By whose say-so are boards
> of directors authorised to play God?[77]

Yet, adds Heilbroner, business people are less than keen on the Friedman position, not because it potentially limits their power but because they are averse to such explicit recognition of their self-interest. They 'recoil from the implication that they are "only" moneymakers ... capitalists do not like to act like the creatures of pure self-interest that they are supposed to be'. Heilbroner also identifies three major failings of Friedman's position.

First, there is little evidence of pure profit maximisation in the real world because this would not be socially responsible, but socially irresponsible. Heilbroner suggests that Friedman's position 'does not squarely face up to the consequences of its own First Rule: for if corporations in fact sought to maximise the profits of their stockholders, we would find General Motors lowering the price of its cars enough to drive Chrysler and even Ford to the wall'. This, of course, explains why the first position on the extent of social responsibility continuum described above is profit maximisation and social irresponsibility. Second, Friedman's position assumes that the rules of the game can be established without cheating, in spite of the influence of business. Heilbroner cannot accept the assumption that government makes the rules independently of business or that business will willingly acquiesce to such rules if it has no part in the making of them. He cites previous regulatory attempts which show that the rule-making agencies of government are almost invariably captured by the industries which they are set up to control; a point which the Friedmans acknowledge in *Free to Choose*, but then use to justify deregulation. So on this point, Heilbroner concludes that Friedman's proposals are not 'anything more than a license for business to define its "social responsibility" behind the respectable screen of a government front, after which it will indeed more or less live up to its own standards'.

Yet perhaps the most important argument against Friedman's position is Heilbroner's third point. Here he observes that such a view of social responsibility rests on a curious conception of modern capitalism. One must be aware of the context in which Friedman's position is advanced: a restatement of the tenets of classical capitalism, the competitive model of capitalism described in the previous chapter. Can Friedman realistically claim, using such a model, that the rights of shareholders should predominate? Such a position assumes property rights which hardly seem applicable when the 'ownership' exercised by the shareholder over his or her corporation is so different from that of the small businessperson over his or her property. The stockholder is no longer a significant source of venture capital, 'merely a passive holder of certificates of varying degrees of risk and potential return', with little knowledge of the real performance of 'his' corporation. Surely the other stakeholders deserve some return?

Bell's rejection of Friedman's argument also questions shareholder ownership. He asks: 'Is the corporation primarily an instrument of "owners" – legally the stockholders – or is it an autonomous enterprise which, despite its particular history, has become – or should become – an instrument for service to society in a system of pluralist powers?' He concludes that today ownership is simply a 'legal fiction' and while 'the corporation may be a private enterprise institution ... it is not really a private property institution'. Hence 'One can treat stockholders not as "owners" but as legitimate claimants to some fixed share of the profits of a corporation – and to nothing more.'[78] Heilbroner goes further and suggests that the labour force, management, and the firm's customers should be viewed as more legitimate claimants.

Recognition of corporate response and responsibilities to a number of stakeholders as well as the stockholders clearly weakens Friedman's position. Banks suggests that the 'most trenchant scholarly rebuttal to Friedman'[79] is Jacoby's Social Environment Model, of which 'The most important characteristic ... is the explicit recognition that corporate behavior responds to political as well as to market forces.' Jacoby writes of Friedman's position that, 'Unfortunately , Friedman failed to add that social involvement is consistent with self-interest, and that corporate managers need a sophisticated understanding of business-societal relationships in order to operate on that principle.'[80] This failure to recognise the context of corporate action is referred to by Johnson as the 'Friedman Misconception' – 'the view that the enterprise is altogether and solely an economic organisation, divorced from its sociocultural setting'.[81]

So it can be seen that the argument that the social responsibility of business is to make a profit is more sophisticated than it might at first appear. It is about more than simply asserting the property rights of shareholders and fulfilling their expectations of maximum returns on investment. Both Friedman and Hayek, as prime exponents of this argument, are concerned not only about these rights but also about managers having an area of discretion in decision-making relating to social issues. They ask 'How is a manager to know what his or her social responsibilities are?' and 'What right has a manager to assume social responsibilities – by what mandate?' Valid though these concerns may be, they both ignore human nature and the inevitability of managerial discretion in practice. Within the classical economic model there is scope for Friedman's position but even then one must be wary of business influence when government intervention in the market is inevitable. Moreover, as discussed in the last chapter, this model assumes that material progress is the most important goal of the economic system in bringing welfare for all, whereas latter-day affluence may suggest that other goals are now more important. In other words, profit may not be able to provide the means for achieving today's social goals. Outside the classical economic model, in the real world of mixed markets, Friedman's argument is a misconception. Yet shareholders must be permitted some return. More importantly, some control must be exercised over managerial discretion on social issues. There must then be social control of business. Prior to looking at the mechanisms for social control of business, it is worth considering management practice and perspectives on social responsibility issues. The chapter concludes with an assessment of the arguments for and against corporate social responsibility.

Management creeds and social responsibility

Profit maximising, trusteeship, and 'quality of life' management

Included within those that fall into the error of the 'Friedman Misconception' would be a substantial proportion of managers, as indicated by the various managerial creeds identified by Hay *et al.*, Silk and Vogel, and Steiner and Steiner. Hay *et al.* identify three phases of corporate social responsibility. They then suggest that each of these phases also represents different managerial values that may be currently found. Phase one, or type one, is profit maximising management. Here 'the individual's drive for maximum profits and the regulation of the competitive market-place would interact to create the greatest aggregate wealth for a nation and therefore the maximum public good'.[82] Such a position is based not only on economic logic, but also society's goals and values: the problem of economic scarcity at the time this phase was predominant meant that economic growth and the accumulation of aggregate wealth were primary goals; Calvinism stressed that the road to salvation was through hard work and the accumulation of wealth. Such a position follows the logic of Milton Friedman. The difficulty in maintaining this position results from the problem in drawing a line between spending the stockholders' money for charity and spending it in the enlightened self-interest of the firm. As Blumberg observes, adhering to the neoclassical standard is difficult because the rules of the game have changed – with increasing government intervention and changes in public attitudes. Both of these factors require response, whether regarded as public relations techniques or socially responsible conduct.[83] In other words, changes in the rules of the game demand some sort of social response from business, however such a response may be justified and defined.

Phase two, or type two, is trusteeship management. This notion has already been touched upon in the earlier discussion of corporate social

responsibilities to various constituencies or stakeholders. As Hay *et al.*
put it: 'In this view the manager was seen as a "trustee" for the various
contributor groups to the firm rather than simply an agent of the
owners.'[84] They suggest that this phase emerged in the 1920s and 1930s.
They attribute it to two factors. First, the separation of ownership and
control, discussed earlier. The 'trusteeship' concept provided an answer
to the question prompted by the increasing diffusion of ownership of the
shares of American corporations: 'To whom is management
responsible?' According to this concept, management was responsible
to all contributors to the firm. The second factor is the emergence of a
largely pluralistic society. Pluralism implies a trusteeship role. Hay *et
al.* suggest that this type is currently predominant, with the majority of
business managers today adhering to a phase two concept of social
responsibility. They suggest that 'these individuals understand the pluralistic nature of our society and are generally committed to being
equitable in dealing with the various contributors to the firm and the
concerned outside pressure groups'.[85] Others concur and a number refer
to Franks Abram's 1950 comment, as Chairman of Standard Oil, that the
manager should conduct his affairs 'in such a way as to maintain an
equitable and working balance among the claims of the various directly
interested groups – stockholders, employees, customers and the public
at large'.[86] Blumberg describes this view of management duties to various groups as managerialism and suggests that this is held by both the
British Institute of Directors and the Confederation of British Industry.[87]

The third phase identified by Hay *et al.* is the 'quality of life'
management. This, perhaps not surprisingly, is a little more nebulous
than the other two phases. They suggest that this phase has become
popular in recent years within an affluent society in which the aggregate
scarcity of goods and services is no longer the fundamental problem.
Referring back to this author's typology of extents of corporate social
responsibility, this would constitute the 'championing' position,
category 4. For the firm this means that it 'becomes deeply involved in
the solution of society's major problems'.[88] Yet, as in the typology, Hay
et al. also stress the importance of profitability. Profit is necessary for
social responsibility and, indeed, economic well-being is the first
responsibility. However, the importance of the role of profit
notwithstanding, Hay *et al.* do claim that a growing number of business
executives and academics seem to be accepting the phase three position.
This, they suggest, has resulted in a number of large US corporations
becoming involved in major social action programmes – such as IBM,
Chase Manhattan Bank, Xerox, Eli Lilly, and Coca Cola. Such actions
are justified in terms of enlightened self-interest. This, they suggest, is a
major intellectual concept for convincing profit-maximisation-oriented

managers to be aware of and include societal considerations in their decision-making.

Hay *et al.* define enlightened self-interest 'as an action by a firm which cannot be clearly justified on the basis of cost and revenue projections but is taken because it is believed to be in the best interests of the firm in the long run'.[89] There are three positive dimensions to this: the recognition that anything a firm does to produce a better environment for society will at least be of long-term benefit to it; the enhancing of the public image, as a form of institutional advertising, in providing a recruitment advantage with idealistic students, and in giving employees a sense of doing something worthwhile; and the provision of possible profitable market opportunities, such as in pollution abatement equipment. There are also three negative dimensions to enlightened self-interest; insensitivity will eventually lead to government intervention, such as with worker safety issues and the resultant health and safety at work legislation; harassment by social action groups and other critics, such as boycotts or demands at annual general meetings, is averted; and insensitivity may result in lower stock values through ethical investments.

To conclude on the Hay *et al.* analysis of managerial creeds: it can be seen that they claim a shift in managerial emphasis: from owners' interests, under the Adam Smith and, latterly, Friedman notion of general welfare resulting from the pursuit of self-interest – a profit maximisation model; to group interests, under the pluralist notions of the trusteeship model; to, most recently, society's interests, in accord with a recognition of affluence permitting a concern for a wide range of social issues – a quality of life model. On the current state of social responsibility of management, they suggest: 'Each new phase has not merely replaced the earlier phase but rather has been superimposed on it. Thus, a modern view of social responsibility would to some degree incorporate essential parts of all three phases of the concept.'[90] So the concept of social responsibility has gone through each of the three distinct phases described above, each phase corresponding to a particular set of managerial values. In practice, the extent of social responsibility will depend on whether the manager is type one, two, or three, at least in so far as he or she is permitted discretion. But as already noted, this area of discretion can be quite considerable. Hay *et al.* suggest, somewhat optimistically perhaps, that type three is becoming increasingly popular.

Business ideologies and classical, managerial, and consent creeds

The managerial creeds described by Silk and Vogel, and Steiner and Steiner, are similar in many respects to those described above. Steiner and Steiner link changes in the concept of social responsibility with different managerial creeds, but only two types are identified that correlate with the Hay *et al.* model. They refer to these creeds within a discussion of managerial ideologies.[91] Steiner and Steiner's two types are the classical business ideology, which they suggest has dominated business thought and action for two hundred years, and the modern socio-economic managerial ideology. The former extols the values of individualism, private property, free competition, and limited government. The description of the competitive model of capitalism in the last chapter covers most of the facets of the classical ideology as described by Steiner and Steiner. It is, of course, comparable to Hay *et al.*'s phase one profit-maximising management. The modern socio-economic managerial ideology is comparable to an amalgam of Hay *et al.*'s phase two and phase three, with a leaning toward the latter. Steiner and Steiner note that the new ideology is not as well articulated, complete, and specific as the classical one, but claim that there is little doubt as to its growing in general acceptance in the future. They suggest that its origins go back perhaps a hundred years, but that it is only within the past two decades in the United States that it has become accepted by businesspeople. Even so, there are some who suggest that expressions of social responsibility within this ideology are little more than empty rhetoric: a 'more or less transparent defense of privilege masquerading as philosophy, the search for sanction cloaked as a search for truth'.[92] Steiner and Steiner conclude:

> For the great majority of business institutions, most of which are comparatively small companies, the classical ideology is accepted today by society and business people in those companies and probably will be for some time into the future. Most people do not expect a person whose business is desperately striving to break even to concentrate on much else besides making a profit, so long, of course, as that person abides by the law. For larger organizations, however, society expects much more, and leaders of such corporations accept the challenge of the socioeconomic managerial ideology.[93]

But this may not be the case for many of the managers within organisations. Steiner and Steiner suggest that for the vast majority of managers in large corporations, their personal ideology will be a mixture of the classical and the new position and this is likely to persist for some time.

Silk and Vogel identify three creeds: the classical, the managerial, and the consent creed. The first two creeds are as identified by Sutton *et al.* in *The American Business Creed*, a source also used by Steiner and Steiner. The classical creed is the phase one position of Hay *et al.*, and the classical ideology position of Steiner and Steiner. The managerial creed is the trusteeship management of Hay *et al.*, and the essence of Steiner and Steiner's socio-economic managerial ideology. The consent creed seems unique to Silk and Vogel. It emphasises the legitimacy of corporate power, or rather, the requirement for legitimacy. It assumes that 'the privileges of business will depend on the extent to which corporations listen to, correctly interpret, and effectively respond to the political and social preferences of the American people'.[94] It is based on the idea of popular sovereignty, the notion as expressed by John Locke, of a government only ruling with the consent of the governed. (Vogel has elsewhere written about the corporation as a private government and explained such a connection.[95]) In illustration of this creed, Silk and Vogel quote one executive at the meetings of the Conference Board as saying: 'The social responsibility of business is to create material abundance, but to do so on the basis of the ground-rules that society sets.'[96]

However, this was by no means the predominant creed at the meetings of the Conference Board and, as both Hay *et al.* and Steiner and Steiner observe, such creeds are superimposed on one another:

It is important not to exaggerate the sharpness of the ideological divisions within the business community. Only a relatively few executives articulate a perspective that could be classified unambiguously into one or the other category. Each of the three creeds here named – classical, managerial and public consent – is best understood as an 'ideal type', useful in demonstrating and clarifying the range and variety of contemporary business opinions. Most executives probably include elements of all three positions in their thinking. Among the senior executives at 1974-75 conferences, the classical strain seemed dominant.[97]

Silk and Vogel also suggest that the split between the creeds may be less between different factions than within the minds of individual businesspeople.

So, in conclusion, it would seem reasonable to claim that distinct managerial creeds are identifiable and that they guide decision-making. Because of the area of discretion permitted to managers in matters of social responsibility it would follow that socially responsible actions will be determined by the particular creed which the manager favours or is dominant in his or her thinking at the time. Of course, some might argue that where guided by a managerial creed, the manager is being socially responsible within the terms of that creed. However, the absolute extent of social responsibility is defined within the model given earlier. In practice, Steiner and Steiner and Silk and Vogel claim that most managers adhere to the classical creed. Hay *et al.*, perhaps a little optimistically, claim that they adhere to the trusteeship model. However, like so many issues in this area, this is not clear. Following the model of the extent of social responsibility, it would seem likely that in practice most managers are at position 2, profit maximisation tempered by the 'moral minimum' through self-regulation. In view of Hay *et al.*, Steiner and Steiner, and Silk and Vogel's observations, there is at least a tendency towards position 3 and perhaps even position 4. Managerial recognition of social responsibilities and action in accordance with this, while it may not resolve the problem of the legitimacy of corporate power, does point to a form of control of that power. Self-control is indeed a solution to the problem of corporate power and is advocated by Beesley and Evans and many others, including business itself.

Arguments for and against corporate social responsibility

There are five principal arguments against corporate social responsibility: the problem of competing claims (the role of profit), competitive disadvantage, competence, fairness, and legitimacy. Each will be considered in turn.

Competing claims – the role of profit

Friedman argues that the notion of social responsibility in business 'shows a fundamental misconception of the character and nature of a free economy'.[98] Business's function is economic, not social. Accordingly, it should be guided and judged by economic criteria alone. Action dictated by anything other than profit maximisation, within the rules of the game, impairs economic efficiency and represents a taxation on those bearing the costs of such inefficiency, most notably the stockholders. The role of the corporation is to make a profit and maximise social welfare through the efficiency which that entails, and as Simon *et al.* put it, 'consideration of any factors other than profit-maximising ones either results in a deliberate sacrifice of profits or muddies the process of corporate decision-making so as to impair profitability'.[99] So, to quote Silk and Vogel, 'In short, the corporation will best fulfill its obligation to society by fulfilling its obligation to itself.'[100] However, this argument falls down in a number of ways. Simon *et al.* identify four reasons. First, it emphasises the profits of the individual firm as opposed to the corporate sector, which may not mean the highest efficiency from society's point of view. Second, there is the distinction between the short term and the long term. Social goals may be profitable in the long term, for the reasons considered in the discussion earlier of enlightened self-interest. Third, there are other indicators of well-being besides profitability. Because of the uncertainty about what will be profitable, corporate goals in practice place profitability second, seeking an assurance of a required minimum profit.

Fourth, and finally, there is the concern for the efficient use of national resources. Because of social costs, profitability is not necessarily the best measure of effectiveness. Indeed, they argue, 'the argument for efficient allocation of resources would appear to require the corporation to locate and regulate the social consequences of its own conduct'.[101]

Furthermore, Simon *et al.* suggest that if these arguments are not accepted, the negative injunction against social injury would, at least, have to be respected. In other words, Friedman ignores the moral minimum: 'most of the debate on corporate responsibility, by rather carelessly focusing on what we have termed affirmative duties ... has obscured what seems to be the fundamental point: that economic activity ... can have unwanted and injurious side-effects, and that the correction of these indirect consequences require self-regulation.'[102] (There are some similarities here with Heilbroner's point that pure profit-maximisation could amount to social irresponsibility, as discussed earlier.) Essentially, the main criticism of this argument against corporate social responsibility – the need for profit maximisation – is its basis in an inappropriate economic model, the competitive model of capitalism; particularly because of social costs and the question of who the profits are for. Noting the argument about the separation of ownership and control and the consequent limited influence of shareholders over the conduct of professional managers, Ackerman quotes a statement by the chairman of Xerox which pointedly illustrates the inapplicability of the notion of profit-maximisation for shareholders: 'If we ran this business Wall Street's way, we'd run it into the ground ... We're in this business for a hell of a long time and we're not going to try to maximise earnings over the short run.'[103]

Competitive disadvantage

The competitive disadvantage argument against corporate social responsibility suggests that because social action will have a price for the firm it also entails a competitive disadvantage. So, either such works should be carried out by government or, at least, legislated for so that all corporations or industries will be subject to the same requirements. Mintz and Cohen show that such a consideration was paramount in Alfred Sloan's 1929 decision not to fit safety glass to Chevrolets, 'one of the single most important protections ever devised against avoidable automotive death, disfigurement and injury'. Sloan was concerned about public anxiety over automobile safety and did not wish to publicise hazards. In his correspondence with Lammot du Pont over the possible supply of safety glass he observes that despite General Motors La Salles and Cadillacs being equipped with safety glass, sales by Packard, one of their competitors, had not been materially affected. So

Sloan wrote, 'I do not think that from the stockholder's standpoint the move on Cadillac's part has been justified.' Sloan was still reluctant even when he recognised that such a feature would come in the end, he did not want to hurry it along: 'The net result would be that both competition and ourselves would have reduced the return on our capital.' Even when Du Pont noted that Ford had started to fit safety glass in the windshields of all their cars, Sloan observed: 'it is not my responsibility to sell safety glass.'[104]

Green notes that Sloan's rejection of safety glass because it would add slightly to price and because his competitors lacked the 'lifesaving technology' should not be possible today because companies could go to the government to urge minimum standards and thereby avoid placing the firm at a competitive disadvantage.[105] And as Simon *et al.* observe, the competitive disadvantage argument against social responsibility is difficult to accept when the social injury is caused by one firm but not its industry peers – as in Sloan's refusal to fit safety glass even after it was fitted to the windshields of all Ford cars. But if the social injury is not unique to one firm then 'the individual corporation can at least be expected to work for industrywide self-regulation within the limits of anti-trust laws; or the individual firm can work for government regulation'.[106] What this ignores, however, is that many industries are ultimately in competition with other industries and there may then be a competitive disadvantage for the industry as a whole in relation to substitution goods. This issue of inter-industry competition aside, the criticism of the competitive disadvantage argument is essentially sound. In approbation of his position, Friedman quotes Adam Smith's comment: 'I have never known much good done by those who affected to trade for the public good.' While healthy scepticism might be desirable, the oligopolistic form of most markets and increased consumer knowledge and awareness makes such a position inappropriate. There are other reasons besides. Ackerman's observations on the advantages and disadvantages of early corporate response to social demands suggest that an early response, while it may seem unnecessary, does provide flexibility. Perhaps more significant, though, is his recognition that the area of discretion within which managers act is quite broad and as competition is conducted on many fronts there is scope for an early response, particularly when the potential benefits are also considered.[107]

Competence

Friedman asks, 'If businessmen do have a social responsibility other than making maximum profits for stockholders, how are they to know what it is?' This implies the competence argument against corporate social responsibility. Simon *et al.* identify three ways in which, it may be claimed, a firm is not competent to deal with social issues. First, there is the claim that corporations do not have the technical skills to deal with social issues. This, they suggest, will vary from case to case and, given the notion of last resort in the Kew Gardens Principle (discussed earlier), can only be valid if some other party can do the job better. Second, there is the claim that corporations do not know what is good for society and some other institution, such as government, knows better. But, they observe, 'a corporation's alleged lack of insight into the nature of the good is not a reason for objecting to its social activities unless they are deliberately coercive'.[108] Third, there is the claim that incompetent attempts to resolve social issues waste shareholders' money. But, suggest Simon *et al.*, this is only true if management acts in accord with its own predilections, in which case management needs to be made more accountable to the shareholder. Alternatively, such a claim could be countered by pointing to the separation of ownership and control and the role of the professional manager. These factors notwithstanding, the argument of competence can only be applicable to affirmative actions; there is still, as Simon *et al.* note, the moral minimum of the negative injunction against social injury, for which competence cannot be an issue.

Bradshaw, a practitioner writing in this area (as President of Atlantic Richfield Company), does point out that 'corporations cannot cure all social ills, and, indeed, in many areas should not even try ... This nation is richly endowed with many and varied institutions. Social change is, I believe, accomplished through these many institutions and not through any one.'[109] He goes on to argue that businesspeople should stick to their competencies, but, bearing in mind his observation that the rules of the game are changing, work 'within those competencies [and] become a prime mover for change at the rule-making level, whether it is in national government, regional areas or states'. Similarly, Silk and Vogel report the comments of the executives at the Conference Board meetings who contended that if they try to operate outside their special area of competence they will invariably get into trouble: 'We shouldn't accept responsibility for what we don't know about.'[110] Elsewhere, Vogel observes that many social issues do not present much scope for solution by business. Moreover, it is not realistic to expect the business community to assume a leading role in balancing social needs with economic imperatives, because it would be inconsistent with the political views of business: 'The social reforms whose enactment have so dramatically improved the lot of the average American over the last 75 years mostly were adopted in spite of business lobbying, not because of it ... if business is to perform as well as it can, it requires pressure from those outside it.'[111]

So on the competency argument one must conclude that while there is the moral minimum, social actions beyond this are constrained by what business is able, competent, and willing to do. As Rockefeller notes: 'No one sector of our society is competent to deal with these problems ... The only answer is that all sections must become involved, each in its own distinctive way, but in full and collaborative relationship with the others.'[112]

Fairness – domination by business

Friedman asks, 'is it tolerable that these public functions of taxation, expenditure, and control be exercised by the people who happen at the moment to be in charge of particular enterprises, chosen for those posts by strictly private groups?'[113] This is the fairness argument against corporate social responsibility. Heilbroner's concern about corporations playing God has already been noted. In a similar vein, Davis and Blomstrom observe, 'combining social activities with the established economic activities of business would give business an excessive concentration of power ... [which] would threaten the pluralistic division of powers which we now have among institutions, probably reducing the viability of our free society'.[114] As Levitt notes, 'The corporation would eventually invest itself with all-embracing duties, obligations, and finally powers – ministering to the whole man and molding him and society in the image of the corporation's narrow ambitions and its essentially unsocial needs.'[115] Big business acting in accord with notions of social responsibility gives managers more discretionary power over the lives of others in three ways, as Simon *et al.* observe: by political action (lobbying), the creation of private government (within the organisation), and by a smothering effect – domination by business values.

However, they counter, if business does have this power then the problem is to control it, not think it presents a problem only in the social policy context. One must also consider what is worse: a lack of self-regulation may be more arbitrary in its effects:

> We grant that even corporate self-regulation may have some spill-over effect – that the attempt to avoid or correct a self-caused social injury may have some influence on the freedom of action of others. Such effects will, we think, be relatively insignificant when compared to the benefits of self-correction.[116]

Moreover, they ask that even if affirmative modes of corporate social responsibility involve manipulation, should one fault genuine efforts to help? Besides which, the distinction between leadership and manipulation is a fine one. They conclude on this issue: 'we are convinced that the type of corporate self-regulation we have proposed will help to limit the arbitrary and oppressive impact of corporate activity, rather than the opposite, and therefore does not present a fairness problem.'

Legitimacy – the role of government

The final principal argument against corporate social responsibility is legitimacy: social issues are the concern of government. Or, as one executive commented at the Conference Board meetings: 'We pay the government well. It should do its job and leave us alone to do ours.'[117] As Silk and Vogel comment, the businessperson feels 'non business' contributions should be voluntary and government has legitimate social concerns which business supports in the payment of taxes. Simon *et al.* identify three positions in this argument. First, unless business acts then government will act, with all the attendant disadvantages of government intervention cited by critics of government encroachment of private spheres. Moreover, corporate social problem-solving may be preferable because it is pluralistic and is therefore likely to be preferred by the people. This position seeks to minimise the role of government. Second, as Levitt and Friedman suggest, corporate involvement in social problems is likely to be bungled, which in itself will lead to government intervention. This has the disadvantages of both government and business interference in the private sphere: again, a position which can be employed to support business action to minimise government's role. The third position claims that only government can deal with market imperfections. This is because some encroachment is viewed as necessary (the mixed market position) and there needs to be an orderly division of labour. They counter that again these positions against corporate social responsibility reflect only on the affirmative duty and not on the negative injunction against social injury. In any event, there is still a case for self-regulation because the duplication of effort cannot in itself be harmful, federal agencies tend to represent industry interests anyway, and much corporate activity is overseas and outside government jurisdiction.

Simon *et al.* conclude on these five principal arguments against corporate social responsibility:

> These points do carry weight with respect to some affirmative
> modes of corporate social action, but we find these objections
> unpersuasive in application to self-regulating activity. Whatever
> debate there may be over more expansive notions of corporate
> responsibility, a self-policing attempt to take into account the
> social consequences of business activity and at least an attempt to
> avoid or correct social injury represents a basic obligation.[118]

The problem of competing claims, competitive disadvantage, competency, fairness, and legitimacy are the principal arguments against corporate social responsibility. Other arguments include: the public being misled about who bears the cost of corporate social action, believing it to be free; the problem of determining benefits, costs, and priorities; the weakened international balance of payments – reduced efficiency raises costs and may put companies at a competitive disadvantage internationally; and the lack of a broad base of support among all groups in society.[119] Also, as Beesley and Evans observe, Friedman's argument must be seen within the context in which it is presented, as 'part of an argument holding that property rights, as for instance manifest in company shareholdings, and, more fundamentally, the right to engage freely in economic activity are necessary (but admittedly not sufficient) conditions for the maintenance of Western-style political freedom'.[120] This is the argument about political freedom considered in Chapter 1. Essentially this argument, the others briefly mentioned, and the principal arguments have been answered and found to be lacking. This is due mainly to their dependence on an inappropriate socio-economic model of contemporary society, and their failure to account for social costs and the moral minimum of the negative injunction against social injury.

The arguments for corporate social responsibility are implied above. They emphasise changes in public expectations of business; enlightened self-interest; the avoidance of government intervention; the extent of corporate power and the need to balance this with responsibility in self-regulation; and business resources.[121] It is worth concluding this chapter by quoting Steiner and Steiner's summary in review of the arguments for and against corporate social responsibility:

> Business decision-making today is a mixture of altruism, self-interest, and good citizenship. Managers do take actions that are in the social interest even though there is a cost involved and the connection with long-range profits is quite remote. These actions traditionally were considered to be in the category of 'good deeds'. The issue today is that some people expect – and some managers wonder whether they should respond to the expectation – that business should assume a central role in resolving major social problems of the day in the name of social responsibility... Business cannot do this, nor should it try. Larger corporations, however, clearly feel that the old-fashioned single-minded lust for profits tempered with a few 'good deeds' must be modified in favour of a new social concern. Society also expects its business leaders to be concerned. The issue is not whether business has social responsibilities. It has them. The fundamental issue is to identify them for business in general and for the individual company.[122]

The identification of these responsibilities and ensuring they are met – as well as the continuing problem of corporate power ignored by Steiner and Steiner – demands social control of business. The mechanisms for this, including the market, are considered next.

Chapter three

Social control of business : from responsibility and philanthropy to accountability

Preview

> You think you are helping the economic system by your
> well-meaning laws and interferences. You are not. Let it be. The
> oil of self-interest will keep the gears working in almost
> miraculous fashion. No one need plan. No sovereign need rule. The
> market will answer all things.
>
> Paul A. Samuelson[1]

> Today the grounds of legitimacy for corporate power are shifting.
> The impact of corporations on their social and physical
> environments has become too great for the exercise of managerial
> power to be justified by the legal rights of property ownership
> alone. The conception of the marketplace as a sphere of activity
> where an impersonal mechanism would hold power accountable is
> a slim fiction for critics.
>
> George A. Steiner and John F. Steiner[2]

Samuelson's précis of Adam Smith's message is a statement of how the market operates as a social control mechanism, or, at least, how it works within the competitive model of capitalism. The quotation from Steiner and Steiner is a suitable riposte. No longer, it seems, is the market an adequate control, as discussed in the previous two chapters. Yet is the corporation's social role limited to its own attempts at self-regulation and benevolent gestures? The claim here is that there are other social control mechanisms as well as self-regulation, and there is still a vital role played by the market – a role which gives credibility to the notion of ethical purchase behaviour as an attempt to make business socially responsible.

Benevolent gestures in the form of donations to charity and other arbitrary measures might be business's view of social responsibility.

This is not, however, social responsibility as defined in Chapter 2; it is philanthropy. This, as a consequence of self-regulation, is insufficient. Moreover, the problem of corporate power is not resolved without accountability. Hence this chapter develops the argument by moving from responsibility and particularly responsibility as philanthropy, to accountability. The question now posed is 'How may social responsibility in business be ensured?' Or, 'How may business be made accountable for its actions?' The answer lies in an examination of the mechanisms for the social control of business.

The problem of corporate power is not new. Concern about monopoly distortions reducing efficiency and the treatment of labour both gave rise to proposals for improving social control of business. Current concern, however, is far greater, focusing on the very legitimacy of corporate power. Many solutions to the problem of corporate power have been proposed but they all, it is claimed here, involve government intervention, market control, or self-regulation. Radical solutions involving an end to the market economy are not relevant here, but those which would maintain the market economy include breaking up the larger firms, nationalisation, and market socialism. Yet none offers an effective solution because the problem of power stems from the economic requirement for large-scale organisations and operations. Less radical, piecemeal solutions seek either to achieve gradual change from within or from without. Solutions based on change from within seek changes in corporate governance. Solutions based on change from without emphasise increased disclosure, by legislation, social audits, ethical whistle-blowing, and the activities of pressure groups. This, of course, is where the role of pressure groups in the marketing system and ethical purchase behaviour fit into the social control of business.

A simple model is proposed classifying the forms of social control of business according to the type of power involved: condign, compensatory, or conditioned. Each corresponds to the forms of control, as identified above, of legislation, the market, or moral obligation. Each is examined in turn and its strengths and weaknesses considered. Legislation can be effective but not always, and there are limits to its use. The market has already been shown to have many drawbacks as a social control mechanism, but it is not totally ineffective. Moral obligation resulting in self-regulation, while having some effect, seems 'unfair' in the creation of élites and insufficient as it does not involve accountability. The conclusion is that if the legislation mechanism is overloaded and potentially damaging to market economies, and that moral obligation is inadequate or undesirable, then further social control of business might come from the market mechanism. This suggests a case for ethical purchase behaviour, for consumer boycotts, and a role for pressure groups in the marketing system. It is also in keeping with the current politico-economic climate, in the UK and the United States at least, in arguing that one should 'let the market work'. Chapter 4 follows on from this chapter by examining pressure groups.

Solutions to the problem of corporate power

A wide range of perspectives

A great many different solutions to the problem of corporate power have been advocated. As the previous discussion of corporate social responsibility indicated, one solution is self-control by business: in other words, the practice of social responsibility by business. This will be considered further. The problem, however, as with all forms of social control of business, is ensuring accountability. For Medawar, power demands accountability: 'in a democracy, decision-makers should account for the use of their power ... their power should be used as far as possible with the consent and understanding of all concerned.'[3] But as Silk and Vogel show, even the most socially responsible of the managerial creeds does not actively seek accountability. Having noted that the consent creed 'seeks to apply to the corporation the legitimating concept of John Locke that a government rules only with the consent of the governed', they add that 'no American business executive really wants to hand over direct control of the corporation to the electorate ... They declare that they are prepared to be "accountable", but are not clear on what forms their "public accountability" should take or what social mechanisms should be used to insure it.'[4] The recognition of this points to other solutions to the problem of corporate power.

The discussion of managerial creeds has reported the belief that many managers hold, and is a feature of the classical position: that the market is the mechanism by which the control of business is or can be realised. Traditionally, business was the servant of the market. A number of sources note that although the issue of social responsibility in business came to the fore in the 1960s, it is not a new concern. Originally, concern focused on ensuring competition, on keeping business as the servant of the market. Monopoly wastage through the assumed misallocation of resources was the issue. But as Heilbroner writes, 'Recently, however, technical studies by economists have considerably lessened fears about the degree of resource misallocation ... the average percentage of profit on sales during the 1960s has been around five per cent. This does not seem a piratical margin.'[5] He continues by suggesting that concern then moved on to the exploitation of labour, although now 'it is difficult to believe that labor relations was once a burning issue with respect to corporate responsibility'. He reminds the reader of the abuse of labour common at the turn of the century and later, and the anti-union position and activities of companies until government intervention, when 'the unthinkable came to pass in the institution of collective bargaining'. Although labour exploitation is still an issue in some quarters, concern now centres on the legitimacy of corporate power.

This concern about competition and the later issue of labour exploitation was met with government intervention (which in itself limited the validity of the classical position). Government intervention and regulation is, then, another way in which the social control of business is realised. Thus far, three forms of social control of business have been identified: self-control in social responsibility, the market, and government intervention. Indeed, as this chapter later shows, these are the major forms of social control of business and all other solutions to corporate power are either variations or are so radically different that they amount to a solution to the problem of corporate power that effectively does away with the problem by removing the corporation. In other words, they present an alternative economic system to capitalism.

Jacoby identifies a typology of corporate criticism, grouping business critics into three categories.[6] First, there are the reformist critics, 'who accept the basic institutional framework of the contemporary American economy and society'; second, the leftist critics, who 'seek to substitute authoritarian socialism for the capitalistic system of competitive private enterprise'; and finally, the utopian critics, who 'reject both capitalism and authoritarian socialism and seek to establish new social orders based upon different human values'. The concern here is principally with the first category, not only because they are, as Jacoby notes, the majority, but also because the argument expressed in this study assumes a market-based economy and would therefore be largely irrelevant to the changes sought by the latter two categories of critics. Unlike Jacoby, this is not an all-too-swift dismissal of the criticisms and aspirations of such critics, merely recognition that their proposed solutions to the problem of the social control of business go outside the status quo and outside the scope of this work. Jacoby lists five major theses of the corporate critics, the reasons for the current concern about corporate power. He suggests big business corporations are alleged to:

(1) Exercise concentrated economic power contrary to the public interest;
(2) Exercise concentrated political power contrary to the public interest;
(3) Be controlled by a self-perpetuating, irresponsible 'power elite';

(4) Exploit and dehumanise workers and consumers;
(5) Degrade the environment and the quality of life.

He then examines these allegations in detail.[7] The essence of their allegations, however, is that corporations have excessive power which is abused and requires some form of social control. This argument was presented in the previous chapter. Many different solutions to this problem of corporate power have been proposed. The more prominent proposals will be considered here: first, the more radical solutions, which although maintaining the market economy would involve major change; then, secondly, the 'piecemeal' solutions.

Radical solutions within the market economy

Heilbroner – having considered the Friedman solution which he describes as doing nothing[8] and has been amply covered, and the solution of self-control which will be considered again later – then looks at other solutions.[9] One approach might be to break up the big firms: after all, corporate power and the problems of corporate power have come about through the growth in big business (as reported earlier): 'in many industries the minimum plant size to permit efficient operations is much smaller than the average firm size ... Hence the suggestion to fragment large companies into plant-size companies, retaining all the efficiencies of assembly-line production, but removing the agglomeration of financial strength from which corporate power emerges.' This would be technically possible in the United States through the rigid application of anti-trust laws. However, Heilbroner does identify two major drawbacks to this solution. First, it is politically unacceptable: 'a rejuvenated anti-trust movement might go so far as to split General Motors ... But the possibility of splitting these (still immense) companies down to the size of a simple plant seems certain to encounter such a barrage of business opposition that its chances for political passage are nil.' Second, diminishing size would not necessarily increase responsibility, if only because of the precondition of profit, as earlier discussed. The showpieces of the economy are, as Galbraith notes (and Schumpeter, but for different reasons), the large firms; whereas 'the models of powerlessness – the highly competitive textile or coal industries, for example – have also been the models for industrial backwardness, characterised by low research and development, low wages and long hours, anti-unionism, company towns, etc'. And not only does Heilbroner accept a relationship between size and efficiency, and also profitability and responsibility, but he also sees, somewhat paradoxically, an advantage to corporate size for the social control of business: 'The power of the corporation to work social good or evil would not be lessened by fragmenting it. It would only be made less visible and hence, in the end, less accountable or controllable than by bringing it out into the open at the top.' A third drawback to this solution – which Heilbroner does not mention – would be the loss of economies of scale in marketing and other operations. The proponents of this solution seem to assume that economies of scale are only realised in production.

Beesley and Evans, in considering attempts to increase competition, note that not only does the regulator have the problem of being sure that such a move will necessarily benefit the consumer, but also that there is the difficulty of reconciling the interests of the other parties involved, for 'it is impossible in practice to confine the attention to the consumer ... the regulator inevitably concerns himself with other interests such as the shareholders and employees'.[10] Galbraith's favoured solution to the problem of corporate power is nationalisation. Although he acknowledges that 'in nearly all of the non-Communist world, socialism, meaning public ownership of industrial enterprises, is a spent slogan',[11] he does see advantages to this form of organisation, for 'public ownership increases the amenability of the firm to social goals'.

Both Galbraith and Heilbroner write approvingly of British nationalisation policies following World War II. They suggest that nationalisation can provide the funds and management for failing industries and put them on an efficient footing, and a single nationalised firm can serve as a standard bearer for an industry when in competition with other private companies. So, 'the nationalisation of inefficient industries or of individual misperforming firms may indeed serve as a means of raising the general level of social performance'.[12] In this respect, Beesley and Evans suggest they 'may even provide a model of social responsiveness for the private industrial sector' as their purposes are wider than the purely commercial.[13] However, they also note that as models for managing social responsiveness, the nationalised industries are lacking because of their ambiguous and changeable relationship with government. For Heilbroner, there is also a problem in that difference in ownership need not mean greater responsibility:

> The effect of nationalising a firm is to transfer its effective 'ownership' – i.e., the control over the disposition of its surplus, as well as the control over the nature of its operations – from a group of private individuals mixing their desire to make money with a confirmed set of social 'ideals', to a group of public officials mixing their desires to make careers together with their confused ideas as to social ideals.[14]

There is also, as he continues, the inefficiency that seems to result from nationalisation:

To be sure, the motive of social service or public service is preferable to that of private profit-seeking. On the other hand, the curbs over profit-seeking – in the form of competition or of displacement by dissatisfied power groups who 'raid corporations' – probably provides more active controls over the efficiency of private enterprise than can be exercised over public enterprise.

It is not that Heilbroner wishes to write off nationalisation as a misguided ideal, merely that he wishes to sound a note of caution: 'It may be that the deficiencies of public ownership and operation are preferable to those of private enterprise.' However, he suggests that it does not solve the problem of corporate responsibility for 'it merely makes explicit the ultimate nature of that problem, which is how to exert effective political control over an economic institution'.

Public ownership of corporations need not be restricted to the nationalisation of weak and strategic industries, or those that prove to be insufficiently socially responsive. Socialism, with the public ownership of all corporations, seems an attractive proposition. Lindblom explains it thus:

> As an alternative to private enterprise, market socialism is, in principle at least, easy to establish. Merely remove top management from all existing corporations and put government officials in their places. Or put the same managers back in their jobs, but make them government officials. Instruct them to carry on as before: produce and sell whatever customers will buy, pay for whatever inputs are necessary, avoid losses, cover costs. An appropriate new rule might be: Make money but don't practice monopoly. Since corporate managers are already salaried bureaucrats, they should find it easy to operate under the new rules, very imperfectly, of course, as in any system.[15]

However, while some point to Sweden or Yugoslavia as illustrations of a form of socialism along these lines working effectively, many others have doubts. Obviously the merits of capitalism versus socialism and vice versa – even market socialism – cannot be considered here. But the essence of the argument against market socialism is as with nationalisation, but more so: the problem of inefficiency which results from removing or, at least, weakening market pressures, and the likelihood of the social responsibility of the organisation not being greatly enhanced anyway, especially when placed under the political shelter of the government. For Heilbroner, this solution to the problem of corporate power merely dodges the issue: 'the corporation, with its vast powers at best half controlled, is a form of social organisation from which there will be no escape for many generations to follow.'[16] Big organisations are required by the technology of the time. Hence, they cannot be avoided and neither can their consequences. Heilbroner concludes that there is only the stark choice between big organisations operating through the 'motives of acquisitiveness' or through 'bureaucratic conformity'. Either way, they exert dominion over men. He sees little escape from bigness: 'In the small-scale communities, men co-operate. But men can no longer live in small communities on this crowded planet, even if they wanted to. In large communities, men contend, and some means must be found to concert their energies to the common needs of survival.' Unfortunately for socialism, as a collectivist ethic, the only way in which this concert of energies seems to be achievable is in appeals to acquisitiveness or to patriotism.

Aside from these quite radical – within this context – solutions to the problem of corporate power (smaller economic units, nationalisation, and socialism), and as well as more radical solutions still (such as the corporate state or even communism), there are what might best be termed 'piecemeal' solutions. They either seek to change corporate governance and make management more accountable, or seek to apply some form of external control. Again, it is not possible or, indeed, appropriate to consider these solutions in any detail. But they do need to be noted and are therefore briefly considered next. Moreover, ethical purchase behaviour and especially boycotts would most accurately be described as piecemeal solutions to the problem of corporate power.

Piecemeal solutions

Piecemeal solutions constitute some of the less radical proposals for the solution of the problem of corporate power: changes in corporate governance, increased disclosure, ethical whistle-blowing, and so on. These solutions attempt to solve the problem gradually, by degrees. Changes in corporate governance tend to focus on the inclusion of various stakeholders of the firm on the boards of directors: workers,[17] for example, or consumer representatives, or minorities.[18] However, not only is the solution viewed as impractical because of the inevitable conflicts of interest and the problem of identifying all significant interests,[19] but it also assumes that decision-making is at this level. A number of studies suggest that the board may be merely a 'rubber-stamping authority', as Brookes reports (but questions).[20] Another suggested change in corporate governance is chartering, as favoured by Ralph Nader.[21] These and other piecemeal solutions seek to increase pressure for social responsibility from within the organisation. There are also other piecemeal solutions which seek to increase the pressure for social responsibility from without. One major category of solutions that falls within the latter includes methods for increased disclosure.

Increased disclosure is favoured by many as a means for enhancing social control of business, both indirectly by allowing regulation of business to operate and to a lesser extent market control, and directly by embarrassing the firm into action. It can, then, enhance social control of business by all major forms of control: by regulation, by markets, and by moral obligation (self-control in social responsibility). One way of increasing disclosure is the social audit: 'a commitment to systematic assessment of and reporting on some meaningful, definable domain of a company's activities that have social impact';[22] or, as Medawar puts it: 'presenting the accounts of a company to show not what cash it spent or earned for itself – but what, in social terms, it cost or gave to the community.'[23] However, the very notion of a social audit is flawed in the assumption that there are objective standards by which social performance can be measured.[24] In principle, social audits are attractive; in practice they are problematic, if not impossible. Sturdivant suggests that the term social audit should not be used (quoting George Steiner) 'because measurement of social performance does not now and probably never will approach in accuracy and acceptability the accountant's audit of economic performance'.[25] He prefers the notion of a Social Assessment System; whereas one executive at the Conference Board meetings, reported by Silk and Vogel, observed: 'The social audit is a device for consulting firms to make money.'[26]

Another way of increasing disclosure is ethical whistle-blowing. As Nader argues:

> An allegiance to one's employer should not, as corporations would
> have us believe, supersede that of an individual to society, or to a
> higher moral authority. This does not mean that an employee
> should subvert or be disloyal to this corporate employer. But if an
> employee brings a specific safety or health hazard to the attention
> of his superiors and it is ignored because profit is placed above
> public safety, it then becomes the employee's duty to go outside
> the corporate structure and reveal the hazard to the authorities or
> private citizens who are in a position to expose and correct the
> situation.[27]

However, this obviously presents problems for the whistle-blower, as Sturdivant points out,[28] and as recent cases illustrate.[29] Revealing corporate misdemeanours may also be ineffective if the authorities are partisan, as an event in the UK Sizewell Inquiry would seem to bear out.[30]

Increased disclosure may also be realised through legislation, forcing corporations to report on hiring practices, anti-pollution measures, and so on. This is one proposal advocated by Ralph Nader's Center for the Study of Responsive Law, and the Project for Corporate Responsibility.

The problem here, though, is the selective nature of such an approach. As Beesley and Evans observe in considering enforced disclosure of the rate at which complaints are received:

> If disclosure results in coercive responses, then the possibility of unfair bias arises ... The number of complaints, for example, could be bolstered by an enthusiastic group of critics of the company, or depressed by the absence of an adequate complaints mechanism. A raw number of complaints would need to be related to the number of customers, the type of product and so on, to avoid bias. Though the obvious result of distortion is to penalise the company, it also runs against the consumer's interest, in that the information on which he is to make his judgement does not reflect the service which would actually be provided for him.[31]

Disclosure may also be realised by the actions of interested pressure groups. This in itself provides an argument for internal social audits, either to refute an allegation or check information that a pressure group has obtained.[32] One such group is the Council on Economic Priorities: 'a non-profit organisation established to disseminate unbiased and detailed information on the practices of US corporations in areas that vitally affect society, including equal employment, environment quality, military production, political influence and consumer practices.'[33] Commenting approvingly on their research, Heilbroner notes that the Council believes the most effective weapon against corporate irresponsibility is unfaultable research. It has the aim of making both managers and investors more aware of the social consequences of their actions. As Beesley and Evans observe on this: 'Directors do not like to be singled out as socially irresponsible citizens any more than anyone else; and at least some kinds of practices can be lessened simply by making the generals aware of what the troops are doing.'[34] The second aim is ethical investment. This involves either the sale of stock in 'bad' companies and the buying of stock in 'good' companies, or, as Simon *et al.* suggest is preferable, keeping stock in 'bad' companies but using it to demand greater social responsibility.[35] Analogous to ethical investment is ethical purchase behaviour. Although no source has been found employing this term, a number of writers in the area have suggested it as a solution. So, for example, John Tepper Marlin advocates that the public should 'support socially responsible businesses in the marketplace by taking into account social performance in its buying'.[36] Other advocates of ethical purchase behaviour are considered in subsequent chapters.

This examination of specific solutions to the problem of corporate power has considered some of the proposals advocated, from major changes in the economic system to making the current system work better through greater disclosure. Other solutions have been advocated: this examination has merely looked at some of the more frequently occurring proposals. This chapter now turns to the forms of social control of business, how control is currently realised, and how it may be enhanced within the current system. As well as providing an answer to the question identified in the Preview – 'How may social responsibility in business be ensured?' – it provides a basis for classifying ethical purchase behaviour and boycotts as social control mechanisms, and for their comparison with other mechanisms.

Forms of social control of business

Types of power and a model for classifying forms of social control of business

Although unable to propose a paradigm for the business and society field, Jones does put forward an integrating framework for research in business and society. This is based on the methods of social control of business and is described as 'an attempt to provide a research agenda for this emerging discipline'.[37] His matrix categorises social control mechanisms along two dimensions: the level (or scope) of control and the mode (or philosophy) of control. Boycotts are identified by Jones under the level of the individual firm/industry and the mode of countervailing power; a categorisation which will subsequently be shown to be highly appropriate in its emphasis on countervailing power. This model does have value, but a simpler model can be identified. The notion of social control of business implies that society has, or could have, some power over business. Power is a concept for which there is some debate on definition, principally because it can be studied in many different ways and in many different circumstances. Here Russell's definition of power is preferred to that of Mills quoted earlier, namely: 'the production of intended effects.'[38] Russell goes on to identify three kinds of power:

> The most important organisations are approximately distinguishable by the kind of power that they exert. The army and the police exercise coercive power over the body; economic organisations, in the main, use rewards and punishments as incentives and deterrents; schools, churches and political parties aim at influencing opinion. But these distinctions are not very clear-cut, since every organisation uses other forms of power in addition to the one which is most characteristic.

Most studies of power generally acknowledge three types of power in line with the above: force, inducement, and manipulation. Etzioni has coercive, remunerative, and normative power,[39] whereas Galbraith, in a more recent study, suggests condign, compensatory, and conditioned power. Little difference between his categorisation and the many that have gone before somewhat belies his observation: 'It is a measure of how slightly the subject of power has been analyzed that the three reasonably obvious instruments of its exercise do not have generally accepted names. These must be provided: I shall speak of condign, compensatory and conditioned power.'[40] Of course, given the concerns expressed in Galbraith's earlier work, noted previously, it is not surprising that Galbraith writes in this book about corporate power and the absence of consumer sovereignty:

> Much exercise of power depends on a social conditioning that seeks to conceal it. The young are taught that in a democracy all power resides in the people. And that in a free enterprise system all authority rests with the sovereign consumer operating through the impersonal mechanism of the market. Thus is hidden the public power of organisation – of the Pentagon, the weapons firms, and other corporations and lobbyists. Similarly concealed by the mystique of the market and consumer sovereignty is the power of corporations to set or influence prices and costs, to suborn or subdue politicians and to manipulate consumer response. But eventually it becomes apparent ....[41]

However, although the emphasis in Galbraith's work is on the power that business exerts over society, the three types of power can also, it is proposed here, be seen in the way in which society exerts power over business. This indicates a simpler model of the social control of business.

Table 3.1: Social control of business – a simple model

Form of Control	Type of Power
Legislation (government intervention)	Coercive Force Condign
Market forces	Remunerative Inducement Compensatory
Moral obligation (self-regulation)	Normative Manipulation Conditioned

As Table 3.1 shows, and as the previous and following discussion supports, the social control of business is achieved by virtue of legislation, market forces, and moral obligation; or, respectively, force, inducement, and manipulation. This model will provide the basis for the analysis of ethical purchase behaviour, including boycotts, as a social control mechanism.

By legislation: condign power

Legislation over business is society exerting power by force. Business has to act within the law or face sanctions. Recognition of this within society ensures legitimacy for the corporation providing it is generally believed that the legislature and judiciary are effective: that is, that there are suitable laws which are adequately enforced. As Beesley and Evans put it, 'Legislation is seen as achieving its effect through the serious prospect of enforcement.'[42] They also note that legislation may take the form of prescription or provide a framework for regulations 'to guide and legitimise the detailed interventions of the regulators, and to make them accountable to enforceable terms of reference'.[43] Furthermore, legislation can work in other ways. In particular, it can provide a framework within which people can regulate each other's activities without recourse to litigation. Not surprisingly, perhaps, business complains that there is excessive regulation of its activities. It complains that regulations 'threaten the functioning of a "free" economy and its ability to innovate and respond rapidly and creatively to economic opportunities'.[44] Weidenbaum goes further and suggests there is a cause and effect relationship between government regulation of business and the diminution of business performance.[45] He then identifies five costs of government regulation:

(1) The cost to the taxpayer of supporting a galaxy of government regulators.
(2) The cost to the consumer in the form of higher prices to cover the added expense of producing goods and services under government regulations.
(3) The cost to the worker in the form of jobs eliminated by government regulation.
(4) The cost to the economy resulting from the loss of small enterprises which cannot afford to meet the onerous burdens of government regulations.
(5) The cost to society as a whole as a result of a reduced flow of new and better products and a less rapid rise in the standard of living.

Of course, in addition to ignoring the possible benefits of regulation, the above list does assume costs that will not occur in every case. Obviously business will seek to minimise the constraints within which it must act. But in so doing it can claim, through spokespersons such as Weidenbaum, and somewhat paradoxically, that it is helping society as a whole even though it is society that seeks to apply the constraint. As Weidenbaum explains: 'a reversal of the current trend of ever-increasing government intervention in business is essential not so much from the viewpoint of business, but primarily from the viewpoint of enhancing the welfare of the individual citizen.'[46] For similar reasons, Foxall pointed to the costs of consumerism in an attempt to introduce a sober and more balanced view of consumerism in contrast with the academic euphoria of the time.[47]

However, for many of the critics of business, regulation is insufficient or inadequate. Medawar notes, in illustration, the inadequacy of the UK Canned Meat Products Regulations 1967. They do not require that the percentage of meat content should be declared, only that the percentage of meat content should correspond to one of the nine different descriptions that a tinned meat should be given. So while 'chopped meat' must not contain less than 90 per cent meat, 'meat loaf' must not contain less than 65 per cent meat.[48] But 'poor' law is perhaps less of a problem than no law at all. In the Office of Fair Trading report for 1976, only about 14 per cent of the 470,000 complaints referred by local authorities, Citizens Advice Bureaux, and other sources were covered by existing criminal legislation.[49]

Some of these complaints were probably covered by industry established and controlled voluntary codes. Such codes are often established in anticipation and, so the industry hopes, avoidance of legislation. The Press Council and the Advertising Standards Authority are two UK examples of bodies established to administer voluntary codes of conduct, both of which proclaim their independence and effectiveness, with great frequency, while their critics suggest they are self-serving watchdogs without teeth.[50] Medawar suggests that self-regulation of this sort fails to provide a clear frame of reference by which conformity with given standards can be judged, fails to define or enforce high enough standards, and fails to gain general acceptance: 'As such, many codes evolve and exist mainly as means of allowing business to proceed with minimum interference from outside.'[51] For Medawar, the major problems with both legislation and voluntary codes are:

(1) By defining what is unacceptable, by implication everything else is acceptable: 'you also provide a framework outside of which "anything goes".'
(2) Codes and laws only establish minimum levels of performance, identifying behaviour which falls short of the required level. They do not measure performance.

(3) The associated costs (the point made by Foxall and Weidenbaum, referred to above).
(4) The problem of defining corporate social responsibilities (as discussed earlier).

Added to these problems is the increasing belief in the ineffectiveness of government,[52] which in turn limits the effectiveness of legislation for the social control of business. Partly in recognition of the limited effectiveness of government, there has been a movement (in the UK and US) towards letting the market work. These moves reflect a recognition of the limits to regulation and how it can impair the market mechanism. Beesley and Evans, in advocating self-regulation by business – 'corporate social responsibility' – observe that society's control mechanisms are of limited capacity and substitutable. Hence self-regulation might be encouraged so as to reduce the load on legislative measures: 'corporate social responsibility can now be regarded as one of a package of mechanisms through which a pluralistic, self-regulating social strategy can be sustained.'[53] Similarly, Lord Limerick, as Parliamentary Under-Secretary of State at the Department of Trade and Industry (DTI), has pointed to the limited capacity of regulation:

> The community must not ... look on the DTI as an all-purpose fire brigade to be called in with their hoses whenever anything goes wrong. Still less is it realistic to expect that my Department will install automatically triggered sprinkler systems in companies up and down the land. The primary responsibility for exercising surveillance over companies in which they have an interest lies with its members themselves.[54]

This view, expressed at the BIM conference on social responsibility in reference to forthcoming legislation on activities such as 'insider trading' and 'warehousing', was no doubt heart-warming to the businesspeople attending. As the Chairman of the conference noted in response to a discussion on worker directors: 'Personally, I think it would suit the British scene better to do it on a more pragmatic basis. That may take several years ... But in the final analysis the board of directors must have the authority ....'[55] A typical example of how a powerful group in society can, when that power seems threatened, find justification for avoiding the issue? However, there are still very real limitations on the effectiveness of regulation.

Friedman and the Chicago School reiterate the classical position on regulation. They express the criticisms of government regulation as voiced by Weidenbaum. They argue that goverment's natural function is to make uniformly applicable rules within which markets can operate, and to serve as an umpire if these rules are violated. Other than that, government's only other duty as far as business is concerned should be with monopolies, externalities, and the protection of those unable to protect themselves. Anything beyond this is considered an unreasonable intervention. Their criticism of government intervention has an unusual ally. Consumer advocates are critical of government intervention not in theory, but in the form it takes in practice. Advocates are concerned more with equity than efficiency, but they are suspicious of regulatory agencies because, as Marlin, for example, has noted, they tend not to serve the public, to raise prices, and to reduce output, creating bureaucratic and unresponsive industries. Consequently, Marlin observes: 'The concept of the agency itself as the representative of the public should in most cases be buried without further ceremony.' His solution is 'stop waiting for government'.[56] These criticisms are in addition to those cited above by Medawar. So, while regulation clearly does have a part to play in the social control of business, this can only be up to a point. As Heilbroner writes:

> The businessman ... is supposed to have a clear-cut mission – to make profits; and a clearly defined boundary of responsibility – to conduct a law-abiding business enterprise. As the legal profession will testify, this narrow authorisation is difficult enough to delimit – there is an immense body of law as to what a business can and cannot 'legally' do in its lawful quest for profit. But beyond this ill-defined economic domain stretches the much larger and still less clear domain of the social and political responsibilities that reside in the lawful conduct of a profit-making business.[57]

What happens, what forms of control can society apply *Where the Law Ends?*[58]

By markets: compensatory power

The market as a mechanism for the social control of business is society exerting power by inducement. Simply stated, it is a method by which society rewards corporate responsibility with profits and irresponsibility with losses. If one accepts that the market can work in this way both in theory and in the 'real world', then one has a ready explanation for ethical purchase behaviour and boycotts in particular. However, Chapter 1 showed this view of the market to be unacceptably simplistic. It was shown that it must be examined as an ideology, for the market is more than merely 'a technical device for discovering preferences', as the Institute of Economic Affairs claims. Social responsibility by virtue of market forces assumes the exercise of purchase votes, as Gist puts it:

A fundamental tenet of our economic system is that scarce economic resources are ultimately allocated by the preference patterns of final consumers; that is, we as consumers vote, as it were, for particular types of institutions and for particular types of products and services. We vote by purchasing things we wish to encourage in institutions we wish to encourage. We vote by not buying things we wish to discourage.[59]

As might be expected, given the earlier discussion of managerial creeds, Silk and Vogel found that businesspeople viewed the market as the arbiter for social responsibility: 'Business is the most responsible institution by far. I resent Ralph Nader calling his organization a public service organization. My company is a public service institution. Critics of business claim to represent the public, but they have forgotten that business does what the public wants.'[60] Of course, the origin of this perspective lies in classical economics, and particularly Adam Smith, as revealed in the oft-quoted passage about how individual greed is, through the market, transformed into collective good. For Smith and for Friedman, however, collective good or 'what the public wants' seems only to be material welfare. While this was no doubt reasonable in Smith's day, it is insufficient given society's current affluence. Yet the market does provide a big incentive for business to do as people want. As Weidenbaum drily observes: 'More purchases by willing customers do tend to generate more profits and greater accumulation of capital.'[61]

Yet, despite this, and for all the reasons discussed in Chapter 1, 'The conception of the marketplace as a sphere of activity where an impersonal mechanism would hold power accountable is a slim fiction for critics.'[62] To some extent, however, there is social control of business achieved through the market. As Lindblom observes, the market is not dead. Control might only be limited to economic goals, as Friedman argues and clearly favours; or it might extend to other goals as Gist implies above, which, of course, is a major theme of this study.

By moral obligation: conditioned power

The social control of business by virtue of moral obligation is society exerting power through conditioning, resulting in self-regulation. As Berle writes, 'Corporate managements ... are constrained to work within a frame of surrounding conceptions which in time impose themselves.'[63] There will inevitably be cultural precedents to business action. So Ackerman, for instance, has written about the requirement to institutionalise social responsiveness within the business organisation;[64] while in the UK, the Confederation of British Industry has stated: 'While the law establishes the minimum standard of conduct with which a company must comply if it is to be allowed to exist and trade, a company, like a natural person, must be recognised as having functions, duties and moral obligations that go beyond the pursuit of profit and the specific requirements of legislation.'[65] This 'moral imperative' comes from the environment within which managers work. As one practitioner writes, they must be guided by the 'consensus of opinion'.[66] It is this that must guide managers in that area of discretion discussed earlier. As Silk and Vogel note, 'The problem that has always troubled critics and would-be reformers of the modern corporation is by what criteria executives should make judgements about what is in the best interests of the various constituencies of the corporation or of society.'[67] Again, the criteria are determined by what is socially expected. So, for example, even profit-maximising managers will maintain a respect for the rule of law and work within it.

Heilbroner – while recognising that 'power is thrust irrevocably and inescapably into the hands of business management, who must exercise it according to some criteria' – notes that Berle's thesis of management guided by a 'corporate conscience' is élitist and 'therefore places more confidence for social progress in the benevolence of the upper classes than in the common sense of the lower'.[68] This is corporate social responsibility in the sense of self-regulation. Yet is it sufficient that managers should be guided by what they think is best? Is this social control of business or a convenient (and élitist) ideology to mask naked self-interest? These questions cannot be directly answered. They are probably also the wrong questions to ask. First, managerial discretion on social issues is, as Chapter 2 showed, unavoidable. Second, it is misleading to imply that this discretion is extensive, at least in all cases at all times. Limits on managerial discretion are quite considerable, as a little thought about any suitable issue and the stakeholders involved will indicate. Third, and perhaps most importantly, as the term moral obligation implies, managers will be guided by social norms. Self-regulation involves more than conscious management decision-making on the basis of defined criteria. Self-regulation also involves, as Berle seems to convey but not to Heilbroner's satisfaction, the unconscious guidance of what society expects. Put crudely, managers, like all members of society, are conditioned in such a way that constrains their behaviour. So the extent to which they have discretion on social issues depends on circumstance and the social conditioning limitations on all human choice behaviour.

However, where there is discretion – and that is not denied – there will always be the argument that this power is 'unfair', or unwarranted. But if, despite Friedman's arguments, there is nothing that can be done about it, if it is unavoidable, then efforts must be concentrated upon limiting the extent of that power and ensuring that those who exercise it, as Medawar and others have commented, do so under conditions of accountability. Limiting the extent of corporate power involves restrictions on managerial discretion in decision-making on social issues. Yet as has been seen, the government, through legislation, can only do so much. The legislative mechanism can become over-burdened. It is also not always effective. Moreover, government intervention threatens the market economy system. An alternative approach might be to ensure that self-regulation operates more stringently by having, as Ackerman argues, institutionalised corporate social responsibility and as others have advocated, the professional manager. Professionalism, in this respect, would involve conformity with a code of ethics and other guidelines on social responsibility. But is such a notion realistic? It could never be meaningfully legislated and business would be unlikely collectively to act and institute, voluntarily and effectively, such a major constraint on its practices, even if the notion of professional practice could be defined.

Ensuring accountability is equally and similarly problematic. If even under the perhaps inaptly named consent creed, managers are not prepared to accept accountability, what likelihood is there of self-regulation ever producing accountability? Public outrage and condemnation at corporate atrocities such as Thalidomide or the Bhopal poison gas leak provide some measure of accountability, or at least the potential for accountability. But as already noted, atrocities are not the central issue. It is not sufficient to argue that public displeasure following an atrocity amounts to true accountability, even when that displeasure may be supplemented with legal action against the corporation as a whole and its executives individually. So the mechanism of legislation seems overloaded, limited in effectiveness, and potentially threatening to the market economy system. Self-regulation seems 'unfair' and also to be inadequate. One possible conclusion is that there is a requirement incumbent upon the market to play a greater role in the social control of business. The final part to this chapter considers a way in which this could be achieved.

Social control of business and consumer sovereignty

Purchase votes and social responsibility in business

If the market mechanism is to be effective in the social control of business in non-economic ways, as previously suggested, how can this be achieved? Put another way, can consumer sovereignty ensure social responsibility in business and in what way? The answer is in ethical purchase behaviour. But while such a claim as made here seems reasonable in theory, to what extent can it be realised, and has it been realised, in practice? The theoretical justification for the answer of ethical purchase behaviour has been given in Chapter 1. It is based in the competitive model of capitalism and the notion of consumer sovereignty. But how far removed from reality is the ideology? The quotation by Samuelson in the Preview to this chapter suggested that the market will answer all things. Its way of doing this is through consumer sovereignty: by providing purchase votes – 'We vote by purchasing things we wish to encourage in institutions we wish to encourage', as Gist was quoted earlier. If this does not happen one is without the rationale for capitalism. In practice, however, consumer sovereignty will exist to varying degrees depending (principally) on choice through competition, and information. Consumer sovereignty in ethical purchase behaviour, as in all purchase behaviour, will depend on informed choice.

Social responsibility in business, it has earlier been noted, means different things to different people. At the risk of over-simplification, one could claim that the literature on social responsibility in business falls into one of two categories: either advocating corporate social responsibility, how to be a good corporate citizen; or criticism of business, how many firms fail to be good corporate citizens. The distinction is subtle. Both categories are normative, but one advocates a doctrine while the other identifies shortcomings. The former category seeks self-regulation while the latter typically seeks greater government intervention. So the notion of social responsibility can mean a form of self-control or it can mean saying what business should be doing, delineating a social role for business.

Social responsibility may not only mean different things to practitioners and academics; it is likely also to mean different things to consumers, whose purchase behaviour is here to be harnessed to this vague, amorphous notion of social responsibility in business. Different people will have different ideas as to what is socially responsible. Consider, as a simple example, the production of contraceptives. One group of consumers may view this as socially responsible, while another group may view it as socially irresponsible. Yet this is not a disadvantage to the notion of ethical purchase behaviour; it is simply indicative of the essence of consumer sovereignty and the right to choose. Social responsibility in business will not and need not be defined here, by this author. It will be defined by the consumer in the market-place. Definitions by consumers of social responsibility will be the outcome of many factors and influences. However, the particular influence of concern here is the pressure group.

A role for pressure groups?

Ethical purchase behaviour requires choice and information. Choice will be largely a function of competition in the market-place. However, the choice criteria employed by the consumer will depend partly on the information available. Ethical purchase behaviour is dependent on informed choice, on the consumer being aware of the ethical issue and it therefore acting as a potential influence on the purchase decision. While information on ethical issues can come from many sources, the concern here is with a source that is organised and directed towards providing such information, the pressure group. The pressure group and its potential influence on purchase behaviour is examined in detail in the next chapter. Its role in the marketing system is considered more explicitly in Chapter 6. Here the concern is to show why such groups are relevant to the social control of business.

In discussing the role of conditioning in the social control of business it was recognised that managers' decisions on social issues will be guided by their understanding of society's expectations. But what happens when these expectations change? Will managers necessarily recognise and accept changes in society's expectations of their behaviour? It is not certain that managers will acknowledge such changes, at least voluntarily. Pressure groups are often prominent in social change. They can attempt to alert managers to changes in society's expectations of corporate behaviour. Most likely, however, they will play a role in convincing or coercing managers into accepting change. They are for this reason likely to be a major force in providing the information necessary for ethical purchase behaviour, if not organising ethical purchase behaviour in boycott action. The pressure group seems likely to be a major influence in consumer definitions of social responsibility in business, which may subsequently prompt ethical purchase behaviour.

Ultimately, whether business is socially responsible depends on the effectiveness of the three forms of social control of corporate power identified. All three forms have a part to play. When they are perceived as inadequate, corporate legitimacy is questioned. Pressure groups are likely to be evident in demonstrating the inadequacies of the social control mechanisms and seeking to enhance them. One way they go about this is in organising boycotts of business. Following the examination of pressure groups in Chapter 4, later chapters then turn to boycotts of business, very specific instances of ethical purchase behaviour, organised by pressure groups. This to some degree answers the question about the extent to which ethical purchase behaviour can and has been realised in practice.

Chapter four

Pressure groups and pluralism

Preview

> The chief social values cherished by individuals in modern society
> are realised through groups ... the individual has meaning only in
> his relations with others.
>
> Earl Latham[1]

> There is more to democracy than the occasional vote, and there is
> more to democracy than political parties. Pressure groups, offering
> an alternative form of expression, are a healthy component of
> genuine democracy.
>
> Des Wilson[2]

The previous chapters have examined consumer sovereignty under
capitalism and the extent to which it may be employed, along with other
mechanisms, in the social control of business. Choice and information
have been shown to be vital for consumer sovereignty and it is suggested
that pressure groups could be a principal source of the information
required by consumers for ethical purchase behaviour. Consumer
boycotts, the most manifest form of ethical purchase behaviour, are of
course predominantly pressure group inspired. A role for pressure
groups in the marketing system has therefore been identified, but little
has yet been said about the nature of pressure groups. This chapter
addresses the question 'What is a pressure group?', considering the
pressure group role in the political process and pluralism.

Whilst it has been claimed that pressure groups are a central feature
in the political process, it soon becomes apparent that this is only true
for a certain category of pressure group. There is a great diversity in the
types of pressure group which may be found in terms of a number of
dimensions, but particularly the subject of the group's concern, the way
that concern is exhibited, and the group's influence. A typology of

pressure groups shows that promotional pressure groups with open membership and high political specialisation are of most relevance to this study. Promotional pressure groups, despite the role which might be attributed to them in pluralistic models, do not seem to have the influence afforded to sectional pressure groups. Because of their limited resources, particularly their weak strategic location, they do not have 'insider' status and therefore must rely on public opinion as their primary avenue of pressure. The other avenues of pressure, the executive and Parliament, are very often closed to them. However, a fourth avenue of pressure, often overlooked in the literature, might be corporations, especially given the acknowledgement of corporate power in the previous two chapters. Corporations may be an avenue of pressure as an ultimate target of pressure group activity in their own right – so as to change corporate behaviour. Alternatively, they may be an avenue of pressure intended to influence the public authorities indirectly, either by motivating public opinion or by employing the 'insider' status of business.

Corporations as a target of pressure group activity are most likely to be influenced by direct action tactics, one such tactic being the consumer boycott. This brings the argument full circle. Promotional pressure groups have grown rapidly in recent years, offering the scope for greater political participation. However, they lack influence because they are rarely afforded 'insider' status and must therefore work outside the conventional channels. Direct action may compensate for their weak strategic location and the consumer boycott may indeed be a tactic which with a well-supported pressure group suggests a stronger strategic location. Given the earlier argument about consumer sovereignty as the rationale for capitalism, it would be highly appropriate if the boycott tactic were to provide greater political participation. A potential for pluralism through direct action by pressure groups seems to be indicated. While the previous chapters demonstrated the case for ethical purchase behaviour and the need for information provided by pressure groups, this chapter, in addition to identifying the nature of pressure groups, shows that promotional pressure groups are in need of effective tactics; the consumer boycott tactic seems particularly appropriate because (in an economic sense) it strengthens the group's strategic location and has the legitimacy of consumer sovereignty to justify it. Political participation can in this way be increased, with the market at least attempting to 'answer all things'. Pressure groups may then *wish* to assume a role in the marketing system, for not only does ethical purchase behaviour need pressure groups, but pressure groups may need ethical purchase behaviour.

The role of pressure groups

A paradise of groups

Pressure groups, at least within pluralistic interpretations, are an integral and legitimate part of the fabric of society and the politial process. Indeed, one school of thought in political science (the 'group theorists') claims that understanding the role of groups in politics is essential to explanations of the political process, with Bentley going so far as to suggest, in an oft-quoted passage: 'When the groups are adequately stated, everything is stated.' For Bentley, the analysis of group activity offered a complete understanding of politics. Earl Latham, building upon this, suggested that public policy is the equilibrium reached in the struggle to accommodate conflicts of group interests.[3] In *The Governmental Process*, in 1951, Truman observed that: 'Without some working conception of the political role of interest groups ... we shall not be able adequately to understand the nature of the political process ... The puzzle cannot be solved if some of the pieces are virtually ignored.' Willetts, in quoting this passage, claims that it applies with equal force today.[4]

This emphasis on the role of groups is the classical pluralist position. Kimber and Richardson, in presenting this in their introduction to *Pressure Groups in Britain*, are bound to concede that it is, at least for the moment, out of academic favour. They note that Crick is critical of the emphasis on politics as a process, and that for many it is too simplistic a view, taking no account of other factors such as reason, logic, or – dare one say it – principles; although for Kimber and Richardson, many such criticisms seem to be founded on value judgements which question the desirability of politics based on 'might is right'. They temper the group theorists' claim, that the constant and shifting struggle between competing groups in society is the central feature of the political system, by suggesting that although there may be more to it than this, the political process cannot be understood without giving serious attention to the role of pressure groups.[5] Pluralism is considered further, later on in this chapter. Of importance here is the point that political scientists, and those of a pluralistic disposition in particular, ascribe a major role to pressure groups in the political process.

Some pressure group analysts go further than this. Wootton's analysis of pressure politics in Britain starts by considering the role of groups in British society – all groups, including the subclass of pressure group. He quotes Sir Ernest Barker's reference to England as a 'paradise of groups'. He then claims that pressure groups are, like other groups or civil associations, an integral part of the fabric of society. In this respect he suggests that 'pressure groups are essentially *the* civil associations out to achieve some of their objectives by political means' (Wootton's emphasis).[6] Placing pressure groups within the context of all groups in society indicates the diversity of pressure groups, as well as their importance. The *Directory of Pressure Groups and Representative Associations* lists organisations 'that exist to promote the interests of a particular group of people or to gain acceptance for a particular point of view' under seventeen major categories. Seemingly every aspect of society is represented by some group, be it the National Council for Civil Liberties (aims: to defend and extend civil liberties within the United Kingdom) or the British Goat Society (aims: to circulate knowledge and general information about goats). This list of six hundred groups must only be considered a starting-point. Excluded are those for whom promotional or representational work is not their primary concern; and the many groups which quickly form because of a specific issue (such as the referendum on British membership of the EEC) and just as quickly disappear, one could not expect to be included, nor the multitude of local groups.[7]

It is apparent from the above discussion that problems of definition are likely to abound. Groups have been shown to be a pervasive and central feature of British society and politics. Yet while this is a reasonable claim for the class of phenomena known as pressure groups, it is less meaningful to suggest that this applies equally to all pressure groups. As can be seen from the above two examples, different types of pressure group exist. Not only is there a great diversity in terms of the subject of their concern, but also in the ways they exhibit that concern. Before examining these definitional problems further, it is useful to consider political participation and the role of pressure groups. This will provide additional and less abstract evidence of the importance of pressure groups, and also point to the type of pressure group of most relevance to this study.

Political participation and pressure groups

Political participation in Britain amounts, for the most part, to the grand act of casting a vote every five years or so: a gesture which may be particularly futile in all but marginal constituencies within an electoral system that lacks proportional representation. The vast majority of the population seems untroubled by political concerns or, at least, unable to participate directly in the decisions on such matters other than in the use of the ultimate sanction at the ballot-box. As Coxall reports, beyond voting in general and local elections, 'only a small minority of the population have a greater political involvement: a mere five per cent of the electorate are individual members of political parties and an even smaller proportion are party "activists"'.[8] Yet this need not be

Ethical Purchase Behaviour

considered as depressing as some commentators claim. As Coxall goes on to note, most people believe – including politicians – that elections make the government pay attention to public opinion. Moreover, the British political system as a parliamentary democracy (as opposed to a direct or populist democracy) provides essentially for indirect participation, notably through one's representative in Parliament.

While such mechanisms for participation, both directly and indirectly, might exist, they do not dispel the impression of mass political apathy. However, in contrast with this, and somewhat refreshing, is the growth of pressure groups; a phenomenon welcomed by academics, other commentators, and even party politicians such as Tony Benn. In recent years involvement in political parties has declined. Coxall and others suggest that many people have joined pressure groups instead, with the 1960s and 1970s witnessing what he describes as 'an explosion of pressure group activity'. This is significant in that, as he continues, 'for social reformers, protesters and for those who simply wanted to protect their own interests, pressure groups had become a genuine and attractive alternative to political parties'.[9] Finer, using an electrical engineering analogy, has appropriately described pressure groups as 'an auxiliary circuit of representation'.[10] There are, of course, some who express doubts about this type of political activity; though as Wallace's historical analysis shows, it goes back at least as far as the eighteenth century,[11] and as the previous section demonstrated, pressure groups are an integral part of British society. What is new however, is the growth in the number of pressure groups and pressure group activity in recent years. And as will be seen, it is a certain type of group which has grown in numbers and activity, with significant consequences for political participation. It is these groups in particular which are most relevant to this study.

The increase in the number of pressure groups is difficult to quantify. Many groups are either too informal, too ephemeral, or too local to come to sufficient prominence for measurement. However, many writers in the area have commented on the increase in pressure group activity. Marsh observes that the last twenty years have seen 'a rapid expansion' in the number of groups, particularly those he terms 'ideological' groups. Referring to the first edition of the directory of pressure groups mentioned earlier, he notes that half of those organisations which gave a date of formation were formed after 1960. Moreover, given the concern of this section with political participation, he comments: 'most of these new ideological groups are liberal, reformist and radical – that is, they advocate legislative change in a liberal direction. There are of course exceptions, for example the anti-abortion groups, but the overall pattern is clear.' He suggests that the directory would indicate that no new 'economic' interest group was formed in the last twenty years

102

which was not a merger of existing groups.[12] Pym has suggested that pressure groups had at least something to do with the changes of the late 1960s (including the legislation on abortion and divorce) that caused journalists to write of Britain as the permissive society, even if the extent of that influence is difficult to estimate.[13] While Wallace observes: 'the emergence of new organisations alongside the established pressure groups of British politics has served to involve a great many new people in political activity at a time when activity through parties has been declining, and as such has contributed in itself to the democratic process'.[14]

Writers on pressure groups in the United States have also observed an increase in pressure group activity. Milton Kotler writes of the power of organised citizen action, observing that the contributions received by pressure groups exceed the legitimate support enjoyed by the national political parties.[15] Whereas Berry, although not willing to attribute the disaffection from party politics to the growth of pressure groups, does observe that they represent constituencies that have been 'chronically unrepresented or underrepresented in American politics'. He suggests that 'in an increasing number of issue areas, public interest groups have become part of the political environment, and thus part of the equation that explains public policy outcomes'.[16] Writers in the management area have also commented on an increase in pressure group activity, such as Sadler;[17] and the European Societal Strategy Project, under Ansoff, predicted further increases;[18] although this latter group, if the observations by Kenny are anything to go by, would seem to be less enthusiastic about the rise of pressure groups. Contrary to most writers in business and society (admittedly, it would seem, better informed), he suggests that pressure groups are a threat to democracy rather than a vital stimulant and part of it.[19] Finally, pressure group activists have also documented the increase in pressure group activity and the importance of this for political participation. Des Wilson, reputedly Britain's best-known, most experienced, and effective campaigner, former Director of Shelter and involved with other prominent pressure groups (including CLEAR, Friends of the Earth (FoE), and the 1984 Committee for Freedom of Information), has referred to the 'mushrooming' of pressure group activities in the 1960s and subsequently, suggesting that the role of pressure groups is to 'guard the guards'.[20]

The growth of direct political involvement through pressure group activity is generally welcomed by those favouring pluralism. However, before considering the implications of this growth in terms of pressure group influence in the market-place, it is necessary to consider what is meant by the term pressure group and the types of pressure group that exist. Pressure group terminology is examined with the targets of pressure, for the terminology employed in the literature makes a somewhat suspect assumption on pressure group targets that needs to be remedied.

Pressure group terminology and targets

Despite an established and long-standing role for pressure groups, the term pressure group carries unfortunate associations. It is popularly used in an emotional and derogatory way that denies the role of such groups. It is all but a term of abuse for the ill-informed – Kenny's denigration of pressure groups, referred to above, is an apt illustration of this. Wootton, in noting the tendency of the term to raise hackles, refers to an instance where a leading TUC official objected to the TUC being referred to as a pressure group.[21] Other writers in the area make similar observations, and Roberts attributes the 'unsavoury overtones' associated with the term to the lurid exposures of the concealed influence of pressure groups on political decisions. Yet he goes on to suggest, 'in attempting to describe and analyse the workings of the British political process, it is impossible to ignore the extent to which it relies on non-party groups, and it is almost equally difficult to avoid employment of the terms lobby, pressure group and interest'.[22] The term and notion of a pressure group is particularly emotive and threatening to those of an individualist (rather than collectivist) disposition. Such a response is in fear of an organised group within society furthering its interests against the 'general will'. Yet many such critics are likely to belong to at least one pressure group. As Rose notes, approximately half the electorate belong to one or more organisations which sometimes seek to influence British government.[23]

Hence, although pressure groups are a central feature of the political process and many of the population are members of pressure groups, they are viewed with suspicion. This writer would also suggest that some of the more recent antipathy towards the term and notion of pressure groups is related to, as Marsh has observed, the rise of 'ideological' groups of a liberal and radical disposition. Current popular usage of the term pressure group is more usually in reference to (and derision of) the 'woolly hat brigade' at Greenham Common, than the sober-suited gentlemen of the Confederation of British Industry. In a similar vein, Mrs Mary Whitehouse has criticised the influence of pressure groups, not realising that her organisation, the National Viewers and Listeners' Association, is itself a pressure group.

The discussion of the scope and importance of pressure groups indicates the difficulty in providing a comprehensive definition that goes beyond the somewhat loose definitions taken from Wootton and Shipley and employed up to this point. Moreover, the foregoing discussion has also revealed a multiplicity of terms used to describe such associations: pressure group, interest group, lobby, and public-interest group. The term employed here, and most widely used in the British context, is pressure group; a term indicative of the role of the group.[24] The term lobby is particularly inappropriate, in reference to an organisation, because of its association with group attempts to influence government. For the most part, the concern here is with attempts to influence corporate behaviour. This points to a major weakness in much of the pressure group literature. While power in society may ultimately rest with government, it is in the first instance highly dispersed, and notably in the hands of business, as the previous two chapters demonstrated. Yet the notion that power exists outside government, and in corporations in particular, does not seem to have been appreciated by many political writers.[25] Consequently, the target for pressure group activity is in almost every case assumed to be government. So Wootton defines pressure groups as 'those (not counting political parties) that influence or attempt to influence the public authorities, mainly the central government'.[26] Of course, the failing of such a definition – and it is not unique to Wootton – is the assumption that such groups seek only to influence public authorities. As the evidence presented later shows, there are many groups that try to influence corporate behaviour and this is increasingly the case. Pressure group targets are considered further. However, as yet, the definitional problems surrounding pressure groups have not been resolved. They can only be adequately dealt with, as far as this study is concerned, by considering a typology of pressure groups.

A typology of pressure groups

Sectional and promotional pressure groups

The question 'What is a pressure group?' cannot be simply answered. A single definition is inadequate. The question can best be approached by considering the various types of group – what one might prefer to call a taxonomy. This chapter may then focus on the characteristics of the particular type of pressure group relevant to the study. Mackenzie observes that groups can be identified by the type of interest at stake, the type of body whose decision is influenced (the pressure group target), the internal structure of the organisation, and the methods it uses.[27] However, the dominant criterion used is the type of interest at stake. This is perhaps because all the other criteria seem to stem from this. So Coxall distinguishes between two types of pressure group: the 'leading interest' or 'sectional' groups, and the 'promotional', 'cause', or 'attitude' groups. In the former groups, 'membership is based on the performance of a specific economic role: for example, work as a miner or a company director. Sectional groups "protect" the interests of their members.' On the other hand, promotional groups 'are held together by a shared attitude; they seek to promote a particular cause; Shelter and the Child Poverty Action Group are good examples'.[28] As Kimber and Richardson put it: '*Sectional* pressure groups seek to protect the interests of a particular section of society, while *promotional* pressure groups seek to promote causes arising from a given set of attitudes.' [29]

This distinction, while found throughout the literature, is not always made employing the same terms. In his historical analysis of pressure groups, Wallace distinguishes between those moved by self-interest and those moved by idealism. He refers, in illustration, to the issues and groups organised over free trade and the right to combine in trade unions, as a nineteenth-century example of the former category. Groups organised for the abolition of the slave trade is an eighteenth-century example of the latter category. Such examples both support his claim about the long-standing nature of pressure group activity (he suggests that many pressure group causes and methods would be familiar to a nineteenth-century activist; only the context of group activity has changed), and this typological distinction in particular.[30] In *Pressure Politics* (a 1983 publication claimed to be the first full analysis for over a decade of the influence and importance of pressure groups in British politics), Marsh identifies similar historical origins and distinctions to pressure groups, although he employs a continuum of pressure group types from the powerful 'economic' groups such as the British Medical Association (BMA) and the National Farmers Union, to the single-issue 'ideological' groups, such as the abortion lobby. He writes, 'Economic interest groups protect and promote the specific economic interests of their members, while ideological groups promote or defend legislative or administrative change for ideological reasons rather than to forward their members' particular financial interests.' Of course, the typology falls down in the implication that groups such as the BMA are not in some sense ideological, but the notion of a continuum is useful even if one has to accept that the term economic or ideological only refers to the group's primary characteristic. It does at least avoid the artificial boundaries one has with discrete categories.[31]

Marsh's typology differs little from the promotional/sectional distinction found elsewhere. But there are weaknesses to this. Recognising the inadequacy of this two-fold classification, R. T. McKensie suggests three categories: sectional groups, promotional groups, and all other groups.[32] A rather more helpful contribution is that by Willetts. He examines the role of pressure groups in the global system, suggesting that they have a significant impact transnationally as well as nationally. In so doing, he offers a typology which employs the promotional/sectional distinction, but identifies different types of group within each category.[33] While this indicates the pervasiveness and diversity of pressure group activity, it is perhaps a little broad. In essence, Willetts includes all civil associations. However, all these groups could indulge in pressure group activity and such an all-embracing typology no doubt provides support for his thesis about the transnational impact of pressure groups. Willetts concedes overlap between his categories but, for the most part, it is the groups within his last category, 'specific-issue promotional groups', that are of relevance here. His comments on such groups are worth noting:

> By the nature of their work, specific-issue groups are likely to be challenging orthodoxy. Often they are either raising new issues, which have not before appeared on the political agenda, or are trying to change the way existing issues are handled. Thus they usually concentrate on influencing public opinion and the media and so they become household names.[34]

The part played by public opinion in the achievement of pressure group aims is widely acknowledged and will be considered further. However, Willetts's typology, although more comprehensive than others considered (perhaps too comprehensive), is not particularly robust. Groups differ in the extent to which they are 'political', in particular. Some may only rarely, if at all, exert pressure and be pressure groups in that sense. This is not clear from Willetts's typology and definitional problems remain. The National Council for Civil Liberties and the British Goat Society, to refer to the earlier examples, would come under his last category, but they are substantially different.

Wootton's typology is required to resolve this issue of degree of political specialisation. This typology is less inexact, recognising that the political involvement of some groups may be greater than that of others. Wootton starts with the distinction between 'interest' and 'idea' groups, which he attributes to Harwood Childs of Princeton, and dates back to 1935. He then observes that Potter's late 1950s development of this is the most influential classification in Britain. This, again, is the promotional/sectional distinction: 'sectional groups (whom one stands for), and programmatic or promotional groups (what one stands for) ... congruent not only with Childs' [distinction] ... but with the one drawn by the groups themselves between organisations *of* and organisations *for*'.[35] But the groups within each of these categories may not only differ in terms of political involvement (he contrasts, in illustration, the National Farmers Union and the Tomato and Cucumber Growers Association), but also some ostensibly promotional groups

107

may have a distinctly sectional character. These are elsewhere referred to as 'anchored', for although they may present themselves as promotional groups, they are grounded in and financed by sectional ones. Some groups are more discreet (misleading) about their anchorage than others, a prominent example being the Genetic Study Unit, found to be closely tied, to many people's surprise, to London Rubber Industries (now London International, the leading condom manufacturer in the UK). Wootton's typology takes account of this.

His typology is expressed as a two by two matrix, as shown in Figure 4.1. One dimension accounts for the political involvement of the group, the degree of political specialisation. The other dimension accounts for whether the group is 'of' or 'for', which is the degree of openness of membership. Examples of each category and a title for each category are shown in Figure 4.1. Anchored groups are included with the parent group. So Transport 2000, for example, would be included with the National Union of Railwaymen (NUR) 'on the assumption that those who pay the piper call the tune'. Also worth noting is the inclusion of the Wing Airport Resistance Association (WARA) and the Welsh Language Society under cell two. Although this cell in its closed membership dimension appoximates to the sectional group classification, these groups become included contrary to other analysts, because with distinctive local roots, and in defence of their territory, they will be more like 'of' than 'for' groups. Wootton refers to the groups in the bottom row as 'self-created', as opposed to the top row of 'given' groups. And, in confirmation of Marsh and Wallace, cited earlier, he suggests only cell three is a recent development, with the other types of group existing at least as early as the end of the eighteenth century. He suggests cell three groups have arisen from the perceived solidary (intrinsic rather than instrumental) benefits.

Wootton's typology resolves the definitional problems which plagued much of the earlier discussion of pressure groups. It has been noted that the promotional or ideological type of group is of most concern here (though, as will later be seen, sectional groups also become involved in influencing purchase behaviour in the market-place), and within Wootton's typology, it is particularly the groups that come under cell four. These groups he terms propagational. Having considered pressure groups in general, it is appropriate to consider the characteristics of the type of group relevant to this study, given that adequate distinctions can now be made.

Promotional pressure groups

While sectional pressure groups will be seen to be of some relevance to the study, they do not warrant a detailed analysis. Of greater concern are

Figure 4.1: Wootton's typology of pressure groups [36]

		Political specialisation	
		Low	**High**
Closed		1	2
		T & G, NUR	TUC
		British Aircraft, Burmah Oil, London Rubber Industries, House of Fraser, Hill Samuel	CBI, ABCC, NFU, British Road Federation
		Law Society	British Legal Association
		Townswomen's Guilds, Women's Institutes	National Joint Action Campaign for Women's Equal Rights
		National Federation of Pakistani Associations	League of Overseas Pakistanis (Tower Hamlets)
M e m b e r s h i p		Urdd Gobaith Cymru (Welsh League of Youth)	Welsh Language Society
		Saffron Walden Countryside Association	Saffron Walden Anti-Airport Committee, Stansted Working Party (etc.), WARA
		(operational)	*(representative)*
Open		3	4
		National Trust, Georgian Society, Ulster Architectural Heritage Society, Association for the Protection of Rural Scotland	Conservation Society, FoE, Population Stabilisation
		Friend	Campaign of Homosexual Equality
		Society of Individualisation	Justice, Amnesty, NCCL
		National Allotments and Garden Society	Child Poverty Action Group, Shelter
		Workers' Educational	CASE; FEVER; PRISE
		(expressive)	*(propagational)*

the promotional pressure groups. Wootton's typology forms the basis for the study, but as an academic schema, it does not say a great deal about the groups' characteristics. Rather than refer to his discussion of groups in illustration of his typology, a rounder picture can be gained of the groups of interest here by considering Wilson's description of what he terms 'our kind of group';[37] for Wilson writes about and for promotional pressure groups. These are the groups which, as Willetts notes, spring most readily to mind when the term pressure group is used. They are the groups to which one is making reference when the term pressure group is used in everyday language. They are the groups which have become increasingly more numerous, more prominent, and perhaps even more influential over the past twenty years. They are the groups which provide scope for political participation and to which an increasing number of the population are turning for this reason. Finally, they are the groups which tend to be lambasted by the popular press because of their liberal and sometimes radical position and, as this writer earlier suggested, figure largely in the current emotive response to the term pressure group because of this. It is perhaps because many of these groups are on the fringes of respectability that they are given less attention in the academic literature than the sectional groups. Although it seems as likely that this is due to the shortage of work on pressure groups in general in recent years – the period of ascendancy for promotional groups – and the greater influence of sectional groups.

Wilson makes the distinction between sectional and promotional groups, using these terms and others. His preference seems to be for the terms which indicate the former groups as 'bad' and the latter groups as 'good', although he is in keeping with Mackenzie in the use of the distinction 'selfish' and 'do-gooders'.[38] This is indicative of what might be termed the caring characteristic of promotional groups. As Wilson puts it:

> Because when we talk of pressure groups we mean *our kind*, we speak of pressure groups approvingly and positively ... however, we are only one kind of pressure group and often we are the least effective. For it is not only the poor who have pressure groups – so do the rich; not only the environmentalists and conservationists – so do the polluters and the squanderers of resources; not only the civil libertarians – so do the forces of authoritarianism. Thus ... there are two kinds of pressure groups – those whose motivation is a concern for the health and well-being of the community, and who usually campaign to change or improve priorities or policies, and those with vested interests, whose cause is usually maintenance of the *status-quo*, or furtherance of policies beneficial to them, irrespective of the implications for the community.[39]

110

This position, identifying the sectional groups as 'self-regarding' and the promotional groups as 'other-regarding',[40] although not usually expressed in such forthright terms, does find support within the academic literature. However, one must be wary of the claim of such groups – when self-appointed – to represent the community. In particular, there is the criticism of the middle-class bias of promotional groups. One must consider whether their campaigns to change priorities or policies are a reflection of community concern, or class interests and priorities. For example, conservation of green-belt areas may be at the loss of low-density housing; or the costs of the prevention of environmental pollution such as acid rain from coal-burning power stations, may in being passed on to all consumers have to be borne by those who would, voluntarily, have chosen to spend their money in other ways.

Wilson's preferred term for his kind of pressure group is 'community cause' pressure group. Within this, he identifies three categories:

(1) Single-issue pressure groups, having one objective or seeking to further one particular cause. For example, CLEAR; its sole aim is to reduce and if possible eliminate lead pollution.
(2) Issues-in-context pressure groups, pursuing a number of objectives or issues but within an overall context. For example, FoE.
(3) Practice-based pressure groups, these may be either of the above categories but, in addition, include groups that have aid or direct service in their make-up. For example, a 'charity-cum-pressure group' such as Shelter, which provides direct assistance to the homeless in addition to campaigning.

This does not prove to be a robust classification, but it does indicate tendencies and is useful for this reason, as will be seen.

In the earlier quotation, Wilson makes the point about the limited effectiveness of promotional pressure groups. Later, he writes of the distinction between the 'Davids' and the 'Goliaths': 'The advantage, in terms of money, economic and relative strength, is heavily weighted to the powerful pressure groups. As a result, the pressure groups for whom this book is intended – those of and for the community – are more often than not the "Davids" involved in an unequal fight with industrial or governmental "Goliaths".'[41] It is this limited effectiveness of promotional groups, and their part in political participation, which makes the consumer boycott tactic particularly worthy of study. It is argued in this study and elsewhere that greater use could be made of this tactic, and it is especially appropriate for promotional groups with their limited resources. Given more such resources, promotional pressure groups could be more effective and contribute to political participation in the way Wilson suggests in the quotation given in the Preview to this chapter.

The avenues of pressure

Insider' and 'outsider' status

The avenues available to pressure groups by which they may attempt to exert influence will vary according to the type of group. Group strategies and tactics will then vary in accord with this. As Roberts puts it: 'leaders of groups act on the basis of a "target structure", i.e., an appreciation of the most suitable parts of the political system on which to exert influence or "pressure".'[42] Of particular importance is whether the group has 'insider' or 'outsider' status. Pym suggests this is the most important dividing line between groups. She distinguishes between in-groups and out-groups as follows:

> Out-groups are out because they propagandise for unpopular causes or minority interests, or because they are judged unrepresentative of those they claim to speak for. In-groups, that is to say those readily and regularly admitted to consultations with government departments, may derive their legitimacy from their indispensability to the economy, because they speak for acceptable causes like animal or child welfare or because, like church groups, they have become over the years simply part of the British way of life.[43]

As a general rule, sectional groups have insider status, while promotional groups have outsider status. This difference in access to decision-makers is no doubt what prompts Wilson – as a spokesperson for outsider groups – to distinguish between the two types by saying that 'the "outsiders" threaten "the system" itself, whereas the "insiders" are more likely to wish to strengthen the *status-quo*'. He goes on to refer to Benewick's three 'worlds' of pressure groups, where each 'world' has a different degree of access.[44] It is more complex than this however. Coxall refers to groups which are legitimised, that is recognised by government as having the right to be consulted. The basis of this recognition, he suggests, is the representativeness of the group and the cases of rival groups claiming to speak for the same interest. But in exchange for recognition, restraint and consideration is expected of the group, a rare exception to this being the National Union of Students, a group maintaining an aggressive and critical stance but still seen as legitimised. The benefits of recognition for the group are the opportunities to influence policy or, at least, gain advance information about governments' intentions. The government benefits from getting advice and information, acquiescence in, or even assent to, their proposal, and possibly assistance in the administration of policy.[45]

Finer has suggested three principal avenues of pressure, approached by groups in sequence. These are the executive, Parliament, and public opinion. The sequence, it is suggested, is reversed for promotional groups. This is due to the insider/outsider status differences of sectional as against promotional groups, discussed above. Indeed, one can rationalise such a sequence by presuming that while recognition for sectional groups is almost always automatically conferred because of the resources available to them (as later examined), promotional groups are required to demonstrate the need for recognition of their case by first mobilising public and then parliamentary opinion. According to such a model, promotional pressure groups thereby become legitimised and acquire insider status, and therefore potential influence with the executive. Sectional groups, on the other hand, need not necessarily lose their insider status when they turn from the executive, to Parliament, and then public opinion. While this is a possibility, the move may only be as a means of demonstrating support for their position in their dealings with the executive or perhaps done in concert with the executive, as critics of corporatism would presume, so as to maintain a show of democracy.

Yet again, however, the reality of pressure group activity is probably even more complex than this, despite the face validity of such a model. Kimber and Richardson, having described Finer's model, contend that pressure group activity is generally much more complicated than this and that such a straightforward scheme only applies in some cases, with many groups trying to use several avenues simultaneously.[46] The model is based quite safely though on the inevitable differences in status of pressure groups, and particularly promotional groups as compared with sectional groups. It can perhaps be most appropriately seen as a distinction between ease of access for any particular group of different avenues of pressure. This may in turn influence the emphasis rather than the sequence of pressure group activity. Yet there may be a fourth avenue of pressure worth considering.

Corporations as an avenue of pressure

Coxall observes, reaffirming the quotation at the beginning of the last section from Roberts: 'if they are to succeed, pressure groups must clearly understand how power is distributed in society.'[47] Somewhat disconcerting is that having made this remark, Coxall then refers solely to pressure group attempts to influence government. Business power, both independent of and in relation to government,[48] goes unrecognised. Even Kimber and Richardson, although having recognised that business may be a target for pressure group activity, fail to provide any explanation or justification for such a target. Business power independent of government was adequately demonstrated in the previous two chapters. Hence, it is proposed here that there are four principal avenues of pressure: the executive, the legislature (Parliament), public opinion, and corporations.[49] Corporations are an avenue of pressure in the sense that action involving corporations may spur them into acting in support of legislative demands by lobbying on behalf of the group, or by lobbying on the group's behalf as a complement to the group's own lobbying activities. So the groups employ the insider status of business (see the later discussion of American civil rights and anti-war protests, for example). Alternatively, of course, corporations are a target of pressure group activity not so as to realise any indirect influence with the executive (as an ultimate target), but simply to achieve changes in corporate behaviour; that is, the corporation is both the avenue and ultimate target of pressure group activity.

Having the corporation as an avenue for pressure group activity is due not only to its independent power and its potential influence, but also to the limited access available for most promotional groups to other avenues. Marsh observes that the late 1960s and early 1970s saw a formalisation of interest group representation with a distinct move away from the use of Parliament, and parties in particular, as the channel of access to government. This, he suggests (and is supported by Des Wilson in this), is due to disappointment with the Labour Party. This period of rapid growth in the number of promotional pressure groups seems, at least in part, attributable to the failings of the Labour Party to implement policies promised on various 'causes'. (Although pressure groups try to avoid being too closely linked with any particular party, so that they may try to have dealings with whichever party is in government, the tendency is to have closer links with the Labour Party because of the greater compatibility on the whole of promotional pressure group causes and Labour Party policy.) But if radical policies cannot be achieved through parties directly, can they be achieved via pressure groups? The problem is that radical groups are unlikely to be afforded insider status. Moreover, they may not even want it, in fear of being co-opted or, as Marsh puts it, 'concerned about the possible emasculation of their radicalism if they become too closely involved with government'. He suggests that this leaves little alternative but to try and influence public, or rather élite, opinion, 'a strategy which in most cases had limited effect'.[50]

This discussion of the avenues of pressure seems depressing from the promotional pressure group perspective. Of the three principal avenues of pressure traditionally identified, they seem for the most part to be able

114

only to rely on public opinion. While government action may be influenced by public opinion, this is not always the case, as shown, for example, in the abolition of capital punishment and the lifting of restrictions on homosexual relations – both without the support at least initially of the majority of the public[51] – and, more recently, the siting of cruise missiles in the UK. The identification of corporations as a fourth principal avenue of pressure may be a cause for some optimism. It could be that the increasing emphasis on pressure group activity directed at corporations reflects both a recognition of their power but also the access difficulties with the other avenues. The limited influence of promotional pressure groups is a function of their resources. This is considered next, as an essential precursor to the subsequent examination of pressure group strategies and tactics.

Pressure group resources

Commitment, cohesion, and strategic location

The executive is the ultimate target of pressure group activity in most analyses of pressure group behaviour. It is there that the most important decisions are taken, and although some pressure groups have achieved their aims through Parliament directly, as in the use of private members' bills, this is often subject to the assistance or at least passive approval of the executive (known as 'withinput'), as illustrated by the 1967 legislation on abortion and homosexual relations.[52] The avenues of Parliament and public opinion are primarily employed to bring pressure to bear on the executive indirectly. Access to these avenues of pressure depends upon pressure group resources.

Rose identifies three major resources of pressure groups: commitment, organisational cohesion, and strategic location.[53] Commitment of members is one of a pressure group's most important resources because the greater it is 'the more confident a group's leaders can be that they speak with a united membership behind them and that any bargain reached with government will be accepted by the group itself'. Cohesion is important because the 'more durable, the more frequent, the more numerous, and the more intense the contacts among individuals, the easier they are to organise for cohesive political action'. The cohesive groups are preferred by Whitehall for this reason. Commitment and cohesion can be influenced by the group's efforts. Strategic location, however, depends on the group's activities. 'An organisation occupies a strong strategic position if it commands resources – energy, money or food – that are indispensable to the conduct of a society.' Various factors affect the degree of strength of the group's position, notably whether it is a monopoly in the provision of a service (contrast, for example, the railway workers and the power workers), and whether it provides a professional service with professional norms which may inhibit exploitation of its monopoly position, as with doctors, nurses, and teachers.

Rose suggests that the resources of money, votes, and publicity 'are of relatively limited importance in England', an assertion which is certainly contentious, if not naïve. He accepts that money can ensure that an organisation exists and is necessary to employ experts to present the group's case with technical issues, but argues that money does not buy favours from parties or MPs; 'it is given openly in recognition of mutual interests.' This is a reasonable position on first inspection, but questionable when examined more closely. Rose quite simply understates the importance of money for effective pressure group organisation, research, and activities. This is particularly the case with promotional pressure groups, as Wilson and others have argued.[54] Of course, the welfare activities of the practice-based pressure groups are entirely dependent on income, but as the anti-nuclear power lobby has found, advancing a particular argument may also depend on financial resources, especially at public inquiries.[55] As for votes, Marsh and Chambers show that, at least for the anti-abortion lobby, while publishing a list of the past voting records on the issue of MPs standing for re-election had a minor effect on election voting patterns at most, it did at least politicise MPs on the issue and possibly incline wavering MPs to abstain or vote for amending legislation on the issue when elected.[56]

However, it is Rose's dismissal of publicity which is most suspect (and, of course, money plays a part in this). Promotional pressure groups, as shown, have frequently little option but to attempt to influence public opinion, for which publicity is required. Case studies of pressure group activity where publicity was vital to pressure group success are given later, but before considering public opinion in more detail, it is useful to look further at pressure group resources. In particular, it is worth considering the disparity between sectional groups and promotional groups. This lends weight to the discussion about the importance of public opinion and the potential importance of corporations as an avenue of pressure.

Sectional and promotional groups compared

Pressure group commitment and cohesion, as resources over which the group may have some influence, are worth considering together. There is a substantial body of literature exploring the benefits of pressure group membership. Olson, in what is commonly regarded as a seminal work, questions why people join pressure groups when there are costs associated with membership but the benefits are collective and will be received by the individual, as a member or otherwise. He argues that the logic of collective action is such that:

> unless the number of individuals in a group is quite small, or unless there is coercion or some other special device to make individuals act in their common interest, *rational, self-interested individuals will not act to achieve their common or group interests*. In other words, even if all of the individuals in a large group are rational and self-interested, and would gain if, as a group, they acted to achieve their common interest or objective, they will still not voluntarily act to achieve that common or group interest.[57]

This, of course, contradicts the conventional wisdom that groups of individuals with common interests usually attempt to further those common interests. As Olson shows, this argument is based on the assumption that individuals in groups act out of self-interest, but is flawed in presuming that groups will act in their self-interest as a consequence. Such a presumption is dubious because all the individuals in a group would gain if the group objective were achieved, regardless of the input by any specific individual. Obviously groups do act to further group interests. Olson's explanation for this is that the motivation lies not in the recognition of group interests, but in the selective incentives also offered by groups. However, 'the only organisations that have "selective incentives" available are those that (1) have the authority and capacity to be coercive, or (2) have a source of positive inducements that they can offer the individuals in a latent group'.[58] Such incentives are available to pressure groups such as unions, the large economic groups. (Indeed, understanding of Olson's argument reveals the importance to unions of closed shop agreements.) Few such incentives are available to what Olson terms the 'forgotten groups': 'Groups of this kind fit the main argument of this book best of all. They illustrate its central point: that large or latent groups have no tendency voluntarily to act to further their common interests.'[59] Such groups, he claims, are amongst the largest groups in the nation and with the most vital common interests, while exerting no pressure. He cites in illustration taxpayers, consumers, and the 'multitudes with an interest in peace'. The weakness of consumers in this respect is particularly important within the context of this study.

While it is apparent that not all promotional groups are 'forgotten groups', there is a great disparity between sectional and promotional groups in terms of the selective incentives – which Olson claims are essential for survival – available to them. Pressure group resources of commitment and cohesion are therefore influenced by such incentives.

117

On the basis of this analysis, the commitment and cohesion in promotional pressure groups must rely on three factors: solidary incentives, small group size, and altruism. Solidary incentives are the benefits derived by individual members as an intrinsic rather than instrumental function of membership, for example, regular association with others sharing similar attitudes. As Forbes notes in reference to Moe, Olson restricted his assessment of benefits solely to economic returns.[60] Olson recognises that small groups may act voluntarily in support of group interests, although he suggests such action will be sub-optimal. Of course, small groups by virtue of their size are likely to be less influential, if only because they are seen as unrepresentative. However, organisations may be structured in a way that exploits small group benefits, by having relatively autonomous tiers. So this may be why CND, for example, is organised on a local, area, and national basis. Similarly, FoE is successful in having local groups that are relatively autonomous provided they adhere to a few basic principles, as well as a national organisation. Olson's argument refers only to the action of individuals acting out of self-interest; altruism may be a powerful motivator for promotional groups. As Colby observes in a recent paper, many public interest groups are similar to social movements, which suggests a modification of Olson's argument because of the role of altruism with, for example, staff who 'may well "work cheap" because of their own belief in the cause'.[61] Yet it must be concluded that collective action by promotional pressure groups is influenced by this restriction on the resources of commitment and cohesion.

When organised and with a membership willing to act on behalf of group interests, promotional pressure groups then face the problem of their weak strategic location. What sanctions can promotional pressure groups employ in support of their demands? Sectional groups use their structural position in the economy, promotional groups can use only certain types of direct action (or the threat of it) if their argument is insufficient. Typically, such actions are designed to appeal to public opinion via meetings, rallies, marches, or demonstrations – though there are types of direct action which are intended to be, at least in part, a solution to the demands of the group. The release of animals involved in laboratory experiments is a good case in point. Consumer boycotts are another type of direct action seeking a more immediate solution as well as possible publicity benefits. Here, however, there is potentially an attempt to utilise the structural position in the economy of the group's members and supporters. This, when considered alongside the earlier arguments about consumer sovereignty, is indicative of the latent promise of consumer boycotts for promotional pressure groups. In contrast with the acts of animal rights and anti-vivisectionist groups which have been violent and patently illegal, boycotts are a form of Non

Violent Direct Action (NVDA) which may be technically illegal (although they need not be, as discussed later) but are unlikely to result in prosecution because of the interests of the companies involved.

In sum then, promotional pressure groups are at a disadvantage *vis-à-vis* sectional groups in terms of resources. Commitment and cohesion will be difficult to realise and maintain without selective incentives. More importantly, given an organised group that is committed and cohesive, the weak strategic location of the promotional group is likely to mean that with failure of their argument to convince the powers that be, there are then few effective sanctions at their disposal for more forceful persuasion. Despite Rose's claims to the contrary, publicity (and, therefore, money) is seen as vital to promotional pressure groups – surely Rose was thinking only of sectional groups. Publicity can, by influencing public opinion, strengthen a group's argument. It is, moreover, both necessary for and an aim of direct action.

The role of public opinion

In fairness to Rose, his argument about publicity should be given in more detail. The use of publicity by some pressure groups and the value of the media in this is recognised here:

> Pressure groups with a weak strategic position and few other organizational resources may turn to the media. Media publicity gives the appearance of mass support by the multiplying effect of mass circulation. The simplest and cheapest publicity device is to issue a press release or write a letter to *The Times* signed by prominent persons, for names make news.

However, he continues: 'But any publicity, even free publicity, is of little avail, in so far as it is a sign that the group in question is unable to advance its claims through quiet negotiations in Whitehall.'[62] Does this mean that groups without insider status are then without influence or, for that matter, deserve to be without influence?

Rose, of course, assumes that the pressure groups seek only some action by government (subsumed from the dominant idea within politics about the location of power in society), and that pressure group action cannot in itself produce a direct solution (a possibility discussed later in relation to direct action). Essentially his claim is a variation on the supposed truism that once an issue is on the streets it is lost. Shipley, in expressing the same supposed truism, makes an important qualification in reference to attempts to appeal to public opinion: 'The less sympathy a group has in Whitehall, the more likely it is to embark upon a mass campaign ... When an interest with established access to official circles sets itself on such a course, it is usually a sign that the normal channels have failed.'[63] This suggests that while such a claim may be true for established pressure groups normally afforded insider status, it does not necessarily hold for the outsider groups. One must ask what alternative there is for the outsider group other than to attempt to influence public opinion. To gain access to the executive or even the legislature, it must demonstrate public support. This is particularly true of promotional groups because their representativeness cannot be demonstrated by referring to a clearly identifiable membership (as recognised in Wootton's typology). Their supporters are drawn from the public at large, and public support is necessary to endorse the group's demands. Direct action is the only other alternative but this is even more of a last resort, as is later shown.

Public opinion, as Roberts eloquently puts it, creates 'a climate of possibility'.[64] Even if it does not provide the group with an input on decision-making, it can at least put the issue on the political agenda, as Ward claims for the anti-nuclear lobby.[65] Many writers in the area emphasise the importance of expert pressure group use of the media. Wallace writes, echoing Rose, 'Politicians ... easily mistake Press agitation for aroused public opinion.'[66] Wilson writes extensively on the use of the media and his CLEAR case study provides a good example of pressure group use of the media and public opinion to achieve its aims, by prompting appropriate government action.[67] But there are drawbacks to attempts to mobilise public opinion in support of the pressure group. Coxall identifies two forms of public campaign. First, there are long-term educational and propaganda campaigns intended to produce significant shifts in public opinion. Second, there are short campaigns designed to mobilise public opinion against a specific threat and, if possible, avert it. In the former case, there is the distinct likelihood of counter-groups being formed to oppose the campaign. With short campaigns, a hostile public reaction might ensue because most people's minds are already made up. These problems are in addition to any that may result from upsetting a relationship the group may have with government, as a consequence of going public.[68] Public opinion also tends to be conservative, which severely restricts the possibilities for mobilising mass public support for the radical pressure group. Indeed, this provides such groups with a major incentive to use direct action. Coxall suggests attempting to influence informed rather than mass opinion.[69] In a similar vein, Klein identifies the paradox that 'it is precisely those who want the greatest social changes who should be most elitist in their approach'. Though general public opinion might be more effective for some pressure groups, as he continues: 'Populism could be an effective ally of a right-wing radicalism: this would exploit public opinion on such issues as immigration and hanging and flogging.'[70] All of this discussion, of course, assumes public opinion does in fact influence government policy. Returning again to the issue of capital punishment serves as a reminder that this is not always the case.

Promotional pressure groups strategies and tactics and the factors in their success

Appropriate strategies and tactics for promotional pressure groups

The previous parts of this chapter have identified the characteristics of promotional pressure groups (the type of pressure group of most relevance to this study), and the avenues of pressure and pressure group resources. On the basis of this, certain strategies and tactics are indicated for promotional pressure groups, which will be reviewed here. The apparent weakness of promotional pressure groups has somewhat called into question the earlier claims about the role of such groups in the political process and the likelihood of the growth in these groups' increasing political participation. While few would suggest that promotional groups are entirely without influence, it is accepted that their influence is, in general, far less than that of the sectional groups. This has been shown to be attributable to their lack of resources and, for most promotional groups, their outsider status. Because of this, promotional pressure groups have to adopt particular strategies and tactics both within the conventional political process and outside it. Corporations may then become a target of promotional pressure group activity as these groups seek ways to enhance their position, as well as being a target because of perceived abuse of corporate power. It is worth repeating the earlier observation that much of the pressure group literature concentrates solely on pressure group influence on public authorities (and for the most part, sectional group influence). Hence consideration will be given initially to the strategies and tactics for promotional pressure groups seeking only to influence public authorities, then subsequently to the influence of corporations. In keeping with the earlier discussion and much of the literature, this analysis will consider the pressure group role within a pluralistic model of the political process.

Colman suggests that the individualistic conception of democracy, as espoused by Rousseau and most philosophers of the classical liberal tradition, gave way to pluralism with the increasing scale and complexity of the governmental process following the industrial revolution. He refers to Wolff's description of the modern 'vector-sum' conception of democracy, 'which views the government as a pivotal point of forces exerted on it by pressure groups throughout the nation, its function being to resolve these conflicting forces into a single balanced policy'.[71] This does not occur for a number of reasons. As Colman observes, and

121

perhaps most importantly, governments are motivated by principles as well as interests. For some issues, such as capital punishment, principles may be indivisible, denying scope for give-and-take. A pressure group faced with principled government policy on the issue at hand, and seeking to change that policy, can either induce the government to modify the principles which guide the existing policy or modify the policy in spite of the principles, in the interests of expediency. The former course is open to any pressure group, involving persuasive attitude change directed at the decision-makers or the public at large. However, it is the latter course which is more frequently successful, but which is only available to groups possessing some measure of power over the government through, for example, their control over resources which the government depends upon. This involves an exercise in bargaining. While these are ideal types, contrast, for example, the National Union of Mineworkers, the Provisional IRA, or the British Medical Association, with Friends of the Earth or the Campaign for Nuclear Disarmament.

While Colman is guilty of generalisation and over-simplification – the earlier discussion has shown the picture to be far more complex than he suggests – and many would dispute the notion of a government trying desperately to adhere to principles in the face of coercion, his description of pressure group influence on policy seems basically accurate. In other words, to summarise the earlier discussion in this chapter and Colman's observations above, promotional pressure groups, because of their weak strategic location, must rely on persuasive attitude change. Promotional pressure group strategy is based on the need to change public and informed opinion, but Colman is not very optimistic about such an approach. He concludes by declaring the importance of persuasive appeals:

> Pressure groups which do not command the necessary resources to bargain directly, which is the case with most promotional or cause groups, are ... bound to restrict their efforts to attempts at persuasion ... they cannot bargain, because the government does not depend upon them in any concrete sense. The success of their campaigns therefore rests solely on the effectiveness of their persuasive appeals.

This is correct in so far as it refers to groups working only within the conventional political process. Promotional groups do, though, work outside it, employing direct action. While direct action (including boycotts) may be intended to gain publicity and influence opinion, it may also be intended to seek a more immediate solution on the issue. However, before considering direct action of this sort, it is useful to look at the types of strategies and tactics available to promotional pressure groups seeking to change public or informed opinion.

Mobilisation of legitimacy for the cause

Willetts suggests that pressure groups are formed and then work through a process of changing perceptions, socialisation, and recruitment.[72] Their ability to apply pressure is through the 'mobilisation of legitimacy for their cause'. As he observes:

> Winning support by changing people's perceptions of the issues is done by presenting arguments and information. An argument that there must be sanctions against South Africa because the regime is oppressive, or that nuclear power cannot be used because it is dangerous, depends upon convincing people that South Africa is oppressive or nuclear power is dangerous. Both topics may seem very remote from the everyday lives of those who are not immediately involved.

If promotional groups are to rely on their argument they require sound information. So Wilson counsels: 'Whatever you do, don't economise on research.'[73] Because of the importance of source credibility in influencing opinion and the likelihood of a pressure group being considered biased, reliable information is vital. Willetts notes that the 'processing of information is always a major activity of pressure groups and often it is overwhelmingly the most important activity'. Government dependence on information for its decisions may even mean that the pressure group acquires insider status, or is at least consulted by government, once it has established a reputation for reliability. It becomes, in Mackenzie's words, of 'administrative necessity'. He suggests the appeal to reason is the most effective of all techniques, but it is necessary to ensure the information 'is that the best people believe to be best'. Civil servants may, as he notes, be generalists, but they can at least assess the reliability of information.[74]

Pressure groups will then be concerned not only with influencing public opinion, but also élite opinion. They compete for the public's attention through the media, by publishing literature, and by setting out their cases at meetings, conferences, and demonstrations. Their information is of two sorts: that for mass communication – press conferences and releases, advertising, newspapers, magazines, pamphlets, and through spokespersons and interviews on radio and television; and that for specialist requirements – research documents, background information, briefing materials, technical journals, and giving advice.[75] The former is intended to influence public opinion, possibly targeted on opinion leaders in society given Lazerfeld's two-step model of the flow of information, while the latter is aimed at informed and influential opinion, principally government, though some may usefully reach opinion leaders in the public at large.

Ethical Purchase Behaviour

Willetts is careful not to attribute too great a part to pressure groups in changes in public opinion and consequent changes in government policy: 'we must be careful not to attribute too much influence directly to the pressure groups. They do help to mould attitudes within society, but at the same time they are a reflection of society. If a cause is totally at variance with the prevailing social norms, it would be unlikely that any group could be formed or that it could obtain much publicity.' Hence, public support is vital for the group to become organised. He does, however, continue by recognising the role of public opinion in influencing government and other targets: 'If, nevertheless, a group is formed which cannot evoke a response in the wider society, even if by pressure group standards it achieves a large membership, then governments and other targets will usually be able to afford to ignore it.'[76] Presumably then, governments cannot afford to ignore widespread public support for pressure groups. It is worth noting at this point that the size of a pressure group's membership is not indicative of the group's representativeness or support. This of course relates to the comment about the pressure group as a reflection of society. While with sectional groups the membership comprises for the most part the bulk of the group's supporters, this is unlikely to be the case with promotional groups. This is conveyed in the preferred American term for promotional groups: public interest groups. By definition, promotional groups do not represent a definable social or economic interest (ignoring the issue of middle-class bias), theoretically – recalling Wootton's openness of membership criterion – the whole population could join them. Most promotional groups will claim to speak for the interests of society at large; even if their opponents dispute such a claim they will at least acknowledge that the extent of the group's support goes beyond the fee-paying membership. This point is made throughout the literature.

Wilson rather neatly describes 'our kind' of pressure groups as 'advocates in the court of public opinion'.[77] This captures the view of promotional pressure groups as representatives of the public, but also, in order to be both effective and truly representative in this role, the requirement to gain popular support. Wilson describes at length, from A to Z, a great number of tactics that can be deployed in this purpose – too numerous for mention here. Other (academic) writers tend to refer to tactics only in passing (always assuming that the reference to promotional groups is more than a passing one). The case studies used by Wootton, Frost, Marsh, and others all identify tactics but do not attempt to evaluate and compare, or even classify. Perhaps this, and the lack of literature on promotional groups in general, is indicative of the ineffectiveness of such tactics. The difference between American and British politics has entailed the use of predominantly British sources in this chapter on pressure groups; it is perhaps because of the greater effectiveness of pressure group tactics in America that an American source must now be employed to present a reasonable categorisation of pressure group strategies and tactics.

Berry's categorisation of strategies and tactics

The more open American political process presents, it is argued, greater opportunity for pressure group influence. It is not possible to consider this issue here, but it is widely accepted that the British political process is relatively closed with much criticism of the inadequacy of disclosure in this country. Shipley suggests that interest groups in Britain have, in comparison with the United States, 'cultivated closer, more effective contacts with government departments'. (This, as later discussed, is sometimes viewed as corporatist.) The closer relationship between pressure groups and the executive is counterbalanced in the United States by pressure group influence with the legislature.[78] These differences between the United States and Britain both point to a greater influence for promotional pressure groups and a greater effectiveness of promotional group tactics in the United States, but also the difficulties likely to be encountered by an outsider, promotional group in Britain. Yet the strategies and tactics employed by American and British groups would not seem to differ greatly. Indeed, as Marsh observes, many British promotional groups are influenced in their strategies and tactics by the experiences of their American and continental counterparts.[79]

Berry defines strategy as 'broad plans of attack, or general approaches to lobbying', and tactics as 'the specific actions taken to advocate certain policy positions'.[80] His categorisation of pressure group strategies and tactics is based on interview research with staff lobbyists in 83 public interest groups. He identifies three categories of tactics.[81] First, direct lobbying, those techniques that are characterised by direct communication between lobbyists and government officials, such as personal presentations and testifying at congressional hearings. Second, methods by which groups lobby through their constituents, such as political protests (demonstrations, picketing, sit-ins) and letter writing. Finally, trying to change governmental policy by influencing elections or altering public opinion, the techniques of indirect lobbying, such as releasing research results and public relations. He found personal contact to be the most highly regarded tactic. But it would seem likely that not only should lobbyists' views of tactic effectiveness be judged with caution, as Berry concedes, but also the notion of taking any tactic in isolation from the rest is suspect because any outcome will be the consequence of the totality of pressure – that is, all the tactics employed – and moreover, is unlikely to be solely attributable to the pressure group's activities. As Berry notes in his conclusion (but not, unfortunately, in qualification of his claims about tactic effectiveness), 'the problems of distinguishing the influence of interest groups upon policy makers, as distinct from other influences such as the press, general public opinion, and other political élites, remain rather substantial'.[82] Perhaps British analysts of pressure groups have been wise in avoiding evaluations of pressure group tactics! His study should be seen to be primarily of value in its attempt to categorise pressure group tactics rather than assess their effectiveness.

This comment also applies to pressure group strategies, although it seems likely that groups have less discretion on their choice of strategy and often, indeed, employ more than one of the four strategies Berry identifies.[83] These are: the use of the law, embarrassment and confrontation, information, and constituency influence and pressure. They are given in a decision-making framework. Berry's determinants of strategy – goals and capabilities, and structure of the environment – are in keeping with British writers in the area who refer to organisational and environmental determinants of strategy. Some refer only to environmental considerations, largely in recognition of the great constraints faced by promotional groups: as Willetts writes, 'The choice of what strategy to adopt is made pragmatically on an estimate of what is more likely to be successful.'[84] Others acknowledge organisational as well as environmental considerations, including Berry. He even questions whether pressure groups assess different possible strategies and their subsequent effect: 'To them, admitting their ineffectiveness was not an acknowledgement of their organisations' failures, but a reaffirmation of their commitment to the cause.'[85] He suggests that the most important decision on a given issue is not the selection of strategy or choice of tactics, but the decision to become active on the issue in the first place.

Pressure group strategies and tactics are a consequence of the type of group and the circumstances in which it finds itself: which, for promotional groups and particularly in Britain, entails a dependence on influencing public opinion. Without insider status and with a greater emphasis on the executive rather than the legislature in the political process, they are obliged to adopt the strategies and tactics that will affect public opinion on the issue. For British outsider groups, the greatest hope lies in the embarrassment and confrontation strategy. While such a strategy still requires the effective use of information by the pressure group, it is used as a weapon against the public authorities rather than as a tool employed in co-operation with government. It is premissed on the belief that, as Berry puts it, 'sufficient exposure of bad policy will act to stimulate governmental officials to change such policy ... if a minimum of publicity can reveal what people in government are doing, those same people will find themselves under a new set of circumstances for future actions in that their behaviour will be critically scrutinised'. The group works to sustain controversy on the issue, making the official or department respond to the group's charges, which in turn gives the group greater legitimacy. Berry attributes this strategy, indirectly, to outsider status:

> Groups imbued with this strategy have a rather hostile, untrusting view of government. Of the variables previously discussed, the one that is probably most important in pushing a group toward this strategy is the perceived receptivity of targets. Groups adopting this strategy have long accepted that they are not going to be institutionalised into the policy-making process. Rather, they must force people in government to listen to them through protests, news leaks, whistle-blowing, and other similar tactics.

Additionally, of course, there is the force of public opinion. However, it is this strategy of embarrassment and confrontation and these tactics that force government to listen, which are also employed against corporations. They have within their perceived role as private institutions no recognised obligation to listen to pressure groups and are unlikely to be receptive targets of pressure group criticism.

Protest tactics and the corporation

The notion of corporations as 'private governments' might in itself suggest a comparability between pressure group attempts to influence the corporation with attempts to influence government. Regardless of whether the corporation is viewed as a political institution in this way, the limited access to corporate decision-making for the promotional pressure group at least suggests that it is reasonable to view the promotional group's position *vis-à-vis* government. Given the paucity of literature on pressure group activities directed against corporations,[86] this perspective can provide some useful insights. Moreover, not only will the corporation be a target for pressure group activity because of perceived abuse of corporate power, but also to strike indirectly at government. As seen earlier, the limited opportunities available to many promotional groups oblige them to consider any possible target.[87] The visibility of corporations and their concern for the corporate image suggests they are particularly susceptible to protest tactics, especially corporations in consumer markets (contrast, for example, RTZ's limited concern over criticism of their involvement in Namibia with that expressed by Barclays). While the use of information and particularly the release of research results will play an essential part, protest tactics will often be employed to draw attention to alleged corporate misdemeanours. It should be recognised that there is a distinction which is rarely made in the literature, and is not always clear, between protest tactics and direct action, where the pressure group is actually doing something to solve the problem directly. Although direct action has this specialised meaning, it is used in some of the literature to refer to protest tactics, such as demonstrations, which are for publicity purposes. Of course some, if not all direct action, is intended to be partly for publicity purposes, hence the confusion. Here, direct action will be considered separately.

The intention of protest tactics to obtain publicity demands that they should be of interest to the media. Such tactics will, as earlier noted, indicate that the normal channels, if ever available to the group, have failed. They must then maximise the publicity in a way that enhances the group by demonstrating and increasing public support. With good tactics 'the argument is in the action';[88] such as demonstrations outside a London shop selling furs, by protesters dressed in safari suits holding a sign saying 'help exterminate species – shop here'. Such action should be good-humoured, or public opinion may be alienated, and by being original both in itself and in conveying the message of the group, will capture media attention. The need for innovation and originality becomes ever greater the more protest actions there are. Berry's comment that demonstrations generally decrease in newsworthiness the more they occur[89] seems applicable to all protest tactics. Des Wilson, in his work with Shelter in particular, has shown himself to be remarkably adept at producing interesting events, and conveys the importance of this and the ways in which such an effect can be achieved throughout his book.

Meetings, rallies, marches, and demonstrations are direct methods of appealing to public opinion if the more passive methods referred to earlier, such as press releases, advertising, and so on, prove ineffective. Etzioni, in his study of demonstrations, suggests they are a legitimate form of political expression. His conclusion that they are necessary because other avenues of pressure are closed is in keeping with the argument presented here and probably applies to all protest tactics: 'demonstrations democratize in that they increase the *equality of political opportunity* by providing a tool with a built in advantage for those for whom the other tools of democracy are somewhat unwieldy and, not infrequently, relatively inaccessible'.[90] For protest tactics not only appeal to public opinion but also provide political leverage. As Berry writes, the strategy behind demonstrations is threefold: to expand public awareness of an issue through press coverage, to make government officials more sensitive and cognizant of a particular point of view on an issue, and finally by press coverage 'strengthen the group's hand and give it more leverage in the political process'.[91] Elsewhere, Michael Lipsky has referred to protest as a political resource along the same lines as Etzioni: 'protest is correctly conceived as a strategy utilised by relatively powerless groups in order to increase their bargaining ability.'[92] And commenting on the tactics of Saul Alinsky, Bailey writes, 'To compensate for the absence of power resources that depend upon either wealth or special access, protest is used.'[93] (Alinksy's tactics are principally direct action and this point about leverage applies even more forcefully to direct action and particularly with direct action involving corporations.)

Political leverage achieved by protest tactics is far more likely if there is violence involved. As Etzioni recognises and Hain noted in *Stop the Seventies Tour,* both media and political attention increases with violence. Governments at least take note if there is 'fighting in the streets'. Fortunately, many groups are ideologically opposed to the use of violence and employ non-violent direct action. However, the Stop the Seventies Tour group, while adhering to NVDA, could not prevent violence being used by rugby stewards in co-ordination with the police.[94] The authorities may even deliberately provoke violence, not to provide the group with political leverage but to deny it popular support.

In conclusion, it can be seen that the factors in the success of pressure groups and the circumstances faced by promotional groups point them towards certain strategies and tactics. As the latter discussion indicates, this may mean direct action and even violence if their attempts to change public and/or informed opinion – the only strategy likely to have any chance of success for most promotional groups – are unsuccessful. This would seem to apply also to actions against corporations. Moreover, the lack of opportunity to influence government may make corporations a target for pressure groups so as to strike indirectly at government.

Direct action and the corporation

Direct action refers to actions outside and probably in conflict with conventional democratic processes. There is a distinction between direct action and publicity stunts. However, much direct action is for publicity. A good case in point is the return of non-returnable bottles to Schweppes, dumped in a colossal pile outside the Schweppes office by supporters of Friends of the Earth. Wilson describes this as a classic piece of direct action, but notes that it was also an effective media event. It did, of course, involve a corporation as a target. The corporation can become the target of direct action because of some perceived corporate misdemeanour (and plenty of examples of such actions are considered later involving boycotts); because it is tangentially involved in some activity, but the real target is government, which although seen as being responsible cannot be reached directly; and, finally, because the corporation is a handy target. As will be shown later, the choice of the corporation and any specific corporation may be entirely arbitrary, or simply on the basis of prominence, susceptibility, and accessibility, rather than any perceived assessment of corporate 'guilt'. The likelihood is that corporations will be subject to direct action ever more frequently in the future.

It is, for most groups, the intransigence of the authorities to a pressure group's case which prompts demonstrations, direct action, and possibly violent direct action. With most groups, direct action is viewed as a last resort. FoE, for example, is reluctant to use direct action and has refrained so far on the nuclear power issue. Ward identifies a threefold strategy at work: to bring issues directly to the attention of the public by the activities of local groups and the publication of high quality publicity material; to influence the public through well organised media events; and finally, by direct access to lobbying Parliament and giving testimony to Royal Commissions and public inquiries. It is this faith in being 'incorporated' that has militated against the use of direct action. This reluctance to use direct action has led to many activists forming local anti-nuclear groups and affiliating to the Anti-Nuclear Campaign. And while Ward suggests that FoE's activities have put the issue of nuclear power firmly on the political agenda, FoE has never really obtained insider status, but acted as a 'legitimating gloss on corporatist politics'.[95]

Ward's case study was written in 1983. In late 1983 and early 1984, Greenpeace, which sees involvement in public inquiries as largely futile, successfully employed direct action against the nuclear power industry. While attempting to 'cap' a pipe discharging radioactive material from Sellafield (Windscale) into the sea, they came across an extremely high level of discharge, well in excess of the level permitted by the government and which Greenpeace was (illegally) trying to prevent. There was a government investigation of this accident which blamed the Sellafield management, making 23 recommendations for improvements. The outcome, in addition to the mobilisation of public opinion, was promises by British Nuclear Fuels Ltd. to reorganise its management, discipline some employees, spend an extra £12 million to improve safety, and accelerate plans to reduce radioactive discharges into the sea. Greenpeace observed that this accident may not have been the first and still sought an end to all radioactive discharges. They could at least claim a partial success and the likelihood of a complete success in the near future is considerably enhanced. Greenpeace had used the conventional channels to no avail. Obliged to use direct action, it was relatively successful.[96] Similar successes have been achieved by Greenpeace, using direct action, over the dumping of hazardous chemicals at sea and whaling. Marsh suggests there are 'certain signs that direct action may increase'. Although direct action is alien to the

British tradition, he notes that the influence of American and continental experiences is prompting many British promotional groups in that direction, particularly as some are American offshoots.[97]

Promotional groups may find governments intransigent and unresponsive. Yet there may also be little governments can do, particularly as regards multinational companies, or at least little they would wish to do, because of their fear of offending them. This is particularly true of governments in the Third World.[98] Promotional groups must then act directly against the cause of their complaint. This will often be business. Another interesting instance of direct action against a corporation is the (falsely) claimed poisoning of Mars chocolate bars by the Animal Liberation Front, over the alleged involvement of Mars in experiments on animals. This supports the claim about how intransigent, unresponsive, or ineffective government behaviour on an issue may push the group into direct action, and how corporations may increasingly come under attack. The year 1984 witnessed a number of direct actions against firms by this group, justified in this way: 'The traditional animal welfare movement has been around for decades, and it has not been very effective. It is only through direct action that people can see something has been achieved.' The group also recognises ethical purchase behaviour, as 'Notes slipped into the wrappers said the Front did not wish to harm human life, but people eating "cruelty-based products" should be responsible for their own actions.'[99] It seems, however, that they would wish to deny people the right to choose in their purchase behaviour. Direct action and the corporation will be further considered in the next chapter. This chapter concludes with a brief examination of pressure groups and pluralism and the role of direct action in this.

Pluralism through direct action?

If public policy is to be the equilibrium reached in the struggle to accommodate conflicts of group interest, how may promotional pressure groups play a part? Their limited resources and consequent limited influence would seem to militate against the pluralistic ideal. There are many interests which, because of their weak strategic location or because they are not organised, have no opportunity for participation in the political process. Interests which are not organised must, it would seem, rely on their particular concerns being recognised and accommodated by the authorities. For organised interests, however, a number of solutions seem to present themselves on the basis of the analysis here. If these interests are organised as a promotional pressure group they will find it unlikely that they are able to influence the authorities directly, by involvement in decision-making. Even if they

131

desire insider status and achieve it, only rarely do such groups have much influence. They lack the sanctions by which they can make demands in the way that is available to the sectional groups. They must then rely on the mobilisation of legitimacy for their cause by gaining popular support, and/or the support of influential people. Alternatively, or additionally if possible, they must attempt to improve their strategic location so that their demands may be backed by sanctions or coercion.

The strategies and tactics for influencing public and élite opinion have been discussed. They include the consumer boycott as a protest tactic. This approach may be unsuccessful, however. Groups are then placed in the position of waiting for a more amenable administration – perhaps indefinitely – or using direct action. Direct action is a last resort for a number of reasons. It may alienate some of the popular support for the group and probably any support that may exist within government. It may be illegal and violent. As a form of coercion it may offend some groups' preferences for what they view as democratic procedures; although one might question whether coercion by a promotional group is any different to the coercion previously exerted by a variety of sectional groups from the National Union of Mineworkers to the British Medical Association. More coercive tactics may also entail loss of control for the group's leadership as action in support of the cause gets out of hand. Hence, there are risks associated with direct action. Direct action may, however, be preferred by some groups for ideological reasons. The activities of the Irish Republican Army (IRA) are an extreme example, in their rejection of the legitimacy of British rule.

The imbalance in the pluralistic model in favour of sectional groups may, potentially, be redressed by direct action. All the possible forms and the desirability of this cannot be explored here. However, one particular form is considered, with good reason to assume it may be desirable. This is non-violent direct action in consumer boycotts, assumed to be desirable because of the employment of consumer sovereignty. That is, such a tactic of direct action is legitimated by the role of consumer sovereignty as the rationale for capitalism (as discussed in Chapter 1). If consumer sovereignty provides the customer with a 'purchase vote', then it may appropriately be used as a form of political participation. The outcome of this form of ethical purchase behaviour may provide political participation in three ways. First, as a form of direct action, the boycott may, by putting pressure on the firm, stop a corporate digression. Second, and particularly if the firm has little control over the digression, it can put pressure on government via the firm to meet the group's demands. It will provide political leverage for the group, perhaps even enhancing the strategic location of the group by giving it some degree of economic power. Third, as a protest tactic, it can at least mobilise and express public opinion, which may also provide political leverage and even insider status and influence.

Corporations may then become involved in pressure group activity both because of their perceived abuses of power, but also because they represent a convenient target which can be employed to put pressure on government. The previous chapters have shown that further social control of business may be achieved through the market, indicating a role in the marketing system for pressure groups. This chapter, in addition to examining the nature of pressure groups, has shown that promotional groups may not only wish to employ the market to correct corporate digressions, but also to improve their weak strategic location in their dealings with government: in other words, by using the boycott provide sanctions which may support their demands and possibly even coercion to force them in extreme cases. Some pressure groups would not even differentiate between the government and some corporations. In such instances, the distinction above is artificial. The 'military-industrial-complex' and the close relationship between the government, the UK Central Electricity Generating Board and the nuclear power equipment manufacturers are cases in point.

Promotional groups are rarely the sole cause of changes in public policy or corporate behaviour. Public policy changes are usually the result of a number of influences, possibly including promotional pressure groups. Of those promotional groups that can claim to be successful, few can seriously suggest they have done more than put the issue on the political agenda. Influencing corporate behaviour, while also the result of a number of forces, may be easier and perhaps more appropriate. The American corporate accountability movement, dissatisfied with government efforts, attacked corporations directly, including the use of direct action. Pressure groups in this country may do likewise. The increased use of direct action will, in itself, mean corporations are more likely to be the targets of pressure group activity. Do boycotts represent a form of direct action likely to be successful? Chapter 1 would suggest, in their basis in consumer sovereignty, that they are a legitimate tactic. The next chapter considers boycotts as a tactic in detail.

Chapter five

The boycott tactic

Preview

> ahimsa ... is not merely a negative state of harmlessness but it is a
> positive state of love, of doing good even to the evil-doer. But it
> does not mean helping the evil-doer to continue the wrong or
> tolerating it by passive acquiescence. On the contrary, love, the
> active state of ahimsa, requires you to resist the wrong-doer by
> dissociating yourself from him even though it may offend him or
> injure him physically.
>
> Mahatma K. Gandhi[1]

> This great reform, as you can see, can be achieved without
> shedding a drop of blood, without violence, without breaking any
> law – English, human or divine. But if a man does take a farm from
> which a poor tenant has been evicted, I conjure you to do him no
> bodily harm ... Act toward him as the Queen of England to you ...
> She would not regard you nor your wife nor your children as her
> equals. Now imitate the Queen of England, and don't speak to a
> landgrabber nor a landgrabber's wife nor to a landgrabber's
> children ... If a landgrabber comes to town and wants to sell
> anything, don't do him any bodily harm ... If you see a landgrabber
> going to a shop to buy bread, or clothing, or even whiskey, go you
> to the shopkeeper at once, don't threaten him ... Just say to him that
> under British law he has the undoubted right to sell his goods to
> anyone, but that there is no British law to compel you to buy
> another penny's worth from him, and that you will never do it as
> long as you live.
>
> James Redpath, in 1880[2]

Earlier chapters have put forward the case for ethical purchase
behaviour: its apparent basis in consumer sovereignty and its actual and
potential role as a mechanism for the social control of business with an

information role identified for pressure groups. The previous chapter examined pressure groups, showing that not only may ethical purchase behaviour require pressure groups, but also that pressure groups may need ethical purchase behaviour. Promotional pressure groups are in need of effective tactics: one possible tactic which they could usefully use may be the consumer boycott. This chapter examines the boycott tactic, including (and briefly at this point) the consumer boycott, the most manifest form of ethical purchase behaviour and the form of principal concern to this study, and a tactic which may enhance the strategic location of promotional pressure groups.

Ahimsa is the term Gandhi employed to describe non-violent direct action (NVDA). In keeping with this, Gandhi organised consumer boycotts of salt and British cloth. For Gandhi, this philosophy of non-violence was a way of life – it later brought him into conflict with those who thought of it simply as a strategy. NVDA has proved effective both when used within a non-violent philosophy and simply as a strategy alone. It is adopted by promotional pressure groups for ideological reasons, but probably also because it is the more acceptable form of direct action. It would seem likely that if direct action is to increase, as the previous chapter suggested, then NVDA may become much more commonplace.

Consumer boycotts are the form of NVDA considered in this study. The term boycott originates in the ostracism of an Irish land agent, Captain Boycott. It was first written by Redpath, who describes the tactic above. As this quotation shows, the term boycott refers to more than not buying from an unfavourably viewed seller. Various types of boycott are identified here, including the form of international economic sanctions such as the Arab boycott. Hence this examination of the boycott tactic is not restricted to the consumer boycott, as the consumer boycott needs to be seen within the context of all boycott tactics and NVDA generally. Other types of boycott also suggest implications for the use of the consumer boycott and for management response.

Non-violent direct action

The above quotation about ahimsa reveals the underlying philosophical basis to NVDA. This is important because direct action can appeal for ideological reasons and the use of NVDA and boycotts in particular can reflect this. The IRA's use of violent direct action is at least in part ideological, for its justification is that it is fighting a war, with the British troops in Northern Ireland seen as an army of occupation. Similarly, the use of NVDA by other pressure groups is ideological, in the rejection of the legitimacy of violence. In some cases, consumer boycotts involve not only the avoidance of certain products but also the welcoming of others, in the embracing of a more appropriate subculture or 'alternative' society. However, before considering this philosophical basis to NVDA, it is worth summarising the main points about direct action as a pressure group strategy and as they relate to boycotts of business, as indicated in the pressure group literature and discussed in the previous chapter. First, and most importantly, direct action is a last resort for the majority of pressure groups. It would be incorrect and misleading to suggest that the following discussion of NVDA, as a philosophy, represents the outlook of all or even most pressure groups. Yet it is becoming increasingly prevalent among promotional groups faced with intransigent and unresponsive authorities.

The second point is that direct action is likely to increase as more groups find their demands not being met or ignored, in addition to those groups employing direct action for ideological reasons. Those groups in the former category are likely to prefer NVDA because the weapons used by a group to advance its cause must be appropriate to the character of its aims. An obvious example is CND. As a pacifist organisation, it could not possibly endorse violent direct action. So NVDA is likely to become more commonplace. A further point is that corporations will be increasingly involved. They are attractive targets either as contributors to the wrong which the group is striving to right, or perhaps even as valuable potential allies to be won over, particularly given their insider status. Finally, direct action may be symbolic, designed to gain public attention (but possibly losing public sympathy) and demonstrate strength of feeling or breadth of support. In so doing, the group has the sense of being active and morale is raised and maintained. Alternatively, or additionally, direct action may be designed to achieve concrete results in itself. The actions by Greenpeace referred to in the previous chapter and the advocacy of squatting by groups for the homeless are typical examples of direct action with both symbolic and concrete intentions. The symbolic forms of direct action, however, may be more accurately described as publicity stunts or protest tactics. Demonstrations and perhaps even strikes are a recognised part of the political process and should not perhaps be described as direct action, as the earlier discussion of definitions indicated.[3]

In sum, then, promotional pressure groups often find themselves obliged to turn to direct action in the last resort, because of their relative powerlessness. Corporations are likely to become increasingly involved and, given the probable preference for non-violent direct action, this involvement could well feature consumer boycotts. This chapter examines the boycott tactic including boycotts of business, an examination which continues in Chapter 7. First, however, it is necessary to look at non-violent direct action as the incorporating philosophy and strategy for boycotts.

Non-violent direct action provides groups with a particular form of power. It gives the group and its supporters moral superiority. This is where the distinction between violent direct action and non-violent direct action becomes apparent (though this may be more often in theory than in practice, and not always in the public's perception of events). Violent direct action employs violence. However, NVDA involves more than the refusal to employ violence. A non-violent action requires the participants neither to use violence initially nor respond with it when provoked, nor even when it is used by the authorities. Moreover, the participants must not retreat in the face of violence as this would show that violence always succeeds. In so doing, as Gandhi found, the non-violent protester achieves moral superiority over the opponent. This is described by Richard Gregg as moral jiu-jitsu:

> The non-violence and goodwill of the victim act in the same way that the lack of physical opposition by the user of physical jiu-jitsu does, causing the attacker to lose his moral balance. He suddenly and unexpectedly loses the moral support which the usual violent resistance of most victims would render him. He plunges forward, as it were, into a new world of values. He feels insecure because of the novelty of the situation and his ignorance of how to handle it ... The user of non-violent resistance, knowing what he is doing and having a more creative purpose, keeps his moral balance. He uses the leverage of a superior wisdom to subdue the rough direct force of his opponent.[4]

The successes of the American civil rights movement under Martin Luther King are generally attributed to his adherence to the principle of non-violence. He wrote 'I had come to see early that the Christian doctrine of love operating through the Gandhian method of non-violence was one of the most potent weapons available to the Negro in his struggle for freedom.'[5] Yet this should not give the impression that Gandhi's use of non-violence was entirely pragmatic. For Gandhi, ends and means were coincident. His use of non-violence was both because he realised it was an effective conflict technique, and also because of his preference for it as a way of life, rooted in his moral and religious beliefs. Gandhi's philosophy and his use of NVDA is described in detail in Joan Bondurant's *The Conquest of Violence*.[6] She suggests that the method of satyagraha, the name Gandhi used to describe his actions, is the key to understanding his political thought. Her work is a widely acknowledged classic on NVDA, but is only part of an extensive literature. Sharp's *The Politics of Nonviolent Action*, published in 1973, is probably still 'the most comprehensive attempt thus far to examine the nature of non-violent struggle as a social and political technique, including its view of power, its specific methods of action, its dynamics in conflict and the conditions for success or failure in its use'.[7] The politics of NVDA can only be considered briefly here, but they should be seen as the essential backdrop to boycotts.

Sharp emphasises that NVDA may be used as a strategy by pressure groups but this need not necessarily be based on a principled rejection of violence. Accordingly, Sharp's study does not attempt to convert the reader to a new faith, or to describe some non-violent philosophy. He is concerned with the effectiveness of NVDA in an attempt to find alternatives to violence. It should be appreciated that, as Sharp notes, 'Nonviolent action is just what it says: *action* which is non-violent, not *inaction*.'[8] However, actions are not simply violent or non-violent, there is in effect a continuum of violence. The point is important because consumer boycotts are to be justified because they are non-violent. However, as a coercive action, they are most accurately seen as being on a point well towards, but not at, the non-violent extreme of this continuum. Indeed, non-violent alternatives to violence need not be greatly different from violence in the way in which they operate. As Schelling comments: 'The violent actions and the nonviolent are different methods of trying to make it unrewarding for people to do certain things, and safe or rewarding to do other things.'[9] Consequently, the application and motives of either method may be incorrect or 'bad'. Such an observation is obviously true of the particular form of non-violent action of concern here: boycotts, and all types of ethical purchase behaviour, may be for 'good' or 'bad' motives. The user's intention is based on his or her perception of 'good' or 'bad' and may even be deliberately evil.

The Politics of Nonviolent Action comes in three volumes. The first, *Power and Struggle*, examines political power and the characteristics and achievements of non-violent struggle. Sharp shows that the assumption that power derives from violence and can be controlled only by greater violence is misplaced. He identifies a long history of non-violent action, from ancient Rome to the civil rights struggles in the United States. He specifically refers to non-violent action by working people in the late nineteenth and early twentieth centuries to improve conditions and gain greater power, using as later discussed, the strike in conjunction with the consumer boycott. So, while he describes Gandhi as 'the outstanding strategist of nonviolent action', he recognises that non-violent action in various forms has been used by many others at many different times and not just by Gandhi, to whom the notion of non-violent action is so often attributed. Underlying and therefore uniting all these various actions is a particular perspective on power: 'implicitly or explicitly, all non-violent struggle has a basic assumption in common and that is its view of the nature of power and how to deal with it.'[10]

Sharp argues that obedience is at the heart of political power, involving an element of reciprocity and mutual dependence. Obedience is then essentially voluntary as it rests on a combination of a fear of sanctions and free consent, the latter largely arising 'from a more or less nonrational acceptance of the standards and ways of one's society, or from a more or less rational consideration of the merits of the regime and the reasons for obeying it'.[11] Accordingly, if power rests on obedience, which is a consequence of both coercion and consent, that consent may be withdrawn if the legitimacy of the ruler is called into question and his or her power position threatened. This logic was employed by the American corporate accountability movement in regard to the power of corporations. Somewhat earlier, this understanding of the potentially fragile nature of power led to Gandhi arguing the need for a psychological change away from passive submission to self-respect and courage, for recognition by the subject that his assistance makes the regime possible, and for the building of a determination to withdraw co-operation and obedience. Gandhi said his speeches 'are intended to create "dissatisfaction" as such, that people might consider it a shame to assist or cooperate with a government that had forfeited all title to respect or support'.[12] Sharp shows that the use of non-violent action has brought ordinary people higher wages, a breakdown in social barriers, changes in government policies, frustrated invaders, paralysed an empire, and dissolved dictatorships.

Direct action and the corporation

The likelihood of direct action being increasingly used in this country, involving the corporation with ever growing frequency, may be illustrated by reference to a recent survey. Boyle reports a Gallup opinion survey, specially commissioned for the BBC programme 'Inquiry – Protest and the Suburban Guerilla'.[13] This found surprisingly high proportions prepared to break the law on issues where national interest could take precedence over their local needs. Fifty-five per cent said they would be prepared to contemplate breaking the law to stop a motorway near their homes; 67 per cent regarded lawbreaking as a potentially legitimate tactic to stop a nuclear power station. These figures were presented within the context of a programme showing that direct action tactics were no longer the prerogative of minority and unrepresentative pressure groups, but were also appropriate to 'middle-class folk who had already climbed the ladder of protest, found the system wanting, and were prepared to countenance hard-line direct action if all else failed'. This, of course, not only points to the growing acceptance of direct action, but also to the much wider issues of political participation, disclosure, and the role of pressure groups, considered in the previous chapter.

One must accept that this type of television programme contains an element of sensationalism. However, the facts of events that have occurred at public inquiries (direct action), the opinion survey findings, and the views of former senior officials, should not be lightly dismissed. Moreover, corporations are involved to various degrees from being a potential target when constructing motorways, to an active party lobbying for its own interests in conflict with local interests, such as the British Airports Authority at Stansted and the CEGB (*et al.*) at the Sizewell Inquiry. Oil companies hoping to drill in the Home Counties found themselves up against a group called Save Our Surrey who, until prevented by the Independent Broadcasting Authority, had an anti-advertisement featuring Conoco on the local radio station. This was at least partly intended to be pressure group influence on purchase behaviour. One protester commented, 'I used to think Friends of the Earth were a bunch of long-haired layabouts ... until I discovered Conoco!' So there seems to be some degree of popular support for direct action and the corporation is most definitely involved.

NVDA and the consumer boycott

Sharp goes to considerable lengths to identify the different types of NVDA. Three broad classes of methods are identified: symbolic actions, withdrawal of co-operation, and direct intervention. Boycotts are classified as withdrawal of co-operation. Three subclasses are subsumed under this class, which Sharp refers to as non-cooperation: social non-cooperation, economic non-cooperation, and political non-cooperation. The methods of economic non-cooperation Sharp divides into economic boycotts and strikes. A full list of the categories and types of economic boycotts identified by Sharp is given in Table 5.1.

However, Sharp's categorisation of economic boycotts is not in itself adequate for direct application to this study. He includes actions which are beyond the scope of the investigation and interest here, such as the actions by governments. The concern here is restricted to actions by individual or organisational customers, not countries via their governments; although such actions may be, arguably, ethical purchase behaviour. The distinction that is made is between all economic boycotts – 'the refusal to continue or to undertake certain economic relationships, especially the buying, selling, or handling of goods and services'[14] – and the consumer boycott, defined here as the organised exercising of consumer sovereignty by abstaining from purchase of an offering in order to exert influence on a matter of concern to the customer and over the institution making the offering. The distinction is

Table 5.1 : Sharp's categories of economic boycotts

---

1 Action by consumers:

- consumers' boycott
- nonconsumption of boycotted goods
- policy of austerity
- rent withholding
- refusal to rent
- national consumers' boycott
- international consumers' boycott.

2 Action by workers and producers:

- workmen's boycott
- producers' boycott.

3 Action by middlemen:

- suppliers' and handlers' boycott.

4 Action by owners and management:

- traders' boycott
- refusal to let or sell property
- lockout
- refusal of industrial assistance
- merchants' 'general strike'.

5 Action by holders of financial resources:

- withdrawal of bank deposits
- refusal to pay fees, dues, and assessments
- refusal to pay debts or interest
- severance of funds and credit
- revenue refusal
- refusal of a government's money.

6 Action by governments:

- domestic embargo
- blacklisting of traders
- international sellers' embargo
- international buyers' embargo
- international trade embargo.

---

partly the result of the difference in perspectives. Sharp's concern is with all non-violent action, particularly in this case, that involving the withdrawal of co-operation in economic relationships. The concern here is with a specific form of non-violent action because it is a type of ethical purchase behaviour and is therefore based in consumer sovereignty. As earlier noted, this study is ultimately an investigation of the extent of consumer sovereignty. All forms of economic boycott would seem to be included in Sharp's schema. It may then be suggested that a consumer boycott is one type of economic boycott. However, it is not then possible to say that it is comparable to a specific category identified by Sharp. It is more than his category 1, action by consumers. It is, because of this difference in perspective, all actions identified in Sharp's schema where the participant is employing his or her power in the market-place as a customer, that is, using consumer sovereignty.

To conclude this brief examination of NVDA it is worth considering how NVDA may work, in the British context in particular, and the possible role of the consumer boycott in this.

NVDA in Britain and a role for the consumer boycott

Sharp emphasises the importance of preparation for non-violent action, and the likelihood that the challenge will be repressed but that with solidarity and discipline (particularly in ensuring that actions remain non-violent in the face of violence) a form of jiu-jitsu may operate, as earlier noted. He identifies three mechanisms by which non-violent action produces victory: by conversion, which he suggests is the least likely; by accommodation, where concessions are granted but the opponent is neither converted to the activists' point-of-view nor coerced into action; and, third, by non-violent coercion. Sharp's analysis concludes with the claim that non-violent action can contribute to long-term social change by redistributing power. Power becomes diffused as non-violent action involves a decentralisation of power. This political ideal permeates Sharp's analysis but not, it seems, to its detriment. (It is hoped that such an observation is true of this study and the expressed concern for the slightly less ambitious ideal of greater political participation. Of course, this ideal is not altogether unrelated to that expressed by Sharp.)

The classic non-violent action results from severe oppression, often stemming from the participants being unable to do anything else, as Gandhi recognised in India and South Africa. In such circumstances, as Lakey suggests, 'The task of the non-violent campaigners, then, is to get the opponent to see them as human beings.'[15] Yet how relevant are such classic actions to contemporary Britain? The government may attempt to portray CND as 'crackpots', but they are still viewed – perhaps even by the government – as human beings. Blacks are relatively dis-advantaged in this country, but – with the possible exception of a small extremist minority – they are still viewed as human beings and could not be reasonably described as heavily oppressed. Circumstances of severe oppression may dictate the use of NVDA. In such cases it may be possible to organise mass actions, producing the classic or 'grand' non-violent campaign – such as Gandhi's salt satyagraha. But there are few causes in this country, for the moment at least, that seem to either warrant such action – it is, after all, a last resort – or would command mass support. One may ask, for example, what happened to the mass civil disobedience that was promised on the arrival of cruise missiles? CND has one of the largest memberships, if not the largest membership (110,000 in 1984)[16] of any pressure group in this country: if they cannot fulfil such a promise over what they claim to be a life and death issue, who can?

Hence one must distinguish between actions resulting from severe oppression and those that are more typical of the promotional pressure group in this country. This would be where pressure groups arc attempting to get the authorities (including corporations) to listen, by employing their last resort strategy. In such a case, action is likely to be by a committed few, the inner core of the pressure group membership and those some may term fanatics. In the former case, the action is more likely to involve far greater numbers – the Montgomery bus boycott in the 1950s and the more recent Ciskei bus boycott in South Africa are good examples. Having made this distinction, it is useful to illustrate it by considering the more typical non-violent action in this country. In so doing, it is worth noting the observation in the previous chapter and repeated earlier in this chapter, that direct action may involve a symbolic element. It was suggested that direct actions might not be accurately so described if they were simply symbolic acts. Yet if one recognises that most non-violent actions in this country amount to small-scale pragmatic non-violence, one also acknowledges that they are largely symbolic. This is not claimed for all non-violent actions that have taken place in this country to date, nor will it, as a generalisation, necessarily apply to all future non-violent actions.[17] The point, however, is important for the assessment of consumer boycotts and will be considered further; for are boycotts, as non-violent actions, to be judged by their economic effect when they are principally symbolic acts?

Wilson is not an advocate of conscientious non-violence. He does, however, suggest that no cause justifies the use of violence in Britain. He therefore supports the use of pragmatic non-violence. In so doing, he offers six guidelines for direct action:

(1) If possible it should be relevant to the injustice so that a clear message emerges from the action;
(2) It should have imagination and humour;
(3) It should enlist the sympathy of people, not alienate them;
(4) It should be non-violent;
(5) It should be seen to be an expression of genuine injustice, and not the first but rather the last resort;
(6) Wherever possible it should be within the spirit of the law.[18]

This captures the flavour of most NVDA by pressure groups in this country. Importantly, as will be seen in relation to boycotts, he also notes in support of these points that 'Direct action can ... be justified in many circumstances although it becomes less effective the more it is employed and the earlier it is employed.' And, further, that 'Direct action, to be defensible, should always relate to the cause itself, and wherever possible, the only victims of it should be the perpetrators of the injustice.'

The Stansted protesters referred to above are intending to use civil disobedience within the law. They have in mind such actions as lying down in front of bulldozers. This is comparable to the frequent actions organised by groups such as Friends of the Earth to protect conservation areas.[19] The principal point made in 'Protest and the Suburban Guerilla' was that some of the more unlikely people are now becoming involved in such actions. This applies too to many of the current supporters of CND. This group is now prepared to use tactics that involve breaking the law. In June 1984, for the first time in a CND demonstration, there were (two thousand) people breaking the law. This, the programme suggested, was a product of the example set by Greenpeace and the Greenham Common protests. One CND demonstrator commented: 'I've tried everything else – done all the democratic things.' Yet for all the talk of guerilla action and law-breaking, it is unlikely that this is an indication of a growing radicalisation of the masses – not even the middle-class masses.

Law-breaking is arguably morally justifiable when the law is 'wrong', illegitimate, or *in extremis*. As Wilson notes, 'the police themselves tend to interpret the law differently on different occasions ... at their best, they seek to act "within the *spirit* of the law"'.[20] This, he argues, should be the position adopted by pressure groups. In illustration, he suggests that if protesters were to breach the law of trespass as in the above example of the defence of a Site of Special Scientific Interest (as well as presumably causing an obstruction), this would be within the spirit of the law as it would be to prevent the breach of what is perceived to be a more serious law. The actions by the suffragette movement were similar in this respect. The law was breached to change the law. Boycotts as a pressure group tactic can be illegal. Yet, as with the sort of actions described above, they are minor breaches of the law. One might perhaps compare them to the breaches of Sunday trading laws. Laidler, in a study of the boycott in labour struggles, argued the law was wrong (in the US, in 1913) in making boycotts illegal.[21] Protesters against nuclear arms might argue that because the issue is so vital to human survival, their minor breaches of the law are justifiably *in extremis*. Finally, and perhaps most convincing, is the claim that the law is illegitimate in certain circumstances. This is why the case for NVDA must rest on such actions being a last resort. This argument on legality is not sophisticated, but it does seem acceptable. Returning to Etzioni, the most sensible position seems to be, as he advocates, recognising and tolerating protest – including that which may be in minor breach of the law – as an important form of political expression.

Etzioni defends peaceful demonstrations as a legitimate political act. It also seems a sound basis for defending consumer boycotts and – bearing in mind that NVDA is more than just civil disobedience – many other non-violent direct actions. As Etzioni puts it, 'When people have institutionalised channels to express themselves and channels which are effective, why should they take to the streets?'[22] Could consumer boycotts not work in a similar way for expressing concern about corporate misdemeanours? Having examined boycotts as non-violent direct action, and what is meant by this, it is now appropriate to consider further various types of boycott. The remainder of this chapter considers the origin of the term boycott, the different types of boycott, the boycott in labour struggles (including the consumer boycott), the boycott as an international economic sanction, and how the boycott can affect business.

Various types of boycott

Captain Charles Cunningham Boycott

There are a great variety of boycotts, from social ostracism to consumer boycotts. Laidler, and Nelson and Prittie, explain the origin of the term.[23] The word is the surname of a notoriously severe rent collector of the Earl of Erne, Captain Charles Cunningham Boycott, of County Mayo, Ireland. The Irish peasantry had long been suffering from the excesses of the British landlord class. Lands had been confiscated, homes of the peasants destroyed, starvation wages paid. The famine of 1878 encouraged an increase in the number of evictions, for ever more trivial reasons. To oppose this move to clear the states, the Land League was formed to represent the peasants. The situation demanded direct action.

In the summer of 1880, Boycott sent his tenants to the fields to cut oats. However, instead of offering the regular wage of 62 and 37 cents a day for men and women respectively, he offered only 32 and 24 cents. His tenants refused to work. The Boycott family and servants attempted to harvest the crop but gave up after a few hours. The tenants finally returned to work after pleas from Mrs Boycott, but on rent day they were served with eviction papers. The outraged workers held a meeting and secured pledges from those present, including the servants, herders, and drivers, to cease all relations with Boycott and his family. Boycott requested assistance, and a relief expedition of seven regiments and fifty hired men was rushed to the estate. The crops were gathered, but at a cost well in excess of their value. The term boycott was thought up three days after the decree of social ostracism by James Redpath, an American journalist, and Father O'Malley, an Irish priest. It was first used publicly by Redpath in August 1880, in the village of Deenane. (Redpath's explanation of the device was quoted in the Preview to this chapter.)

On this occasion at least, the boycott proved successful. No one would work for Boycott, speak to him, or supply him with goods or services; ultimately he was driven out of his home, and out of Ireland. More importantly, the boycott action made many people in England and Ireland aware of grave injustices. However, this was not the first use of the boycott tactic, even if it was the first so named. As Chapter 7 shows, there is a historical precedent for boycotts dating back well before 1880.

The boycott of Captain C. C. Boycott involved the ceasing of all relations with Boycott and his family. It included the social boycott and various types of economic boycott as identified by Sharp. However, the use of the boycott need not be so blunt; it may be more selective. While all the possible and various types of boycott were employed against Boycott, it is more usual to find a more restricted application of boycotts. So Wootton, in this regard, identifies a continuum of boycotting, from the most limited application to the most extensive.[24] He defines the boycott as 'abstaining from using, buying from, selling to or otherwise dealing with a person or institution in order to exert influence'. His emphasis is on the use of the boycott by sectional groups. At one extreme he has political strikes; at the other, withdrawal of participation from voluntary schemes. Wootton is not clear about the basis on which his continuum operates, but he usefully illustrates how boycotts may differ and as far as this study is concerned, it seems sufficient to view the continuum of boycotting as being based on the degree of ostracism involved. So a continuum can usefully be conceived along which various types of boycott may be found which represent greater or lesser non-cooperation.

Boycotts in labour struggles

The boycott was of major importance in organising labour, in the United States at least. Historians attribute a central, if not determining, role to boycotts in the labour struggles for unionisation. The basis for much of their accounts of the part played by boycotts lies in the analyses of two contemporary writers: Laidler, whose *Boycotts and the Labor Struggle* was first published in 1913; and Wolman, whose *The Boycott in American Trade Unions* was published in 1916. Their studies will be used directly here in a brief consideration of the role of the boycott in labour struggles and also in Chapter 7, as their examination of the mechanism of the consumer boycott does not seem to have greatly suffered over time.

There is an appealing logic to the use of consumer boycotts in labour struggles, neatly expressed by Laidler in comparing strikes and boycotts: 'The strike aims to gain better conditions for labor by depriving the "unfair" employer of the labor power necessary to produce goods; the boycott, on the other hand, seeks these same ends by depriving the employer of the market for those goods which labor has created.'[25] Laidler argues that the boycott is a natural and necessary partner to the strike. However, before examining the role of the boycott in unionisation, it is important to clarify the meaning denoted by the term boycott. Wootton observes that where sectional pressure groups such as solicitors or teachers refer to a policy of non-cooperation, they are simply using the polite name for a boycott. He also refers to the political strike as being at one end of the continuum of boycotting, and given his definition of boycott, it would follow that industrial action such as strikes or working to rule are types of boycott. What then does Laidler mean when distinguishing, as above, between strikes and boycotts? Of course, the concern in this study is solely with the 'not buying from' types of boycotts, by customers. This too is Laidler's main concern, as the above quotation would indicate, although he is insufficiently explicit in this respect.

Laidler defines boycotting as 'an organised effort to withdraw and induce others to withdraw from social or business relations with another'.[26] The basis for his subsequent classification of types of boycott is not, however, the explanatory discriminator of the source of power which the type of boycott seeks to employ – as in this study, in the reference to consumer sovereignty – but the group in society using the boycott. So Laidler, for example, identifies the consumers' boycott 'used chiefly as a protest against the high cost of living'; the employers' boycott, 'an organised effort of employers of labor and monied interests generally, to induce others of their class to cease business relations with those who, in their opinion, are too active in the cause of labor'; and a variety of the employers' boycott known as the blacklist, 'an agreement of employers to refuse employment to certain workmen obnoxious to them, generally on account of their activities on behalf of labor'. Wolman acknowledges and more satisfactorily resolves this problem of definition. He defines the boycott as 'a combination formed for the purpose of restricting the markets of an individual or group of individuals'. However, he goes on to exclude strikes and similar actions on the basis of the chronological priority of the terms already used. Hence, 'the term boycott will be used to describe the efforts of labor combinations to restrict the markets of employers in the purchase and sale of economic goods, whether these goods be raw materials, materials in a partial state of completion, or finished products about to be sold to the ultimate consumer'. In other words, he restricts the term to actions involving product markets rather than labour markets.[27]

Different types of boycott are identified as having been used in labour struggles, even when the term boycott is restricted to product markets. For the most part, these terms and their meanings are still current and can usefully be considered here. Both Laidler and Wolman refer to primary, secondary, tertiary, and compound boycotts. Laidler defines the primary boycott as 'a simple combination of persons to suspend dealings with a party obnoxious to them, involving no attempt to persuade or coerce third parties to suspend dealings also'.[28] Simply stated, this is where the employees of a firm abstain from purchasing the firm's products, probably in conjunction with strike action, but with no attempt to persuade others to do likewise. He suggests that this form is ineffective and consequently rare. However, his exclusion of attempts to influence third parties would probably have belied practice, although such boycotts would not be illegal whereas those involving attempts to influence third parties could be. This may explain his definition. It does, however, differ in this respect from Wolman's definition: 'the action is directly against the offending employer, the members of the organisation simply withholding their patronage ... and inducing their fellows to do the same.'[29] While this definition may include legal and illegal actions (the legality of boycotts is a complex issue), it would seem better to reflect practice and current usage.

Secondary boycotts involve attempts to get wider support, defined as 'a combination of workmen to *induce or persuade* third parties to cease business relations with those against whom there is a grievance' (Laidler's emphasis).[30] They become compound boycotts when coercive and intimidating measures are used, involving either threats of pecuniary injury or actual physical force and violence. Laidler identifies three important points of attack against a boycotted employer in the use of the secondary and compound boycott. The first is inducing or coercing his employees to quit working for him, perhaps using picketing. The second is inducing or coercing suppliers to stop providing supplies to the employer (and, as examples show, this may involve threatened or actual strike action at the suppliers). The third and 'the most important method of injury is the inducing or coercing of customers to withdraw their patronage from the obnoxious concern'. This may include suppliers of the initial target for attack, as well as the initial target; as is made clear in Wolman's definition.

Wolman defines secondary boycotts as 'a combination to withdraw patronage from a person in order to force that person in turn to withdraw his patronage from that individual or firm with whom the union was primarily at odds'.[31] They involve injury to those not directly involved in the dispute. He does not use the term compound boycott to refer to instances where pecuniary or physical injury is threatened, as Laidler, suggesting the terms secondary boycott and compound boycott are synonymous. This again would seem to reflect practice, as a boycott without the threat of pecuniary or physical injury seems a rather abstract notion; although again, Laidler's distinction seems geared towards accommodating different legal consequences of boycott action. Wolman suggests that 'it is perhaps better to use the expression compound boycott to describe boycotts against all persons not involved in the original dispute, whether these boycotts be secondary, tertiary or even of a higher order, whereas the primary boycott denotes that simple form in which the boycott is imposed directly upon the offending employer'.[32] This reflects current usage, excepting the preference for the terms primary and secondary, rather than primary and compound. Tertiary boycotts are somewhat loosely defined by Laidler. Essentially, as the previous quotation from Wolman indicates, they are still further removed from the firm with which the union has a grievance. For reasons of simplicity and in keeping with current usage, it is preferable to include tertiary boycotts and those of a higher order under the term secondary boycott.

Boycotts can be negative or positive. Negative boycotts involve purchasing from recommended sources: 'The primary purpose of negative boycotts is to secure for "fair" firms the patronage of labor and its friends. Indirectly, they divert trade from "unfair" employers.' This involves the union label, placed on goods 'as a guarantee to the trade unionists and to the public generally that the goods are produced under conditions favourable to the unions', exemplified in the California grape boycott case later. 'White' or 'fair' lists are also used.[33] Wolman refers to negative boycotts as indirect boycotts. The positive boycott involves the 'unfair' or the 'We don't patronise' list. These lists, Laidler notes, were published in trade union journals under these captions, or posted at trade union headquarters. He suggests they became of little importance after 1908 (and two important court rulings on boycott legality), but they are still employed today in boycott actions such as the Arab boycott[34] and the boycott of goods and services from companies associated with South Africa. This form of boycott Wolman describes as the direct boycott.

Wolman claims the boycott to be 'the most effective weapon of unionism'.[35] Laidler also has a high regard for the boycott, arguing that 'its future role is destined to be a potent one'.[36] Yet in spite of this, trade union historians make little mention of its use other than during the period examined by Wolman and Laidler of the late nineteenth and early twentieth centuries. This apparent demise of the consumer boycott would seem to go unexplained by the historians. Reference is made to the impact of legislation, but Wolman had indicated that legislation would simply involve the use of the boycott in secret and illegally. Yet it is possible to speculate with some certainty on the decline in importance of the boycott, on the basis of Wolman and Laidler's analyses. For it seems that once organised, labour no longer required or was able to use the consumer boycott. However, according to Wolman and Laidler, it was in this organisation of labour (in the United States) that the boycott played such a vital role.

The adoption of the boycott by unions stemmed from the difficulties experienced in controlling labour supply when labour was unorganised. As Wolman writes: 'The essence of trade union success is its ability to control the labor supply in particular trades.'[37] Where this is not possible, the unions sought an alternative way of exerting pressure on employers, and thereby achieving organisation. Both Laidler and Wolman recognise that the importance of the boycott lay in the difficulties in using strike action. Wolman suggests two conditions under which the boycott is likely to emerge: where organisation of the labour force is impossible, and where organisation is fraught with such difficulties as to make it unlikely. In the first case he refers to boycotts upon prison products, and in the latter to the difficulties faced where employers used espionage to detect those employees recruited to the union and dismiss them, and where workers, particularly women and children, are indifferent or opposed to organisation. Therein, however, lie the causes, it would seem, for the demise of the boycott; changes in these conditions – largely brought about through the effective use of the boycott – meant that strike action or the threat of it could be used effectively. Many examples of the use of the boycott in both Wolman and Laidler illustrate the extent of its effectiveness. For example, during the boycott of D. E. Loewe and Company by the United Hatters' Union, sales fell for the year by $160,000–$170,000, from $400,000 in the previous year, a drop of 40 per cent.[38]

Not surprisingly, boycotts were roundly condemned by the employers. They were described as blackmail and contrary to the American tradition of free trade – despite their use against Britain in the War of American Independence, and their use in one form or another by employers against employees. Eventually, the assistance of the courts was sought to outlaw boycotts. Laidler, writing prior to impending legislation on the legality of boycotts, argued in favour of legalisation. Wolman, writing after legislation was passed severely restricting boycotts, suggested they would continue, but 'no longer be employed with impunity'.[39] Yet it seems he was wrong. Was there sufficient incentive for unions to risk litigation in support of their action or of others – with consequences for individual members – when their own industry was organised? Was the boycott necessary when labour reached a certain degree (critical mass) of organisation? Laidler notes the following reply by a union official to his questionnaire survey on the use of the boycott: 'We don't have to boycott any more. We control the skilled workers. Employers desiring skill must employ our members.'[40] Despite his plea for the legalisation of boycotts, he unwittingly anticipated their demise as a union resource, writing at one point: 'the thorough organisation of labor often renders boycotting unnecessary.'[41] The boycott was of the utmost importance in organising labour. Once that task had been largely achieved, it declined in importance.

Boycotts as international economic sanctions

The enthusiasm for the boycott evident in the writings of Laidler and Wolman can also be found in writings of the same period about the economic boycott as a sanction used by governments. Just as Laidler and Wolman wrote of its potential in furthering labour's struggles, others advocated its use in preventing or replacing war. World War I, it will be recalled, was the war to end wars. Its horrors led to a renunciation of war: 'The "balance of power", that fundamental concept of European diplomacy, was called by President Wilson, "the great game, now forever discredited". Men spoke now of a "Concert of Powers" and a "League of Nations". The limitation of armaments and the destruction of militarism were everywhere declared to be the aim.'[42] How could such a concert ensure peace without recourse to military action? The need for a coercive measure was not dismissed. Instead, an economic rather than a military weapon was to be employed if found necessary. This was expressed in the Covenant of the League of Nations, which, at the insistence of President Woodrow Wilson, formed part of the peace treaty agreed at the end of the war. In explanation President Wilson said in 1919: 'If any member of the League breaks or ignores these promises with regard to arbitration and discussion, what happens? War? No, not war but something ... more tremendous than war ... Apply this economic, peaceful, silent, deadly remedy and there will be no need for force ... The boycott is what is substituted for war.'[43]

Such a remedy was not new to American presidents, even if the term was. In 1793, Jefferson wrote that 'nations may be brought to do justice by appeals to their interests as well as by appeals to arms', which would 'relieve us too from the risks and horrors of cutting throats'.[44] The use of the boycott in this way is neither recent nor redundant, but it seems that the greatest faith in such a weapon was held during the period following World War I. This is revealed in the writings of the time. John Foster Dulles, who became an American Secretary of State, wrote in

1932 in *Boycotts and Peace*: 'The great advantage of economic sanctions is that on the one hand they can be very potent, while on the other hand, they do not involve that resort to force which is repugnant to our objective of peace.'[45]

Accordingly, Remer, in *A Study of Chinese Boycotts*, justified his 1933 analysis by saying that 'in a world which has renounced war, it may be worth while to examine the efforts of the Chinese in the field of non-violent coercion'.[46] Remer's study is worthy of consideration for reasons other than historical interest, despite its age. It reveals not only the contemporary view of the great potential for peace through the use of the boycott, but also certain elements in its use which are relevant to current use of the boycott as an international economic sanction and in the form of the consumer boycott.

Three end results sought are identified: publicity, punishment, and a policy change within the boycotted country. The boycott is viewed as a weapon and assessed in this sense. In this assessment, the important distinction is made – which applies to all economic boycotts – between success and effectiveness: 'for it is plain that a boycott may be effective in cutting off trade without being successful in, bringing about the desired change in policy.'[47] He continues by suggesting that a boycott is not likely to be successful unless it is effective, although this must surely be less important where the end result sought is only publicity.

His study examines Chinese boycotts between 1905 and 1932. However, these Chinese boycotts were not directly comparable to the boycotts envisaged by the League, as he notes, nor are they identical to the international economic sanctions employed today. The essential difference is that the Chinese boycotts were not the formal or official acts of the Chinese state. They are for this reason closer to consumer boycotts than international economic sanctions, as will become apparent.

What form did the Chinese boycotts take? It would appear from Remer's analysis that they involved an almost spontaneous reaction by many of the Chinese people against the goods of countries which aggrieved China. So, for example, the 1905 boycott against the United States followed American restrictions on Chinese immigration, and the 1932 boycott against Japan followed Japanese policies in Manchuria. Although in a sense spontaneous, they were not without organisation, yet this did not come from the government, at least in any official capacity. Their origin, organisation, and possibly effectiveness have cultural explanations. Passive resistance had long been practised by the Chinese against their governments and officials. This tradition of passive resistance and the structure of Chinese society provide the cultural precedents for the Chinese boycotts. Remer suggests that the rise of Chinese nationalism in the early twentieth century led to the increasing use of passive resistance on international issues, in boycotts of foreign goods. However, only the international dimension was new, 'The boycott is a means of carrying on a dispute, a weapon, a technique, which has a long history in China.' Chinese nationalism fulfilled two conditions necessary for boycotts to extend beyond domestic issues: 'The feeling of solidarity which lies behind the boycott had to spread beyond family, village, guild, or association, to the whole Chinese community and the feeling that resistance was necessary had to spread from the desire to resist a group of foreign merchants or a particular governing body to a desire to resist a whole nation.'[48]

Remer's study of Chinese boycotts is instructive and in many ways relevant to this study. It is worth mentioning that the methods used in the enforcement of the boycott have a remarkable similarity to those used in labour struggles and current consumer boycotts. Remer observes that the early boycotts were enforced by the ordinary group methods familiar in China with the addition of some coercion from aroused public opinion. However, over time other methods were adopted: advertising and propaganda for the boycott by burning 'inferior' or 'enemy' goods, picketing, posters, public demonstrations and speeches, and extra-legal fines on merchants dealing in boycotted goods which resulted in them being paraded through the streets and even placed in cages in the street. Remer also highlights the requirement for organisation and solidarity in boycott actions. This is in keeping with Laidler and Wolman's analyses, discussed above.

Remer's conclusions on the boycott are that it can be both effective, in securing a restriction on trade (although this is not always immediately obvious from trade statistics), and successful, in producing policy changes. He anticipated increasing use, although he acknowledged disadvantages. He suggests the weapon is a blundering and awkward one, it leaves the initiative with the opposition, it is slow, it is costly, and it is uneconomic, as losses fall on many who are not involved in the dispute. One contemporary commentator described it as 'a double-edged knife which injured Chinese even more than Americans and other countries quite as much', in reference to the 1905 boycott against America.[49] Yet not only can it be successful because of its economic effectiveness, but also because of its psychological or emotional effect.[50] It is also an effective form of publicity: 'It brings to the attention of the world the acts of which the boycotters complain and the policy behind the acts against which the boycott is ultimately directed.' Moreover, by employing passive resistance, the nation 'is likely to secure, in addition to publicity, the sympathy of the rest of the world'.[51] In the introduction it is asked whether the boycott is an effective weapon of retaliation or merely a theatrical sword. It seems that it may be both. Fifty years later, this conclusion seems equally valid in the assessment of the current use of international economic sanctions when more recent examples and analyses are considered. Again there are observations which seem applicable to consumer boycotts, perhaps pointing to boycott principles.

Examples of the current use of international economic sanctions as boycotts are hardly required, its current use being quite extensive: Russia boycotted, by the United States in particular, over the invasion of Afghanistan; the boycott of Rhodesia over UDI (Unilateral Declaration of Independence); and the oil and arms embargo against South Africa, to name but a few recent examples. Others are identified by Roberts.[52] He suggests that the view of the boycott as an effective alternative to war stems from its effectiveness within states, in consumer and other boycotts. However, he finds only limited evidence of the economic effectiveness of international boycotts. He attributes the failure of sanctions to the fact that foreign trade was not affected as much as might be expected, to the support given by non-boycotting states, and to the growth of solidarity within the receiver state. Yet the use of economic sanctions continues. This, Roberts suggests, is not only because they are not entirely ineffective, but also because they have an expressive function. They convince the aggrieved state that it is 'not taking things lying down'. This motive is criticised by Dekker as an irrational moralistic attitude. Finding that the boycott and embargo is unsuccessful in most cases, Dekker suggests that success is probable only with an unstable regime and when the action is sudden and drastic.[53]

However, not all analyses are so sceptical of the economic effectiveness of previous or future economic boycotts. Losman, on the basis of an analysis of boycotts against Cuba, Israel, and Rhodesia, concludes that boycotts may be economically effective but are unlikely to be successful. He, like Remer, makes the important distinction between success and effectiveness:

> A successful boycott is one which results in the acceptance by the 'target state' of the conditions specified or implied by those applying the sanctions ... Effectiveness thus measures the degree of economic damage felt by the target state ... boycotts can be highly effective, yet still fail in terms of their basic political objectives. In short, effectiveness is a necessary but not a sufficient condition for success.[54]

His conclusions on the Cuban boycott are that the cost of sanctions was great (for example, export earnings, 60 per cent of which were with the United States, fell from $625m in 1959 to $167m in 1961), but Cuba was rescued by the Soviets, with much of the cost being borne by Cuba's communist allies. The United States general economy was unaffected. Yet while the boycott was economically effective, Losman does not feel it was politically successful: 'if it was Castro's "communism" which led to the American embargo, today he is very much more a communist and a part of the communist bloc than he was before.'

On the Arab boycott of Israel, Losman concludes that it has been most effective in potential foregone, particularly in denying Israel the role of trading centre for the Middle East, which Palestine's pivotal location would have ideally suited. The Arab states have suffered through applying the boycott, which explains its uneven enforcement. The effects of blacklisting are, he claims, completely indeterminable. Yet what is the outcome of the boycott? As Losman writes, 'In Israel, the population stands resolute in its determination to succeed, regardless of sanction-imposed difficulties.' Presumably, the boycott gives the Arab states some sense of actually doing something, however futile it might seem. Finally, on the Rhodesia boycott, events following the publication of his paper have to some extent weakened Losman's argument. His conclusion was that there was little internal political pressure upon the Smith regime to capitulate. The costs of economic sanctions were at first quite heavy, particularly with the loss of export revenue from tobacco sales, but over time the state adapted and, in effect, the economy suffered 'a "one-shot" slow-down'. Because the brunt was borne by tobacco farmers, staunch supporters of UDI, by the African population employed in the tobacco industry, and by business profits, political pressure was minimal. Losman saw little prospect for resolution of the Rhodesia situation. In all three cases, Losman thought it unlikely that success would materialise despite economic effectiveness. Yet he did introduce a caveat which was quite sensible in view of the Rhodesian sanctions subsequently proving not entirely unsuccessful: 'If agreements are reached, the more probable causes will not be economic but changed political bases for compromise or the imminence of military, rather than strictly economic warfare.'

In other words, boycotts in themselves are inadequate. Galtung would largely support Losman's analysis, but see it as incomplete. His sophisticated and detailed analysis, which concentrates on the Rhodesia boycott, is still generally negative about the likelihood of success with economic boycotts, but identifies the conditions under which the boycott can be both effective and successful and recognises that success may be in terms other than the defeat of the regime of the boycotted state. Galtung defines international economic sanctions as 'actions initiated by one or more international actors (the "senders") against one or more others (the "receivers") with either or both of two purposes: to punish the receivers by depriving them of some value and/or to make the receivers comply with certain norms the senders deem important'.[55] So, in contrast to Losman, Galtung recognises that the rationale behind economic sanctions may involve an attempt to punish as well as to coerce. This, of course, is closer to Remer's analysis, and Galtung comes closer still. Galtung suggests the view that punishment is a necessary condition for compliance is simplistic, yet he acknowledges the prevalence of a punishment-oriented attitude. The use of negative sanctions in politics has much to do with a desire for retribution, along the lines of 'If compliance is not obtained, there is at least the gratification that derives from knowing (or believing) that the sinner gets his due.'

Galtung suggests that the situation faced by the receiver is less bleak than it might appear. He identifies a naïve theory of the process by which the boycott is intended to work. This postulates a goal of political disintegration of the enemy so that compliance is achieved, a goal realised by value deprivation. However, in economic warfare as in military warfare, deprivation is not necessarily directly proportional to political disintegration. Indeed, the theory is naïve because value deprivation can initially lead to political integration and only later – perhaps much later or even never – to political disintegration. This is because of adaptation: 'that which seems unacceptable at the beginning of the conflict becomes acceptable as one gets used to life under hardship.' The case of Rhodesia illustrates this well. Political disintegration did not prove to be a consequence of value deprivation, and it was also counteracted. Adaptation proved to be self-reinforcing, providing unintended benefits; sacrifice became desirable in the form of conspicuous sacrifice; while smuggling introduced an element of excitement into life. In such ways were economic effects minimised; while the moral criticism implied in sanctions was dealt with by acts of transposition. So, for example, Prime Minister Wilson became viewed as a communist, while jokes served to ridicule the sanctions. Government action included partial censorship to promote pluralistic ignorance, as well as attempts to minimise economic effects and demonstrate the legitimacy of its position.

Galtung's conclusion is that what works at the individual level does not necessarily work at the level of interaction between nations. Yet this does not preclude success. Adaptation may not survive into the long term and the threat of boycott may often be sufficient. The point is that success depends on more than whether the sanctions were universal and therefore economically effective. Moreover, there is the punishment aspect: 'the value of at least doing something.' Galtung, after recognising the ways in which states minimise their vulnerability to boycotts, wonders if other types of sanctions might be more appropriate. He seems, however, somewhat optimistic in thinking they might be applied, given his identification of the dominance of a punishment-oriented attitude in world politics. Perhaps punishment is the most realistic of aims for economic boycotts; or, in keeping with Remer, punishment and publicity. Such actions are not entirely futile. As

Galtung writes: 'If the sanctions do not serve instrumental purposes they can at least have expressive functions. Thus, as a highly dramatic (and costly) way of reinforcing international morality, economic sanctions may be useful.' If the senders themselves are deprived, this purpose, Galtung claims, may be even better served.

In looking at international economic sanctions one can, given the above conclusions, see evidence of ethical purchase behaviour. The Chinese boycotts, although considered under the heading of international economic sanctions, seem to have had a lot more in common with consumer boycotts; they also have important implications for consumer boycotts. Finally, the notion of boycotts as a way of reinforcing morality, of having an expressive function, has been introduced. This approach is particularly attributable to Galtung, but the other analyses considered above have also contributed to the idea that consumer boycotts cannot be assessed in terms of economic effectiveness alone. Some general principles in the use of boycotts have also emerged. It now seems important that in analysing consumer boycotts there should be the distinction made between success and effectiveness; between goals seeking compliance and those seeking only punishment and/or publicity; and between economic effect and psychological or emotional effect. In the latter case, for example, it might well be that one can equate the 'hurt' felt by Japan at being boycotted, as identified by Remer, with the reaction of business to boycotts. This may in turn be as important a factor in success as economic effectiveness.

The Arab boycott

The Arab boycott is the use of the boycott as an international economic sanction. Separate consideration of it here is justified by its predominance in the literature and, more importantly, because of its central feature of boycotts of business. It is probably the most significant boycott currently affecting business. The Arab boycott also offers some support for the concept of ethical purchase behaviour, in its apparent futility and the nature of its administration, and also in the response it has engendered from Jewish organisations and others. Moreover, it is interesting to consider the issues of social responsibility in business raised by company compliance with boycott demands and also the way in which companies responded to the boycott as a possible general indicator of management response to boycott action. Much of the following is based on the comprehensive analysis of Nelson and Prittie, *The Economic War Against the Jews*.[56]

The Arab boycott was set up by the League of Arab States in 1945. The Boycott Committee declared, 'Products of Palestinian Jews are to be considered undesirable in Arab countries. They should be prohibited and refused as long as their production in Palestine might lead to the realisation of Zionist political aims.'[57] Boycott offices were established in League members' capitals with a central office established in 1946 in Cairo, which moved to Damascus where it is currently based, in 1949. In that year, following the proclamation of the State of Israel on 14 May 1948, the Arabs closed their frontiers with Israel and declared themselves to be in a permanent state of war with that nation. In 1952 the boycott was extended to foreign companies doing business in Israel. Over the next few years the task of the Central Office for the Boycott of Israel was clarified: 'to monitor international trade and implement a primary boycott of Israel and a secondary boycott of foreign firms assisting Israel. It developed a tertiary boycott requiring foreign firms not to deal with other firms already on the blacklist. The tertiary boycott would also apply against businessmen and other individuals considered to be Zionists.'[58]

During this period up to the mid-1950s, the Arab states were relatively weak. But over the following twenty years, particularly with Soviet support, there was greater aggressiveness. The blacklist grew, with *Business International* claiming there were 53 American companies on the list in 1960, 134 in 1962, and by 1970 there were 1,500 American companies (including Sears Roebuck, Coca-Cola, Ford, Xerox, and many other major companies) according to a list revealed five years later by a Senate committee.[59] The boycott resulted in discrimination against Jews in employment. The American Army Corps of Engineers admitted that on the Dhahran Airfield project in the early 1950s and on subsequent projects, American Jews had been barred. While in Britain, in the 1960s, the Jewish peer Lord Mancroft was forced to resign from the board of directors of Norwich Union because of company fears that the Arabs might blacklist shipping companies insured through them. However, undoubtedly, if not inevitably, it was oil and the recognition of the power that it provided, that gave the boycott significance. Support for Israel by the West during the 1973 Yom Kippur War led to an oil embargo. Despite Arab fears of retaliation by the West there was disarray, and the relative unity of OPEC enabled the Arabs to demand massive increases in oil revenues. This oil wealth provided great purchasing power which, together with fears of further disruption in oil supplies, gave potency to the boycott.

Congressman Jonathan Bingham, who sponsored anti-boycott legislation, reports in the introduction to *The Economic War Against the Jews* that in 1974 there were 785 business transactions involving the demand for boycott compliance by American firms. By September of 1975 there were 7,545 such transactions. Over the next six months there were 25,000 such transactions, with acquiescence by the American firms in 90 per cent of cases. Figures for the number of firms on the blacklist vary because of the secrecy surrounding it. Hotaling claims that the list he appends is probably very close to the list held in the Boycott Office at the time. He shows 5,000 firms blacklisted internationally in 1977, the US list the most extensive of all. The exact figure is unimportant; an idea as to the magnitude is all that is required. More recent newspaper reports[60] and the response to the survey questionnaire (discussed in Chapter 8) suggest that the effects of the boycott remain at this level. This is despite anti-boycott legislation in the US and France.

The operation of the primary boycott is quite straightforward. The secondary and tertiary boycotts are more complicated because they function in a more convoluted fashion. As found in the boycotts in labour struggles, the further removed the boycott is from the grievance, the more difficult it is to control and enforce. It also appears less legitimate. Consequently critics of the Arab boycott such as Nelson and Prittie accept the primary boycott against Israel – Arab states should be able to choose their trading partners – but view the secondary boycotts and particularly the tertiary boycotts as insidious. Yet despite the difficulties in imposing higher order boycotts experienced elsewhere, the Arabs seem remarkably successful. This success seems to stem from their oil wealth derived purchasing power. It should be noted that the boycott does not prohibit the sale of goods to Israel, as is commonly assumed. Winchester writes that the boycott 'seeks to minimise trade with Israel by asking any firm that trades in Arabia to declare full details of its business with Israel. If the trade is significant, or if there are "known Zionists" on the firm's board, then the Arabs will not, in theory, do business.'[61] This is largely correct.

Enforcing secondary and tertiary boycotts demands strict policing or powerful disincentives to discourage breach of the boycott provisions. So powerful are the disincentives in this case that companies go out of their way to ensure that they remain 'clean'. Hotaling refers to a policy of self-regulation, noting that the conglomerate Inchcape and Co. has a total embargo on Israeli or Israeli-connected companies. Nelson and Prittie describe this as a voluntary boycott; not even waiting to be pressured by the Arabs, companies decline to do business with Israel: 'They anticipate Arab objections and act without having received letters or questionnaires from Damascus or elsewhere; before they even make contact with potential Arab customers and clients, they make sure they are "clean" by Arab standards.'[62] British companies are particularly guilty of this, it seems. They are described as 'the willing victims'. Britain, of course, has long been involved in the Middle East. It bears a great deal of the responsibility for the troubles there and sponsored the formation of the Arab League. It was for many years Israel's second trading partner, after the United States.[63] Winchester reports that Britain's share of Israel's import market is currently 6 per cent, whereas it was 85 per cent thirty years ago. This is attributed to the boycott.[64] And British complicity with the boycott is not restricted to companies, for the Foreign Office continues to authenticate negative certificates of origin.[65]

The Arab boycott, although not a consumer boycott as defined here, does have a number of implications for the arguments proposed regarding consumer boycotts and also ethical purchase behaviour and social responsibility in business. The use of the boycott in this way by the Arabs is arguably ethical purchase behaviour. Many of its characteristics point to this, but the vagueness and ideological approach to its administration and, perhaps above all, its apparent futility, are the strongest indicators. One might not support the Arabs' cause or admire their methods, but their purchase behaviour when guided by the boycott has to be recognised as being strongly influenced by ethical rather than commercial considerations. Of course, there have been occasions where the boycott provisions have been ignored for commercial reasons, but they are exceptions rather than the rule. Also, one could argue, the willingness to comply of the firms involved has reduced the sacrifice required, but there are still around 5,000 firms whose products in most cases the Arabs choose to deny themselves. One might say that given their oil wealth, it is easy for the Arabs to refuse to deal with what they view as tainted firms, just as it was earlier argued that social responsibility in business is easier when profits are high and very difficult when 'one's back is against the wall'. This is probably true, yet it does not make their purchase behaviour any the less ethical; their ethical concerns in purchase behaviour are simply more easily accommodated. The futility of all this must be apparent. Losman, as noted, refers to the determination of the people of Israel to succeed. As important, however, must be the support Israel receives from other countries, particularly the United States. The destruction of Israel, which is after all the goal of the boycott, would be politically unacceptable to the West. The actions of the Arabs are therefore in ethical condemnation. But to what end?

Although Britain's trade with Israel has fallen quite considerably, Israel's trade with the rest of the world has never stopped growing and Israel claims 'the world's record in economic growth'.[66] Losman's balance sheet approach, assessing the economic effect of boycotts, suggested that foregone potential was the most serious economic impact of the boycott. The blacklist must entail losses to Israeli trade. Yet the costs of the boycott are also borne by others, as in most international economic sanctions. In this case business bears a lot, if not most of the costs. No doubt this serves to discredit Israel, or at least provide a platform for Arab grievances. In this way the boycott has an expressive function, as with other international economic sanctions. But in its economic effectiveness it also seems an effective punishment of Israel and those viewed as its supporters. However, this apparent effectiveness does not seem to give rise to success. The goal of the boycott seems impossible to achieve regardless of boycott effectiveness.

If this futility of the Arab boycott and its other characteristics seem an inadequate basis for claiming ethical purchase behaviour, one need only turn to the response to the boycott by Jewish organisations and their supporters for a more convincing example. The anti-Jewish aspects to the boycott have particularly incensed Jewish feeling in the United States and in Europe. Attempts to fight the boycott were primarily aimed at securing anti-boycott legislation. This is documented in both Hotaling and Nelson and Prittie. Other actions were also initiated, no doubt with legislation as their long-term aim; these included counterboycotts and shareholder actions. Often, however, organised counterboycotts were unnecessary, as many consumers responded spontaneously in immediate rejection of the offerings of firms complying with the boycott. So strong was the feeling that what for the Arabs was a blacklist became for many a white list, a 'roll of honor', with one American Jewish group 'urging Jews to buy the products and patronise the services of companies blacklisted by the Arabs'.[67] They created a 'negative' or 'indirect' boycott. Counterboycotts were organised. The decision by Brown and Williamson, a subsidiary of British American Tobacco, not to sell its cigarettes to Israel led to the following widely distributed announcement:

> If you smoke Viceroy, Raleigh ... and other products of the British
> American Tobacco Company, YOU ARE SUPPORTING THE
> ARAB CAUSE ... The British American Tobacco Company,
> owners of Brown and Williamson Tobacco Company, has
> knuckled under to Arab pressure ... Don't give them your support!!

Individual Jews switched brands and the company's cigarettes were not distributed at community dinners and similar functions. Loss of sales resulted in a fall from fifth to tenth place in market share. This together with being publicly pilloried resulted in a change of policy. Today the company sells to both Israel and the Arab states.

Similar action was taken against Coca-Cola for its reluctance to invest in Israel. Five million dollars worth of sales were lost within a week. Coca-Cola conceded, a plant was built outside Tel Aviv, and Coca-Cola was blacklisted by the Arabs. Public protest was considered a more important factor in this change of policy than the effects of the counterboycott. Nelson and Prittie quote Uval Elizur's comments on the counterboycott: 'It is not the only, or even the most effective weapon to

161

be used by friends of Israel. A display of public protest hurting the company's reputation and pressing it to prove its integrity – achieves more'. Of course, concern for the company's reputation is not unrelated to sales. The distinction between boycott effects and corporate image effects, if one need and can be made, is simply the short term against the long term. The action did not deny cola to the Arabs. Pepsi-Cola carefully avoided Israel, allegedly because of insufficient demand. This too resulted in consumer action.

One particularly active group was the American Jewish Congress (AJC). It organised a shareholder action reported by Hotaling, and Nelson and Prittie, and considered in detail by Vogel because 'it represented the largest shareholder campaign ever mounted'. He notes that the AJC action was primarily intended 'to help place the issue on the agenda of the governmental process'. Given the earlier discussion on the likely achievements of pressure groups this seems a realistic objective. The action succeeded in securing public attention and interest, as a consciousness-raising exercise, and also was directly successful in getting companies to change their policies. Probably most important though was, as Maslow comments in Vogel, 'the millions of shares that were voted in support of our resolution helped create the national climate that resulted in overwhelming support in the House and Senate for strong anti-boycott legislation'.[68] Examining the AJC action leads directly into the social responsibility implications of the boycott. What, one must ask, should a company do that wishes to trade in the Middle East and be a good corporate citizen?

Nelson and Prittie point out on a number of occasions that where Arab need for a particular product or service is great the boycott provisions and blacklist will be ignored. In such a case, it is easy for a company to be a good corporate citizen. So American Express, for example, had closed its operations in Israel apparently because of the boycott. Partly due to pressure from the Anti-Defamation League of B'nai B'rith (ADL), it reopened its Israeli offices despite Arab threats. The company suggested this was because 'one's reputation in business still counts'. The outcome? 'Today, the company enjoys good relations with all parties, an indication again that the Arabs won't actually blacklist a company which ignores the regulations if they want what it offers.'[69] Some have suffered from adopting such an approach. GEC, for example, claimed to have lost twenty million pounds worth of business in 1975, for 'regarding it wrong to cut off profitable and legal trade with any customer'.[70] The majority of companies, it would seem, however, comply with the boycott provisions, either voluntarily or on request.

So the answer to the question about how the good corporate citizen should respond to the Arab boycott would seem to be that it should ignore the boycott altogether, viewing it as unfair and unreasonable discrimination (if only in commercial terms). It should also express this position if called upon by the Boycott Office to explain its Israeli connections. Indeed, to follow the line of argument given earlier on social responsibility in business, one might expect the good corporate citizen to lobby for legislation or an industry-wide agreement prohibiting compliance with the boycott. Yet few companies seem able or willing to adopt this position. One must then enquire as to the basis on which they defend their compliance with the boycott. This is easily identified. It is a recognised position on a company's social responsibilities, if not the predominant or, at least, traditional position. It is based on the argument, thoroughly explored earlier, that a company's sole social responsibility is to make a profit. As Nelson and Prittie put it, 'commercial considerations' are paramount.

In analysing the Arab boycott the concern must be with the majority of companies, whose activities are less clear-cut than the principled exceptions referred to above. For the majority it is, in social responsibility terms, a more murky world. These are the companies which might usefully be described as more pragmatic. Their decisions might seem clear-cut when considered in the light of their relatively straightforward cost–benefit analyses. They are, however, when the strict economic parameters have been removed, complex if not exceedingly muddy. If this behaviour is the norm, it should at least be acknowledged that it results from a feeling of being unable to afford less than pragmatic behaviour or perhaps, as Friedman would argue, not knowing nor having a mandate for other forms of behaviour. Of course, if this is the norm, one must also expect managers to feel bound to work within it. Yet should commercial considerations alone be allowed to prevail? On this particular issue Nelson and Prittie argue that the consequence is an anti-Semitic revival:

> Anti-Zionism has been a convenience to bigots, for it permits
> anti-Semites to pose as anti-Israeli, while denying any anti-Jewish
> bias. In much the same way, the Arab economic war against the
> Jews allows the 'outside' world to pursue anti-Israeli and even
> anti-Jewish policies, while pleading that no anti-Semitism is
> intended, or that business considerations, remaining paramount,
> compel them to cooperate in this war against the Jews.[71]

The argument that commercial considerations should dictate compliance or otherwise with the boycott has been both suggested to government in attempts to fight anti-boycott legislation, and suggested by government. A representative from the US Commerce Department told Congress that 'American firms should not be restricted in their freedom to make economic decisions based on their own business interests.'[72] While in Britain, in the House of Commons, a government spokesman said that the government deplored all trade boycotts other than those internationally supported and sanctioned by the United Nations; but 'How firms should act in any particular case is a matter for the commercial judgement of the firm concerned.'[73] It would appear that this continues to be the British government's position given the Foreign Office willingness to authenticate negative certificates of origin. Nelson and Prittie suggest that this is in part due to Britain's historic ties with and guilt feelings about the Arab world, 'But more operative, without doubt, is Britain's unwillingness to take a moral stand even on a boycott the government said it "abhorred", because of the desperate need to promote exports to the oil-rich Arab world.' It was earlier argued that one approach for the firm in identifying a socially responsible position could be to follow the example of the government. Can this be advocated here given the British government's less than unequivocal stance on the boycott and, indeed, its actual complicity?

The options facing a firm trading in the Middle East are given an additional dimension by the anti-boycott legislation. The argument that local business standards should dictate behaviour is weakened because the impact, if only by virtue of the legislation, is domestic as well as overseas. Many more issues are raised as compliance with the boycott can entail breaking the law. Does the good corporate citizen exploit loopholes, or make an assessment as to whether the benefits of compliance outweigh the potential costs of fines as well as other costs previously considered? Many other issues of social responsibility in business are raised by the Arab boycott. The above discussion is but an indication of the complexity of the situation facing the manager when the rules of the game have changed from the simple formulation expressed in the competitive model of capitalism, with its axiom of profit maximisation.

To conclude on the Arab boycott, it seems that as an international economic sanction it is effective. Yet the boycott cannot be credited as successful. Nor is it necessarily a peaceful form of coercion. Nelson and Prittie refer to the paper by Roberts, earlier cited, and show that with the Arab boycott Roberts is correct in suggesting that 'economic sanctions are not so much an alternative to war as a prelude or even accompaniment to it'.[74] By example, they refer to the Suez Crisis of 1956, as well as the various Arab–Israeli armed conflicts. Peace in the Middle East is in the interests of all. Nelson and Prittie suggest that this will only come with the recognition of Israel. While this must be a long term goal, they do make more immediately useful suggestions, including strong anti-boycott legislation. Referring to this they argue: 'Businesspeople need this kind of "shield" to protect them, and such shields should be internationalised.'[75] This, of course, is a familiar argument and was explored earlier. (Suffice to note here as a reminder,

Friedman would probably disagree with their argument.) While Nelson and Prittie would wish to deny ethical purchase behaviour to the Arabs, they advocate it in the fight against the boycott:

> Public opinion could be mobilized far more than it is today. Lists of foreign companies that comply with the boycott could be widely publicized; American workers and consumers could, for example, be provided with periodic lists of imported products whose foreign manufacturers comply with the boycott and thereby endanger American jobs.[76]

Finally, to conclude on the implications of the Arab boycott for boycotts in general, it can be seen that the boycott will not be used only by those advancing 'good' causes, that submission to boycott demands may involve a breach of corporate social responsibilities. It is, when discussed by those who disagree with the boycotters' demands, a weapon of blackmail. Where then does this leave the firm? It must respond to demands from many sources which will often, as this case illustrates, be in conflict with each other. Should the firm act in accord with a pluralistic model, balancing various interests as if within a microcosm of the political process (at least as it is perceived by pluralists)? The response of business does seem to support such a model, where decisions of this sort are made on the basis of which response will minimise damage to the corporate image and trading interests of the firm. Even the so-called principled firms may respond in a principled fashion because that is what is demanded when an assessment is made of the potential damage to the corporate image and it is recognised that part of that image is based on an expectation of principled action. Of course, all such dubious decisions need to be kept as far away from public scrutiny as possible. Meanwhile, pressure groups seek to expose such corporate action because that is in their interests.

Business and the boycott tactic

This chapter has deliberately avoided concentration on the consumer boycott, for this is to be addressed in Part Two. The boycott tactic has been examined within the context of non-violent direct action and the non-cooperation form of NVDA in particular. Various types of boycott have been considered, especially the economic boycotts such as international economic sanctions and the boycotts used in labour struggles (including the consumer boycott). This has provided more than background and an introduction to the consumer boycott. It indicates what may be general principles applicable to all boycotts.

The boycott tactic is a form of direct action. Although a last resort, the use of direct action by pressure groups seems likely to increase, especially NVDA. Corporations are likely to be increasingly involved and even if the economic effects may be small, because of the likelihood of mass actions being low in the affluent West, the detriment to the corporate image in symbolic direct action may be sufficient to obtain corporate compliance. The three end results sought in international economic sanctions, as identified by Remer, probably apply equally to consumer boycotts: publicity, punishment, and policy change. The distinction between success and effectiveness is also important; though effectiveness, because of corporate image fears, may not be a necessary criterion for success, as some have suggested of international economic sanctions. Publicity as a result of the consumer boycott may be sufficient for success, as a powerful theatrical sword. The Arab boycott illustrates this where companies choose not to comply with the boycott for fear of adverse publicity at home. If nothing else, the analysis of international economic sanctions suggests that perhaps all boycotts may have a useful expressive function. This is somewhat similar to Etzioni's observations, noted at the outset of this chapter, on demonstration democracy.

Chapter six

Pressure groups in the marketing system

Preview

In the factory we make cosmetics. In the store we sell hope.

Charles Revson[1]

Every purchase of a product or service could become a 'vote' for a marginal change in the shape of society, as well as for the product purchased. For example, Procter and Gamble and Unilever share the detergent market in this country, and to all intents and purposes, despite differing advertising, their products are the same. But the social impacts of these two companies differ substantially. If they chose, or were compelled to broadcast those social impacts, detergent buyers in their purchasing could vote for their preferred set of social impacts ... Armed with social impact data, adequately presented by firms, the public at large could truly participate in shaping society by the exercise of purchase votes.

Raymond E. Thomas[2]

As yet little attempt has been made to in some way explain ethical purchase behaviour at the micro level. Consumer sovereignty offers a justification for such behaviour but little in the way of explanation as to why any individual consumer would wish to so act. A proposition made here and explored in the empirical work of the study is that there is negative product augmentation. Levitt has described how products may be augmented positively, referring in illustration to the quotation by Revson above. It is here suggested that products may also be augmented negatively. This may be seen in terms of a legitimacy element in the marketing mix. The quotation above by Thomas calls for ethical purchase behaviour by suitably informed consumers exercising their purchase votes. His argument is for social impact data to be presented by firms. This is viewed here as somewhat Utopian, largely because of the acknowledged problems in social audits and, as Beesley and Evans show, the difficulties in making sensible comparisons between firms. However, this data could be presented by concerned pressure groups, in a way laudable to the advocates of pluralistic politics. This is advanced here in the form of a model of pressure groups in the marketing system. Management responses in this are considered. The origins of the term ethical purchase behaviour – the outcome of the model – are also given here, and a review made of the previous very limited work in this area.

This chapter concludes Part One by briefly considering some of the preliminary conclusions and propositions that have emerged and that constitute the theoretical argument for ethical purchase behaviour. This summary provides the basis for the more detailed examination of consumer pressure for corporate accountability in consumer boycotts, which follows in Part Two.

Pressure groups in the marketing system: a model

Negative product augmentation and legitimacy in the marketing mix

What is a product? Twenty years ago Fisk answered this question by defining a product as a cluster or 'bundle of psychological satisfactions'.[3] However, this is an observation long recognised in marketing thought. Bartels refers to the study of buying motives by psychologists at the turn of the century, the very beginning of what he considers to be marketing thought.[4] A product then is more than the physical and most immediately tangible attributes of an offering; it is also the intangible attributes. For the consumer, the product is 'a bundle of perceived benefits'.[5] As Foxall puts it, 'a product is not simply a physical entity but a bundle of attributes which promise certain satisfactions, physical, social, psychological, economic, to the buyer'. He suggests that although only one element within the marketing mix, 'it is of immense importance in that it encapsulates the great majority of the benefits expected by the customer'.[6] Foxall goes on to explain how the various attributes of a product can be conceived as dimensions in multi-dimensional space. If some of these attributes are absent – the salient attributes – then consumer perceptions of the product will alter. For example, elsewhere Foxall refers to an experiment on blindfolded beer drinkers which found that they were not capable of distinguishing brands of beer. Not surprisingly, given the conception of the product as a package or bundle of attributes, it was found that 'labels and their associations did influence their evaluations'.[7] So, as these, and many other sources show, the product is conceived within marketing as being a package of benefits or values; that are intangible as well as tangible, social-psychological and physical, or expressive and instrumental; and which the consumer expects to receive on purchase.

Levitt goes as far as to say that 'People don't buy products; they buy the expectation of benefits.' His augmented product concept is the explicit recognition of the conception of the product described above. It is frequently cited and his articles describing it are widely republished.[8] He writes:

> Whether the product is cold-rolled steel or hot cross buns, whether accountancy or delicacies, competitive effectiveness increasingly demands that the successful seller offers his prospect and his customer more than the generic product itself. He must surround his generic product with a cluster of value satisfactions that differentiates his total offering from his competitors'. He must provide a total proposition, the content of which exceeds what comes out at the end of the assembly line.

Hence his reference to the quotation by Revson in the Preview to this chapter and his claim that despite factory sales of cosmetics in 1968 of $3bn, 'in 1968 not a single American woman bought a single penny's worth of cosmetics'. Those cosmetics were, via product augmentation, transformed into something else: '"Hope" is the extra plus – the special promise of customer-satisfying benefits – that gives cosmetics their special appeal ... What is important is not so much what Revlon puts inside the compact as the ideas put inside the customer's head by luxurious packaging and imaginative advertising.' Levitt goes on to explain how such an approach also applies to industrial products such as pressure valves or polypropylene, whereby product differentiation through augmentation can be equally important, even if glamour is not the added ingredient. As Levitt puts it, 'By augmenting his generic product with unsolicited extras that produce extra customer benefits, the seller produces for himself extra customers.'

Levitt recognises that the marketing concept views the customer's purchasing activities as being problem-solving activities. His argument for product augmentation seeks to differentiate generic products by the provision of benefits or attributes that offer solutions to consumers' problems beyond those offered by the generic product alone. In this way, the producer acquires a 'competitive plus' – in other words, competitive advantage – in highly competitive markets. Yet Levitt does not acknowledge that a producer can acquire a 'competitive minus', a competitive disadvantage, through the provision of attributes not sought by some customers. The concern here is not with the planned provision of unsolicited extras that do not provide customer benefits but add to the cost, or detract from some other feature of the product. It is with the unintended provision of product attributes, or, at least, where product attributes result that are not the consequence of a deliberate attempt at product augmentation. Consider, for example, the boycott of Saran Wrap, which is manufactured by Dow Chemical, over Dow's involvement in the Vietnam war in the supply of napalm to the US military. The boycott of this product (a cling film for wrapping food) was promoted by the organisers distributing leaflets which informed shoppers: 'If you buy Dow products, you help kill. *Do not* buy Dow products – buy substitutes as long as Dow makes napalm' (Vogel's emphasis).[9] Saran Wrap was augmented in a way entirely unintended by Dow; it became, for some people at least, associated with charred infants. While the provision of this product attribute was not entirely unintended, in the sense that Dow made the decision to supply napalm despite possible ramifications for their other product lines, it was not a deliberate attempt to augment the product. Product augmentation, however, was the result.

Management may have less discretion or control over whether this form of product augmentation occurs. Manufacturers of goods in South Africa, that are South African companies, can do nothing about the origin of their goods short of entirely locating elsewhere. However, importers and retailers have more discretion in that they can choose not to deal in South African goods because of the way they are, for some consumers, augmented with the imagery of brutal oppression and racial discrimination against the majority population in South Africa. The product is a package, as Levitt puts it above: 'a total proposition, the content of which exceeds what comes out at the end of the assembly line.' Extending this concept further, it is possible to argue that the product is augmented in various ways whether the seller wants it or not. The augmented product may be augmented to the disadvantage of the seller. Levitt writes about how products may be deliberately and positively augmented. It is proposed here that products may be unintentionally and negatively augmented. This is negative product augmentation.

This author has elsewhere written about the legitimacy concept as an element in the marketing mix.[10] Essentially, this paper expresses two ideas concerning the marketing mix. First, the notion of legitimacy as a further element in the marketing mix in addition to the four Ps (product, price, promotion, place). It is argued that, in certain circumstances, purchase behaviour may be influenced by the relative legitimacy of a company's offering to the market-place. The would-be customer finds some component of the offering inappropriate (illegitimate) because he or she thinks it socially undesirable. Second, that the marketing mix should be defined from the customer's perspective, not the producer's.

Adopting such a perspective would be in keeping with a consumer orientation rather than a producer orientation, reflects consumer practice, and would justify the incorporation of legitimacy in the marketing mix even where managerial discretion on this element was limited or non-existent.

Legitimacy is the extent to which society has conferred approval on certain thought and behaviour, relative to other thought and behaviour. The legitimacy concept operating in purchase behaviour – and giving rise to ethical purchase behaviour – can be found where some prefer domestically produced goods. Many private and fleet car buyers continue to buy only British, for as British Leyland has stated in its advertising 'British cars means [*sic*] British jobs.' Country of origin may affect the legitimacy element in other ways, such as some failing within the country of origin, apartheid in South Africa for example, or some action taken by the country of origin against the importing country. During the Falklands crisis, not only did sales of Argentinian goods suffer (particularly corned beef and wine) but also sales of Kerrygold Irish butter because of Ireland's refusal to support the British government.

This paper was written some time before the full conceptualisation of the argument expressed here on ethical purchase behaviour; indeed, before this term had been thought of. The debate about whether or not to include legitimacy as a separate element in the marketing mix alongside the four Ps, or any other number and type of elements in the marketing mix that have been identified, seems on reflection irrelevant and pedantic. It is sufficient simply to recognise that there is a legitimacy element which may influence purchase behaviour. Further, the criticism of definitions of the marketing mix for emphasising the producer's concerns is naïve. Kotler's definition typifies this emphasis: 'The set of controllable marketing variables that the firm blends to produce the response it wants in the target market.'[11] This definition is now accepted as appropriate, for although it could be argued that the marketing mix is the total proposition presented to (and therefore perceived by) the consumer, this does not assist practitioners. The marketing mix is the term used by marketing teachers to explain to marketing practitioners how they may go about (which variables they may employ in) attempting to meet consumer needs. Legitimacy – which will inevitably be defined by the individual consumer – is one variable which practitioners may employ or have to take into account. As the Marks and Spencer example in the paper shows, practitioners may be able to enhance the legitimacy of their offering.[12] So, to follow the line of argument above, negative product augmentation will result from perceived shortcomings in the legitimacy of the offering. From the producer's perspective, attempts to deal with this would involve manipulation of the legitimacy variable in the marketing mix.

171

A further observation can be made here. It is clear that the product is not just a bundle of benefits, as the product attributes may be seen as disadvantages as well as advantages by the consumer. The product is more accurately conceived as a package of benefits and costs. One cost may be a legitimacy shortcoming, as the quotation from *New Society* (given earlier) aptly illustrates: 'Times are surely hard for the consumer with a conscience. That Chilean wine may have a military bouquet, but can we afford the alternative?' The next section considers negative product augmentation and legitimacy within a model of pressure group influenced ethical purchase behaviour.

The model

One can refer to a marketing system, as Fisk and others have done.[13] This is not currently fashionable, however; probably because it is not very useful in teaching practitioners, but also because of its positivistic implications and limited explanatory value. Accepting these drawbacks, though, one can refer to pressure groups in the marketing system. A system is 'any set of interacting variables'.[14] One variable, it is argued here, which has a legitimate role in the marketing system is the activities of pressure groups. The claim that pressure groups have a part to play in the marketing system is based on the need for information for consumer sovereignty, the power of business, and pluralistic interpretations of pressure group activity; in other words, the arguments advanced in earlier chapters. A model can now be proposed, on the basis of the concepts proposed above and the analysis of boycotts, which describes how pressure groups influence purchase behaviour. The model proposed is a simple one. Efforts could be made to incorporate communications theory and the psychology of influence which would make it to some extent explanatory. But that would go beyond the parameters established for this study. The model proposed is a description of the process which results in pressure group influenced ethical purchase behaviour. A five-stage model is proposed:

(1) Firm's marketing system stable: firm (F1) is matching its resources with the wants of its customers; promotional pressure group (P) is concerned about an issue (X).
(2) Pressure group awareness of firm's failing: P becomes aware of F1's undesirable (as judged by the pressure group) impact on X.
(3) Pressure group response: P approaches F1, other organisations (the media, government departments, etc.) and the customer to seek an end to the impact by F1 on X.
(4) Firm's marketing system becomes unstable: the firm's customers become aware of the impact of F1 on X. This threatens the

exchange process because X becomes a part of the organisation's offering to the customer through negative product augmentation.

(5) Ethical purchase behaviour: some F1 customers, spontaneously or in response to a call for a boycott by P, take their custom to another firm (F2). F2, without the legitimacy shortcoming of impact on X, better matches its resources with those customers' wants.

Various other stages could follow, depending on management response. The model is, of course, very simplistic. It does not, for example, account for the behaviour of customers concerned about X who remain with F1 but receive less utility as a consequence, or those that go to other firms (F3 or F4). It does also assume brand loyalty, competitive market conditions, and so on. However, on the basis of this and previous chapters, it is thought likely to describe the general pattern of events. Its validity is explored in Part Two.

Management response to pressure groups in the marketing system can be considered in two ways. First, anticipatory management action, where management recognises that pressure groups are a feature of the marketing environment and takes this into account in its decision-making. This suggests a proactive role for management. Second, management action in response to a pressure group action directed at the firm. This suggests a reactive role for management, although this may be inevitable where pressure group issues are fundamentally in conflict with some or all of the firm's activities (and possibly other pressure groups, such as on the issues of contraception and abortion) or where the firm's proactive role was insufficient or inadequate.

Most of the relevant literature falls into the first category – how management can take preventive action. It need not be concerned solely with boycotts as the management task is essentially the same regardless of the specific form of the potential environmental threat. Management has been urged to scan the environment,[15] to recognise and accept the role of pressure groups,[16] to match performance with public expectations,[17] and even to communicate and co-operate with pressure groups.[18] In other words, management seeks to maintain the legitimacy of its offering. It recognises that there is a legitimacy element in the marketing mix and does all it can to avoid shortcomings and perhaps even tries to enhance its performance on this variable. Ackerman's work, referred to earlier, is useful in a general way in offering guidance on management response to social demands. He describes the process whereby response to social demands can become institutionalised as necessary because 'Edicts from on high and staff activity don't affect change; it has to be institutionalised in the operating units.'[19] There is then an important distinction between social responsibility decisions (presumably possibly including responses to pressure group demands) made at the corporate level and at the operating level. He argues for social responsiveness to be included within the organisation's reward and punishment system.[20] Again, this is more concerned with preventive action rather than response to a specific demand.

One paper which does consider management response to a specific pressure group demand regarding the firm's products is by Ford and Vezeridis.[21] They propose a six-stage model of environmental conflict:

(1) Peace – 'the products are marketed regularly'.
(2) Skirmish – 'little activity. An article may appear in a scientific magazine or on the inside pages of newspapers.'
(3) Conflict – escalation: 'the issue receives increasing publicity ... the controversy is taken up by a social organisation which starts to pressurise companies.'
(4) Three possible outcomes to the previous conflict:
   a. Company defeat – product completely withdrawn, voluntarily, under pressure, or as a result of legislation.
   b. Tactical withdrawal – company makes modifications or concessions, voluntarily or by force of law.
   c. Pressure defeat – pressure lifted because product shown to be harmless, discredit or failure of a pressure group, or external factors which mean that 'the environmental costs of a product must be incurred'.
(5) Victory from defeat – following from 4b – 'company takes advantage of the changes in its products or methods which have been forced or have resulted ... "environmental safety" of the modified product becomes a positive feature of the company's marketing policy'.
(6) Pre-emptive strike – company learns its lesson: 'products are designed to alleviate or at least not to exacerbate environmental problems.'

The last stage of course is preventive action, management seeking to maintain the legitimacy of the offering. The three possible outcomes suggested at the fourth stage are those that follow on from the model proposed above. The firm may give in to pressure group demands by withdrawing the product or by making all necessary modifications (or, as a compromise, some modifications only). Alternatively, it may fight the pressure group. Put in terms applicable to pressure group demands not relating to the environmental threat of the firm's product, the company may give in to the pressure group and cease and/or remedy the perceived grievance, or it may fight and attempt to justify its action (the grievance). Again, Part Two will assess the validity of these claims.

While having presented the argument for ethical purchase behaviour, Part One has not considered why such a term should be used, nor any previous work in the area recorded in the relevant literature. This is examined next and before Part One is concluded with an overview of the argument advanced here.

Refining the concept of ethical purchase behaviour

Defining ethical purchase behaviour

The term ethical purchase behaviour came about in an effort to provide a unifying concept for very different influences on purchase behaviour. Indeed, one person may practise ethical purchase behaviour by not buying a product, another by buying that same product (as was the case with the Saran Wrap boycott, and this frequently occurred during labour boycotts). Inspiration came from the literature on ethical investments. An activity which often has similar motivations, but is found in product markets rather than investment markets, could be suitably described as ethical purchase behaviour. The two activities are quite closely analogous. Those responsible for investing the funds of unions, universities, professional associations, and others have over the past twenty years been regularly urged 'to consider the social consequences of corporate activities from which these institutions derive an endowment return'.[22] Vogel and others have written extensively about ethical investment in the United States.[23] Prominent of late are demands for institutions to disinvest from companies involved in South Africa. But actions on other issues continue, even if they are no longer in the limelight, as Vogel's recent review shows.[24]

Ethical investment has even acquired some prominence in Britain. Prompted by the British Medical Association (BMA), which acted on the basis of a report by Social Audit, charities and health organisations recently sold off their shareholdings in tobacco companies, causing a noticeable fall in tobacco share prices.[25] The BMA had previously severed its links with unit trusts investing in tobacco companies.[26] The National Union of Mineworkers trustees of the miners' pension fund attempted, but were prevented by legal action, to refuse to back investments in overseas markets or in energy related interests which compete with coal.[27] Further, the Trades Union Congress (TUC) has urged trade union trustees of pension funds to press for a complete ban on direct pension fund investment in South Africa. Recognising the legal difficulties involved in trustees attempting to make ethical investments on behalf of others, the TUC counselled that South African investments are commercially ill-advised because of the increasing instability of the country.[28] Meanwhile, the Church of England General

Synod passed a resolution in 1982 calling for total disinvestment from companies involved in South Africa, though this has not been implemented. The Church favours a policy of 'positive engagements', whereby through maintaining contact with firms' managements it may influence policy. In 1984 it sold its £4·4 million holding in Carnation, the United States dairy products company, because despite contact with management it was dissatisifed with the wages paid to the company's South African workers.[29]

These examples show how ethical investors can operate by selling off investments or by keeping them and using them to press for changes in the companies concerned. Another form of ethical investment is positive rather than negative. This is where investors only invest in ethical concerns, as distinct from disinvesting or pressing for changes in un-ethical concerns. The counterpart in ethical purchase behaviour is the purchase of an ethically acceptable product. In the United States, invest-ors may invest in a number of ethical investment institutions, such as Working Assets Money Fund[30] or Shearson/American Express.[31] In the UK, there is Mercury Provident, Friends' Provident, and The Ecological Building Society.[32] Unity Trust, a union bank established in 1984 in conjunction with the Co-operative Bank, has a prohibition on dealing with South African interests and all its lending is confined to the United Kingdom to support domestic enterprise.[33] The Quakers refuse to invest in liquor, drugs, nuclear energy, weapons, pollution, firms with bad labour relations, and South Africa. They played an important part in recently establishing in Britain the Ethical Investment Research and Information Service (EIRIS), to 'meet a long-standing need on the part of institutions and individuals who want to know more about the enterprises in which they invest than the rate of financial return'.[34] Similar institutions have existed in the United States for some time.[35] EIRIS recognises that ethical investment decisions require information. However, they do not seek to identify 'clean' investments; it is for the investor to decide what constitutes 'clean'. They merely provide details on those activities of the companies concerned that might be of interest to a potential investor. In other words, they do not attempt to define what is ethical. The same principle applies to defining ethical purchase behaviour.

Ethics is about what is right and wrong in human behaviour. There are, however, no absolute standards. Ethics may be defined as 'a theory or morality which attempts to systematise moral judgements, and establish and defend basic moral principles'.[36] When applied, such systems are expressions of what people think ought to be. There are many bases for such systems, or rather, commonly used principles. Steiner and Steiner identify fourteen, such as Kant's categorical imperative: 'one should not adopt principles of action unless they can, without inconsistency, be adopted by everyone else'; the utilitarian principles of philosophers such as Bentham and Mill: 'the greatest good for the greatest number'; the Golden Rule, found in every great world religion: 'Do unto others as you would have them do unto you'; the means–ends ethic, most commonly associated with Machiavelli: 'worthwhile ends justify efficient means'; and the might-equals-right ethic, as expressed in Nietzsche's understanding of master-morality: 'What is ethical is what an individual has the strength and power to accomplish.'[37] These different possible bases for ethical systems are in themselves indicative of likely divergence of opinion on whether an action is ethical or unethical. There are many further factors leading to an individual's judgement, including the individual's values, cultural experience, and information on and understanding of the circumstances of the action. Some philosophers such as A. J. Ayer have, because ethics are so individually determined, concluded that ethics and moral judgements do not exist, but are meaningless expressions of emotion.[38]

Ethics is a complex subject of profound philosophical enquiry. Of importance here, however, is simply the recognition that defining one behaviour as ethical and another as unethical is the outcome of an individual's moral judgement, an act of moral reason, and, as such, likely to differ from person to person. For this reason, ethical purchase behaviour is in itself also an outcome of an individual's moral judgement. It could then result in different responses to the same product by different individuals who are yet both consciously indulging in ethical purchase behaviour. This observation is also true of ethical investment. Responses by practitioners to an article by Purcell on ethical investment made this clear. One respondent commented, 'Were there no ethical investors ten, five, or two years ago? Of course there were.' This respondent's view of these earlier ethical investors is probably that they were ethical in the sense of fulfilling their duties to those who had entrusted capital to them. He continues by asking if there is a magical dividing line between ethical and unethical investors, observing that some draw the line at investment in South Africa, while others at between unionised and non-unionised companies. In the latter case, 'they outlaw three-fourths of private employment in America'.[39] For these reasons, EIRIS does not identify 'clean' investments and no attempt can be made here to say what is ethical purchase behaviour in any specific case. Yet there is some consistency to such behaviour indicating common standards, even if they are only emotional responses or expressions of the values of the ruling élite. So while there are no absolutes, there are shared perspectives on ethical behaviour, some of which are more prevalent than others. Purcell's reply to his critics recognises this: 'People differ in their philosophical and theological reasons underlying ethics, but I think there is fair consensus about *applied ethics*, a kind of a garden-variety definition meaning integrity, virtue, and consideration for others, which I think most HBR readers would share.'

In the case of EIRIS, the ethical judgement is simply implicit rather than explicit. For one must ask how they provide the information necessary for their clients to make ethical judgements. They, of course, assess the performance of companies on what they define as ethical issues: involvement in armaments, nuclear power, South Africa, and so on. They permit some flexibility, as a range of issues is considered, but a moral judgement is still made, which largely reflects the concerns of the church groups responsible in setting up EIRIS and its clients. Many of the issues prompting ethical purchase behaviour and ethical investments are common. Some of these issues are considered in the next section, which looks at forms of ethical purchase behaviour previously examined. This section has shown that ethical purchase behaviour is an expression of the individual's moral judgement in his or her purchase behaviour. As such judgements are individual, ethical purchase behaviour may involve a considerable variety of possibly conflicting issues and priorities, but some consensus can be expected.

Some forms of ethical purchase behaviour previously examined

It has already been noted that ethical purchase behaviour is largely unrecognised in the literature. However, *some forms* of ethical purchase behaviour have been recognised, though not by this name, and this should be acknowledged. These various forms previously identified come together under the all-embracing term ethical purchase behaviour, together with other forms not already identified. Within what may be broadly described as the marketing literature, this study follows in the tradition of the work of Anderson and Cunningham, Kassarjian, Kinnear *et al.*, and others, on socially responsible or ecologically concerned consumption. They consider some forms of ethical purchase behaviour, but their concern is principally with identifying, for segmentation purposes, who the consumers are that practise this. So Engel and Blackwell include this work under the heading 'Catalysts to Consumerism', suggesting it has identified socio-psychological variables associated with an interest in consumerism activities. For them, the contribution of this work is in having helped to describe 'socially conscious consumers', that is, 'those persons who not only are concerned with their own personal satisfactions, but also buy with some consideration of the social and environmental well-being of others'.[40]

Webster[41] refers to the 'socially responsible consumer' and suggests 'In general, he [sic] has been found to be a pre-middle-aged adult of relatively high occupational, economic and social status. He tends to be more cosmopolitan, less dogmatic, less conservative, less status conscious, less alienated, and less personally competent than the less socially concerned citizen.' He points out that these discriminators are more problematic than demographic variables and 'the task of developing workable definitions of segments will be a difficult one'. Webster then goes on to discuss phases in market development and changes in the marketing concept as a system of economic exchange, where the focus moves from the market, to the seller, to the buyer, and finally to the public. In the final phase, 'the revised marketing concept is not fundamentally new or different from the old one. It merely represents a fine tuning to make sure that public needs are consistent with private wants, a piece of unfinished business under the old marketing concept.' This is an early statement of Kotler's societal marketing concept,[42] though less adequately expressed. It seems – but this is not made explicit – that Webster assumes that socially responsible consumption is, or will be, the norm, in spite of having identified it as being particular to a market segment. So his justification for a revised concept of marketing rests on the notion of socially responsible consumption. Unfortunately, it comes across as little more than wishful thinking. He writes:

> How else could business enhance the quality of life except by offering goods and services that find value in the market-place and return profit to the shareholders? That is the only function of business! But as the definition of value changes, so does the criterion of marketing effectiveness change, that for which profit is the reward.

Webster argues, in other words, that value in the market-place now includes social considerations, suggesting a revised concept of marketing. It pays to have a broader social purpose because consumers demand it. This is a remarkably convenient argument given that it was written at a time when criticism of business was at its height. It is, however, unacceptable. A quantum leap is made between some very limited evidence of socially responsible consumption by some consumers, to an ideal solution to the problem of social responsibility. Yet while such an argument is so obviously flawed, the concept suggested – the societal marketing concept – is thought to be valid. As the next section shows, the argument presented in this study attempts to fill the gap between the well-intentioned rhetoric of the societal marketing concept and examples of ethical purchase behaviour. It eventually provides some support for such a concept, not unqualified, but at least fully justified. Webster does, to be fair, recognise some of the implications of socially responsible consumption, even if he does overstate them and fail to acknowledge any of the intervening considerations.

Both Webster, and Engel and Blackwell, cite the paper by Anderson and Cunningham on the socially conscious consumer.[43] (Indeed, this is the only paper Webster cites in support of his claim for socially responsible consumption!) It is important to note that although Anderson and Cunningham claim to have identified an image of the socially conscious consumer, this is not based on any observation of socially conscious consumption; the dependent variable was the score on a social responsibility scale, for 'it can be assumed that socially conscious individuals, whose orientations are reflected in a variety of socially responsible behaviours, would manifest social consciousness in consumption decisions'. Consequently, despite their large sample and sophisticated multivariate data analysis, they have to concede: 'It would be useful to determine whether consumption patterns are different between high and low scorers on the Berkowitz–Daniels Social Responsibility Scale, particularly with respect to products and/or brands which claim environmental benefits.' Their claims are further weakened by the likely collinearity of the dependent and independent variables and their dubious use of discriminant analysis.[44]

Kassarjian's paper on incorporating ecology into marketing strategy, cited by Anderson and Cunningham, comes a little closer to socially responsible consumption by looking at behavioural intention. He was mainly concerned with measuring attitudes towards air pollution and whether people say they would pay more for a pollutant-free gasoline, that is, their behavioural intention. He shied away from attempting to find out whether those with a concern for air pollution actually did pay more and buy the pollutant-free gasoline, offering only extremely limited circumstantial evidence to suggest that they did. He suggests that 'With a *good* product based on ecological concerns, the potential for a marketer seems to be impressive'.[45] This, however, conflicts with a study reported by Engel *et al.* where 'In spite of aggressive marketing by the refiners, the no-lead/low-lead gasolines received less than half of the 10 per cent volume expected of them.'[46] They suggest the discrepancy may be due to the acute pollution experienced by the respondents in Kassarjian's study, but also comment, 'Possibly consumers are concerned about pollution generally but do not perceive their own consumption of gasoline to be serious enough to result in a problem that would generate extended problem solving.' Moreover, 'an individual consumer risks paying for societal benefits while other consumers can get away without paying'. In other words, a problem of the logic of collective action where, as discussed in Chapter 4, it is often found that voluntary collective action is unlikely even if the would-be participants could anticipate collective good. Consequently, Engel *et al.* write that voluntarism has its limits, that, 'There is, in the literature of consumerism, a persistent belief expressed that consumers ought to voluntarily act in a way that is beneficial to the society they live in. At the same time, there is persistent evidence that they will act in a way that is beneficial to themselves as individuals.'[47] The belief they refer to is to be found in the previously mentioned papers and others,[48] but the evidence either way is scant.

The point about all these studies – and there are more[49] – is that they assume ethical purchase behaviour, even if it is referred to only in part, as ecologically concerned consumption or socially responsible consumption. They offer only limited evidence of ethical purchase behaviour and mostly in an indirect way. No explanation is offered as to why or how such purchase behaviours may come about. This omission is redressed here, in the provision of direct evidence and an argument for ethical purchase behaviour. Moreover, ethical purchase behaviour is more than socially responsible or ecologically concerned consumption. Others have come nearer to a wider definition and this work, although conceptual rather than empirical, is worth considering here.

Thomas, for example, has written about purchase votes on social impacts, allowing consumers to express their social preferences in the market-place with firms broadcasting their social impacts.[50] More realistically, perhaps, he has also written about those impacts being broadcasted by 'informed partisan groups'. His 'Consciousness Four' marketing sees 'consumers as accepting (or rejecting) the total social impact of an organisation'. He is not clear about how this will come about – for example, who these informed partisan groups are and their role in practice – but his use of Lindblom's concept of disjointed incrementalism gives credence to the notion of each individual consumer's vote contributing towards some change in the socio-economic system. The type of purchase behaviour he has in mind is broader than socially responsible consumption: 'Individual consumption decisions today require us both to determine our "needs" and to consider an intricate pattern of social, economic, legal and ecological variables.' Even in this paper, however, Thomas is primarily advocating organisational broadcasting of social impacts.[51] In *Can the Market Sustain an Ethic?* Yale Brozen suggests that markets reflect the ethics of participants, in which case one might presume he would argue that there already is ethical purchase behaviour. He refers, by example, to American firms that refuse to sell goods to Russia although they would, at least in the short run, profit from doing so. Their justification, he suggests, lies in the belief that in the long run they could be conferring benefits on a government which may become an enemy in some future situation. Alternatively, there are those that choose to trade with Russia, not so much for profit, but in the hope that economic interdependence will reduce enmity and the chances of a future war. So he sees a place for ethical conduct in the market:

181

In terms of whether or not some kinds of transactions occur, a free market simply reflects the notions of right and wrong already possessed by participants. The market does not mechanistically determine any kind of conduct. Moral or ethical choices are made by individuals. In a free market, responsibility for such choices is left in the hands of each person. To that extent, a free market places responsibility on each for his or her own conduct.[52]

In *The Public Use of Private Interest,* Schultze argues that greater use could be made of the market, in preference to increased government intervention, on social issues. In acknowledging the problem of self-interest overriding social concern, he suggests, 'the prerequisite for social gains is the identification ... of the defects in the incentive system that drive ordinary decent citizens into doing things contrary to the common good'. Yet he still wishes to employ self-interest in addition to any 'preaching' that might lead to more appropriate behaviour (ethical purchase behaviour). So he writes, 'If I want drivers to economise on gasoline usage, advertising appeals to patriotism, warnings about the energy crisis, and "don't be fuelish" slogans are no match for higher prices at the gas pumps.'[53] Schultze is a great believer in the market: 'Harnessing the "base" motive of material self-interest to promote the common good is perhaps *the* most important social invention mankind has yet achieved.'[54]

Robin Wight is another with great faith in the market. He suggests that 'power grows out of the shopping basket' and that consumerism is in recognition of this. He makes frequent reference, in illustration, to consumer boycotts: 'a militant method of responding to an unsatisfactory product as perfect competition says one should';[55] while Vogel[56] recognises that consumer sovereignty need not be limited to responses to unsatisfactory products. Referring to both ethical investments and consumer boycotts, he writes that although in theory consuming and investing 'are "economic" decisions ... legitimately guided by only self-interest ... [there is] an increasing consideration of social factors in both investment and consumption decisions ... citizens are beginning to consider the possibilities of employing "public" standards of judgement in the economic arena'. He suggests that the distinction between the 'public' act of voting in the political market-place, which is public and political because it involves an attempt by the individual to advance a perception of the general good, is becoming blurred when ostensibly 'private' acts of voting in the economic market-place, guided entirely by self-interest, are beginning to incorporate social factors. He refers to consumer boycotts on the production of war materials (by ITT and Dow), investment in Angola (Gulf), and participation in the identity card system in South Africa

(Polaroid), by way of example. Such boycotts 'have become a major vehicle of popular protest against business', and it seems that he is in favour. He refers, moreover, to ecologically concerned consumption:

> As environmental concern increases, there is a tendency – still more celebrated than measurable – for 'ecologically responsible' citizens to express their identification with the public interest by their private purchasing decisions. People can thus influence environmental issues by 'voting' with their dollars, as well as with their ballot. In effect, they are taking seriously the analogy between 'dollar' votes and political votes, which forms the basis of the corporate defense of consumer sovereignty. Thus, one is encouraged to purchase biodegradable detergents, smaller cars ...

It was noted earlier that socially responsible consumption is but one form of ethical purchase behaviour. It is concerned with, as Vogel shows in this quotation, the environmental impact of consumer purchases. It is limited to non-returnable bottles, high-phosphate detergents, leaded petrol, and so on. In other words, socially responsible or ecologically concerned consumption seeks to limit the pollution created by the consumer in consumption. Ethical purchase behaviour is concerned with these and much wider social impacts. The arguments for such behaviour, by Thomas, Brozen, Schultze, Wight, and others, recognise that consumer sovereignty need not be so restricted. Of course consumer sovereignty can be employed to express concern about and possibly remedy product defects and products that pollute; but why not, as these conceptual contributions seem to imply, all the social impacts of the firm? Vogel differentiates between the types of consumer boycotts he earlier referred to and ecologically concerned consumption: 'Ecologically "responsible" consumption differs from purchasing which is politically or ideologically motivated chiefly in that for the former, the relationship between what is consumed (or not consumed) and the social problem being addressed is direct.' Yet there is no need to so differentiate. It is all ethical purchase behaviour, as here identified and defined.

Ethical purchase behaviour and the societal marketing concept

The application of the concept of legitimacy to marketing is not without precedent, for Kotler writes of the importance of legitimacy in describing the 'higher purpose of marketing':

> Ultimately, the enlightened marketer is really trying to contribute to the quality of life ... Profits will still be a major test of business success in serving society. However ... profits are really a

183

by-product of doing business well and not the moral aim of business. Business, like other institutions of society, prospers only by maintaining legitimacy in the eyes of consumers, employees and the general public. Legitimacy is grounded in the institution's commitment to serve higher moral aims.[57]

This perspective is reflected in his societal marketing concept,[58] wherein there are three underlying premisses:

(1) Consumers' wants do not always coincide with their long-run interests or society's long-run interests.
(2) Consumers will increasingly favour organisations which show a concern with meeting their wants, long-run interests, and society's long-run interests.
(3) The organisation's task is to serve target markets in a way that produces not only want satisfaction but long-run individual and social benefit as the key to attracting and holding customers.

Kotler's societal marketing concept, particularly in the latter two underlying premisses, implicitly recognises ethical purchase behaviour. He suggests consumers will be influenced in their purchase behaviour by social issues. Yet is all this talk of a higher purpose of marketing and a societal marketing concept simply empty rhetoric? The answer to this question on the basis of the argument presented here would seem to be negative. A case for ethical purchase behaviour has been presented, based on the nature of consumer sovereignty, the requirement for social control of business via the market-place, and the growing influence but need for effective tactics of promotional pressure groups. The use of the consumer boycott tactic, it is argued, represents an attempt to achieve ethical purchase behaviour and instances of this have already been considered. Further instances are examined in Part Two. So the first and foremost conclusion at this point must be that there is a case for ethical purchase behaviour and some evidence of it. There are other preliminary conclusions. These can best be considered by reviewing the theoretical argument for ethical purchase behaviour.

The theoretical argument for ethical purchase behaviour

Chapter 1, in exploring the nature of capitalism and consumer sovereignty from an economic and political perspective, provides a philosophical basis for ethical purchase behaviour. Consumer sovereignty is shown to be the rationale for capitalism; its expression in ethical purchase behaviour is therefore appropriate to market societies. Yet consumer sovereignty may in practice be limited, which raises doubts about the competitive model of capitalism, the marketing concept, and the likelihood of ethical purchase behaviour. Political-economic systems are distinguished by their dependence on the market mechanism. In market societies decision-making is decentralised and power can be said to lie with consumers in the form of consumer sovereignty. By looking at the origins of capitalism it can be seen that market society brings with it the benefits of material progress and freedom. Economic and political freedom is said to accrue, though this depends on an interpretation in accordance with the philosophy of individualism. This philosophy forms the basis for the competitive model of capitalism, first advanced by the classical economists, and subsequently by business and the neo-classical economists. The material progress under capitalism is not disputed, but the competitive model of capitalism, although constituting the dominant ideology, is not always preferred or considered to be accurate. Marx, Keynes, Schmitter, and others have offered different interpretations, particularly the crisis, compromise, and corporatist models of capitalism.

Economic systems may be assessed by the criteria of efficiency, freedom, equity, and altruism. The competitive model of capitalism, although impaired by market imperfections such as externalities and imperfect information, does rate highly on the criterion of efficiency. Within acceptance of the philosophy of individualism it also rates highly on the criterion of freedom. It is on the criteria of equity and altruism, which almost seem in conflict with efficiency and freedom, that it may be most criticised, especially in an affluent society. Accordingly, the suggestion that 'the market will answer all things' is disputed. Capitalism might have brought material progress but this may no longer be the most important social goal. There is also increasing concern over the associated social costs (externalities). Yet, it is argued here, consumer sovereignty may be employed to address these failings.

Critics of the competitive model of capitalism have different preferences or priorities to its adherents, but they also highlight its inaccuracies, particularly the notion of consumer sovereignty. Galbraith's Revised Sequence, for example, refers to a producer sovereignty. In mixed markets it is more accurate to refer to degrees of consumer sovereignty, dependent, most notably, on choice through competition, information, actions by the state, and individual wealth. So two forms of consumer sovereignty emerge, an absolute form as found in the competitive model of capitalism, and a more restricted form where consumer sovereignty is viewed as a technical term to refer to degrees of consumer authority. The marketing discipline subscribes to the competitive model of capitalism. Consumer sovereignty may even be a paradigm for marketing. Yet as a feature of perfect competition it is theoretically irreconcilable with marketing strategies. Perfect competition does not exist in the 'real' world and, if it did, there could not be marketing strategies. The centrality of consumer sovereignty to marketing points to the ideological nature of marketing thought. Marketing's response to consumerism is one illustration of this. So Chapter 1 shows that, while ethical purchase behaviour as an expression of consumer sovereignty is in keeping with the competitive model of capitalism and marketing, it may be restricted by the limited degree of consumer sovereignty. Moreover, how does society control business if not through the market?

Chapters 2 and 3 consider the social control of business. The limits to society's control over business by the market were indicated above. Ethical purchase behaviour, especially in consumer boycotts, is an attempt at the social control of business via the market. It may result from externalities or a difference in priorities – equity or altruism preferred to efficiency. In any event, social goals other than material progress are sought. Chapter 2 examines the social role of business – what society might expect from business and, in corporate social responsibility, what it receives. Business and society is the discipline concerned with business's social role. Its analysis of the relationship between business and society, however, provides few certain answers; the issue is complicated, particularly by the different ideological positions that may be brought to its analysis. Yet by approaching the issue in terms of the social control of business, a meaningful focus may be adopted which brings clarity and reduces ideological bias. Business digressions, such as ITT's involvement in an attempted coup in Chile, emphasise the need for social control of business. They reveal corporate power without accountability. Yet all corporate actions may be so criticised, for the exercise of power by business lacks legitimacy. Claims to property rights are no longer sufficient, given the separation of ownership and control; though the extent of corporate power is considerable, business essentially identifies the issues for which it is responsible and the priorities to be attached to them. This exercise of power is defended by reference to corporate social responsibility – to the self-regulation of business. Corporate social responsibility has become something of a shibboleth; all firms practise corporate social responsibility. Beyond the rhetoric, however, if firms have a social role, then clearly they have responsibilities. In which case, how may these responsibilities be defined or identified? How does management determine their relative priority? How far does corporate social responsibility extend? And how does management actually act in practise?

Corporate responsibilities may be identified by looking at the social costs created by the firm, externalities for which it could assume responsibility as it has caused them. But social costs are not always immediately apparent or readily acknowledged. Responsibilities may also be identified by examining the impact of the firm's activities on its stakeholders. But this method is also problematical. The firm may not be aware of all its stakeholders and some, such as the shareholders and the community, may be in conflict. Business is therefore still left with determining priorities even when it has identified its responsibilities. Related to the priorities problem is the question of the extent of corporate social responsibility: How far should business go in helping to resolve the problems of society? Four positions are identified in a model proposed here, which combines corporate goals and responsibilities: profit-maximisation and social irresponsibility; profit-maximisation tempered by the 'moral minimum' through self-regulation; profit as a necessary but not sufficient goal, with affirmative action extending beyond self-regulation; and, finally, going beyond this to include the championing of political and moral causes unrelated to the corporation's business activities, as long as profitability permits. Many, however, would argue against social responsibility of any form beyond profit-maximisation. Yet such a position, the 'Friedman Misconception', is founded in the competitive model of capitalism with all its flaws, and, in particular, ignores the reality of managerial discretion on social issues.

Management practices and perspectives on social responsibility may be considered in terms of managerial creeds or ideologies. One may distinguish between profit-maximising management, trusteeship management, and 'quality of life' management; of which the second type is said to be predominant. The third type, equating to the fourth position in the model on the extent of corporate responsibility, might be becoming more popular. Similarly, one may refer to classical, managerial, and consent creeds, or to the classical ideology and the modern socio-economic managerial ideology. The creeds to which managers adhere will determine their response on social issues. While there may be a trend towards adopting greater responsibilities, it is thought likely that the majority of managers are still only at the second position in the model, of profit-maximisation tempered by the 'moral minimum' through self-regulation. Business practices and perspectives on social responsibility are then largely in keeping with Friedman's admonitions.

Yet profit-maximisation as the sole social responsibility of business should not be simply dismissed as self-serving. A closer analysis of Friedman's case reveals five principal arguments against corporate social responsibility: competing claims (the role of profit), competitive disadvantage, competence, fairness (domination by business), and legitimacy (the role of government). However, while important, the counter-arguments are considered more so. They acknowledge the inaccuracies of Friedman's model of capitalism, managerial discretion, the extent of corporate power, the 'moral minimum', and the relationship between enlightened self-interest and the long-term profitability of the firm. So social responsibility may be a doctrine to which management adheres in the absence of any other basis for action. Yet corporate social responsibilities may be identified and even addressed by management. The doctrine of corporate social responsibility is a form of social control of business. There are other forms that seek corporate accountability.

Chapter 3 examines the social control of business mechanisms, turning from the doctrine of corporate social responsibility and philanthropy to corporate accountability. Various solutions to the problem of corporate power have been advanced over many years. Those solutions which would maintain a market society include radical solutions, such as nationalisation, and more piecemeal solutions. The latter involve pressure from within the organisation for social responsibility such as changes in corporate governance, and pressure from outside the organisation through increased disclosure by, for example, social audits or ethical whistle-blowing. Ethical purchase behaviour, particularly in consumer boycotts, constitutes a piecemeal solution involving pressure from outside the organisation. Despite the great number and variety of solutions proposed to the problem of corporate power, those, at least, that would maintain the market system may be said to involve three forms of control over business: legislation, the market, and self-control. According to this analysis, a simple model may be proposed corresponding to the type of power involved. Studies of power generally acknowledge three types: force, inducement, and manipulation. Galbraith, in looking at the types of power business exerts over society, identifies condign, compensatory, and conditioned power. Yet, it is claimed here, society exerts power over business in a similar way. Condign power or force operates through legislation. Compensatory power or inducement operates through the market. Conditioned power or manipulation operates through moral obligation and self-regulation. All three types have strengths and weaknesses. Legislation may not always work and there are limits beyond which it cannot be sensibly applied. It may also threaten the market system. The market, as Chapter 1 concluded, is in itself insufficient. While moral obligation, in self-regulation, has in Chapter 2's examination of the doctrine of corporate responsibility, been shown to be problematical. It is, in particular, élitist and does not involve direct accountability; though it is acknowledged that this form of control amounts to more than conscious efforts by the firm to endorse social responsibility, as it incorporates social conditioning – management action in accordance with social norms.

The conclusion reached on the social control of business is that further control is required and this may be achieved, perhaps necessarily, through the market. So it is argued that consumer sovereignty could attempt to ensure social responsibility in business. This would be in keeping with, or at least only a slight distortion of, the competitive model of capitalism. In 'letting the market work' it would also be appropriate to the current politico-economic climate in the West. But while ethical purchase behaviour sounds a good solution, in practice it may be difficult. It demands informed choice. Only then could consumers vote in the market-place on those social responsibility issues about which they are concerned. Choice requires competition; while information on social issues may be provided by organisations specially concerned with those issues: pressure groups. So Chapter 3 has examined the mechanisms for the social control of business, proposed a model within which they may be incorporated, and found them lacking. The market, perhaps overlooked by business and society analysts, may offer further potential for the social control of business in ethical purchase behaviour. But given the already acknowledged limitations to consumer sovereignty, this solution is not without its drawbacks. Pressure groups, however, who are already acting on business and on social responsibility issues, might serve to enhance consumer sovereignty. Chapter 4 examines pressure groups and their potential in this respect.

Pressure groups have an important role in the political process and society. They have been described as an 'auxiliary circuit of representation'. Yet there are many different types of pressure group, some having more influence than others. In particular, there is the distinction between groups that are 'of', the sectional groups, and groups that are 'for', the promotional groups. Within this distinction, there is also a difference in their degree of political specialisation – in how political they are. The concern here is largely with promotional pressure groups of high political specialisation, such as the Campaign for Nuclear Disarmament. They are the groups which have grown in numbers and influence over recent years and, for advocates of pluralism, are therefore viewed favourably and as contributing to political participation. Promotional pressure groups, however, are often of limited effectiveness because they lack the necessary resources. Three principal avenues of pressure are traditionally identified: the executive, Parliament, and public opinion. But few promotional groups achieve 'insider' status, even if they desire it, and have largely to rely on public opinion. This reflects and exacerbates their absence of resources, especially their weak strategic location, problems in ensuring commitment and cohesion – they are dependent on solidary incentives, small group size and altruism – and their limited finances. Public support endorses a group's demands but may not be forthcoming for more radical groups; the only alternative then is direct action. The politics literature tends to ignore corporate power and, perhaps accordingly, the literature on pressure groups focuses on pressure group action against governments rather than business. Yet business may be a fourth avenue of pressure. Pressure groups may seek to change corporate behaviour or, alternatively, use business as an avenue of pressure to influence the public authorities indirectly, motivating public opinion or employing the 'insider' status of business. An increasing pressure group emphasis on corporations may be in recognition of corporate power but also because of limited access to the other avenues of pressure.

Promotional groups, for the most part, operate by mobilising legitimacy for their cause. They do this by providing information; directly, in the form of reports or their literature, but also in their actions, such as demonstrations. They hope thereby to influence public and elite opinion. Different groups and different environments demand different strategies and tactics. Strategies include the use of the law, embarrassment and confrontation, information, and constituency influence and pressure. There are many tactics, from letter writing to sit-ins. The strategy of embarrassment and confrontation is most likely to be used against the firm, for although it may be conceived as a 'private government', not all strategies and tactics employed against the public authorities are appropriate. The prime concern here is with pressure group use of the consumer boycott tactic against business. But the pressure group literature has little to contribute on this. Of importance, however, is that the factors in pressure group success and the circumstances promotional groups find themselves in, push these groups towards particular strategies and tactics. As these groups are largely tied to public opinion and this may be difficult to influence or be ignored by the authorities, then the increasing number of promotional groups will be ever more likely to seek direct solutions to the issues they address. Business will then become increasingly involved and, given its visibility and consequent vulnerability to embarrassment and confrontation strategies, protest tactics and direct action employed. This may happen regardless of corporate 'guilt', simply because corporations constitute a convenient target.

The consumer boycott may take the form of a protest tactic, merely to gain media attention. But it is more appropriately seen as direct action. Direct action is a last resort, deservedly so in its extreme forms. Consumer boycotts as a form of non-violent direct action and legitimised by their basis in consumer sovereignty may provide promotional pressure groups with an effective and attractive tactic where their other efforts are frustrated. So Chapter 4 shows that while ethical purchase behaviour requires the provision of the necessary information, pressure groups, whose role is to provide such information, are in need of effective pressure tactics. Pressure groups may then seek a role in the marketing system. In doing so, political participation may be increased and the exercise of power in society becomes more diluted.

Chapter 5 examines the boycott tactic in detail, as a form of non-violent direct action and as it is used by pressure groups and others. Features of the boycott and principles in its use and response to it emerge as common, whether it takes the form of the consumer boycott or as an international economic sanction. In particular, it is an expression of disassociation with some repugnant thing – a moral act – and can be symbolic as well as effective. The increase in direct action by promotional groups is likely to be in NVDA. Direct action appeals to some groups for ideological reasons. In consumer boycotts, products may be avoided because they are seen as tainted; NVDA may be more appropriate to most promotional groups' aims, as a rejection of violence. Yet its use may be pragmatic as well as principled, for NVDA has proved highly effective. It provides power through moral superiority. The exercise of power depends on obedience, so NVDA recognises and challenges that obedience, taking power away from immoral authorities and giving it to their critics. This may involve the firm when acting in concert with government, such as Tarmac in its involvement in cruise missile silo construction (see CND case), or independently, with the firm seen as a 'private government'. A Gallup survey confirms the conclusion that direct action is set to increase, with business ever more involved. This is most likely to be in NVDA, including consumer boycotts.

Sharp's comprehensive study of NVDA identifies three classes of action, the withdrawal of cooperation being the most prevalent. Economic boycotts are classified under economic non-cooperation and Sharp offers a typology which includes the consumers' boycott as one action by consumers. There are weaknesses to his analysis, however, and an alternative definition of consumer boycott is proposed which emphasises consumer sovereignty. So, a consumer boycott is the organised exercising of consumer sovereignty by abstaining from purchase of an offering in order to exert influence on a matter of concern to the customer and over the institution making the offering. Sharp suggests that NVDA is successful by achieving conversion of the opponent; though this is less likely than accommodation or non-violent coercion. It has to be acknowledged that the consumer boycott, although non-violent, does have coercive features. Sharp favours NVDA as it can achieve a redistribution of power. Yet how relevant is NVDA to Britain? Much of the literature concentrates on the classic actions over civil rights or by Gandhi. It is suggested that most NVDA in Britain is small-scale pragmatic non-violence and likely to remain as such, in which case a role for the consumer boycott is again indicated. More importantly, the issue is raised as to whether boycotts should be judged by their economic effects when in this country they are likely to be principally symbolic acts. The likely illegality of many common forms of NVDA, including consumer boycotts, is dismissed, as they amount to only a minor breach of the law comparable to breaches of Sunday trading laws and tolerable as a valuable form of political expression. With consumer boycotts in particular, their appropriateness to market society reinforces this judgement.

The term boycott originated in 1880 with the ostracism of Captain C. C. Boycott, an Irish land agent, over the treatment of his tenants. He, and his supporters, were boycotted in a number of ways. A continuum of boycotting may then be identified according to the extent of the ostracism involved and, because of this, and the many different parties that may use or be subject to the boycott, there is considerable variety in the types of boycott that may be found. Some types are more extreme and less acceptable than others, while some boycott actions are not referred to as such, strikes or 'blacking', for example. The concern here is with the 'not buying from' types of boycott. Although strikes or blacking are more commonly used by unions today, consumer boycotts were more important before labour, in the United States at least, became organised. Consumer boycotts appear to have been the key to unionisation. When this goal was achieved they were no longer necessary as the union could more effectively use the strike. The use of the consumer boycott by unions – and its effectiveness – is evidence of the use of the market to control business.

The international economic sanction is another type of boycott and often referred to as an economic boycott. It achieved considerable prominence under the League of Nations following World War I, when it was considered an effective alternative to war. Hopes for the boycott in such a role were not fulfilled, but economic sanctions continue to be used and have proved effective and successful. An interesting variant is to be found in Remer's study of Chinese boycotts. The Chinese boycotts, although international in scope, were not officially organised by the government and were said to be largely a spontaneous reaction by the Chinese people. In this way, they are more like consumer boycotts than international economic sanctions and so have some particularly useful contributions to make here. The methods in their enforcement and promotion, such as picketing and posters, were to be found in the labour boycotts reported (and in more recent consumer boycotts). Remer suggests that their objectives may be publicity, punishment, and policy change. Their outcome may be effectiveness and success, though psychological impact may be as important in success as economic effectiveness. (He makes the distinction, found elsewhere, between economic effectiveness and the achievement of objectives, success.) A boycott may be useful in bringing publicity and, as a passive measure, sympathy. Accordingly, it may be both a weapon of retaliation and a theatrical sword. (As an international action, there can be protectionist benefits as a spin-off.)

Drawbacks to the boycott are, however, identified. It may be a double-edged sword, with costs for the boycotter. (It can also be slow and cumbersome.) Moreover, organisation and solidarity are identified as important in its effectiveness, perhaps more easily achieved in China. Sharp describes China as the 'classic home of the national consumers' boycott' and Remer refers to a long history of boycotts in China, before the term, indeed, was conceived. There is then the question as to the boycott's cultural appropriateness to the West. The origins, organisation, and effectiveness of the Chinese boycotts have cultural explanations, particularly the cultural precedents of a passive resistance tradition and a highly structured society. But Western boycotts, later considered, somewhat allay these doubts. The Chinese boycotts, and Remer's analysis, point to principles in the use of the boycott and common features. They are found to be applicable to both consumer boycotts and more recent examples of international economic sanctions considered, such as those over UDI in Rhodesia. Analysis of these boycotts also highlights target vulnerability and the role of sanctions to reinforce morality. Boycotts may not be futile because of this latter point, even if they are not effective. They can be used to punish, having an expressive function. Some sources suggest effectiveness may not be necessary for success, especially when success has more to do with punishment and showing that things are not being taken lying down than with policy changes. Responses are principally in the form of adaptation, economic restructuring, and trading with or through other countries. It is suggested that boycotts may in themselves be inadequate.

The Arab boycott is an international economic sanction, probably the most significant and costly boycott involving business, and also, in the Jewish response, involves consumer boycotts. It demonstrates boycott effectiveness, but not success; unless the punishment of Israel is viewed as a sufficient, if costly, success. In its expressive role – as moral condemnation of Israel and its supporters – it is an example of ethical purchase behaviour. The Jewish response, spontaneous and organised counterboycotts, is also ethical purchase behaviour. Boycott methods are indicated too, and the factors in their effectiveness; for example, boycotts are difficult to control the further they are removed from the grievance.

More than this, the Arab boycott is also about social responsibility in business and management response to boycotts. Compliance with the boycott has been condemned – even where firms appear to be following the government line – and resulted in counterboycotts. Some firms ended their compliance partly as a result of the economic effect of these boycotts but also because of the publicity. The conclusion about boycotts in general being successful without being effective seems particularly true in the case of consumer boycotts. This, of course, harks back to the observations in Chapter 4 on pressure group strategies and tactics and the visibility of firms. Moreover, in the achievement of anti-boycott legislation by Jewish groups, it shows how pressure groups most often achieve success, by putting issues on the political agenda. Their consumer boycotts, as well as publicity and shareholder actions, played an important part in this. So Chapter 5 is a thorough examination of the boycott tactic, acknowledging the similarities between different types of boycott as well as its origin and its basis in NVDA. The distinction and relationship between effectiveness and success and the expressive function of boycotts has been emphasised. Boycotts need not achieve policy changes to be successful, punishment may have been the intention. Boycotts may only be symbolic, theatrical – but perhaps double-edged – swords. Examples of consumer boycotts were considered in China and over the Arab boycott, and, in the latter case, involved social responsibility issues in business – illustrating their complexity.

This chapter, as the final chapter in Part One, integrates the theoretical argument. An important part of this is showing how ethical purchase behaviour operates at the micro level by referring to the legitimacy concept and negative product augmentation. This chapter also refines the concept of ethical purchase behaviour. Ethical purchase behaviour is closely analogous to ethical investment. Ethical concerns may influence investment decisions in the same way as they influence purchase behaviour. Yet in both cases, it is not possible to specify what is ethical. Ethics concerns what is 'right' and 'wrong', but while some consensus might be expected, this is individually defined. So ethical purchase behaviour is an expression of the individual's moral judgement in his or her purchase behaviour. Previous work in the area is limited to a few, rather unsatisfactory, empirical studies of socially responsible consumption, and more conceptual work that only vaguely suggests or implies ethical purchase behaviour as identified here. The studies of socially responsible or ecologically concerned consumption assume ethical purchase behaviour and are methodologically weak. They also address only one form of ethical purchase behaviour, that intended to remedy problems created by consumers in consumption, rather than more specifically producer created problems. Others have written about the use of purchase votes on a wider range of issues. But their ideas are not developed, nor are the implications considered.

Reference to consumer sovereignty might offer a theoretical explanation or justification for ethical purchase behaviour, but it does not explain why the individual consumer would wish to participate in a consumer boycott or ethical purchase behaviour generally. It is advanced here that there may be negative product augmentation, the unintended provision of unattractive product attributes. Dow's Saran Wrap, for example, became associated with charred infants because of Dow's manufacture of napalm. This suggests there may be a legitimacy element in the marketing mix. These concepts can be incorporated in a five-stage model describing the process which results in pressure group influenced ethical purchase behaviour: firm's marketing system stable; pressure group awareness of firm's failing; pressure group response; firm's marketing system becomes unstable – through negative product augmentation; and, finally, ethical purchase behaviour – customers seek an alternative firm's product without the legitimacy shortcoming. Management response may involve defeat at the hands of the pressure group or a tactical withdrawal, assuming the pressure group itself is not defeated. Management may take anticipatory action and recognise pressure groups as a feature of the environment in which they operate, accounting for this by sustaining legitimacy within the marketing mix.

So Part One ends by identifying some preliminary conclusions; notably that there is support for the ethical purchase behaviour concept and evidence of it, and support for the societal marketing concept. Popular support is important in boycott actions and because of this, and their limited use in Britain to date, they may be more accurately referred to as having a latent potential in the social control of business. Pressure groups may operate as a countervailing power and seem, therefore, particularly in their enhancement of consumer sovereignty, to have a legitimate role in the marketing system. They may, in organising consumer boycotts, transpose social costs into private costs. Finally, the study shows that consumer sovereignty may have the dimension of domain as well as degree. In turn, ethical purchase behaviour, in the recognition of this, offers the potential for greater political participation – though not all political issues can be decided on in markets.

In conclusion, three dominant themes have emerged in the presentation of the case for ethical purchase behaviour and the examination so far of consumer boycotts, one form of this. First, on consumer sovereignty and its extent. It was established as the rationale for capitalism and hence of great importance to market societies. It is identified here as having two dimensions: degree, the amount of consumer authority in the market-place; and domain, the jurisdiction of that authority. The latter dimension constitutes a radical perspective on consumer sovereignty and is in acknowledgement of consumer interest in purchase beyond the more immediate characteristics of the product, as shown in ethical purchase behaviour. Yet despite the significance of consumer sovereignty, it may be limited on both of these dimensions.

The second theme concerns the social control of business and the role of the market in this. Classical economic theory, still predominant in business ideologies, suggests 'the market will answer all things', including the problem of the control of business. While such a role for the market is advanced here, it is in a different way to that envisaged by the classical and neoclassical economists and their adherents. Their belief in the market's capacity to deal with social issues falls down most notably on two points: in externalities (social costs), and in assuming efficiency and freedom to be more important than equity or altruism as the criteria by which the market's performance should be assessed. On the latter point, it was noted that material progress may have been the most important social goal in the classical economist's day, but its relevance for affluent society is questioned. Moreover, within their argument, there is the assumption of a substantial degree of consumer sovereignty, which may not always exist. Here it is suggested that, by acknowledging the domain of consumer sovereignty dimension and ethical purchase behaviour, the market may assume some responsibility for social issues and the social control of business in affluent society – in a way not envisaged by classical economists.

The third theme concerns the part to be played by pressure groups in this scheme, by politicising the market and having an impact on the firm's legitimacy element in the marketing mix. The shortcomings in consumer sovereignty – at least in its domain – may be remedied by pressure groups. They may function to enhance consumer sovereignty by providing information on grievances of concern to consumers and involving business. Such a role would be in keeping with pluralist models of politics and, in the form of the consumer boycott, may provide promotional pressure groups with a needed and effective tactic. The pressure group role also involves the identification of firms' responsibilities (a problem raised in Chapter 2) and, in a pluralistic fashion, their priorities and the extent of corporate responsibility. Firms may also as a consequence be less concerned about their undesirable externalities, as these social costs may be converted into private costs.

Part Two provides the evidence for the argument in a more detailed examination of consumer boycotts, particularly in case studies produced as a result of empirical work by the author. The evidence for ethical purchase behaviour – and here, in contrast to the studies on socially responsible consumption, direct evidence is offered – lies in an examination of such behaviour expressed in consumer boycotts.

Part two

The use and effects of consumer boycotts

Chapter seven

Consumer boycotts of business

Preview

> The powers of ordinary men are circumscribed by the everyday
> worlds in which they live, yet even in these rounds of job, family
> and neighborhood they often seem driven by forces they can
> neither understand nor govern. 'Great changes' are beyond their
> control, but affect their conduct and outlook none the less. The
> very framework of modern society confines them to projects not
> their own, but from every side, such changes now press upon the
> men and women of the mass society, who accordingly feel that
> they are without purpose in an epoch in which they are without
> power.
>
> C. Wright Mills[1]

> We have the power, nonviolently, just by controlling our appetites,
> to determine the direction of the American economy. If black
> people in thirty cities said simultaneously, 'General Motors, you
> will not sell cars in the black community unless you guarantee us a
> franchise here next year and help us finance it', GM would have no
> choice but to comply.
>
> Jesse Jackson[2]

These two quotations illustrate, in the first instance, the powerlessness
of the masses, and in the second instance, how this powerlessness can be
transformed by organised consumer action. Jackson envisages, and has
on occasion successfully realised, a harnessing of consumer sovereignty
to bring power to disadvantaged and powerless groups. A fundamental
question is thereby posed by the juxtaposition of these quotations: How
can the masses be without power in the mass consumer society, when
consumer sovereignty is a prominent feature and principal rationale for
capitalism? This is a big question indeed. Yet an answer of sorts lies in

the examination of the use and effects of consumer boycotts which now follows and builds on the argument for ethical purchase behaviour presented in Part One.

This chapter continues the examination of the boycott tactic, but focuses specifically on the consumer boycott. Various types of consumer boycott can be identified, depending on the relationship of the seller to the perceived misdemeanour. These are acknowledged in the literature. This is sparse, but it reveals historical precedents for consumer boycotts in other cultures and also in labour struggles, especially over unionisation (as indicated in Chapter 5). Consumer boycotts can be illegal, but as with strikes, the firm is unlikely to take action. The ascendancy of labour has diminished the importance of the consumer boycott in labour struggles in recent times, although it is used in the Third World and was employed (highly successfully) over the recognition of the United Farm Workers in the early 1970s in the United States. More recently, the consumer boycott has been employed over civil rights, the Vietnam War, and by the corporate accountability movement. This latter use, of course, highlights the relevance of the consumer boycott to the issue of the social control of business. Ethical purchase behaviour, in boycotts, has then played a part in the social control of business.

Consumer boycotts of business: a literature review

Historical precedents for consumer boycotts

Vogel writes, 'Allowing political or moral preferences to influence one's purchase of products is not, of course, an idea that was invented in the sixties.' Unwittingly he acknowledges ethical purchase behaviour. The concern here, however, is to stick with consumer boycotts, a specific form of ethical purchase behaviour. This is also Vogel's interest in his examination of the types of pressures on business in citizen challenges to business authority. He continues, 'Consumer boycotts played an important role in the American colonists' prerevolutionary struggle against England and have been used periodically both by and against various economic and ethnic groups throughout American history.'[3] He refers to a tradition of boycotting, citing an article in *New Republic*, where the author comments, 'It has long been fashionable to avoid purchasing products that appear on idiosyncratically homemade blacklists.'[4]

Chapter 5 referred to Laidler and Wolman's studies of consumer boycotts used by the American labour unions in the late nineteenth and early twentieth centuries. Laidler, although writing in 1913, refers to a lengthy past history to boycotts:

Although the word 'boycott' is of comparatively recent origin, the practice of boycotting, if we disassociate that term from any necessary connection with labour disputes, and define it for the time being as *an organised effort to withdraw and induce others to withdraw from social or business relations with another*, has been resorted to since the dawn of history.[5]

He later refers to its use on a large scale in the Revolutionary War against Britain: 'Following the passage of the Stamp Act of March 1765, the Boston, New York, and Philadelphia merchants resolved to cease importing British goods until this obnoxious measure should be repealed. Retail merchants refused to sell British goods, and customers to buy them.' Other examples are referred to such as the boycott following the tax on tea, which culminated in the Boston Tea Party. He suggests these historical precedents provided justification for its use in labour disputes as they 'indicate its thoroughly American character'. He concludes his review of the past history of boycotts by saying that it has been 'a potent weapon for many centuries in the hands of state and church, organisations of the agrarian population and of political rebels, and, in fact, of all strata of the population'.[6]

Wolman, for his part, also refers to boycotting in the Revolutionary War and earlier uses (citing Laidler). One particularly early use was the boycott imposed in 1327 by the citizens of Canterbury, England, on the monks of Christ's church, involving an agreement not to 'buy, sell or exchange drinks or victuals with the monastery'. He also notes the boycotting of slave-made products as practised by abolitionists. So consumer boycotts can hardly be described as a modern phenomenon! Most of Wolman's analysis of the history of the boycott is devoted to its prior use in labour disputes. He suggests that one of the first instances of a boycott on commodities – 'where the appeal was to the workman not as a producer but as a consumer' – was a boycott imposed in 1833 in Baltimore on master hatters who had cut the wages of their journeymen.[7] This may be a more appropriate historical precedent than some of the others mentioned if by consumer boycott one is referring to a practice found in consumer societies, that is, under capitalism as it is currently known. In other words, given the definition in Chapter 5, which refers to the consumer boycott as the exercising of consumer sovereignty, historical precedents for consumer boycotts should perhaps be restricted to those actions found within capitalist society. As noted in Chapter 1, capitalist society, and therefore some degree of consumer sovereignty, is only to be found after the sixteenth century, and is probably most accurately seen as a nineteenth- and twentieth-century phenomenon.

Early examples of boycotts are, however, interesting. If they may not be correctly described as consumer boycotts, they are at least from the same class of action known as boycotts and have much in common. Wolman's section on the history of the boycott refers to many instances of consumer boycotts, and the whole of both Laidler and Wolman's works may be seen as accounts of historical precedents for current boycott actions, given their age. More recent consumer boycotts include those by the Nazi's against the Jews[8] and many more cited by Sharp[9] and those included in Appendix B. But putting aside the definitional issue above, the consumer boycott is not unique to Western society. If anything, it is more appropriate to the East, as earlier found in considering Remer's *Study of Chinese Boycotts*. The boycotts organised by Gandhi (described, for example, by Joan Bondurant and by Sharp) are classic examples of consumer boycotts and obvious historical precedents.

So to conclude, one can then refer to a tradition of boycotting both as a form of ostracism as practised in all societies since 'the dawn of history', and in the specific form of the consumer boycott in societies where there has been some degree of consumer sovereignty. Vogel suggests an increase in the use of the boycott most recently, in the United States at least:

> Over the last fifteen years, such consumer boycotts have become more frequent, better organized, and identified with a much broader range of issues. Scarcely a month now passes without the public being asked to boycott a particular product or company in order to express disagreement with some decision of the private sector. These decisions include bank lending practices in declining neighborhoods, popularly known as 'redlining'; the employment practices of several local and national firms; the marketing of gold coins from South Africa; and the manufacture of various products held to be detrimental to the environment.[10]

Yet despite this claim of a recent increase in boycott activity and the many historical precedents referred to above, the literature on consumer boycotts is sparse.

References to consumer boycotts in the literature

References to consumer boycotts in the literature include many sources already considered: Vogel, Sharp, Wolman, Laidler, and so on. Brief consideration should, however, be given to some other sources not yet mentioned. This will of necessity be brief, if only because of the paucity of literature on this topic. The reasons for this will also be given some attention. This section can most usefully start by speculating as to where one might find literature on consumer boycotts. Despite their apparent prevalence over time and increased use most recently, they are only rarely shown as a topic in abstracts.[11] Most references to consumer boycotts found by this author were the product of scanning the Press and what may best be described as serendipity, for systematic literature searches proved largely ineffective. References to boycotts in the Press, including the more obscure publications such as *Peace News* and *New Internationalist*, are mainly about specific instances of boycott action. This source produced by far the most references to boycotts, but as they are about incidents rather than methods or explanations, they are considered separately in Appendix B.

One might expect that the pressure group literature would prove a useful source of references on boycotts and offer some analysis in itself. This was not the case. Excluding publications by or for pressure groups such as those referred to above, the pressure group literature offered little analysis of boycotts as a pressure group tactic and few specific references.[12] This comment is also true of the business and society literature. Vogel's works are on occasion cited and it is fair to say that his *Lobbying the Corporation* is a fairly comprehensive catalogue of boycotts in the United States since the 1950s. However, his concern is not with the boycott as a tactic, how it may be employed, and how management should respond, but as a signal and symptom of citizen discontent with business authority. He does provide some useful references however. Business and society texts mention boycotts in passing in a similar way. They are of course almost entirely American,[13] and yet despite this and Vogel's comment at the end of the last section on the prevalence of consumer boycotts, even the most recent editions have little to say about boycotts. One of the better texts in this respect is *Social Issues in Business* by Luthans, Hodgetts, and Thompson. They refer to the Polaroid case (see Appendix B) by way of example. Other texts which are entirely or largely case studies also include boycott examples, such as Hay *et al.*[14]

Luthans *et al.*'s comments on the boycott tactic, though brief, are worth mentioning here. They include 'product or service boycotts' under the general heading of individual social activism, giving little acknowledgement to the role of pressure groups. They do at least recognise that the boycott has been 'successfully applied to a multitude of products', referring to Cesar Chavez organised boycotts of celery, grapes, and grapefruit to improve conditions for migrant workers in California; boycotts of firms doing business in South Africa, though acknowledging that they have not changed apartheid policies; union organised boycotts of companies such as J. P. Stevens, Farah, and Coors because of their anti-union stance; and late 1970s boycotts of sugar, coffee, and meats that led to a reduction in prices. They suggest in their fourth edition: 'The key to a boycott is to have enough consumer support to reduce demand.'[15] But it is far more complex than this.

The consumerism literature, which may be seen as in a category by itself or as a part of business and society, also mentions boycotts. Nadel, for example, refers to the American consumer boycotts over food price increases.[16] Consumer boycotts are, as in Vogel, cited largely in illustration of consumer grievances. Some, however, advocate boycotts as a solution to some of the issues raised by consumerism. This study has been defined as being outside consumerism, as ethical purchase behaviour is not intended to redress the grievances of the buyer but of some other party. However, not all writers on consumerism take this approach and the arguments advocating consumer boycotts over consumerist issues such as product defects are equally applicable to issues further removed from the product, such as investment in South Africa. Stern, for example, explores the possibilities for consumer protection via self-regulation by business. He argues that this is insufficient and that some enforcement power is necessary. One measure suggested is to 'permit collective action among firms to boycott any firm whose products conform to neither the industry standards nor the labeling requirement' (for providing sufficient information for consumer choice), which would be illegal under American law. In this way, he sees the tripod of government action, the activities of consumer advocates, and business self-regulation made more balanced by the latter being more effective.[17]

Boycotts are also advocated by Box, in a paper questioning whether consumerism has any future in an environment characterised by deregulation. This Dutch writer suggests that 'consumer organisations – as they are doing already sometimes – might exert pressure on certain firms selectively, and keep them under pressure in order to come to a solution for certain problems'. It is recognised, as noted earlier, that consumers are not an organised group to the same extent as the unions say, which makes boycotts more difficult to institute. The overall line of Box's argument though is that consumerism has a future with consumer pressure groups trying to influence the market rather than seeking legal remedies: 'consumer organisations could take stronger action as a market party, that is to say as an organisation of consumers in direct contact and negotiating with their natural opponent, trade and industry.'[18] This, of course, is analogous to the suggestion that the market could play a greater part in ensuring the social control of business.

In *The Consumer Interest*, George Smith reviews the state of consumerism in Britain and in Europe. Referring to boycotts, he suggests they could be used more often and with greater effect. Indeed, he sees the choice for European consumer groups as being between using boycotts and government influence to achieve their aims. He refers to a number of highly successful European boycotts to make his point. Some of these are worth mentioning here (although they are included in Appendix B), in particular, the boycotts organised by the French equivalent to the British Consumers' Association (CA), the Union Fédérale de la Consommation (UFC), and those by the Swiss Federation Romande des Consommateurs. The 'dramatic results' achieved by boycotts organised by these two organisations contrasts with the sluggish progress in implementing the Common Market's consumer programme and the failure of the consultation machinery to improve matters. A UFC organised 1976 boycott of food with colourants caused colourant-free alternatives to be introduced; a boycott of red wines contaminated with asbestos fibres from filtration processes prompted four companies to sue the UFC for £400,000, but they lost their case and were forced to promise not to use asbestos in future; and while Shell was more successful when its legal action forced the UFC to desist from calling for a boycott of its products following the Amoco Cadiz disaster, this was not until after suffering a sales cut of 10 per cent. This latter example is particularly interesting because it is closer to ethical purchase behaviour than those examples where the boycott is over some issue directly affecting the consumer in the consumption of the product. This also applies to the call for a boycott on aerosols (because they are hazardous, damaging to the environment, and wasteful), which resulted in a 10 per cent reduction in sales in France when they were rising elsewhere. More typical of the consumerist type of consumer boycott was the boycott of one brand of a company's tyres because they were four times more liable to blow-outs, and the 1980 boycott of veal in protest at the continued illegal use of hormones in fattening calves, which caused sales to fall by 50 per cent within seven days and reduced the price of the fattened calf in Britain from £75 to £26 in a week. The outcome was the promise by the EEC Council of Ministers of a complete ban on the use of hormones by the end of 1980.

The Swiss Federation's 1967 boycott of butter over successive government-sanctioned price increases proved so successful that the price of butter four years later remained lower than in 1967. Its 1977 boycott of food products not listing ingredients persuaded more food manufacturers to list ingredients and speed up legislation. Smith notes, however, that its 'boycotts of inflation (1971), polyphosphates in cooked meats (1972) and high-priced meat (1975) have been less successful'.[19] So, even if different boycotts are not being organised every month, as Vogel suggests is the case in the United States, they are not uncommon in Europe. But how true is this of Britain?

Smith writes that the Friends of the Earth campaign against non-returnable bottles in the early 1970s 'was the nearest UK consumer and allied organisations have come to organising an outright consumer boycott'.[20] If the possible nuances of meaning implied by the word outright are ignored, Smith is plainly wrong, or at least using the term consumer boycott in a way different to its use here. There has been a UK consumer boycott of South African products since 1960 and the many calls for boycotts and boycotts organised that were noted when scanning the Press, referred to in Appendix B, cannot be particular to the two year period surveyed. However, it must be acknowledged that boycotts do seem less common in Britain than in the United States, a point which will be considered further.

Smith writes that 'Although Ralph Nader established "consumption" as a household word, he widened the definition of consumer until it was synonymous with "citizen". He is a moral crusader for the restoration of the participatory democracy ... in which power, whether in business or government, is decentralised, controlled and accountable.'[21] Ralph Nader is also referred to in a comparison between the approach of the Consumers' Association and that of Nader's groups. Smith sees little to commend the CA, noting that it has 'settled for a relatively quiet life on the campaigning side' and 'eschewed the aggressive tactics of Ralph Nader and some of their own counterparts in Europe'. Perhaps in this context Smith's observation on boycotts in Britain can be understood – as a reference to the failure of the CA to employ boycotts. He concludes: 'The CA is now as much a part of the conformist British scene as the House of Lords, tea and the test match.'[22] Yet pressure groups are in this country increasingly turning to direct action, as earlier acknowledged, and the likelihood would seem to be that the use of the boycott will increase. It was even recently suggested in the House of Commons as a means for securing compensation for British children from the Merrell drug company, manufacturers of Debendox.[23]

Robin Wight's *The Day the Pigs Refused to be Driven to Market* is a journalistic but insightful account of some of the features of consumerism in the late 1960s and early 1970s. Indeed, a number of his theories are developed here: social responsibility as a consequence of consumer sovereignty, boycotts as an expression of consumer sovereignty, and political participation through democracy in the market-place; though he does not express them in this way. Wight too is critical of the Consumers' Association: 'its sedate middle-class activity seems really rather out of touch.'[24] He finds, in contrast, much to commend the Japanese consumer group, Shufuren, particularly because of its use of national boycotts which have 'assailed everyone from rice growers charging excessive prices to canned food manufacturers whose labels conceal the truth'.[25] In keeping with the other consumerist sources listed above, his concern is to describe boycott incidents (suggesting, like Vogel, that they are symptomatic of consumer dissatisfaction) and implicitly advocates the use of the boycott. Some of his arguments are interesting, but as part of the boycott literature, he offers little by way of explanation of methods or analysis.

Interesting, but perhaps not surprising, is the acknowledgement of a place for boycotts by the Austrian economist Mises, an acknowledgement Wight might well endorse. This is interesting because it conflicts with Mises's emphasis on self-interest as the essential driving force for the efficient operation of the market. However, it is not surprising given his claims about the supremacy of the consumer and the freedom of the consumer to choose in a free market economy. So he writes, 'The consumers are free to boycott a purveyor provided they are ready to pay the costs.'[26]

Another equally interesting contribution from economics on boycotts is a paper by Rea.[27] He asks: Under what circumstances might a group of consumers benefit from a boycott? In his analysis the distinction is made between what he terms an economic boycott, where 'the objective is to lower the price paid for a product', and a political boycott where 'the objective is to punish the producers or to force the producers into taking some action'. Rea shows that in an economic boycott all consumers, those boycotting and those not boycotting, can benefit. The magnitude of the benefits depends on the elasticities of supply and demand, the length of the boycott, and the number of boycotters. His argument rests on seeing the boycotters as having formed a buying cartel, so they can act like a monopsonist and increase their utility. He does recognise that overall there is a net loss, with a net cost on society as a whole in the loss of consumer surplus by boycotters, the loss that occurs because non-boycotters are consuming goods which have a lower value to them than the original equilibrium price, and a loss of producers' surplus resulting from the transfer of resources to less productive uses. In other words, there are costs to society because the boycotters consume too little, the non-boycotters consume too much, and there are not enough resources devoted to the industry. Additionally, and this may be a further cost though Rea does not see it as such, there is likely to be an increase in the consumption of substitutes for the boycotted good. Their price will therefore rise, with a further loss of consumer surplus. (Rea assumes substitutes have a perfectly elastic supply.) Rea notes that social pressure on consumers, to enforce the cartel, is crucial to boycott effectiveness. He suggests, in keeping with observations made in Chapter 1 in reference to economics and the real world, that 'The economist is likely to ignore the social pressure that enforces the boycott.'

While Rea's economic analysis is restricted to what he terms the economic boycott, he does consider the implications for the political boycott. The economic effects of a political boycott – Rea suggests an example of which would be a boycott in support of a strike or a boycott of the products of a country whose policies are found disagreeable – would be the same as in the economic boycott. However, in the political boycott the boycotters do not consume any of the boycotted good and the benefits of the lower price go to those not boycotting. Hence there is a greater loss of consumer surplus by the boycotters, only compensated for if the boycott is successful – it alters the policy of the firm, industry, or country being boycotted. Rea concludes that 'a boycott is not folly for a group of consumers, but as is true of most political activities, the fact that the benefits are a public good makes it folly from an individual's narrow point of view'. (This, of course, is similar to the argument previously advanced – about altruism – in rejection of Olson's claim about the absence of suitable incentives in some pressure groups.) Rea also identifies factors in boycott effectiveness, considered later.

Occasional references to boycotts are made in *New Society*, while the *New Republic* article referred to above, which identifies a number of contemporary boycotts, also comes from a publication of that ilk. No doubt other similar publications carry the odd article on boycotts, but they cannot be easily traced and do not, in any case, offer much more than a description of boycott incidents. More useful is the article by Krieger in the *Journal of Peace Research*.[28] This sort of publication, generally seen as outside mainstream academic publishing and ignored by abstracting services (though sometimes containing quite reasonable work), may be a useful source of further articles on boycotts but it is difficult to say with any certainty because of the problems in tracing these publications. Krieger describes the failure of the Another Mother for Peace (AMP) consumer campaign and offers some sound analysis. The AMP campaign was a threatened consumer boycott of the consumer products of manufacturers of war products. His analysis is also considered later. The Krieger article was found via the pressure group literature, and it was cited by Berry.[29] As noted above, the pressure group literature offered few references on boycotts. This was also the case with the two sources (other than Laidler and Wolman) which examine boycotts in any detail, Vogel and Sharp. Vogel, in his bibliographical note, observes that 'there has been no comprehensive scholarly treatment of direct political challenges to the corporation',[30] which is further support for the claim here about the paucity of literature on consumer boycotts. He goes on to note that his study had to rely considerably on information from activist organisations, and newspapers and magazines. Sharp proved useful in identifying references on international economic sanctions, but not consumer boycotts. It seems reasonable to conclude that the literature on consumer boycotts is extremely limited. The next section considers types of consumer boycotts. This is based largely on the categorisation used by Wolman and Laidler seventy years ago. As they are extensively cited by Sharp, their analysis seems not only to have withstood the passage of time but also not to have been supplanted by any more recent or superior analyses.

Types of consumer boycott and boycott legality

The classification of consumer boycotts is based on the relationship of the seller to the perceived misdemeanour. As earlier discussed, Sharp's categories of economic boycotts cannot be used in whole or in part. But the terms used here by Laidler and Wolman can. The principal concern is with the distinction between primary and secondary boycotts, and direct and indirect boycotts. Boycott legality is considered here because legality hinges on these distinctions. The discussion of the Arab boycott in Chapter 5 showed that the distinction between primary and secondary boycotts as used by Wolman still holds. Nelson and Prittie write:

> The first – or 'primary' – boycott consists of the refusal by the
> Arabs to trade with Israel in any way ... The 'secondary' boycott is
> aimed at companies that invest in or do business with Israel ...
> Even more insidious is the 'tertiary' boycott, which also operates in
> 'third countries' and which can threaten firms trading with anyone
> who does business with Israel – even with companies that have
> 'Zionists' (read 'Jews') on their boards or in executive positions.[31]

Examples then follow which illustrate these distinctions. The terms primary and secondary boycott are quite widely used (in the limited literature available). Tertiary boycott is more rare, probably, as the latter quotation indicates, because in application the term is more complex and potentially confusing: Is a boycott of a firm which does business with a firm with 'Zionists' on its board a third level boycott as claimed, or a fourth level boycott? Again, when a firm is boycotted for dealing in a 'third country' with another firm which does business with Israel, is this not a higher level boycott than where the deal does not take place in a 'third country'? And what if the firms involved are remote, or less remote, subsidiaries? There can be no hard and fast rules on determining the level of the boycott beyond the tertiary boycott or third level, and even this can be uncertain. It is perhaps better to go with Wolman's analysis and distinguish only between primary and higher level boycotts, which, as in practice, may be uniformly described as secondary boycotts.

So, in consumer boycotts, a primary boycott would be of the firm causing offence – involved in South Africa, manufacturing napalm, or whatever, while a secondary boycott would be of firms dealing with this firm – typically, this would be a retail outlet or a supplier. To some extent the discussion of higher level boycotts is irrelevant to consumer boycotts, because the firm identified at higher levels is too far removed from the misdemeanour to be a legitimate target and therefore in practice such boycotts are rare anyway. This is less true of boycotts in labour struggles, where firms are more readily 'perceived as being 'tainted'. In the California grape boycott, for example, not only were potential customers discouraged from buying Californian grapes, in support of the unionisation of farm workers, but also from shopping at stores selling this product:

> In each of the five boroughs, we organised neighborhood coalitions of church, labor, liberal and student groups. Then we began picketing A. & P. , the biggest chain in the city. For several months we had picket lines on about 25 to 30 stores and turned thousands of shoppers away ...[32]

This illustrates the primary and secondary boycott. It also indicates how secondary boycotts may be organised but remain legal. For the organisers to have called for a boycott of A. & P. would have been illegal. However, a *de facto* secondary boycott may be established simply by picketing the establishment and advancing the case for the primary boycott. By association (of the primary boycott with the picketed establishment) and/or intimidation, customers of the store are discouraged.[33] (The California grape boycott is included as a case study in Chapter 8.) However, boycott legality is not straightforward. Limited experience of boycotts in Britain means there is very little to go on, although as the MAN-VW case shows in Chapter 8, legal counsel can advise on when boycotts are illegal. In the United States, although there is more experience of boycotts, there is still uncertainty as to the legal position. This is due at least in part to the reluctance of companies to take legal action in fear of exacerbating the situation.

Labour use of the consumer boycott is now limited compared with its extensive use in Laidler and Wolman's day. This is attributed to the achievement of unionisation and the possibility therefore of effective strike action – making the boycott largely redundant. However, it is, accordingly, not surprising to find that the consumer boycott is quite widely used in labour disputes in the Third World. Yet despite this diminished use of the consumer boycott in labour disputes in the West, the literature on the legal aspects of industrial conflicts does have something to offer on boycott legality. Generally speaking, primary boycotts are legal, whereas secondary boycotts are not. As Aaron writes:

> In the United States the boycott, which has been an important union weapon since the days of the Knights of Labor, has been

accorded a wide variety of treatment by legislatures and the courts. At Common Law, state and Federal courts applied the terms 'primary' and 'secondary' to boycotts. These two adjectives did not really describe the nature of the boycott, but were merely shorthand terms for legal conclusions: 'primary' boycotts were lawful, 'secondary' boycotts were not.[34]

The suggestion that the terms primary and secondary are not accurately descriptive is misleading; however Aaron does go on to explain that, as concluded above, the term secondary tends to incorporate all higher level boycotts: 'The chief objection to the word "secondary" was and is that it lumps indiscriminately into one category both employers who are truly "strangers" to the dispute, or wholly neutral, and those who have a community of interest with the struck employer and who may, in fact, be his "allies".' Caution must be exercised here in applying Aaron's interpretation of the legal position. For unlike Wolman (to whom Aaron makes reference), the distinction is not clearly made between boycotts on materials, more usually referred to today as blacking, and the consumer boycott; though it is probably safe to assume that the legal position is the same in each case. It seems that the law seeks to protect neutral third parties, though there may be some debate as to their actual neutrality. In the California grape boycott both the materials boycott and the consumer boycott were employed with great success: 'A long and bitter dispute between the Farm Workers Union and California grape growers was recently won by the union, largely as a result of the efficacy of its efforts to persuade both distributors and consumers not to handle or eat "non-union" grapes.'[35]

Referring to the legality of the boycott outside the United States, Aaron notes that 'Britain has no legislation outlawing boycotts as such.' However, in recent years,

conduct that would be called a 'secondary' boycott in the United States has been declared unlawful by the British courts on several different grounds: that no trade dispute existed; that the conduct constituted a 'direct' inducement to breach a contract to the detriment of a third party; or that the conduct constituted an 'indirect' inducement by 'illegal means', namely the breach of individual contracts of employment outside the context of a labor dispute.

He suggests that the boycott is frequently used in Sweden, but hardly at all in France, not at all in Italy, and that in Germany boycotts of goods have practically disappeared because of the impossibility of boycotting goods of an enterprise which does not produce an end product.[36] These observations should be seen as applying only to the use of the boycott in labour disputes.

211

Of course, outside labour disputes, the consumer boycott would be immune to labour relations legislation. Yet the general rule that primary boycotts are legal, secondary boycotts are not, still seems to apply – and again, it seems, on the basis that is unfair to involve neutral parties. In the United States, the Sherman anti-trust legislation could be employed, as in the Arab boycott (which is also supplemented by specific legislation intended to prevent compliance with the boycott). This legislation might, however, mean that any attempt by a pressure group to call a boycott (where, unlike a union there is no contractual arrangement) would be illegal – primary or secondary. This could well be the case in Britain too, as such a call might be construed as being in restraint of trade.[37]

A 1984 paper by Harper[38] and another fairly recent paper by Harris[39] suggest that the law, in the United States at least, is prepared to acknowledge a consumer right to boycott. Harris writes: 'Recognising that organised boycotts can bring about significant changes in governmental policies, business practices and product pricing, consumers today are placing even greater reliance on this economic weapon. Despite the widespread incidence of consumer boycotts, however, only a few federal courts have decided whether consumers' concerted refusals to buy particular items or services violate the Sherman Act.' Her lengthy paper examines the Sherman Act, the First Amendment and consumer boycotts, and case law. She concludes that, in the event of a court seeking to apply the Sherman Act, it would be unlikely to find a consumer boycott to be a violation. The same conclusion is reached in exploring how a consumer boycott might fare under traditional anti-trust analysis. Political, social, and economic boycotts are three types of consumer boycott identified by Harris. But her categorisation, although on the face of it sound, does not stand up to closer examination. The social and political categories are not distinct. Many consumer boycotts have social and political aims as she defines them. Even her so-called economic boycotts might be described as social or political. Yet a bigger criticism would be that of not having identified the distinction between primary and secondary boycotts. It is uncertain as to whether her conclusions on legality are applicable to both. However, this article is a useful contribution to the limited literature on boycotts. It is valuable simply in its identification of boycott actions.

Harper concludes that the consumer right to boycott 'is a right consistent with the best democratic promises of our society'. His paper, also quite lengthy, is particularly worthy of consideration here; not only because it adds some clarity to the issue of boycott legality (in the United States at least) but also because his argument has a number of similarities to that advanced in earlier chapters in justification of ethical purchase behaviour and boycotts. He finds that consumer boycotts are appropriate to market society:

> One justification for such a right comes from micro-economic welfare theory: consumers' full sovereignty over their decisions will help create the particular mix of production and consumption that maximises welfare for a given distribution of wealth and income. One of this theory's fundamental assumptions is that consumers' reasons for preferring a product should be valued equally. Thus, the reason for a consumer's decision not to purchase, whether a distaste for the social or political practices of the producer or an inferior product, should be irrelevant.

He cites Pigou, Pareto, Bator, and Marshall in approbation. This argument about boycotts as an expression of consumer sovereignty and therefore particularly apt in capitalist systems has been asserted throughout the previous chapters.

Harper writes that prior to the Supreme Court's decision in NAACP vs. Claiborne Hardware Co. in 1981, 'the Court had indicated that legislatures, for rational economic policy reasons, could make peaceful consumer boycotts illegal'. However, in this case, 'the Court asserted a new consumer right to engage in concerted refusals to patronize even if such refusals are economically disruptive'. Although this assertion, while necessary to the Court's decision, 'did not rest squarely on any First Amendment or other precedent', Harper shows that 'a consumer right to boycott is nonetheless appropriate for our society, a right in accord with our social and constitutional values', and that this right 'should be cast as a broad political right to influence social decision-making'. So given the Claiborne decision and Harper's analysis, there does appear to be an emerging consumer right to boycott. The justification for such a right – in viewing the boycott as political action – seems appropriate to Britain as well as the United States. It is probable that, given the higher incidence of boycotts in the United States, the right to boycott will become recognised in law there fairly shortly. That is less likely here. However, it is worth noting that many companies might well choose not to seek legal redress in any case. The publicity surrounding an attempt to obtain an injunction against boycott organisers, and perhaps damages, would likely harm the company more than other options. Should the consumer's right to boycott be denied, there is always the remedy of the indirect rather than the direct boycott. This form is exemplified by the use of the union label, where consumers choose goods produced by union labour in preference to non-union labour and are able to do so because they find the union label on those goods.

The corporate accountability movement and boycotts

In establishing the right to boycott, Harper acknowledges the social impact of business. He writes:

> boycotts as protected political acts should not be limited to those aimed at governmental decision making. Even boycotts aimed solely at private decision making should share the status of other political acts such as electoral voting, contributing money and time to an election or referendum campaign, and litigating for social purposes. All of these political actions can be viewed broadly as means by which citizens can influence important social decision making.[40]

He goes on to note that 'casting the right to engage in concerted refusals to patronize as a right to attempt to affect social decisions clearly accords with the ends the Supreme Court has advanced in securing First Amendment rights'; and that 'many important decisions in our society are made through private economic decisions'. This, of course, has been argued earlier in Chapter 2. It is also the argument of the corporate accountability movement. This movement seeks to make corporations more accountable for the social impacts of their decisions. Harper obviously views the consumer boycott as an appropriate tactic for their efforts.

Lobbying the Corporation – 'the first to document thoroughly the origins and development of the movement'[41] – is a comprehensive account of its aims, actions, and achievements and probably still the best source. The term 'corporate accountability movement' is used by Vogel to describe a collection of pressure groups seeking to increase corporate accountability. Perhaps the most important feature of their efforts is that they are trying to achieve their aims through private mechanisms, acting directly on the corporation rather than through government. Hence the subtitle to Vogel's book: *Citizen Challenges to Business Authority*. This, Vogel suggests, is a new form of political expression, a form which he has participated in and which he favours: 'Debate over the social and moral implications of corporate decisions is too important to be confined to the governmental process; it needs to be conducted in as many forums as possible.'[42] Yet despite this professed bias, his work is balanced. He is prepared to acknowledge that the achievements of the movement are limited and that firms have to act within the constraint of long term profitability.

The private mechanisms employed by the movement are consumer boycotts and activist shareholder actions (where concerned groups and individuals buy shares in a business and use their votes at Annual General Meetings and other rights to press for changes), coupled with efforts to increase corporate disclosure. *Lobbying the Corporation* is in three parts. First, Vogel considers the politicising of the corporation as expressed in the works of Latham, Berle and Means, Dahl, and others (mentioned in earlier chapters), interpreting the corporate accountability movement as an attempt to realise in practice what they argue in theory: 'that corporations wield the power of governments and should, therefore, be treated like governments.'[43] Second, and this is the largest part, is his case study and historical analysis. Here he looks at civil rights and anti-war protests, the resurgence of shareholder participation in activist shareholder actions, efforts to increase corporate disclosure to inform shareholders and the public in general, and protest at corporate conduct abroad – in South Africa, the marketing of baby milk to the Third World, and compliance with the Arab boycott. Finally, Vogel concludes with an assessment of the movement's efforts and achievements.

Vogel traces the origins of the corporate accountability movement back to the civil rights protests of the mid-1950s. 'Both of the two critical events that sparked the civil rights struggle involved the efforts of black citizens to pressure business – one public and one privately owned – to end their policy of providing separate facilities for black and white consumers.'[44] The black boycott of Montgomery City Line lasted a year and cost the bus company more than $7,000 a day in lost revenue. The outcome, apart from the near bankruptcy of the bus company, was an end to bus segregation in Montgomery and other southern cities. The protest also marked the national debut of the civil rights movement's most influential national leader, the Reverend Martin Luther King, Jr. When a nationwide boycott of Woolworths and Kress followed their refusal to desegregate lunch counters, this too resulted in a significant loss of turnover and contributed to desegregation; while a consumer boycott of A. & P. stores under Operation Breadbasket, protesting at A. & P.'s black employment record, led to an agreement met by the company on black employment. However, as Vogel notes, in these and other civil rights protests involving business, there was not the anti-business flavour and demands for corporate accountability that characterised the later protests against the Vietnam War: 'business policies were not alleged to be the cause of racial inequalities, only an example of them ... it was the practices rather than the principles of corporate conduct that were at issue.'[45]

The anti-war protests involved a different and more critical perception of business, such that 'corporations were as responsible for the direction of US foreign policy as was the US government – indeed, perhaps more so'.[46] Recognising that while only the government could end the war, it required the cooperation of American business to continue it, anti-war protesters demanded that corporations publicly refuse to supply military material to the Defense Department while their nation was at war. Two particularly prominent targets were Dow Chemical, who manufactured napalm, and Honeywell, who manufactured anti-personnel weapons – both particularly objectionable products 'whose use personified the immoral conduct and continuation of the war itself'.[47] Boycotts and activist shareholder actions were employed against these companies and others. Companies involved in the war were forced to take a stand on the morality of their actions. The executives of Honeywell were even accused of war crimes, on the basis of the principles applied at Nuremberg. At the 1973 Honeywell AGM, Binger, Honeywell's Chairman, was asked: 'Would the company accept a contract to build gas ovens for extermination?'[48] A question he could not answer, but which illustrates the issue of corporate social responsibility in a dramatic and profound way.

Vogel then turns to the attempts by the Project on Corporate Responsibility to make General Motors more accountable for its actions: 'If blacks could get the vote in the south, why shouldn't the constituencies of General Motors also be enfranchised?'[49] Here, then, and in other similar campaigns, the focus is on corporations as private governments. The earlier civil rights and anti-war protests involved pressure groups trying to utilise – as suggested in Chapter 4 – the position of business, ultimately to put pressure on government. These later actions, mostly between 1967 and 1977, were concerned solely with changing corporate practices and policies. The tactic employed in Campaign GM was activist shareholder action through public interest proxy resolutions. This drew attention to the questionable legitimacy of GM's actions, but the main impact was in re-establishing the role of the shareholder, reasserting 'the prerogatives of ownership'. In this campaign and all the other public interest proxy resolutions Vogel considers, the pressure groups were unsuccessful in getting their resolution adopted; they were insufficiently supported. They did, however, get some response from corporations in a number of cases and considerably increased awareness of the issues.

Seen together, these protests and the others documented by Vogel constitute a movement for corporate accountability, an attempt to restore social control of business given the corporation's 'substantial immunity from the constraints of both the market and the state'.[50] In many of these protests the consumer boycott tactic was used. Consumers asserted their sovereignty and used the market to express their dissatisfaction with some perceived failing of a business – its black employment record, investments in South Africa, compliance with the Arab boycott, or whatever. Consumers in the market-place were demanding socially responsible behaviour from the businesses boycotted. Yet it has to be conceded that the achievements of the corporate accountability movement were limited, even though their demands were modest: 'it has not succeeded in becoming a popular political movement capable of mobilizing the populace against the abuse of corporate power';[51] if only because 'corporate accountability *per se* is too abstract an issue to capture the public's imagination'.[52] Its greatest achievement was in increasing public awareness of the issues and thereby indirectly influencing corporate behaviour.

Of particular importance here is the recognition given to the boycott tactic, especially as it was employed in the social control of business. Recalling the distinction made between success and effectiveness, it is found that Vogel's documentation of citizen protests against corporations includes a number of effective and successful boycotts. However, Vogel comments on the boycott:

> With the exception of the early civil rights protests, virtually the only consumer boycotts that have apparently received widespread public support – and thus measurably affected company profits – have taken place as a supplement to union organising drives. The successes of the United Farm Workers in organising farm workers in Florida and California were largely made possible by one of the most extensive, well-organised, and lengthiest consumer boycotts in American history. A similar and equally successful nationwide consumer boycott was instrumental in forcing Farah Manufacturing Company to recognise the Amalgamated Clothing Workers Union.[53]

Unfortunately he does not make the distinction between effectiveness and success. As Appendix B shows, a number of boycotts described by Vogel proved successful in realising the objectives of the pressure group, without having mass support and being effective in terms of influencing corporate profits. Boycotts can be successful without being effective.

Greater effectiveness and possibly, therefore, greater likelihood of success is dependent upon pressure group support and capabilities, it would seem; which is why, unlike Vogel and partly in response to his study, an examination of the role of pressure groups was considered essential here. Vogel's *Lobbying the Corporation* and the corporate accountability movement provide examples of the use of the boycott as a mechanism for the social control of business. More use of boycotts in this way and increased accountability thereby would seem to depend on whether pressure groups continue to grow in number and influence. However, the corporate accountability movement achieved some measure of success with the consumer boycott, and their boycotts and those over civil rights and the Vietnam war are prime examples of ethical purchase behaviour.

The mechanism of the boycott

Although the literature on the use of the boycott is sparse, it is possible to make some observations on the effective use of this tactic. Wolman and Laidler's studies of the boycott as used by early American trade unions are particularly useful in this respect, despite their age. Wolman suggests that there are 'a few general, if obvious, principles in the theory and practice of the boycott'.[54] However, in practice, adhering to these principles could be difficult. Union control was weak and inadequate because in contrast to their roles as workers, the members of a union in their capacity as consumers were difficult to reach. Consequently enforcing boycotts was by persuasive rather than coercive measures. Appealing for support rather than insisting on it was the order of the day. For promotional pressure groups this would be even more likely as they do not have anything approaching the discipline commanded by unions or the possibility of resorting to powerful sanctions. Hence while there are certain principles for the effective use of the boycott, they do have to be tempered by the realisation that support and submission to control may be largely voluntary. As a consequence, Wolman suggests that the decision to boycott was made by judging each case on its merits. The use of the boycott became in this sense *ad hoc*. Once the decision to boycott had been made, each boycott generally followed a similar pattern.

Prior to any decision to boycott would be the threat of boycott. This is important. The union would claim that any boycott would have extensive support from that union, associated unions, and other 'friends of labor'. But, if only because such support could not be guaranteed (although, of course, the employer might also realise this), it was important only to threaten the boycott first. With the impending boycott, the union could obtain important concessions. As Wolman writes: 'the effectiveness of the boycott consists in its potential rather than in its actual accomplishments. The threat is often more effective than the fact.'[55] As a high frequency of boycotts reduces their effectiveness, there is a further incentive for emphasising the threat of boycott.

The first stage in the boycott process is therefore efforts at peaceful adjustment. Should these then fail, the next stage is the inauguration and endorsement of the boycott by the union. The boycott can then be launched, announcing the boycott to the purchasing public. Obviously notice of the boycott must be effective: 'Inasmuch as the success or the failure of this device depends upon the extent to which it can earn the sympathy of consumers, the importance of an effective boycott notice cannot be overestimated.'[56] The union then attempts to enlist as much support as possible, building the boycott until its demands are met. Finally, on agreement and the ending of the boycott, the union may, in the case of a heavily supported action, extensively publicise the termination of the boycott. There is good reason for this, though not acknowledged by Wolman: the effect of the boycott on the jobs of the employees if the boycott is not ended. The long term impact of boycotts surely makes them less attractive than strike action because of this. On the basis of Wolman's study, a five-stage process can be identified:

(1) Attempts at peaceful adjustment.
(2) Inauguration and endorsement of the boycott.
(3) Effective notice of the boycott.
(4) Enlist support.
(5) Conclude boycott when agreement reached and publicise settlement.

The inauguration and endorsement of the boycott is particularly appropriate to union actions because of the importance of procedure. However, this would also apply to a promotional pressure group that is responsible to a larger group, or where the group was part of an umbrella organisation which might provide funding and support but would therefore require consultation. In any group attempting this sort of action, there is at least the requirement for planning the organisation of the boycott, which would be either at this stage or before the threat of boycott action had been made. An important method for providing effective notice of boycotts at this time was the 'We don't Patronise' and 'unfair' lists published in American labour journals. There were drawbacks to this method, however. The problem of control referred to earlier applied not only to individual workers but also to unions within federations. Lists were published monthly in the *American Federationist*, the journal of the American Federation of Labor (AFL), and in the journals of national unions. Yet the AFL list alone has contained more than 125 firms. This in itself is too long, before any consideration is given to other lists. Too many boycotts at any one time dilutes their effect and too many boycotts *per se* reduces their impact. The undue frequency of boycotts made the procedures of the previous stage vital. These procedures attempted to minimise the number of boycotts at any one time and in total. The centralisation of authority to boycott was also important to contain the incidence of boycotts so that it did not unduly affect workers not in dispute. It was found that while workers might be in dispute in one locality, their counterparts in the same firm elsewhere were satisfied, which made a nationwide boycott of the firm unreasonable from their point of view. It was also found that boycotts might be called by one union in dispute with a firm when its members constituted a minority of the employees, the rest of whom were not in dispute. Again, a boycott would seem unreasonable.

219

'Unfair' lists were a way of the union providing notice and retaining some control. But notice of the boycott was also given in other ways. Word of mouth communication, public addresses, and discussion were important, also notices in union offices, letters, circulars, parades, and processions. During the boycott on a restaurant in San Francisco, a man was engaged to walk up and down outside the restaurant bearing a sandwich board advertising the boycott.[57] The 1908 court decisions on boycotts meant that they had to be secret. It was found necessary to discontinue publication of 'unfair' lists. But Wolman notes that this did not mean the cessation of all public notices of boycott:

> in February 1910, the journals of the Metal Polishers, which after the Bucks Stove Company injunctions had stopped printing the unfair list, substituted a list of firms under the following caption: 'Where our members have been or are now on strike and no adjustments have been made.' The list contained the names of eight firms, one of which was the Bucks Stove and Range Company.[58]

Companies would also produce booklets outlining their grievances. But Laidler has doubts about this approach: 'As a feeble substitute at the present time, the labor periodicals now often call attention to and recite the facts of union struggle, leaving it to organised labor to "do the right thing".'[59] Despite these doubts held by Laidler, boycotting continued, and 'an official of the American Federation of Labor admitted in 1913 that the boycotting activity of American trade unions was just as great at that time as during the publication of unfair lists'.[60]

An alternative to the 'unfair' list which was safe from litigation was the 'fair' list and, hence, the indirect or negative boycott. This not only overcame legal objections but dealt with the problem of counter-boycotts, where those opposed to labour organisation 'threw their custom to offset whatever might be lost through the observance of the boycott'.[61] It also meant avoiding the requirement to find a substitute commodity and involved less hostility. The institution of indirect boycotts through the union label however was a more satisfactory method. 'Fair' lists could show only passive supporters, those with whom the union did not currently have a grievance; there were entire industries without organised labour for which no or few recommendations could be made; to avoid offence the list would have to be as exhaustive as possible and therefore inevitably long and unwieldy; finally, there were problems in defining a fair firm.[62]

Once notice of the boycott had been given, attempts were made to enlist the support of the customers of the firm. This involved district organisers of the AFL, special agents of national unions, boycott committees of the central labour bodies, and the boycott committees of the local unions. The special agents would visit customers of the boycotted concern – perhaps retail outlets – and persuade them to put pressure on the firm to yield to the union demands, or to stop buying from the firm. However, they only stayed in a town for a short while, as their task was to organise the boycott over a wide area, while others dealt with details, notably the boycott committees. District organisers furthered boycotts in conjunction with their main and principal duties as union organisers. The methods used to announce the boycott would continue to be used throughout the dispute. Trade unionists would be asked to give funds in aid of the boycott, to send their delegates to dealers in the boycotted articles, and to write letters of protest to the 'unfair' establishments. The effectiveness of the boycott depended on the union's ability to force observance. So fines, in addition to publicity, would also be employed; although, of course, non-observance was difficult to detect and sanction effectively, in comparison with strike-breaking. Approaches to customers were sophisticated, with the use of market segmentation:

> for many commodities there are special groups of consumers
> whose cooperation and active support are essential to the success
> of a boycott. It is not uncommon, therefore, to find that many
> unions, instead of waging a general boycott, attempt first to enlist
> the support of such groups of consumers.[63]

Particularly important would be those supplied by the boycotted firm that depended on public support in their trade, and feared a secondary boycott, especially if the boycotted firm was not dealing in finished products for the consumer market. This approach was highly successful for the print unions, for 'No retailer is willing ... to pay a high price for advertisements whose only result is to drive hundreds of customers from his store.'[64]

The above description of the mechanism of the boycott refers to actions conducted over seventy years ago. And yet many of the points made apply to actions today and can be considered perhaps as principles of boycott action. The five-stage process described above can also be found, as well as the methods used to give effective notice of the boycott and enlist support. Indeed, Remer even reports the use of the same methods in early twentieth century Chinese boycotts. More recent sources make similar observations to those above on the mechanism of the boycott.

Harper's description of the background to the Claiborne case shows that boycotts in the late 1970s differ little from those organised by labour unions nearly a hundred years previously. Technology may mean they can be more effectively promoted: in the UFW organised boycott of Lucky Supermarkets over sales of non-union lettuce, computers were employed.[65] However, for the most part, they are identical. So in the

Claiborne case, 'leaders urged others to join the boycott through public advocacy and personal solicitations, and they used written and oral statements to publicize the names of non-participants', and 'Protesters peacefully picketed targeted businesses.'[66] The actions described by Vogel and those listed in Appendix B also conformed to this approach (in so far as the sources provided sufficient description for this to be checked).

Harris offers some analysis of the mechanism of the boycott in considering boycott legality.[67] She suggests that consumer boycotts are composed of five distinct elements:

(1) Consumers discussing their dissatisfaction with the boycott target in private.
(2) Consumers reaching an agreement to withhold their patronage from the target.
(3) Consumers actually withholding their patronage.
(4) Consumers publicising their dissatisfaction with the target.
(5) Consumers publicising the boycott itself and persuading others to join it.

Her purpose in considering each element is to examine boycotts as a form of expression and therefore protected by the First Amendment. (An argument in defence of boycotts rejected by Harper. He argues that the right to freedom of expression would be insufficient where other forms of expression that are less economically disruptive could be employed.) Harris's list provides further confirmation of the relevance of Laidler and Wolman's analysis.

Factors in boycott effectiveness and success

Laidler explicitly identifies factors in the effectiveness of boycotts as employed by the United States labour unions at the turn of the century.[68] Again, despite its age, his analysis seems valid today. Sixteen 'elements of success in boycotts' are identified:

(1) *Character of the market for the article.* It is important that those likely to support the boycott are in the market for the boycotted article; in this case, whether the market consisted primarily of unionists and sympathizers or of the employing class. 'Bread, newspapers, hats, cigars, beer, stoves, shoes and other necessities and inexpensive luxuries have been very frequently and effectively boycotted ... of the 196 boycotts described in *Bradstreet's* ... 80 per cent center around necessities.' Laidler notes that boycotts of bread and cigars were particularly successful, whereas attempts to boycott commodities sold primarily to the upper middle and

employing classes were generally unsuccessful. Moreover, they might even be detrimental: 'Dealers in such articles certify that they have oftentimes been benefited by the boycott, as their well-to-do patrons have come to their rescue and frequently increased their orders on account of union opposition.'

(2) *Whether the articles boycotted are purchased by men or by women.* Laidler writes: 'It is unusual for the women of the family to feel the keenness of the trade union struggle, and to recognise the utility of inconveniencing themselves in order that other workers might be assisted thereby'; although he did acknowledge increasing interest.

(3) *Strong organisation among the employees of purchasers if the boycotted article is not sold directly to the mass of working people.* Articles sold to employers such as production materials or unfinished goods could not be subject to a consumer boycott by working people. Employing Wolman's distinction between commodities boycotts and materials boycotts, these articles would demand the latter type of action. Hence 'the threat of the solidly organised brewery workers to strike, should their employers continue to purchase non-union barrels and boilers, has time and again forced the unionising of a shop'.

(4) *Frequency and regularity of consumption of boycotted article.* Laidler quotes the Bureau of Statistics of Labor in New York: 'If it is an article which enters into daily consumption, and is of such a character that it can be made the subject of ordinary conversation, it will soon force the employer to spend money in advertising it, in order to counteract the silent influence of the boycott.'

(5) *Character of the population in the locality of the firm.* Where boycotts were of a local nature and the boycotted firm was in the surrounding neighbourhood, the boycott had a greater chance of success if the neighbourhood was working class.

(6) *Strength and capital of the boycotted firm and the nationwide character of its sales.* Firms with nationwide distribution would require an extensive and costly campaign. Those with plenty of capital could more easily withstand the loss of sales entailed by boycotts.

(7) *Extent to which the boycotted firm is a monopoly.* Purchasers are loath to support a boycott when there is no duplicate of the goods manufactured by the boycotted firm, especially if the item is a necessity.

(8) *Degree to which the efforts of the entire labour body are concentrated on one or more important firms.* Unions recognised that this was 'one of the greatest elements in the success of a boycott', and adopted a policy of concentration.

223

(9) *Amount of favourable publicity.* Although advertised in union journals, the public at large rarely heard of the existence of a boycott through the daily Press unless something striking or unusual happened, as in the legal proceedings against the AFL in the Bucks Stove case.

(10) *Character of the distinguishing mark on the goods.* Without the union label, the task of identifying 'unfair' goods was particularly difficult, and is cited as one reason for the failure of the miners to boycott coal.

(11) *Character of the competition.* Purchasers would be unlikely to boycott goods where the alternative goods were undesirable, such as prison made goods.

(12) *Directness of the boycotting attacks.* The more remote the boycott from the grievance, the weaker it is likely to be: 'At times citizens have been boycotted for purchasing goods from stores whose owners rode in trolley cars during a car strike. However, such boycotts soon subside.'

(13) *Causes leading to the boycott.* Society at large will not support causes with which it has no sympathy. 'Boycotts based upon the employment of non-union men rarely succeed, because society is not prepared to assist either in driving men into unions or out of employment', wrote the Commissioner of Labor in Illinois. However, all eight boycotts in that state against prison made goods were successful and 99 per cent of those against the reduction of wages. Appeals to organised labour were simply made on the basis that the boycotted firm had been 'unfair' to labour, the causes of the boycotts were less important. For this reason, the AFL placed greater emphasis on appealing to its members than the general public, unlike its forerunner the Knights of Labor.

(14) *Vigour with which the boycott is pushed at the outset.* The longer a boycott lasts the greater the likelihood of failure, as supporters lose enthusiasm for the boycott and the firm becomes more able to cope. Laidler suggests that vigour at the outset and the effectiveness of the methods employed during the first few weeks of the boycott 'determine, to a very large extent, its ultimate outcome ... a large proportion of those local boycotts which succeeded came to a termination within a few weeks'.

(15) *The attitude of the law.* Unionists were unlikely to be enthusiastic about supporting illegal boycotts if they might have to face civil or criminal proceedings.

(16) *Thorough deliberation and discrimination by the organisation in using the boycott.* Laidler argues that care in the use of the boycott would make it more powerful when resorted to.

Wolman does not explicitly identify factors in boycott effectiveness; not, at least, in such a deliberate fashion as Laidler. However, many factors can be culled from his analysis. Not surprisingly, they are similar to those identified by Laidler. Wolman observes that the boycott 'exhibits its greatest effectiveness under two conditions: first, when a large proportion of the product of the firm is consumed by communities of laborers, and secondly, where there are special groups of consumers who feel that labor can in turn bring to bear upon them effective pressure of a political or economic nature'.[69] The first condition is the same as Laidler's character of the market for the article. Elsewhere, Wolman writes 'Boycotts on commodities are, in general, effective only when imposed upon such goods as are consumed in large quantities by the working classes.'[70] Wolman's second condition recognises the importance of the secondary boycott where the firm with whom the union is in dispute does not deal in a commodity that can be effectively boycotted by labour because it is not a consumer product. So where a firm deals in materials, unfinished goods, or industrial products, and therefore the customers are other employers, or where the firm deals in consumer goods supplied to the employing classes, the primary boycott would be ineffective, if not impossible. Consequently, efforts might usefully be made to institute a boycott of the goods of the customers of the firm with which the union is in dispute.

In illustration of this, Wolman refers to the 1901 action by the Journeymen Bakers' and Confectioners' International Union which imposed a general boycott on all stores, restaurants, and hotels that sold any of the products of the National Biscuit Company, which had itself been previously boycotted. In this way, the effectiveness of the boycott is considerably enhanced: 'Where the commodity boycotted is a foodstuff or an article of clothing that is usually sold in conjunction with other articles, as is particularly the case with many commodities sold in the general merchandise stores of small towns, the boycott on a business is a far more effective weapon.'[71] Wolman suggests two reasons for this. First, that it is easier to teach the consumer to boycott a person than to boycott a commodity. Second, a boycott of the business is more serious for the retailer than the boycotting of a single item. In the latter case, the retailer may continue to stock the boycotted commodity in anticipation of the end of the boycott without active participation, whereas the boycott of the entire business would probably cause a rejection of the 'unfair' item.

The boycott might be extended in a variety of ways if the firm with which the union is in dispute is not itself a suitable target for boycott. An example of a boycott extended to a business associated with the one with which the union was in dispute was that against the Jamestown Street Railway Company of Jamestown, New York. Here there could be no effective boycott because no competitive route existed which passengers could have used in preference to the boycotted route. However, patronage could be far more easily diverted from the amusement park which was also owned by the owners of the railway company. This also illustrates the need for a substitute commodity that can be bought by those boycotting an 'unfair' item. Wolman writes that efforts were made to provide auxiliaries to the boycott under the Knights of Labor, and an adequate substitute for it under the AFL. This is because 'the boycott is in itself, in the last analysis, an incomplete weapon; to be completely effective it must be equipped with a complementary mechanism. Dissatisfaction with one firm implies satisfaction with another.'[72]

Support for the boycott is of principal importance if the boycott is to be successful. This underlies all of Laidler's elements. However, this factor in boycott effectiveness can be more precisely described as solidarity, in the use of the boycott by trade unions at least. This is more than simply ensuring effective communication of the boycott and attempting to sanction behaviour that breaches it. There is recognition of the boycott as a collective action and the importance of a supportive culture: 'Where the laboring community is a closely knit, intimate assembly, the boycott is waged by collective efforts impelled by a collective conscience.'[73] An important factor in support of boycotts is the low cost to the participant, relative to other forms of action such as strikes.[74] Extensive support may also be less important in some secondary boycotts. As noted earlier, unionists were aware that some of a firm's customers were more important than others, and segmented the market accordingly – a strategy which also offered cost effectiveness in the administration of the boycott.

Laidler refers to the directness of boycotts (element 12), and how boycotts remote from the grievance are likely to be less successful. This factor in effectiveness is also considered by Wolman, particularly as it relates to his definition of secondary or compound boycotts and the issue of boycott legality. The extension of a boycott upon an article, to any retailer selling that article say, has already been discussed in this section. What was not noted, however, was that the more boycotts are a result of this sort of extension, the less effective and less reasonable they seem to become. Boycotting a retailer who attempts to sell an 'unfair' item is justified on the basis that his business is, in effect, an agency of the boycotted firm and therefore automatically included in the original action. Yet how far can boycotts be effectively and reasonably extended? Wolman reports that the stone cutters of Bedford, Indiana, for example, boycotted the hotel at which scab stone cutters stayed and then threatened to boycott a theatrical performance because the actors stayed at the same hotel. In such cases, Wolman finds the boycott indefensible:

Since the boycott of the retailer is indispensable to the waging of
the original boycott, this simple form of the secondary boycott
need not be distingished in principle from the primary boycott.
Where, however, the union imposes a secondary or tertiary boycott
which is not essential to the original boycott ... the extension of the
boycott is indefensible in theory and practice.[75]

This expresses both his view on boycott legality but also on
effectiveness, for he then quotes: 'John Mitchell believes that "the
further the boycott is removed from the original offender the less
effective it becomes" because such a boycott is less likely to receive
public sympathy.' There are two final factors Wolman offers for
consideration, both of which are included in Laidler's last element,
thorough deliberation and discrimination by the organisation in using
the boycott. First, there is the requirement for good organisation and
control, the importance of which speaks for itself.[76] Second, there is the
relationship between boycott effectiveness and the frequency of its use.
Wolman's historical study of the use of boycotts identifies three phases,
where changes in the control and frequency of boycotts notably effected
success.[77] He records that this factor was recognised by the AFL and
attempts were made to increase control. Yet this was not easily done:

> Labor organisations have early learned the wisdom of training the
> combined forces of their organisation upon a few firms instead of
> scattering their energies in the prosecution of numbers of boycotts.
> Because this knowledge has, however, not penetrated to the rank
> and file of the labor movement, it is constantly found necessary to
> enact rules designed to limit the number of boycotts.[78]

Essentially, boycott effectiveness is diminished because excessive
frequency dilutes efforts and lowers impact. The point is emphasised by
Laidler on a number of occasions, and he sees this point as 'a vital
truth'.[79]

Remer's study of Chinese boycotts also identifies factors in boycott
effectiveness. In keeping with Laidler and Wolman, he notes that
'boycotting is more powerful against identifiable goods than against
such goods as easily lose their identity ... against consumers' goods than
against goods that enter into industrial processes ... [and] against goods
for which substitutes are produced within China than against other
goods'.[80] Remer also recognises the greater likelihood of failure the
longer a boycott lasts: 'a boycott brings results at once if it is to bring
them at all.'[81] On the problem of identifying goods, Remer notes that
ways round the boycott included remarking and repackaging goods in
nearby territories (allegedly done to Argentinian corned beef in Brazil
during the 1982 Falklands crisis) and smuggling. Yet Remer is keen to

point out (as earlier noted) that economic effect is not the sole intention nor the only consequence of boycott action. Boycotts can have a psychological impact on the boycotted party and can produce valuable publicity. So economic effectiveness may not be necessary for boycotts to be successful.

The recent sources are slightly more forthcoming on factors in boycott effectiveness than on the mechanism of the boycott. As noted earlier, Luthans *et al.* make the basic point that 'the key to a boycott is to have enough consumer support to reduce demand';[82] though this is too simple a perspective. Effectiveness is likely to improve the potential for success, but some boycotts may never be successful however effective; while in some cases effectiveness has not been necessary for success. Rea is a little more sophisticated:

> in practice, the boycott will be effective only for certain kinds of goods. The consumers' cartel is held together by social pressure. The impact of the social pressure depends on four characteristics of the good: the visibility of its purchase, the visibility of its consumption, its durability, and its perishability.[83]

The importance of social pressure is recognised by Laidler and Wolman, with Laidler noting in particular the success of boycotts of food. Rea suggests food items lend themselves to boycott action because of their perishability and because they are purchased publicly, but have the drawback of not being consumed as publicly as clothing and durable goods. But with durable goods, such as cars, while the publicly consumed (conspicuous consumption) feature is strong 'the fact that a consumer buys a car every 2·1 years instead of every 2 years is not readily observable'. So nondurable goods and services, consumed frequently, are more likely candidates. The perishability feature is important not only for frequency of purchase but also because goods purchased publicly but consumed privately – such as toothpaste – might be hoarded in anticipation of a boycott. Mail order presents a problem because it is non-public purchasing and not amenable to picketing. Rea claims 'One can predict that the participation in a boycott will be greatest for goods which are purchased and consumed publicly, nondurable and perishable.' He suggests the services of restaurants, theatres, and other forms of entertainment are an appropriate target because they are purchased and consumed publicly and are totally perishable. Such a boycott would not only be easier to enforce, but also likely to have a more substantial effect on the target as the nature of service products prevents them from being stored for future use. Yet it must be acknowledged that 'The number of goods that lend themselves to an enforceable boycott is limited because those goods which are most conspicuously consumed tend to be durable.'

The *New Republic* article[84] is sceptical about whether consumer boycotts have a serious economic effect but 'They are nevertheless a nuisance.' It refers to Hunt Foods having to send out 'hundreds' of letters disassociating it from H. L. Hunt, with one executive estimating the company loses $1m in sales a year due to the erroneous association of names. But this also illustrates the problem of computing effectiveness – it is unlikely to be disclosed in the annual report – and the difficulty of focusing on specific targets (as well as the injustice that entirely neutral third parties may accidentally suffer). Focusing on specific targets is particularly difficult when there are many consumer boycotts. So, after giving quite a lengthy list of contemporary boycotts, the author concludes: 'It is hard to know whom to boycott, for how long, or to compute the effect. There's nothing available like the Dow Jones morning comment or the racing form.' In other words, it seems that at the time this article was written, there was the same problem faced by the early labour sympathisers: far too many boycotts. If only for this reason, a pressure group need view the tactic as a last resort.

Computing effectiveness is important because of its part in motivating and maintaining the boycotters. This is noted by Laidler. Perceived consumer effectiveness is also recognised as important in one of the few sources that recognises some form of ethical purchase behaviour. Kinnear *et al.*, in predicting whether their respondents were ecologically concerned consumers, used perceived consumer effectiveness: 'a measure of the extent to which a respondent believes that an individual consumer can be effective in pollution abatement.'[85] They suggest that 'The direct relationship between perceived consumer effectiveness and ecological concern indicates that the consumer's lack of belief that he can be effective in the abatement of pollution is indeed an effective deterrent to his becoming personally concerned about ecological issues in consumption.' This comment would seem to be applicable to all forms of ethical purchase behaviour, including consumer boycotts.

The importance of picketing should not be understated. One of the rights Harper views as essential if the consumer's right to boycott is to be upheld is the right to engage in associated peaceful picketing. Picketing on private property would not be defended by the First Amendment, but full protection should be afforded for picketing on public property 'because public streets and ways traditionally have been considered among the most important of our public forums'.[86] Harper recognises the significance of picketing for boycott effectiveness: 'In the first place, boycott organisers have no alternative means of communication, such as newspaper or radio advertising, that are as cost effective as peaceful picketing in front of a business.' The use of consumer segmentation and recognising that consumers are more likely to be interested immediately prior to purchase means that 'the best time to communicate with potential consumers is when a possible purchase is imminent'. Other sites and methods are far inferior: 'Although boycott organisers could communicate through leaflets without actually patrolling a business site, off-site hand-billing is more easily ignored and picketing may have a symbolic persuasiveness for some consumers that handbilling lacks.' There is also, of course, the coercive element to picketing. This, suggests Harper, is insufficient for denying peaceful picketing, even though it may have an emotional and psychological element and may even amount to social ostracism.

Krieger, in analysing the causes of the failure of the Another Mother for Peace (AMP) consumer campaign, suggests that using only letter-writing was insufficient.[87] The letter-writing should have been a supplement to an actual boycott supported by organised picketing and widespread distribution of literature. The grape boycott is the model of the type of action he envisages (see case study). Further, he suggests that the AMP should have focused on one firm, rather than the eight corporations targeted, the firm which appeared to be most vulnerable to a consumer boycott. He suggests that 'If AMP could get just *one half* of its membership to seriously boycott one firm, this could be a great enough cost to the firm to bring about a change of policy ... If the campaign were to prove successful against one large corporation, its threat potential would increase substantially, perhaps to the point of achieving policy change in other firms by negotiation rather than boycott' (Krieger's emphasis). His analysis confirms the earlier points about maximising impact by concentration of efforts and the role of picketing. It also emphasises the use of the threat of boycott action. A new factor is introduced by relating the concentration of efforts and the threatening of boycott action to recognition that success in previous boycotts is likely to make threats more effective. The converse also applies. If boycotts are not supported and are ineffective and unsuccessful then subsequent threats of boycott action are unlikely to be effective. Not only is the reputation of the boycott tactic tarnished, but also that of the organisation promoting the boycott.

George Smith, after having shown how some European consumers' organisations achieved rapid and good results with the boycott, warns: 'Boycotts are a high-risk strategy. When successful they can have quick and dramatic results. Failure can be costly in terms both of the expense of lost law suits, which could disable financially vulnerable independent testing bodies, and loss of prestige.' In the case of these particular organisations Smith wonders whether boycotts in the long term are more effective than quieter committee work. He notes that the Consumers' Association and the majority of private testing bodies, as well as the EC consumers' organisation, BEUC, have preferred the latter route. Yet he sees a place for boycotts: 'Boycotts, which dramatise what are often technical matters, can therefore, if judiciously used, be seen as a useful support and complement to the day-to-day lobbying activities of BEUC.' For many promotional pressure groups, which are often outsider groups, committee work is not an alternative. Boycotts would therefore seem to be highly appropriate to them, on the basis of Smith's analysis.[88] Sharp and Vogel have nothing to add on boycott effectiveness.

So, to conclude, it can be seen that there is support, long established, for a number of factors in boycott effectiveness. Of particular importance are various characteristics of the product boycotted, the organisation and promotion of the boycott (including picketing), the frequency of boycott action, and the directness of the boycott – how remote it is from the grievance. Support in various ways is vital for effectiveness but not in itself sufficient and, on occasion, extensive support may not even be necessary for success.

In sum

The main points in this chapter are worth summarising. It has been seen that there are historical precedents for consumer boycotts – and, therefore, ethical purchase behaviour – with one source identifying a consumer boycott in medieval England. Yet the literature on the topic is sparse. Boycotts, however, seem less common in Britain than in the United States. Consumer boycotts may be classified according to the relationship of the seller to the perceived misdemeanour, giving rise to primary and secondary boycotts. This tends to affect their legality, though while recourse to legal action might be available, firms are loath to use it because of the associated publicity. Interestingly, two American reviews of consumer boycott legality consider the action as a form of political expression; Harper suggests there is an emerging right to boycott. Should a firm obtain an injunction prohibiting a boycott, this may be overcome by merely citing the grievance and thereby implying appropriate action by consumers, or by using the indirect boycott.

The use of the consumer boycott by the corporate accountability movement directly relates this examination of the boycott to the idea of consumer sovereignty to ensure social responsibility in business and the theoretical argument. Vogel's work identifies the efforts by pressure groups to achieve social control of business via the market. He considers their achievements limited, but he fails to distinguish between success and effectiveness in the use of the boycott and the boycott is shown to have some impact as a social control mechanism. The examples cited are, like other consumer boycotts referred to, evidence of ethical purchase behaviour.

The mechanism of the boycott involves a five-stage process: attempts at peaceful adjustment, inauguration and endorsement of the boycott, effective notice of the boycott, enlist support, and conclude boycott when agreement reached and publicise settlement. The importance of first threatening the boycott was noted, as were control problems and the use of market segmentation in directing boycott efforts. Factors in boycott effectiveness and success include various characteristics of the product boycotted, the organisation and promotion of the boycott, the frequency of boycott action, its remoteness from the grievance, and support.

Chapter eight

Consumer boycott case studies

Preview

We told them that the company could not take a political position.
On the other hand, they know that they should follow the customer
the customer is always right. This was OK as long as the
customer was only interested in the taste of coffee. Now, for the
first time, the customer expressed an opinion about something very
different.

> Douwe Egberts' Sales Director
> (on instructions given to
> the sales force)

You see, we have three thousand branches, and they're all on street
corners, they're very vulnerable. We're the easy target. And a lot
of our critics, if you really got them to sit down quietly and talk to
you – and they have done this to me – will tell you that, OK, they
appreciate that Barclays is a damn good employer, they appreciate
that we're trying hard, but we're still the Aunt Sallies of the bunch.
If they knock us down, then maybe others will follow.

> A Barclays Manager

The five case studies presented in this chapter aptly illustrate many of
the points made about boycotts, social responsibility in business, and
ethical purchase behaviour. The two extracts above are typical of the
many telling quotations, events, or responses that feature in the cases.
As evidence for the argument presented here, the case studies speak for
themselves. However, some of the major points are worth highlighting
and are therefore summarised in the case analysis at the end of the
chapter.

233

Case study research

Following a limited survey research investigation,[1] case study research was conducted to seek further evidence for the argument presented in Part One and in addition to that given in the last chapter, by examining five instances of ethical purchase behaviour in the form of pressure group organised consumer boycotts. The survey research showed that ethical purchase behaviour can and has been realised in practice. The cases are further evidence of this, but in their greater depth and detail they reveal the consequences of ethical purchase behaviour, particularly its impact on social responsibility in business, and address other issues raised in Part One. The data collection objectives were to ascertain what happened in each case, how each party operated, and why the events took the form they did. Five cases were found to be sufficient for the purposes here, particularly given the experience of 'saturation'.[2] A case study is defined as 'a detailed examination of an event (or series of related events) which the analyst believes exhibits (or exhibit) the operation of some identified general theoretical principle'.[3] The examination here is founded on primary and secondary data, including semi-structured interviews. It was analysed using a coding procedure in the writing-up.[4]

The cases describe the boycott of Barclays and other firms over their links with South Africa, of Tarmac and MAN-VW over their involvement in cruise missile contracts, of Douwe Egberts over its processing of Angola coffee, of Nestlé over its marketing of baby milk to the Third World, and of California grapes over farm worker unionisation.[5]

Barclays and South Africa

Apartheid in South Africa stirs many people. It is purportedly a system whereby the many races of South Africa may coexist securely and separately, different but equal. (The word apartheid is Afrikaans for separateness or segregation.) Yet it is in effect a racist ideology advancing separate development of the peoples of South Africa to maintain the economic exploitation of the black majority. There are many countries whose inhabitants suffer oppression and indignities at the hands of the state; conditions are arguably as bad in some South American countries as they are in South Africa. However as, indeed, the South African government commented in a series of advertisements in the national Press in the UK in 1983, 'South Africa arouses more controversy than almost any other country in the world.' This is not only due to the extent of the oppression in South Africa but also because of the way in which it is institutionalised. Racism and the exploitation of the black population is firmly embodied within the culture and legislation of South Africa, with, for example, blacks unable to vote, and the Group Areas Act prohibiting people of different races from living in the same area. The immorality of such a system is deeply offensive to countries of the First World (and the whites in South Africa do not wish their country to be seen as part of the Third World). Multinationals operating in South Africa are, as a consequence of doing business there, seen to be implicated in apartheid.

The criticism of corporate involvement in South Africa goes beyond an objection to companies remaining in a country which so clearly flouts the democratic principles cherished in their home countries. The economic function of apartheid and the role of business in apparently maintaining and benefiting from it suggests that those multinationals operating in South Africa bear some responsibility for apartheid. Indeed, it has long been argued that there is a convergence of interest between business in South Africa and the upholders of apartheid – that South Africa's apartheid system has always been a mutually beneficial alliance between a minority government and private business. This is exemplified in apartheid's role in the provision of cheap labour, particularly in establishing a migratory labour system, which even the UK government has admitted 'robs the individual of the basic freedom to seek and obtain the job of his choice. It also causes grave social and family problems.'[6] Accordingly, critics of a Marxist persuasion argue that capitalism has created apartheid. As Charles Longford puts it: 'Behind all the different manifestations of apartheid stands the mighty economic machine of South African capitalism. This machine absorbs cheap black labour, puts it through the wheels of industry, mining and agriculture and then expels it to distant reservations for the unemployed until the system requires more labour.'[7]

While this reference to the effective role of the 'homelands' (where many of South Africa's blacks are forced to live) is largely accurate, this does not confirm a simple causal relationship between capitalism and apartheid. In a recent and thorough study by Merle Lipton, *Capitalism and Apartheid*, a more sophisticated analysis is suggested: 'Apartheid cannot simply be explained as the outcome of capitalism or of racism. Its origins lie in a complex interaction between class interests (of white labour as well as of sections of capital) and racism/ethnicity, reinforced by ideological and security factors.'[8] She shows that while South African mining, agricultural, and white labour interests were generally served by apartheid, often the interests of manufacturing were not. The limits to black advancement have also placed constraints on South African manufacturing industry.

The debate on the extent of corporate culpability for apartheid notwithstanding, involvement in South Africa is a major issue of social responsibility in business. Continuing operations in South Africa are defended by arguing that economic progress will necessitate the incorporation of the blacks and end apartheid, but this is rejected by critics who see little evidence of this happening. Their solution is the armed seizure of control by the African National Congress (ANC), with external pressure applied in the form of various sanctions. While condemning apartheid, Western governments and business have largely resisted the pressure for disinvolvement in the South African economy, advocating constructive engagement to protect their interests.

South Africa is dependent on Western capital in the form of investment and trade. Direct investment has declined because of criticism but has been replaced by indirect investment. Yet trade and investment involves an interdependence. So the West, and Britain and the United States especially, is thereby committed to the stability of South Africa and the maintenance of apartheid, particularly as the trade with South Africa involves strategic raw materials for which South Africa is the major source of supply. This is aside from the country's political and military significance as a bastion against communism. This economic, political, and strategic interdependence makes the use of effective international economic sanctions by the West unlikely (although the recent increased unrest [from 1984 onwards] and its extensive media coverage, strengthened demands for their imposition). Business, in turn, wishes to defend its economic interests and so follows the government's line. International economic sanctions against South Africa, as a type of boycott, are of interest here for the reasons given earlier. More importantly, their use or otherwise is closely tied to the case for and against business involvement in South Africa and consumer boycotts over this. South Africa's reliance on Western trade and investment has led to many calls for economic sanctions. Yet apart from the more recent largely token gestures made in response to the continued unrest in South Africa, there has only been the UN arms embargo and the OPEC oil boycott.

Four principal arguments are advanced against sanctions: the costs for those imposing them, as referred to above; that they would harm the blacks most, but then it is said they are already suffering; doubts as to their effectiveness – historically there is some support for this, particularly when countervailing measures are employed (but then why oppose them?); and, finally, constructive engagement. The latter argument, for 'bridge-building' and change from within, is the most prominent. In accordance with this, corporate involvement is prescribed by codes of conduct such as the EEC and Sullivan codes. These are voluntary but many firms comply to deflect criticism at home, and although they may have raised black living standards, they have not really challenged apartheid. Over 15 years ago, in examining corporate involvement in South Africa and the constructive engagement argument, Ruth First *et al.* wrote:

> In their reply to the suggestion that this involvement puts a special onus on British firms to help to end apartheid, businessmen generally give one of two answers: the first is that business and politics (like sport and politics) should not be mixed, and the second that apartheid may be objectionable, but that business is 'doing its bit behind the scenes' to change it; the alternative to this reform-by-participation would, after all, be to try to bring down South Africa's regime and consequently her economy. So let us opt for reform through business rather than for revolution.[9]

Critics see little evidence of constructive engagement working, and particularly with the recent unrest, it has come to be seen as tacit support for apartheid. With international economic sanctions not forthcoming many consumers choose to support a consumer boycott campaign; it has been suggested that as many as one in four view South African products as tainted. Hence there is probably more consumer boycotting in Britain over apartheid in South Africa than any other issue. Indeed, the Anti-Apartheid Movement's boycott campaign has been running for more than 25 years. (Business has been attacked on other fronts as well, particularly by ethical investment, and is frequently criticised in the Press for having links with South Africa.) The consumer boycott is, as a moral act, an expression by the individual of his or her preferences on the issue, a sanction by the individual as the state is not prepared to act. It also adds to the aggregate of pressure for change. The revitalised boycott campaign has had some recent successes, especially with some retail outlets and the local authorities, but overall, purchases from South Africa (UK imports) have increased rather than declined. The most well-known consumer boycott involves Barclays Bank.

Public criticism of direct investment in South Africa – through companies – and a strategy by the South African government to reduce its consequential vulnerability, have reduced direct investment and brought about a trend towards indirect forms of investment. This is largely through banks and so they have been targeted in the boycott campaign. All the major banks lend to South Africa. The Co-op and some other smaller banks do not. Barclays was singled out for attack because it had a subsidiary in South Africa – Barclays National Bank – which was the largest bank there, with about 1,000 branches. Barclays was vulnerable in Britain because of its visibility; it has three thousand branches on British high streets. Barclays defended its involvement in South Africa using the constructive engagement argument, though its critics could see little other than cosmetic changes as a consequence of Barclays' continued involvement. The principal pressure group active against Barclays was End Loans to Southern Africa (ELTSA). ELTSA operated by applying what its main organiser described as 'moral, public opinion type pressure and economic pressure', pressing Barclays to leave South Africa and end loans. Its materials included a glossy Shadow Report, produced on an annual basis 'to chronicle details of how Barclays' presence in South Africa and Namibia helps sustain the apartheid system'. The Shadow Board was comprised of a number of public figures, including Neil Kinnock, MP and Leader of the Labour Party, and the actress Julie Christie. Many account closures were claimed, individual accounts but also those of non-commercial organisations such as church bodies, local authorities, and others, for example, the British Psychological Society. However, ELTSA felt that the economic impact of this was low. Yet they believed they gave Barclays a 'fairly dirty name' and contributed to the pressure on the bank to leave South Africa.

Barclays' response was in the form of public relations. They produced material designed to reply to what they called their 'puzzled critics'. This suggested that economic ties and investment are the only way for peaceful change – the constructive engagement argument, and they actually used that term – and that a bank cannot simply close down. Interviews with Barclays managers revealed that while little business was said to have been lost, the criticism hurt. Yet in 1985 there seemed to be evidence of a phased withdrawal by the bank. In August, amid deteriorating economic conditions, there was an end to Barclays' majority shareholding. Pressure on the bank – presumably including the consumer boycott – was conceded as a factor in this move. One change forthcoming was an end to the use of the Barclays name in South Africa. However, to what extent ELTSA and the boycott could claim responsibility was difficult to say at this stage. They did at least appear to have created a climate of possibility. Interestingly, the following comment was given by Sir Timothy Bevan in the Chairman's statement for Barclays Annual Report 1985 and reprinted in advertisements in the national Press:

It seems to me that the statement 'we want to crush apartheid itself, not the victims of it' has it about right. To those who take their accounts away from us on ideological grounds, as is their right, I would pose one simple question: 'Do you want us to stand back and wash our hands of apartheid or do you want us to continue to strengthen the tide of change?' Apartheid is unjust and immoral and so rightly condemned; equally it seems to me to be unjust to condemn us as supporters of the system, when in fact Barclays National is amongst the leaders in South Africa in opposition to it.

Barclays plc still had a 40·4 per cent stake in Barclays National Bank which it needed to defend. While, within the same statement, Sir Timothy Bevan spoke of the role of constructive engagement as above, one of the reasons given in explanation of the reduction in shareholding was, 'we and many others deplore the slow movement of the South African Government in dismantling institutionalised racial discrimination'. Barclays was caught in a cleft stick: trying desperately to hold on to the constructive engagement argument to defend its remaining investment in South Africa yet at the same time trying to divest, which was extremely difficult given South Africa's instability. No doubt there was considerable envy of those firms, particularly American firms such as General Electric and Pepsi, who had managed to get out. Yet Barclays could hardly have argued that they had not received sufficient warning.

ELTSA had not accounted for the increasing unrest in South Africa which, during 1984 to 1986, came to be daily portrayed on television and in the national Press. This provided a considerable stimulus to the boycott Barclays campaign, particularly among UK students. Nor had they accounted for any moral dimension in Barclays' decision-making on whether to stay in South Africa. The predominance over this period of the South African situation in current affairs and the pressure on Western governments to impose sanctions on South Africa highlighted Barclays' involvement there. The deteriorating economic conditions in South Africa and Barclays' planned expansion in the United States (where at this time consumer activism on South Africa was greater on the whole than in the UK) added further weight to the case for a clear strategy on South Africa. It was these factors which had led to a reduction in Barclays' shareholding in its South African subsidiary and urged a complete withdrawal from South Africa.

In 1982 Sir Antony Tuke had been succeeded as Chairman of Barclays by Timothy Bevan. Tuke had never been receptive to criticism of Barclays' involvement in South Africa, standing firm on the constructive engagement argument. Bevan, however, was said genuinely to detest apartheid and, moreover, was less susceptible to pressure from Pretoria, as the relative importance of Barclays' South African operations had diminished. Neither did he have a history of long associations with white South Africans and his views were also shared by some of the newer members of the Barclays board. These views became public when, in November 1985, Bevan mounted a critical attack on the South African regime in a speech to branch managers. He, moreover, revealed contacts with the ANC – he had met Oliver Tambo, President of the ANC, in London. The new and dynamic chief executive of Barclays National Bank, Chris Ball, had also been having meetings with black nationalists. Indeed, Ball's radical stance (for a South

239

African business executive) was earning for Barclays National Bank in South Africa an anti-apartheid label! Meanwhile, the corporate exodus was taking hold. *Business Week* reported that three times as many US companies had halted all or part of their South African operations in the year up to September 1985, compared with the previous year. Ford, Apple Computers, and Singer were among the 18 companies disinvesting. As *The Economist* explained, also in September 1985: 'The reason for the flight from South Africa is that no businessman wants to be caught propping up a government whose social policy leads to the sjamboking and shooting of people on television – so, eventually, to money-losing revolution.'

In 1986 Bevan's stance against apartheid – for moral or commercial reasons (or both) – hardened still further. Barclays had, with the other banks, despite a request to do otherwise from the President of the Anti-Apartheid Movement, agreed to a rescheduling of South African debt in March 1986, though on tougher terms than expected by Pretoria. By the time of the May 1986 board meeting it had been decided to withdraw fully from South Africa. In November, agreement was finally reached. Barclays sold its remaining stake in Barclays National Bank, which had a current market valuation of £221m, for £82m (at the financial rand exchange rate) on 24 November 1986. It was bought by Anglo-American and Anglo-American controlled companies. Bevan said the reasons were 'basically commercial'. Ball acknowledged the likely impact on the South African economy but was positive about the opportunities for the South African bank. It was, he said, 'a unique opportunity, giving us the potential to strengthen our position both domestically and internationally'. He contrasted the move with the disinvestments earlier in 1986 of multinationals such as IBM and General Motors by noting that the bank was not dependent on outside supplies. He referred to Barclays' reluctance to take this move and explained, 'They are not doing it to achieve a political objective. They are doing it because they are under political pressure.' In an editorial headed 'Moral pressure in the market' the *Financial Times* clearly attributed the withdrawal to the boycott campaign:

> ordinary people, revolted by what they have learned about the [apartheid] system from the news media, are not much concerned with the sometimes agonizing decisions faced by those actually involved; they want to make their opposition felt, and have proved again that they can bring effective pressure to bear on commercial organisations, even if they cannot move foreign governments. Moral pressure of this kind – whether against apartheid, whaling, the fur trade, vivisection or even the defence industry – is an increasingly important fact of business life.[10]

It had emerged in August 1986, from the leak of an internal Barclays document to Anti-Apartheid, that Barclays' share of the student market had dropped from 27 per cent to 17 per cent between 1983 and 1985. Students are a vital sector of the market for banks because of their likely future prosperity and the high level of customer loyalty within the industry; people generally tend to stay with the bank they first join. Chris Ball later suggested that the drop was even more substantial than the ten percentage points widely cited, explaining the withdrawal as almost entirely due to this loss of business. He did, however, also acknowledge the importance of Barclays' US expansion plans and the limitations placed on them by involvement in South Africa.[11] The 'hassle factor' of continually having to respond to vociferous pressure groups must also have played a part in Barclays' decision to withdraw. It may even have contributed to Barclays' lacklustre performance of recent years and low morale. Anthony Sampson (author of *Black and Gold*) suggests that the impact on South Africa was considerable: 'the withdrawal was perhaps the most fundamental blow so far of those that have begun to rain on the South African economy.'[12] Yet it has hardly forced great concessions out of South Africa. The Anti-Apartheid groups claimed Barclays' withdrawal to be a major success. In many ways for them, it was, although they cannot claim full responsibility for it. It was even a victory for capitalism. As the *Financial Times* also commented:

> The whole merit of the market system is that it is the best system yet devised for recording and satisfying consumer preferences, and if these preferences rank the rights of minorities or humane farming, alongside the elegance of a design or the palatability of a strawberry flavour, it does the customers nothing but credit.

Tarmac, MAN-VW, and the Campaign for Nuclear Disarmament

The boycotts in Britain of Tarmac and MAN-VW over their links with cruise missiles were organised by what at the time was probably the largest and most influential promotional pressure group in Britain. The Campaign for Nuclear Disarmament comprised around 1,500 local groups and 400,000 people. Moreover, according to opinion polls, a majority of the population supported their opposition to cruise. Yet the boycotts were clearly unsuccessful.

The 1979 decision by NATO's European members to site cruise missiles in Europe provided a focal point for the peace movement and CND achieved a forty-fold increase in size. The early 1980s not only saw a tremendous growth in the size of the CND membership, but also the pressure group's importance. The *New Statesman* commented in 1983 on CND:

It has provoked a substantial and so far rather desperate counter-attack by Mrs Thatcher and her government. It is the one organisation that has clearly for the time being 'won' a moral and political argument with that government. Tory policies on other issues – the economy, unemployment, civil rights, immigration – may be incompetent or immoral or both. But attacks on them have not so far managed to upset the facade of Tory confidence. CND has done more than upset the facade. Its campaign has created the situation where the clear majority of the British electorate is now opposed to the deployment of cruise and Pershing II missiles in this country. It has been a remarkable political achievement.[13]

At its previous peak in popularity CND had been divided on the use of direct action; this time its leadership was prepared to tolerate different forms of protest. CND endorsed non-violent direct action and set up working groups to devise suitable campaigns. The more extreme forms of direct action, such as the peace camps, received most publicity, but CND did, in May 1983, announce their intention to boycott MAN-VW, Tarmac, and the National Savings Bank (NSB), and this received extensive coverage. Even at this stage, however, CND had its doubts about the suitability of these targets. Yet although the NSB action was never initiated, the other two boycotts went ahead.

Tarmac was the main contractor for an £11 million contract to provide cruise missile storage facilities at Greenham Common airbase. A peace camp protester had approached the Nuclear Free Zone (NFZ) local authorities about Tarmac, and Southwark Council had already responded to her boycott request prior to CND's announcement. Mr Alan Davis, leader of Southwark Council, said, 'The decision was taken in line with our anti-nuclear policy and in sympathy with the large numbers of people who have been protesting at the siting of cruise missiles at Greenham Common and in support of our general desire to work for peace.' Although Tarmac was specifically named, the council said it intended to ban all companies working at the base. Mr Davis hoped other councils would follow Southwark's lead. Legal advice had been taken before the council passed the resolution on 23 December 1982. The council was Labour controlled and the resolution had not satisfied all of its members. Mr Toby Eckersley, the opposition leader, described the decision as 'an outrageous abuse for purely political reasons of local government powers and responsibilities'. He asked the Local Government Minister, Mr Tom King, to investigate; though the Local Government Office of the Department of the Environment indicated that any challenge to the decision would have to be through the courts. CND was simply picking up on this campaign.

Tarmac's response to CND's announcement of the boycott reiterated its position as expressed when Southwark had reported that it would no longer be using the company. This emphasised that many firms were involved, sought to direct attention towards government, and hinted at unemployment or legal threats. As the campaign gained momentum, other councils wishing to follow Southwark's example found that there was a problem of legality and that they had to be careful how they worded support for the boycott, but pressure on Tarmac continued to grow. Tarmac directors were said to be taking the campaign seriously and tried to deflect attention on to the government:

> We are only one of more than 100 companies involved at
> Greenham Common in addition to the public statutory
> undertakings and feel that the stance against us is unfair ... Tarmac
> respects the views of sincere people who hold strong opinions
> about the morality of nuclear weapons but would urge them to
> direct those views in any responsible lawful way to Government
> who, in the end, are the only people who can respond.

The company also reiterated its concern for job security for its workforce and said it was not for company directors 'to make judgements in political fields'. This latter point in particular was taken up by a local CND group. Marcus Lynch, of West Midlands CND, said 'We believe that Tarmac, other contractors and civil engineers generally should consider the ethics of working on nuclear installations' (which, indeed, they did, within the pages of the profession's magazine, *New Civil Engineer*). He suggested it was impossible for firms to have a neutral view on such matters and asked 'Would Tarmac have tendered for and built Hitler's gas chambers?'

Many NFZ authorities, however, felt they could not publicly support the campaign because of the likelihood of legal action, but some surreptitiously boycotted Tarmac, by not including the firm – one of the largest contractors in the country – on their tender lists. As the campaign did not materialise as CND had threatened (though they did not really do much more than announce the boycott), Tarmac maintained a low profile; but it would have used legal action otherwise. Two authorities were said to have cancelled major contracts but changed their minds because of Tarmac's threats on rates payments in one case and employment (involving 3,000 jobs) in another. But identifying those councils which did blacklist Tarmac is problematic because of their reluctance to be named. Tarmac suggests that there was only 'a handful ... six at the most' where they experienced 'real baulking' and were notably excluded from the tender list. They did not wish to disclose who was involved because (at the time of interviewing) they were doing work for them again.

Tarmac considered that the boycott had ended by early 1984. It is possible that customer resistance to Tarmac because of the firm's involvement with cruise remained for some time after this, as revealed in the firm's decision in July 1985 to close their Peterborough office,[14] but the boycott seemed to fade away. This probably had as much to do with the NFZ authorities' other problems and higher priorities as with CND's failure actively to promote the boycott; though it is worth noting that in October 1986, the Environment Secretary, Nicholas Ridley, announced legislation to stop councils imposing political conditions on their contracts. He specifically referred to discrimination against construction companies involved in nuclear missile sites.[15] This suggests that the boycott had some impact, even if it did not significantly affect the commissioning of the cruise missile base.

CND put far greater effort into the MAN-VW boycott, though the boycott did not have its unqualified support. The launch of the campaign was a series of blunders. CND's announcement of its intention to boycott MAN was made without having had any contact with the firm. The announcement suggested that MAN was involved in supplying the cruise missile launchers, whereas MAN (in Germany) was supplying 40 allegedly standard military tractor units. This confusion was repeated when the boycott was subsequently launched and after the company had been in contact with CND to clarify the point. Moreover, the vehicles were to be delivered by air, not road, and would therefore not be as visible as expected. Finally, when seeking a meeting with the company, the letter from CND Chairwoman Joan Ruddock was sent too late and to the wrong person. Yet this latter blunder was unimportant anyway as the group's demands of MAN (essentially that it should stop supplying truck tractors to the US Army) could not have possibly been realised, at least through MAN-VW (UK), an independent concessionaire. The boycott did not get off to a good start!

MAN-VW was initially quite concerned by the campaign, particularly with the threat of demonstrations outside its VW car showrooms. As a MAN-VW manager commented on Volkswagen's customer profile: 'a large proportion of VW buyers will fall into groups like schoolteachers ... probably one of the areas where there is the strongest groundswell of opinion supporting CND's aims ... so in that sense we could have been regarded as a good target.' When the campaign seemed likely to go ahead the firm urged dealers to be careful not to provoke further publicity. In a letter to its dealers MAN-VW explained its position on the action:

whilst we would not dispute the sincerity and concern of the CND movement's members, we believe their efforts are misdirected. It is unreasonable, in our opinion, to seek to affect the lawful business of our dealers, ourselves and the services we wish to provide to nearly one million customers. The aim of the CND group can only be publicity. We trust your staff and yourselves will ensure that nothing takes place on your part to provide that publicity.

A press statement was also provided for use by the dealers if necessary. It emphasised MAN-VW and particularly Volkswagen's remoteness from the grievance.[16] The launch, which CND said involved 10 truck centres, proved to be a 'damp squib' in the firm's eyes. The boycott organisers thought otherwise and were particularly pleased with their use, at one site, of a motorcade of VW and Audi vehicles led by a MAN truck hauling a dummy cruise missile.

Significantly, the customers for MAN trucks did not include the local authorities (who try to buy British). MAN customers were unlikely to support the boycott, so although there was further picketing, this boycott also faded away. The impact of the boycott was negligible. Its failure is attributed, by the firm, to the tenuousness of its link with cruise and the recognition of this by CND supporters:

> They picked on MAN because the transporters are bloomin' great things with MAN written on the front and I think they had this mental idea that one day this armada of these things was going to come across the Channel, up the A2 to Greenham Common, and everybody would see these huge juggernauts and there'd be thousands of people lying in the streets in front of them to stop them getting to Greenham ... And I'm convinced that's the only reason they singled us out, because they saw it as a publicity opportunity ... I think that that started to destroy their argument.

The firm's response to the boycott was to be as open as possible, emphasising the tenuousness of the link, with legal action, although possible, as definitely the last resort. CND was found to be poorly organised but it had essentially got it wrong. As a MAN-VW manager explained: 'It doesn't matter how effective a publicity or PR machine is, if it's spreading things that are basically not valid, it won't get any further.'

Douwe Egberts and Angola coffee

The Angola Committee was far better organised and more committed to its boycott of Douwe Egberts than was CND on the Tarmac and MAN boycotts. Its demand was also realistic. It wanted the firm to stop processing coffee from Angola, then (1972) seeking independence from Portugal.[17]

245

Before launching its action, the pressure group contacted the company to arrange a meeting. The company reluctantly agreed to this but, following the meeting, did not feel it could give in to the pressure group. This was despite the scale of the action planned, public concern about Angola, and Albert Heijn, the second largest coffee roaster (to Douwe Egberts) and the largest Dutch supermarket chain, having agreed not to process Angola coffee. Two more supermarket chains followed suit before the campaign was launched amid much publicity. Leaflets explained how consumers could support the action:

> Through the coffee purchases in Angola, we cooperate against our will in the oppression and exploitation of the Angolese people. Therefore we should convince the coffee companies that we do not want any more coffee from Angola ... Everybody can support this action by refusing to buy coffee from companies that have not made a commitment to refrain from processing Angola coffee.

Consumer support for the pressure group was clearly demonstrated in feedback from the sales force (as indicated in the quotation from Douwe Egberts' Sales Director, given in the Preview to this chapter) and in a market research study. Picketing of shops and supermarkets ensured that consumers were likely to express this support in purchase. But pressure on the firm also came from other directions. Some of the media supported the Angola Committee, a quasi-government body provided it with funds, and the Dutch Labour Party registered its support. Meanwhile, Douwe Egberts' employees had been under pressure, from picketing by the Committee, but also criticism from friends and family: the union found it could no longer support the management and threatened action.

Under all this pressure, Douwe Egberts finally capitulated and agreed not to process any more Angola coffee because 'consumers have objections'. The company received some criticism for deciding to capitulate. Press interest in the Angola coffee issue continued for a time because of events unrelated to Douwe Egberts, but also because a right-wing extremist politician filed a complaint with the Ministry of Justice against the Committee, accusing it of blackmail against the coffee roasters. However, a police investigation could not find evidence of any illegal practices. *De Telegraaf* launched a counter-attack against the Committee which resulted in the firm receiving some letters in protest at their capitulation, but sales in the long run did not suffer because of this.

Douwe Egberts did not renege on its promise not to buy Angola coffee, at least until 1974 when the Portuguese withdrew from Angola. They did not, however, have cause to do so, as both its price and quality were not exceptional. The management did not, in the end, regret capitulation. They did, however, regret their insufficient flexibility. By giving in earlier (or even taking the lead away from the Committee) they would have avoided a situation where either party had to capitulate. Although critical of Albert Heijn at the time, they regretted not having reacted in the same way. The pressure group's success prompted a similar action against Gulf Oil, which was also successful.

Nestlé and the marketing of baby milk

The Nestlé case is one many are familiar with, though perhaps not the more recent events, including the termination of the boycott.[18] 'Commerciogenic malnutrition', as it has been described, was not the result of the marketing of a bad product, but its marketing in inappropriate ways and circumstances. There was nothing wrong with Nestlé's powdered baby milk; it was simply being marketed to people who could not use it properly and had little need of it. Yet it took Nestlé, one of the largest food companies in the world and the market leader in baby milk, 15 years to resolve the problem fully. For ten years of that period the company was under attack from pressure groups and it was mainly through their efforts that the problem was largely resolved and most of the marketing practices of concern ceased.

At first Nestlé largely ignored the problem. Then, around the early 1970s, there appeared publicity on the issue. The magazine *New Internationalist* carried a number of articles on it and the pressure group War on Want produced a pamphlet entitled *The Baby Killer*. This was picked up on by a Swiss group and translated and produced under the title *Nestlé Kills Babies!* Nestlé responded to this challenge, in 1974, with legal action. It succeeded with a libel suit but the latter attracted much adverse publicity, particularly as the judge in the case was critical of Nestlé's practices. With continued adverse publicity, the baby milk industry attempted some self-regulation. The International Council of Infant Food Industries (ICIFI) took some measures, but these were considered inadequate by the UN Protein-Calorie Advisory Group, and one firm left the Council to take more effective action on its own. As avoidable infant deaths continued, pressure increased for more effective action. In 1977, the Infant Formula Action Coalition (INFACT), a collection of pressure groups concerned about the issue, launched a boycott in the United States of Nestlé. Nestlé was chosen because it was the market leader – with around half the world market for powdered baby milk – and because of its intransigence.

Nestlé representatives met with INFACT in February 1978. The pressure group made four specific demands. These were largely in keeping with the statement of an unofficial World Health Organisation (WHO) working group published earlier in the year:[1]

(1) Stop all direct consumer promotion and publicity for infant formula.
(2) Stop employing 'milk nurses' as sales staff.
(3) Stop distributing free samples to clinics, hospitals, and maternity hospitals.
(4) Stop promoting infant formula among the medical profession and public health profession.

One of the pressure group's first coups was persuading Senator Edward Kennedy to hold a US Senate hearing on the issue. At this hearing well-substantiated evidence was presented which clearly established a relationship between infant mortality and the marketing of baby milk. Yet following this evidence, Nestlé's first words in contribution to the debate were:

> The US Nestlé Co. has advised me that their research indicates this is actually an indirect attack on the free world's economic system. A worldwide church organisation, with the stated purpose of undermining the free enterprise system, is in the forefront of this activity.

This characterised Nestlé's response to the boycott until it began to realise that it was losing the debate. Nestlé then shifted from this antagonistic approach to a softer, PR-oriented approach. It attempted to present its case rather than curtly dismissing any criticisms made.

By the late 1970s the pressure groups had got the World Health Organisation involved. WHO was attempting to put together a code of practice for the industry. Nestlé took an interest in this, and, it has been suggested, attempted to co-opt WHO officials. Meanwhile abuses by the infant formula companies continued to be identified. When WHO finally produced a Code of Practice in 1981 this was endorsed by Nestlé. However, this did not placate the pressure groups. They sought to increase the scope of the boycott to ensure Nestlé conformed to the Code's provisions. INFACT continued to promote the boycott, saying:

> It is important for the boycott to gain strength to ensure that the momentum continues to move in the direction of an end to promotion. The WHO code is important but unless the companies are convinced that they have to abide by it, they will find ways around it. The growth of the boycott is our way of saying that it is in Nestlé's interests to change their practices, to meet with the International Nestlé Boycott Committee, and to honestly commit themselves to abiding by the WHO recommendations.

An article by Doug Clement of INFACT, in a special issue of *New Internationalist* (April 1982) devoted to the boycott, described its progress to date and referred to various actions taken against Nestlé; such as the 'Clip Nestlé Quik' campaign; the 'Stop Stouffers' campaign (persuading consumers not to use Nestlé's Stouffers chain of restaurants and hotels); and the 'Boston Nestlé Party', where a march to Boston Harbour ended with the symbolic dumping of Nestlé products. A copy of a letter sent by a boycott supporter to Nestlé was included in the article. The text read:

My children love Nestlé Quik. My husband and I are virtually addicted to Nescafé. But we will no longer be buying these or your other products. We have learned about the suffering your advertising of infant formula causes. You are a large company. Individually, we don't have much power over your actions. But our outrage joins with that of many others and together we will boycott Nestlé products until you change.

Readers were urged to write likewise to Nestlé and also to government representatives and local papers. The article emphasised that the real strength of the boycott lay in its local base. Readers were, of course, encouraged to stop buying Nestlé products – and tell their grocer why. Various Nestlé products were identified, both Nestlé branded products such as Nescafé and other brands belonging to Nestlé subsidiaries such as Crosse and Blackwell, Libby, Findus, and Chambourcy. Other ways in which supporters could help the boycott included joining or starting a boycott group; inviting friends to a meeting at their home to discuss the boycott; by being a 'codewatcher', completing a questionnaire seeking information on code violations; asking local churches, schools, and social groups to publicise the boycott (with material available from INFACT); and asking organisations to which they belong – local, regional, or national – for an endorsement of the boycott, and making sure the organisation publicises the boycott in its newsletters and stops buying Nestlé products.

In 1982, in response to all this, Nestlé set up the Nestlé Infant Formula Audit Commission (NIFAC), an independent body to monitor its practices, under the former senator Edmund Muskie. At last it began to look as if Nestlé took commerciogenic malnutrition seriously; for the mere issuing of instructions, even when enshrined as company policy, does not necessarily ensure compliance, especially in a large organisation like Nestlé. As Post comments: 'The single most important action that eluded boycott supporters was the creation of a reliable mechanism for enforcement of the Nestlé instructions.'[19] So the creation of NIFAC was not just to show boycott supporters that the firm's marketing practices were being objectively scrutinised, but also to say to the firm's employees that top management was committed to the Code and that every field manager was subject to scrutiny.

Some of the firm's critics then began to accept that Nestlé was doing its best. In January 1984 following agreement between INFACT and Nestlé on four outstanding grievances – and with the intermediation of UNICEF – the boycott was suspended. It was terminated six months later. The success of the boycott has been attributed to its economic impact but, more importantly, its damage to the corporate image, its impact on management morale, and the costs of giving management attention to it. Its success was such that it has been proposed as a model or example for other similar campaigns. As one observer was quoted in *Multinational Monitor*:

> The boycott demonstrates how effective people can be when they analyse the power of multinationals and call them to accountability. Nestlé's agreement to change its practices represents a considerable victory and a model for other kinds of campaigns for consumers.[20]

The California grape boycott

The 1965-70 California grape boycott was both highly effective and successful. It achieved unionisation for farm workers when all previous efforts and methods had failed. But the case is not simply about the right of labour to organise. It also involved minority rights, poverty, pesticide misuse, and civil rights.[21] Steinbeck's *The Grapes of Wrath* (an extract from which appears in the Preview to the Introduction) is an account of the migration of refugees from the dust bowl states to the fields of California and their subsequent degradation and exploitation. Their experiences were not exceptional; farm workers had long suffered injustices. Despite attempts to organise and improve their position, they had been unsuccessful and denied union recognition. Indeed, United States legislation provided for a right to organise for all workers except the agricultural workers. The growth and profitability of Californian agriculture was largely attributed to the resultant low wages.

Strikes had proved ineffective in the organisation of farm workers because of their mobility and the use of strikebreakers. Just as the early US labour unions had found, strikebreaking meant recourse to the consumer boycott. Certain factors in the late 1960s proved to be important in its effectiveness, most notably: popular support for 'la causa'; the structure of the grape market, especially its concentration of sales through the supermarkets, with about 50 per cent of sales in ten major cities; and the relative stability of the table grape farm workers. So great was the support for the union and the concentration of grape sales that an effective boycott of all table grapes was achieved. The growers were coerced into capitulation.

The United Farm Workers Organising Committee (UFWOC), although a fledgling union, was more like a promotional pressure group than a sectional one. This was particularly evident in its having to deal with two constituencies: the mainly 'chicano' (Mexican-American) farm workers in rural California, and middle-class urban America. Cesar Chavez was the inspirational leader that managed, through adherence to Saul Alinsky's principles[22] and NVDA, to unite these diverse supporters in a common struggle. Particularly important were the public confrontations with the growers and their supporters, such as the arrest of the 44 'strikers', which served to highlight the growers' moral failings to those outside rural California. Given the need to build and mobilise popular support for the boycott, the role of the organisers was crucial. The way they operated, as representatives of UFWOC, reflected the union's structure and ethos, which not only avoided the alienation of potential supporters but even enhanced support.

The growers, by contrast, managed to lose support with almost every action they took. Their violence (such as well-documented attacks on picket lines) and attempts to set up company unions are appropriate examples of this. When they finally involved a public relations firm a little more sophistication was employed. The PR firm set up the Consumers' Rights Committee (CRC). This tried to discredit UFWOC and the boycott. It suggested the union was responsible for fire-bomb attacks on supermarkets, later attributed to the Mafia. It opposed alleged picket line intimidation outside supermarkets. One pamphlet said:

> Violence at the supermarket ... why the grape boycott must be
> ended: the techniques developed by New Left anarchists on college
> campuses to destroy higher education – non-negotiable demands,
> threats, assaults, fire-bombing and vandalism – have been extended
> to the supermarket.

More convincing were their arguments on consumer rights to choice, as expressed in the same pamphlet: 'Boycotts are wrong because they violate the basic rights of consumers to choose what they – as individuals – wish to buy or not buy.' The case was effectively made for allowing the consumer choice, but it was too late. Despite the previous bias of the judiciary, the growers also failed to get a ruling prohibiting the boycott. Although they had government supporters, legislation could not be realised to achieve this aim because of divisions among the growers.

The boycott was organised on a large scale, with boycott committees effective in the major North American markets and operating in most American cities. They were comprised of a broad coalition of supporters, from religious organisations to consumer groups, and each could identify in some way with 'la causa'. Picketing and a variety of events, such as the Boston Grape Party, ensured the effectiveness of the primary and secondary boycotts; though this was not achieved overnight. The union had to learn to target the outlets selectively and recognise that different cities demanded different approaches.

The autonomy of the boycott committees was important because every city was found to be unique, often demanding different approaches to the task of stopping grape shipments to it. In New York, for example – the largest grape market in North America, receiving 11 per cent of all grapes sold – the support of organised labour initially cut grape supplies to about 20 per cent of their previous level. Unions in New York were the most powerful in the country, but their refusal to handle 'hot' cargo lasted less than two months, following the growers filing of a complaint to the National Labor Relations Board. Dolores Huerta, the union organiser in New York, then had to turn to the stores. This is how she explained A. & P.'s capitulation:

> In each of the five boroughs, we organised neighborhood coalitions of church, labor, liberal and student groups. Then we began picketing A. & P., the biggest chain in the city. For several months we had picket lines on about 25 to 30 stores and turned thousands of shoppers away. A lot of the managers had come up through the unions and were sympathetic to us. In response to consumer pressure, the store managers began to complain to their division heads, and soon they took the grapes out of all of their stores, 430 of them.

Within six months, all the major chains in New York City, with the exception of a phone-in home delivery firm, had stopped selling grapes. During the entire 1969 season, none resumed grape sales and total shipments to New York were down by 30 per cent.

The growers capitulated because of the demonstrable effectiveness of the boycott. Some even admitted this. Bruno Dispoto, one of the first Delano growers to sign with UFWOC, commented:

> The boycott hampered grape distribution seriously and I wasn't going to tolerate another year of insecurity. My own company suffered some losses as a result of the boycott but not to the extent that we couldn't have continued. All our creditors were extremely concerned about the boycott but they stuck with us and tried to keep us going and I have to admire them for that. But after a point, where they had experienced loss after loss, I don't think they were much in favor of continuing to finance growers who were doing nothing about the union. Something had to be done.

In some markets, grape shipments, and hence sales, were down by more than a third. While the union failed to anticipate the vulnerability of their contracts with the growers and had again to resort to the boycott to consolidate their gains, the 1965-70 boycott was an outstanding success. In *Why We Boycott* Chavez explained the case for this second boycott (which included iceberg lettuce as well as grapes not carrying the union label); he said, 'The boycott is the way we take our cause to the public. For surely if we cannot find justice in the courts of rural California, we will find support with our brothers and sisters throughout the nation.' This boycott was less effective because the issue had become muddied by the intervention of the Teamsters union and their 'sweetheart' contracts with the growers. The issue was finally resolved by California state legislation in 1975; though efforts have continued since then to make further gains and improve the still poor position of the American farm worker.

Case analysis

Identifying factors in boycott success is complicated by problems in determining causality. Factors in boycott effectiveness are more easily identified but the concern here must be with both as the two do not always go hand in hand. Certain highlights of the cases, particularly where they are common or noticeably absent, indicate factors in boycott effectiveness and success. The choice of target and its appropriateness seems influenced by: the link between the firm or product and the grievance, the size of the firm, substitute product availability, product identifiability, firm or product visibility, and the firm's involvement in the market relative to other interests (vulnerability) and in association with the value (to the pressure group) of early capitulation by the firm. The pressure group not only requires dedicated members but also good overall organisation, a network of local groups, the use of market information, and a 'divide and conquer' strategy. Finally, response factors favouring boycott effectiveness and success seem to include the right issue at the right time, moral outrage, and endorsement by important organisations or individuals.

When these findings are considered alongside other studies the following factors emerge as advantageous. On product attributes: a consumer good or service, low cost, frequently purchased, branded, substitutable, perishable, distributed through retail outlets, and publicly (visibly) purchased and consumed. Visibility of the firm may also be important. On the organisation and promotion of the boycott: good overall organisation, control, a network of local groups, promotion of the boycott (including picketing), a 'divide and conquer' strategy, the use of market information, and target firm vulnerability. As the CND case emphasises, the directness of the boycott, its connection with the grievance, is vitally important. This probably prohibits excessive use of

253

the boycott. Finally, support is essential. But, as the case studies demonstrate in contrast with previous work, support may not be simply conceived in terms of reducing demand. Moral outrage, which is important in boycott support, may by putting moral pressure on the firm be more important than economic pressure. The boycott may be successful in this way in combination with other tactics and forms of pressure on the firm. Moral outrage is associated with having the right issue at the right time.

How the firm reacts to the boycott, as the Nestlé case in particular shows, will influence boycott effectiveness and success. Four management strategies were evident in the cases: ignore, fight, fudge/explain, or comply. Barclays' response illustrates the fudge/explain strategy, as does that of MAN-VW. Tarmac used fight and ignore strategies, while the growers and Douwe Egberts used ignore (deliberately or otherwise), then fight strategies. Nestlé moved from a fight, to a fudge/explain, to a compliance strategy. The strategy employed and its appropriateness will greatly depend on the firm's culpability. Within these strategies certain management tactics seem more suitable – effective from management's point of view – than others. Fight strategies can involve counter pressure groups, counterboycotts, co-opting critics and legal action. But these tactics have been seen to backfire, particularly when disclosed. Fudge/explain strategies involve attempts to defend the firm's position, some more credible than others, particularly through public relations. Dialogue with the pressure group will also feature, perhaps persuading the group of the firm's case or achieving a compromise. The dividing line between this and dialogue within a compliance strategy is blurred; for compliance strategies may involve dialogue and negotiations, perhaps supported by social audits, but they may constitute attempts at co-option. It is probable that regardless of the strategy adopted, management may feel hurt or misunderstood. This feeling of hurt – moral pressure – will be important in the likely success of the action.

The model of the process of pressure group influence on purchase behaviour is supported by the cases. Yet more important is the support given to its key elements of the legitimacy concept, negative product augmentation, a role for pressure groups in the marketing system, and, of course, ethical purchase behaviour. The operation of the legitimacy concept and negative product augmentation is well demonstrated in consumer refusals to buy 'tainted' South African produce. A role for pressure groups in the marketing system is evident in all the cases but is seen to be particularly useful in the Nestlé case. This case also shows management reluctance to accept that role. Management should be proactive on these elements of the model by taking anticipatory action. This could even involve attempts to enhance the legitimacy of the offering and establishing relationships with relevant pressure groups.

The boycotts in the cases are moral acts by consumers, confirming the claim that they are ethical purchase behaviour. Moreover, the domain of consumer sovereignty dimension is clearly evident. Negative product augmentation recognises this dimension and the cases, as illustrations of this, thereby show that the consumer can, as, say, in the Douwe Egberts case, be concerned about coffee sources as well as coffee taste.

Finally, the cases are illustrations of the market, specifically in consumer boycotts, being used in the social control of business. The boycott was employed as a social control mechanism. In the Nestlé case, one analyst has referred to balances of power. In the successful cases, the boycott became part of a societal power equation and in the hands of consumers. So consumer sovereignty was harnessed in the way indicated earlier (such as in the Preview to Chapter 7). However, the boycott in itself may not be sufficient, and it may work alongside other tactics. It may not even be appropriate on many issues; many firms are simply not vulnerable to it. However, it can be successful without being effective, particularly given corporate hurt feelings under criticism. This suggests a symbolic type of boycott as well as the more traditional effective (or attempting to be effective) type.

So the case studies and their analysis encompass the three dominant themes in Part One. Answers are provided to the practical questions on pressure group use of the boycott and management response; while evidence has been presented to support the claim that ethical purchase behaviour can be found and seen to operate to ensure social responsibility in business.

Chapter nine

Effectiveness in the use of boycotts and management responses

Preview

Tell it how it is.

Ernest Hemingway[1]

Keep up appearances; there lies the test;
The world will give thee credit for the rest.
Outward be fair, however foul within;
Sin if thou wilt, but then in secret sin.

Charles Churchill, *Night*[2]

This study, as the Introduction explained, started with an investigation of sex-role stereotypes in advertising and the conclusion that advertising would change to reflect consumer preferences on the portrayal of women in advertising. Other sources concluded likewise. While some feminist critics might view this as an inadequate response to the issue, wishing more rapid change, they would be advised to direct their criticism to more important issues. The conclusion reached suggested that an issue of social responsibility in business would be resolved by the market; that consumer preferences in competitive markets could call business to account on social issues. In other words, consumer sovereignty could ensure social responsibility in business. This proposition has been addressed in this study.

This and the final chapter present the study findings on that proposition and related considerations. It suggests consumer sovereignty can ensure social responsibility in business through ethical purchase behaviour and, especially, consumer boycotts. But this is not an unqualified assertion of social control of business via the market; there are important caveats. So, the thesis is that consumers may, in their purchase behaviour, express concern about and attempt to remedy corporate responsibility deficiencies. In order to address this proposition

256

on consumer sovereignty and social responsibility, the study has examined consumer sovereignty, the problem of the social control of business, and the actual and potential role of pressure groups acting on business. This examination provided support for the proposed concept of ethical purchase behaviour. Its increased use in its more deliberate form, the consumer boycott, seems likely with growing promotional pressure group activity and the concern of these groups for effective tactics to use against business. Because of this, and as consumer boycotts are a readily accessible form of ethical purchase behaviour and explicitly concerned with the social control of business, the boycott tactic was considered in detail and a model proposed on how pressure groups may use it. The consumer boycott was also empirically investigated in survey research and case studies.

The principal general conclusions of the study are presented in the next chapter. This chapter concentrates on the more specific conclusions on pressure group use of the boycott tactic and management responses.

Effective use of the consumer boycott tactic

Symbolic and effective consumer boycotts

This chapter is concerned with answering the question: How may pressure groups most effectively employ the consumer boycott tactic and how should boycotted businesses respond? In responding to this, it is vital to distinguish between boycott effectiveness and success. This distinction, found in the analysis of international economic sanctions, is based on the difference between the achievement of an economic impact and realising the objectives of the action. It has equal application to consumer boycotts. Writers on sanctions make the distinction to emphasise that effectiveness does not necessarily give rise to success, as in the case of US sanctions against Cuba. While it is generally assumed that effectiveness is necessary for success, some writers on sanctions, such as Galtung, question this. He observes that the goals in their use may involve punishment and the enforcement of international morality as well as policy changes in the boycotted country. In other words, sanctions have expressive and instrumental functions. So they may be successful without being effective.

Consumer boycotts also have expressive and instrumental functions. Yet this is ignored by the limited previous work on consumer boycotts. This work suggests that effectiveness is necessary for success. This may be excused where the writers were referring to the use of the consumer boycott by early labour unions and where success was entirely defined as forcing compliance from the firm. It does not apply today, however. The case studies reported bear witness to this. A consumer boycott may be successful without being effective. Its use may be to draw attention to an issue and say something about the moral shortcomings of the firm and try and punish it. Remer's study of Chinese boycotts identified publicity and punishment as aims as well as policy changes. He suggests the boycott may be a theatrical sword. This expressive rather than instrumental function means consumer boycotts may be successful in terms other than compliance. In the Anti-Apartheid boycotts, for example, success may be said to have been achieved in so far as firms with links with South Africa are publicised and punished. This is realised without effectiveness. The boycott also contributes to the aggregate of pressure for change and discourages other firms from involvement with South Africa, largely because of the publicity gained.

So consumer boycotts may be successful without being effective because publicity or punishment may have been intended. More importantly, consumer boycotts may be successful without being effective because of company fears for its corporate image or its employees' sense of social responsibility. This points to a second important distinction: there are two types of consumer boycott, the effective and the symbolic. Symbolic boycotts try to punish and publicise a firm responsible for some grievance. Punishment, of course, is closely related to morality. The boycott is a moral act; an expression by the consumer of disapproval of the firm's activities and disassociation from them. In such circumstances, it may not even be appropriate to refer to objectives or effectiveness. As, no doubt, in many consumers' refusal to purchase South African goods, the wish is to avoid tainted (and being tainted by) products of apartheid.

Yet while having this expressive function, symbolic boycotts may also be successful. The firms boycotted are, after all, organisations comprised of people. They too have feelings and morals. Schumpeter may bemoan 'the employee mentality' and the consequent lack of entrepreneurship, but this also brings with it the professional manager for whom profit can assume a lesser importance than the entrepreneur Schumpeter would favour. These managers may be more easily hurt by the criticism implied in boycotts and, with less personal profit at stake, more ready to appease it. Indeed, such managers may have more to gain personally by appeasing such criticism than fighting it. They are also aware of the doctrine of social responsibility in business and various claims made by themselves or others in the organisation about practising it. Looking outwardly, there is the impact of the criticism on the corporate image. This has a bearing on all the firm's business and its long-term survival. Finally, there is always the possibility that a symbolic boycott may become effective and, therefore, economically coercive.

The effectiveness of international economic sanctions is said to depend on the receiving country's vulnerability. This in turn depends largely on the degree to which its trade is concentrated on one or a small number of commodities. It may, for example, entirely rely on the import of oil for its energy requirements. In consumer boycotts, a firm's vulnerability will have an impact on effectiveness and success but in a more complex way than this. In an effective boycott where the boycotted product constitutes much of the firm's business, then clearly success is more likely than where the product is less important. (So, for example, the table grape producers, although able to divert some of their grapes to crush, were dependent on the sale of table grapes. As these sales suffered they came under strong pressure to capitulate.) However, in a symbolic boycott, where moral rather than economic pressure is important, this concentration factor would not matter. Indeed, the reverse may apply, because of the threat to their many other interests, particularly in damage to the overall corporate image.

Related to this is the firm's financial strength prior to the boycott. Traditional boycott analysis would presume financial weakness more likely to give rise to success. In an effective boycott this would be the case, as the economic impact would bite sooner. But because it is more difficult to be socially responsible when 'one's back is against the wall', financial weakness would be a disadvantage in the symbolic boycott. Where the boycott does not have a serious economic effect, the costs of changing the criticised practice may be too great (expensive) for the financially beleaguered firm related to the perceived benefits.

So given this distinction between symbolic and effective boycotts, care must be exercised in referring to factors in boycott effectiveness and success. Accordingly, the next section refers to strategic and tactical considerations in the use of the consumer boycott by pressure groups.

Pressure group strategic and tactical considerations

The factors in boycott effectiveness and success identified from the literature and the case studies were discussed earlier. They can most usefully be grouped as they emerged in the case study analysis: by choice of target, the organisation and strategy of the pressure group, and the response to the boycott. The factors are summarised in this way in Table 9.1. Care must be exercised in referring to such factors. They are desirable or advantageous factors in boycott effectiveness and success rather than conditional factors. In the grape boycott, for example, no directly substitutable product was available. Moral outrage and the appropriateness of the firm are probably conditional factors, but many apparently conditional factors, such as substitutability, may not be important under certain circumstances. Accordingly, the identification of necessary and sufficient conditions for boycott effectiveness and success is problematical. One can note the obvious; that a boycott has to,

Table 9.1: Factors in consumer boycott effectiveness and success

Choice of Target	Organisation and Strategy of the Pressure Group	Response to the Boycott

Appropriateness of firm:
– responsibility for/involvement in the grievance
– vulnerability
– size (market share and/or turnover)
– visibility
– value of early capitulation
 	
Appropriateness of product/brand:
– connection with the grievance (remoteness)
– substitutability:
  • choice (competition)
  • involvement of the other firms in the grievance
  • consumer preferences (brand loyalty)
– identifiable (branded) }
– consumer product   } FMCG
– low cost
– frequently purchased
– visibility of purchase/ consumption
– sold through retail outlets (for secondary boycotts)
	Organisational factors:
	– dedication to the cause
	– good overall organisation
	– control
	– network of local groups
	
	Strategy and tactics:
	– use of strategic/tactical approach
	– promotion of the boycott (inc. picketing)
	– timing of actions in the campaign
	– choice of target, especially:
	  • use of market information (market segmentation)
	  • 'divide and conquer' strategy
	– use of boycott as last resort (frequency of boycotts)
		By consumers (public):
		– moral outrage
		– right issue at the right time
		– willingness to boycott (perceived consumer effectiveness)
		
		By others:
		– management reaction and responses
		– endorsement:
		  • public figures
		  • other firms

and has only to, reduce demand to be effective. But this is not very helpful as many factors may prompt this and it is these various and often different factors that are of interest to pressure groups (and management). Moreover, effectiveness is not necessary for success.

Necessary and sufficient or conditional factors can only be proposed at a relatively high level of generalisation if they are to be robust. Given this observation, it may be suggested that the necessary and sufficient conditions for a successful consumer boycott are support for the issue on which the target firm is involved and consumer sovereignty. Of course, consumer sovereignty is proposed with the meaning given to it in this study. Put otherwise, sufficient consumers must be concerned, willing, and able for a consumer boycott to be successful. They must be concerned in the sense of being aware, having understanding of and sympathy for the cause. They must be willing to express that concern in purchase behaviour (acknowledging the domain dimension of consumer sovereignty). And they must be able to do so by being in the appropriate competitive market-place (the degree dimension of consumer sovereignty).

So, if necessary and sufficient conditions need to be identified this can be done, but only at a fairly general and non-actionable level. It is more sensible to refer to strategic and tactical considerations in the use of the boycott. In doing so, it is recognised that there is a distinction between effectiveness and success and between symbolic and effective boycotts, as discussed above, and that the factors in boycott effectiveness and success vary in importance according to the circumstances of the action. The necessary and sufficient conditions for a successful consumer boycott specified constitute a simple formula for pressure groups. Table 9.1 however incorporates all the major strategic and tactical considerations in the successful use of the consumer boycott by groups, as identified in this study. The table is largely self-explanatory but some comment needs to be made on its less obvious aspects and some of the issues it raises.

Under choice of target there are two categories. This makes the distinction between the firm and the product boycotted; though it does mean that the factor of connection appears twice. There is the connection between the boycotted product and the grievance, which may be different to the connection between the firm and the grievance. Both are important but separate considerations in deciding to organise a consumer boycott against a firm. For example, grapes could be directly connected with the issue of farm worker unionisation. Saran Wrap, however, was more remote from the issue of Dow's manufacture of napalm. Consider the connection between the firm and the grievance in the CND case. Although MAN trucks were closely connected – indeed physically connected – to cruise missiles, MAN-VW (UK), the Lonrho subsidiary, was hardly connected at all. It could not reasonably be claimed that they bore great responsibility for, or could influence, MAN's participation in the supply of trucks to the military that would then be used to pull cruise missiles.

Associated with this is the 'level' of the boycott. Secondary boycotts are more remote from the grievance and therefore less likely to be supported. Yet they may be important in putting pressure on the principal target. So a product sold through retail outlets, which may then be subject to boycott (with picketing) is more likely to give rise to a successful boycott than one sold by mail order. This also illustrates the factor of product visibility in purchase. As Rea notes, visibility in purchase and consumption is likely to make social pressure on consumers greater. Fast moving consumer goods (FMCG) would, because of the factors identified, seem to offer most potential as consumer boycott targets. But, as the Tarmac boycott shows, there is scope for a boycott wherever customers of the firm involved in the grievance are potential supporters of the pressure group.

The vulnerability of the firm was discussed above. It is related to the factor of the value of early capitulation, considered useful in putting pressure on other firms. A firm only marginally involved in the grievance may be more likely to accede to pressure group demands. It may be only marginally involved, in having wider and more important business interests which it would not wish to see threatened. Or the firm may only be a minor culprit on the issue and so has less to lose in making the requested changes. Typically – to avoid the charge of 'why pick on us?' – this would be where a number of firms were boycotted. An example would be of Next's decision to stop stocking South African clothing in their stores, when it only constituted a small proportion of their turnover. Vulnerability also includes financial strength, but this may be an advantage or disadvantage according to whether the boycott is symbolic or effective.

Visibility is a factor in product or brand appropriateness, as discussed above, but also in firm appropriateness. There is the visibility of the firm in association with the grievance, which will be due to the firm's connection with the grievance and public awareness of it. This will be influenced by management reaction to the boycott; contrast, for example, Tarmac's low profile response with that by Nestlé. There is also the visibility of the firm *per se*. A firm such as Nestlé may be a household name, but BTR, which owns among other consumer companies the well-known tights company Pretty Polly, is probably not. BTR has a category A reporting responsibility under the EEC code of Conduct but does not always report.[3] Yet its low consumer visibility may make a boycott organised around its consumer companies of limited meaning to consumers. This of course is related to the connection factor.

Firms may also be visible in particular ways. If they are known or indeed promote themselves on their social responsibility then the threat to the corporate image may be greater and their managers more likely to experience guilt when presented with a consumer boycott. This would make a symbolic boycott more likely to be successful.

Under organisation and strategy of the pressure group, in Table 9.1, there are two categories. There are first those described as organisational factors, which refer to the qualities and competencies of the group. These are fairly straightforward. It need only be noted that, as the pressure group literature suggested and the CND case confirmed, good organisation and control can be elusive for promotional pressure groups. The second category refers to pressure group strategies and tactics in the use of the boycott. It should be emphasised here that because of the nature of most promotional groups the 'deliberateness' that this implies may be largely absent. A boycott may be called because 'it seems a good idea', but with no clear objectives or strategy. It may simply amount to the pressure group asking people not to buy from a particular firm because to do so would be immoral. So the use of a strategic or tactical approach could well be lacking and possibly even considered irrelevant by some groups.[4] Yet, as the cases illustrate, how a group chooses its targets, how it promotes the boycott, and its timing, can be very important. Boycott failure may also tarnish the pressure group, as Hill claimed of CND and George Smith comments (see Chapter 7).

Boycott failure would presumably also tarnish the tactic; though its success in the Nestlé case has clearly added to its credibility. This has meant that the threat of boycott action is all the more important. It may be that the biggest impact of boycotts (and all ethical purchase behaviour) is in their threat or possibility rather than actuality, prompting social responsibility in the first place. Yet there is also a case for groups talking to firms before instituting a boycott. The Angola Committee did this and secured the required concessions from Albert Heijn, giving their campaign a useful and early stimulus. So, by explicitly threatening the boycott on a specific action the group achieved its aims, with that firm at least. There is also the matter of fairness. MAN-VW felt CND behaved quite shabbily in not approaching them before announcing the boycott. Fairness may become important if the group needs to cooperate with the firm in some way. A strategic and tactical use of the boycott by pressure groups would presume some understanding of how boycotts work. The boycott mechanism as earlier discussed identified the threat of the boycott as an important part of the process.

Finally, under response to the boycott in Table 9.1, there are the categories of consumer response and response by others. Consumer response refers to public opinion on the boycott and the attitudes of potential boycott supporters. The factors shown are straightforward and have been discussed. The importance of moral outrage has been emphasised, though it is notably understated or ignored elsewhere. It is worth reiterating the point about symbolic boycotts and how their success is tied to moral outrage and popular support rather than effectiveness.

While a pressure group organising a consumer boycott may be successful without the boycott being effective, it is unlikely that the group will not have economic impact as an aim. Boycotts are most likely to be understood in these terms by the pressure group's supporters. So although two types of consumer boycott are identified here, the symbolic and the effective, this categorisation reflects likely consequences rather than a planned end result. This is the difference between the manifest and the latent. For example, in the Barclays boycott the action had the manifest intent of the firm bowing to economic pressure, but the latent intent of it succumbing to moral pressure. Recognition of symbolic and effective boycotts is important in this context. The factor of willingness to boycott reflects the belief by some that what they see as extraneous influences on purchase behaviour are inappropriate, and it also reflects perceived consumer effectiveness. Unless consumers believe that their purchase decisions will have an impact on the issue of concern, then they are unlikely to participate in a boycott except where they feel so strongly about the issue that they do not wish to be tainted by it. In other words, where an individual's support for a boycott is more pragmatic than moral, then he or she will be concerned about its effectiveness, especially where some personal cost is incurred – going without grapes, for example, or having to buy a less preferred brand. So consumer boycotts have to be promoted as actions intended to have an economic impact.

Having said this, however, it is worth repeating the earlier observation about mass support for NVDA, including consumer boycotts. While individual consumers may practise ethical purchase behaviour on a variety of issues, can they be so organised as to produce an effective boycott? Do boycotts simply constitute a nuisance to management, which, if it were not for the publicity they also brought with them, could be ignored? Certainly, the publicity which boycotts bring means that management ignores them at its peril. It is the publicity and the moral criticism implied that makes symbolic boycotts successful. But effective boycotts are a possibility. Mass support for NVDA is more likely under conditions of great oppression. The recent use of consumer boycotts in South Africa bears this out. They have been very effective, with businesses having to close down. Yet the same outcome was achieved in the grape boycott, where those supporting the boycott were not greatly oppressed. It seems safe to conclude that effective boycotts are possible without conditions of great oppression, given the right issue. Although less likely, this potential for economic impact should then be a further consideration for management beyond publicity and the moral opprobrium. It is also the spur likely to overcome any consumer doubts about effectiveness providing other conditions are met, such as having a suitable target and so on.

Related to this is the cultural appropriateness of consumer boycotts and the issue of consumers as a 'forgotten group'. Non-violent direct action may be more culturally appropriate to Eastern rather than Western peoples, but this does not apply to consumer boycotts. Whereas there may have been more effective boycotts in the East, this may have more to do with the associated oppression and, after all, there have been effective boycotts in the West. Moreover, if the successful symbolic boycotts and the impact on management of the possibility of boycotts (or ethical purchase behaviour of some form) is taken into account, consumer boycotts are probably more culturally appropriate to the market society of the West; though there are differences within the West, between Britain and the US, for example. Perhaps one can refer to a latent promise for boycotts. If consumer boycotts are ethical purchase behaviour then one would expect to find them in a market or consumer society. For this reason, consumers are not 'forgotten groups'; producers in competitive markets cannot afford to ignore them. Anyway, in consumer boycotts, the organisation of consumers *per se* is not important, but their organisation as consumers concerned about a particular issue. Willingness to boycott is not an abstract quality. As indicated above, it is linked quite closely to the issue. It will also be linked to the target of the boycott: there may be embarrassment or difficulties in being committed to a pressure group's aims, publicly demonstrated in supporting some boycotts. It may also be easier to express that commitment in some boycotts than in others. Not buying a brand of toothpaste is likely to be an easier way of expressing commitment to a cause than not buying a preferred make of car.

Before turning to management responses to boycotts, it is worth noting that boycotts should not be seen in isolation and that their use does raise ethical and legal issues. On the former point, it should be emphasised that consumer boycotts are likely to be only one tactic among a number employed on an issue and against any particular firm. Success is likely to be the outcome of all these efforts as well as external factors, and not just the boycott – besides which, it is often not possible to say why success was achieved because of the muddiness of the process; firms are unlikely to acknowledge what prompted a decision to capitulate, if they can be certain themselves.

The legality of consumer boycotts in Britain was raised in the CND case. A firm may have grounds for securing an injunction against a pressure group where the firm's customers are specifically asked not to buy its products. However, Barclays, for example, admitted that they would never sue; though no doubt where boycotts become effective there is greater pressure to do so, as Tarmac suggested. Where the greatest impact on a firm of a boycott is publicity, legal action seems unlikely if not foolish. The pressure group may defend its breach of the law (if such it is) by comparing it to other minor breaches of the law. They might also argue that the law is broken to seek remedy for a more important cause and that, along the lines of Etzioni's argument in *Demonstration Democracy*, the boycott is justified because there are few other forms of expression and that business, as a 'private government', is not in other ways accountable.

The ethics and legality issues are quite closely related, and not just because breaking the law may be said to be unethical. Both legal and ethical doubts about boycotts only become important where boycotts are effective. In symbolic boycotts the action has principally an expressive function. Where symbolic boycotts are successful, management is not so much coerced by as conforming to public or societal expectations. Effective boycotts have a more coercive quality. Although, as Chapter 4 showed, this may be defended as pluralism, pressure groups do need to think through the consequences of their actions where effective boycotts are involved. Other ethical issues in boycotts are considered later, including the issue of intimidation of shoppers by pickets.

So, to sum up on effective use of the consumer boycott by pressure groups: boycotts are more likely to be successful under certain conditions, particularly where the choice of target for the boycott is appropriate, where the pressure group is organised in a particular way and has a strategic or tactical approach, and where there is a favourable response to the boycott. These factors are shown in Table 9.1. Because effectiveness is not necessary for success and there can be symbolic as well as effective boycotts, and because of the different circumstances that may occur, it is not possible to refer to necessary and sufficient conditions for successful boycotts at a less than general level.

Appropriate management responses

Management response strategies and tactics

Management response to a consumer boycott might differ according to whether the boycott is symbolic or effective. As most consumer boycotts are likely to be symbolic rather than effective, for the reasons discussed above, management's concern will probably lie with the potential publicity and moral impact rather than the immediate or short-term economic impact of boycotts. Yet just as pressure groups

Table 9.2: Management response strategies and tactics

Strategies:	IGNORE	FIGHT	FUDGE/EXPLAIN	COMPLY
Some possible tactics	Maintain a low profile – do nothing – stonewall	Fight the pressure group – 'We're right' – legal action – direct attention to government: 'don't mix business and politics' – contact authorities for help • boycott-busting: • promotion – discounts, advertising, etc. • use different brand names/labels • sell to intermediary for repackaging • counter-pickets • attacks on pickets – smear campaigns: • such as 'this pressure group is communist inspired' – various threats: • such as plant closures – 'if we don't others will' – 'look at the others involved!'	Fudge the issue by presenting another case – PR activities – co-option – counter-pressure groups – counterboycotts – endorse firm's position by reference to government policy	Cooperate with the pressure group – dialogue/negotiation with the pressure group – self-regulatory efforts • such as social audits – lobby for industry-wide legislation – use of intermediaries

decreasing   Level of support for the pressure group and corporate culpability indicate strategy and tactic appropriateness.   increasing need to have the intention of organising effective boycotts, management should likewise determine its strategy – by acting as if boycotts could become effective. There are three reasons for this. First, a boycott may become effective. Second, as in pressure groups, those in the organisation may best understand boycotts as potentially economically damaging actions, even if symbolic boycotts only have economic impact in the long term. Third, and perhaps most importantly, strategy should be determined not by an assessment of likely immediate economic impact, but because of the corporate image and morale factors, by an assessment of the firm's culpability and public support for the pressure group on the issue.

So the strategic options remain the same for management regardless of whether the boycott is symbolic or effective. There may be some variation in the tactics employed. Within a fight strategy, for example, boycott-busting tactics may be more important in an effective boycott than trying to direct the attention of the pressure group towards government. But the strategy adopted depends on whether management feels its critics are right and how much support they have. Table 9.2 lists management response strategies and some possible tactics. The four strategies suggested (ignore, fight, fudge/explain, comply) are the only options available to management when presented with a boycott. However, it must be said that they are likely to be only how management's overall approach to the boycott is characterised. They are not mutually exclusive and as the Nestlé case shows, management's approach may change over time. Moreover, the distinctions between the strategies are also blurred when it comes to the tactics employed. Counterboycotts, for example, may form part of a fudge or a fight strategy, just as dialogue may form part of a fudge or comply strategy. So it is not claimed that Table 9.2 is robust, it is merely thought indicative of general tendencies. It also, to some extent, assumes the pressure group is 'right'.

One of the greatest difficulties about this research area, and an important point made throughout the study, is that social responsibility issues are rarely clear-cut. Arguments may often go either way on an issue. Different parties may have different priorities. But if it is accepted that where there is public condemnation of a firm's action then the pressure group is 'right', all strategies other than compliance amount to firms being 'in the wrong' and not being socially responsible. Firms in this position may choose to try to ignore the criticism levelled at it, may openly fight the pressure group, or may fight the group covertly by fudging the issue. The muddier the issue, the easier it is for management to present an alternative case to that of the pressure group. In practice, it may be difficult to distinguish between fight and fudge strategies, though a skilled management will seek to minimise any overtly fighting tactics within a fudge strategy. So, for example, attempts to promote counter-pressure groups and counterboycotts would need to be surreptitious if management were to maintain credibility for the case it was advancing to fudge the issue. Similarly, great subtlety would be needed in attempts to co-opt pressure group members or government officials.

The outward appearance of a fudge strategy would be as close as possible to that of a compliance strategy; though in either case it is not necessary for management to bow to every whim of the group. Compliance simply involves resolving the issue in a way that achieves the aims of the pressure group. Management need not admit to this to follow a compliance strategy. A fudge strategy would reflect this. As Charles Churchill said, 'Keep up appearances; there lies the test; the world will give thee credit for the rest.' However, to account for instances where management has different priorities to the pressure group and to go beyond the simplistic notion of the pressure group as 'right' and management as 'wrong', the fudge strategy may be more appropriately seen as an explain strategy. This gives rise to the suggestion of a fudge/explain strategy as shown in Table 9.2.

The ignore strategy is basically one of keeping a low profile to avoid exacerbating the problem. This may be a first response to pressure group publicity on the issue and the firm's involvement. It is a waiting game that leaves the initiative with the pressure group but is in the hope that the issue will blow over. As noted in Chapter 4, replying to pressure groups gives them legitimacy, and it also adds to the publicity. Of course, an ignore strategy may not in practice be the result of a deliberate policy decision. Management may reject the legitimacy of pressure groups to criticise their activities (this happened in the Douwe Egberts case) or not see them as a threat. This is short-sighted. Regardless of whether the role of pressure groups is accepted, they are a feature of the business environment and are capable of reversing a firm's and individual managers' fortunes.

For similar reasons, a firm may respond with a fight strategy. In its extreme forms, this can involve attacks on pickets, as in the grape boycott, or smear campaigns, as in Nestlé's attempts to brand INFACT as communists. These tactics were patently inappropriate and failed, though they would not always do so. Violence was successfully employed by the authorities in South Africa to defeat the Ciskei bus boycott. Similarly, the grape growers were able to use the communist threat in earlier attempts at unionisation. Tactics such as legal action and arguing 'don't mix business and politics' can be equally inappropriate, even though they are less extreme. They may simply be a gut reaction by managers to 'left-wing loonies'. So a fight strategy may involve the use of the wrong tactics as a result of a failure to make a deliberate policy decision and because of a misunderstanding of the business environment or, as Berle puts it, the 'frame of surrounding conceptions' within which the firm operates. This is not to suggest that a fight strategy will always involve inappropriate tactics or not be successful. The use of a fight strategy may bring success for management in the right circumstances. However, avoiding confrontation does seem more suited to the contemporary business environment. So if management is to respond to a pressure group, but not comply with its demands, a fudge/explain strategy is to be preferred. This would be more appropriate to a participative society which emphasises pluralism. It is also, for this reason, more likely to be successful than an ignore strategy, which may, in any event, prove impossible.

The various strategies described are 'ideal types' in many ways. They may describe effects rather than intentions. The distinctions between them are blurred. They have also been presented on the assumption of management guilt. In practice this will not be so obvious. A fight strategy may be employed because management genuinely feels it is right. The growers in the grape boycott, or some of them at least, believed their workers did not want or need unionisation. Similarly, a fudge/explain strategy may not be the result of Machiavellian management, efforts at political manipulation. Many Barclays managers sincerely believed that constructive engagement was a more appropriate alternative to the disinvestment suggested by pressure groups, and not just out of self-interest. It is important to recognise that these managers may actually be 'right'; that is, not just on their terms, but more generally. Because social responsibility issues are not clear-cut, management may have a case.

It is for this reason that one may refer to explain strategies (as above) and that Table 9.2 includes the continuum of culpability and support for the pressure group. Culpability and support go together because, without support for the pressure group, management need not do anything on the issue. Accordingly, where support and culpability are greatest, a compliance strategy is more likely or, at least, more sensible. Where support and culpability are negligible, an ignore strategy is likely. So, for example, if the pressure group has not got a strong case and lacks support, management may successfully use a fight strategy. But if support is greater, it would be more likely to be successful using a fudge/explain strategy. Within a pluralistic model, culpability would equate with support for the pressure group. The pressure group would receive support in proportion to the guilt of the firm and the importance attached to it. Hence to some extent the decision on the strategy management adopts is made for it. Barclays, for example, could not have defended, even using a fudge/explain strategy, involvement with the Amin regime in Uganda, for example.

However, some managements may not see or be guided by their culpability. Moreover, pluralism in practice has many imperfections. So management may be able to get away with acts that are not socially responsible because of this. Pressure group support and corporate guilt will not always equate and management may successfully employ a non-compliance strategy where there is a shortfall in support relative to great corporate guilt. Where the pressure group is 'wrong', or perhaps has different priorities to management, yet still receives substantial support, then there may alternatively be a shortfall in corporate guilt relative to support. Management may then have to respond to the pressure group demands despite its relative lack of guilt. The strategy adopted has to reflect both assessments of culpability and support if management wishes to achieve its aims. There is, of course, the position that management's aims may include being socially responsible, in which case it would be argued that culpability should be the sole basis for the continuum and for determining strategy. However, this would be naive. Not because management is only socially responsible if it has to be – although this may happen it is not as simple as this because of the role of the manager's values – but because of differences in priorities. It is therefore appropriate that management should be guided by support for pressure groups as well as an assessment of its guilt.

So, to conclude. Four strategic options are available to management if presented with a consumer boycott, or, indeed, any other form of challenge from a pressure group. If management chooses not to comply with the demands made, either because it disagrees with the pressure group on the issue or does not feel it has to or can afford to comply, then it may employ an ignore, fight, or fudge/explain strategy. It may not use one strategy exclusively and its response may change over time. Choice of strategy should be guided by culpability and support for the pressure group, but a fudge/explain strategy is likely to be the most successful. The use of this may reflect a genuine difference on priorities as well as attempts to defeat the pressure group. However, there is a caveat to this. While a fudge/explain strategy may work in the short or medium term, or on a one-off issue or digression, it may not be successful in the long term or on a subsequent occasion. If the grievance is perpetuated and pressure group activities and public interest are sustained, then the firm will be found out. This is evident in the Nestlé case. If a firm successfully uses a fudge/explain strategy to mask a one-off grievance (of the sort described earlier as corporate digressions), it is then less likely to get away with this should another digression occur. The impact on the organisation's legitimacy is then doubled.

Yet at least as far as continued grievances are concerned, fudge/explain strategies may succeed because, as governments well know, pressure groups and their issues are often ephemeral or merely fashionable. So firms, like governments, may simply address the symptoms and not the illness or causes. Rather than dealing with the issue, the alleged lack of social responsibility by the business, the firm may try and placate or defeat the pressure group such that it eventually goes away. A further, human, problem with the fudge/explain strategy, and the others that involve non-compliance, is how they affect the organisation. If people within the organisation no longer believe and accept the firm's defence of its involvement in the grievance, this is likely to influence morale. What sort of organisation abdicates moral responsibility? What sort of people would work in it and would it be a pleasant organisation in which to work? Cigarette manufacturers and firms making arms experience some recruitment difficulties because of the nature of their business. It would seem likely that the same difficulties would be faced by other firms where a pressure group has clearly won the moral argument. In the short term it may prompt the better staff to leave. It could at least influence commitment to the job. Some shareholders would also consider whether it is the sort of organisation in which they would wish to invest. So a consumer boycott may extend beyond the product market and have repercussions in the firm's recruitment and investment markets.

Yet there is a fifth strategy that management might consider. This is not so much in response to pressure group demands but in anticipation of them.

The proactive management strategy

The process model of pressure group influence on purchase behaviour proposed can be extended by including the four management response strategies. One might also, along the lines of the Ford and Vezeridis environmental conflict model, include the stage of management learning from its mistakes. Ford and Vezeridis call this the pre-emptive strike. Here it is more appropriate to refer to a proactive strategy. This need not be the outcome of having experienced a consumer boycott but would be in recognition of the arguments advanced in this study. In particular, it would acknowledge the role of pressure groups in the marketing system, the problem of the social control of business, and consumer sovereignty.

The anticipatory approach for management suggested here goes beyond that advanced elsewhere. It is more than environmental scanning and similar passive activities. It is effectively an open compliance strategy before any conflict has taken place and any pressure is put on the firm, and would include those tactics shown in Table 9.2 under the comply strategy. Although it may not entirely avoid conflict – this is inevitable where there are major differences in priorities –

it will certainly reduce the likelihood of it. Any conflicts that do take place would likely also be less acrimonious and thereby damaging to the firm.

One tactic or feature of the proactive strategy could be the use of the social audit; not, however, the all-embracing social audit that has been suggested, this is not realistic. But companies could audit areas of their activity where pressure groups are active and concerned. So, in contrast to the passive anticipatory management approach, this would involve finding out where potential difficulties are likely to arise for the firm in the business environment, yet also doing something about them. It would, for example, have meant Nestlé identifying 'commerciogenic malnutrition' and, before the issue had even reached the public, establishing NIFAC. One of the problems with a social audit is who actually does it. Whoever it is will have different interests even though the range of these interests would be reduced if the audit focused on a specific issue. Accusations of bias made against NIFAC resulted from the 'who pays the piper calls the tune' argument. Nestlé's critics read the NIFAC reports and replied 'says who?' While different priorities may make some conflict inevitable and such audits would have to be funded by the firm, accusations of bias would have been less likely if the pressure groups had been involved. In other words, a proactive strategy, in doing something about the issue, would attempt to include pressure groups.

Proactive management would welcome pressure groups! There are three principal reasons for this evident from the study. First, pressure groups can have a warning role for management. Many pressure groups achieve little more than provide information on an issue and put issues on the political agenda. Yet in so doing they both identify and contribute to a threat in the business environment of the firm. Assessing the importance of this threat – an established problem in environmental scanning – can be achieved by dialogue with the concerned pressure groups. Whether management chooses to use pressure groups in this way, pressure groups will increasingly be an important factor and potential threat in the business environment. Second, giving pressure groups such a role goes some way towards resolving the problem of identifying the firm's social responsibilities and their priority. Firms that wish to behave in a socially responsible way may also use pressure groups to ensure that their industry counterparts do likewise and that they do not lose competitive advantage by being socially responsible. Finally (though there are ethical considerations here), welcoming pressure groups may bring with it incorporation; or, to be more positive, a greater likelihood of compromise by the pressure groups. Governments use pressure groups to provide information, just as suggested for the firm above. They also involve pressure groups – give them insider status – to achieve incorporation. The pressure group is co-opted. It can result in some power sharing but it is considered worth it. The more tangible, financial costs are also thought justified.

The problem for pressure groups, relative to government and business, is to decide whether they want insider status with the risk of co-option, but the possible achievement of their aims, and whether they are able to demand it. Involving pressure groups in, for example, social audits, is a useful way in which the firm might identify and resolve threatening issues in the business environment. The added costs and risks of this approach seem outweighed by the benefits. From the business and society perspective this also promises some measure of corporate accountability, although whether firms would seek this and welcome pressure groups for this reason is another matter. They are more likely to accept a pressure group role because of the advantages it may bring or because they see it as inevitable.

As well as the pressure group role, management should also acknowledge other features of the process model if it wishes to adopt a proactive strategy. They are: legitimacy as part of the marketing mix, negative product augmentation, and, of course, ethical purchase behaviour. How it should do this – and why – is apparent from the rest of the study, but some comments need to be made here on ethical purchase behaviour within a proactive strategy. A proactive approach would include a marketing strategy that seeks to enhance the legitimacy of the offering, in recognition of ethical purchase behaviour. Anticipatory management would recognise that there can be ethical purchase behaviour and, within this, what is ethical is defined by its customers, regardless of the company's and any other party's perspectives. On such issues, as on more specifically product related matters, the firm must let the customer choose.

Many companies are already doing this. Hirsch, for example, which markets leather watchstraps, produces its own point-of-sale displays which emphasise that its products come from non-endangered species. Similarly, Welleda, and other cosmetics and toiletries companies, note on their packaging, in large print, that their products are not tested on animals. The Body Shop organisation takes a firmer stand on the treatment of animals issue. It even decided to sponsor Greenpeace, because 'We are so naturally akin in our ideals that we feel it will be an ideal match.'[5] Part of this involved the placing of the Greenpeace anti-advertisement for furs in company shop areas;[6] though, of course, Greenpeace is also active on issues not related to animals, such as nuclear power and arms. Another, quite different, example would be Marks and Spencer's policy of buying British, promoting on that, and emphasising its relationship to employment. This, of course, is Kotler's societal marketing concept at work. But, as earlier emphasised, it should be noted that it is not likely to be universal. While all consumers can and will, given consumer sovereignty, practise ethical purchase behaviour, this will mean what they want it to mean. Consumers will not necessarily agree on what is ethical on any one specific issue.

The major implication of this for management is in market segmentation. Previous studies, which may now be classed as in the area of ethical purchase behaviour, focused on socially responsible consumption. Their concern was generally limited to the pollution effects of the product in consumption; leaded petrol, for example. This study shows that there is far more to it than this. These other studies claim, somewhat dubiously, that they have identified the socially responsible consumer. This study argues that it is possible and sensible for management to identify segments concerned about any number of ethical issues that may impinge on the market-place and become manifest as ethical purchase behaviour. It may be that some consumers are more likely to practise ethical purchase behaviour than others. Some sources have identified a consumerist segment,[7] which may be more likely to indulge in ethical purchase behaviour. So, while all consumers can and will practise ethical purchase behaviour, management's concern is to identify those consumers in its market-place that may do so on specific issues relating to its products. On some issues, clearly the majority may feel so strongly as to practise ethical purchase behaviour. The Falklands crisis and its impact on Argentinian products is a case in point. These differences and their expression in the market-place are appropriate to the pluralist model, as later discussed.

So, in sum, management may anticipate pressure group activity, including consumer boycotts, and adopt a proactive strategy. This would involve cooperation with pressure groups and the recognition of ethical purchase behaviour, tempered by the size of the threat posed by the groups. It would also involve acknowledgement of the market segmentation implications of ethical purchase behaviour. The cases emphasise that management needs to be in tune with the rest of society. Firms' misunderstanding of their business environments, evident in the cases with deleterious effects and elsewhere, would best be reduced by a proactive strategy as here proposed.

General boycott principles

The paucity of material on consumer boycotts prompted an investigation of the literature on other types of boycott. This suggested general boycott principles; that there are common features to boycotts whether they be international economic sanctions, materials boycotts (blacking) by trade unions, or consumer boycotts. The similarities between economic sanctions and consumer boycotts – at first glance two seemingly quite disparate activities – were noted above. Elsewhere, other common features to boycotts have been noted or are apparent. It is not the main concern here to identify general boycott principles. However, the more prominent boycott principles can be briefly stated.

First, a boycott, as ostracism, is a moral act. It may be used as a tactic in an entirely pragmatic way, but it is ostensibly at least a moral statement of disassociation. Any boycott is the exercise of the most fundamental action members within a society can take to show disapproval of another or others, by excluding or rejecting them from that society. Boycotts are implicitly, if not explicitly, moral acts. Second, boycotts are statements of disapproval as well as potentially coercive actions. As Galtung observes, they have expressive as well as instrumental functions. So their use may reflect the objectives of punishment and publicity as well as policy changes.

Third, there is a distinction between boycott effectiveness and success. Effectiveness refers to the boycott actually working, and in many boycotts this means economic impact. Success, however, refers to the boycott achieving its objectives. Although, because of the second point, a boycott may be successful by simply saying something about approved behaviour, success is usually conceived as involving acquiescence to a set of demands. The distinction is made between success and effectiveness because one does not necessarily give rise to the other. Boycotts can be effective but not successful, or successful without being effective.

This observation gives rise to a fourth point; boycotts may be symbolic or effective. They may be successful in either case. The symbolic boycott is successful because of moral pressure. The effective boycott is successful for a more coercive reason, depending on the type of boycott. This is usually economic pressure but it could be political pressure, as in the boycott of an election. In both symbolic and effective boycotts success depends on the target's vulnerability to the pressure applied. RTZ, for example, is less vulnerable to a symbolic consumer boycott than Barclays Bank, principally because of the difference in how they present themselves to the outside world and the markets in which they operate. The table grape growers, as one-product companies, were more vulnerable to an effective consumer boycott than, say, BTR. Perhaps because of their less overtly coercive nature, symbolic boycotts are more likely to be successful; though whether a boycott is symbolic or effective has more to do with its effect than the intention, effectiveness will at least be contemplated and even 'promised' by the boycotting party.

Finally, boycotts may be inadequate in themselves. The moral pressure or criticism implied in boycotts may hurt, just as the economic pressure of an effective consumer boycott or economic sanction may hurt. But this hurt may not in itself be sufficient to change the behaviour of the boycotted party. Rhodesia finally became independent; Barclays eventually left South Africa. In both cases, the boycott could only be said to have contributed to the aggregate of pressure for change. Accordingly, they should not be assessed in isolation.

Conclusions

Preview

Chapter 9 has addressed the more practical concerns of pressure group use of the boycott and management responses. The conclusions to the study as an investigation of ethical purchase behaviour are presented below; specifically on the role of the market in ensuring social responsibility in business and on the domain of consumer sovereignty. Conclusions are also drawn on pressure groups as a countervailing power to business and on political participation. The section ends with a summary of the key findings of the study.

Consumer sovereignty, social responsibility in business, and the social control of business

In consumer boycotts

The concern here is with the question: Can consumer sovereignty ensure social responsibility in business and in what way? It subsumes three concerns: whether consumer sovereignty can affect social responsibility in business, the method by which this is achieved, and the success or potential of this method – whether consumer sovereignty does affect social responsibility in business. The method is defined here as ethical purchase behaviour. If the question had been simply 'Can consumer sovereignty ensure social responsibility in business?' then a yes or no answer could have been given. In other words, the question could have been stated as a proposition or hypothesis for 'testing': consumer sovereignty can ensure social responsibility in business. The answer to the simpler form of the question is affirmative and such a proposition or hypothesis could be said to be substantiated. There is evidence presented in the study to show that consumer sovereignty can affect social responsibility in business. However, the method by which this is achieved and its success or potential are important concerns.

Consumer sovereignty can ensure social responsibility in business through ethical purchase behaviour. An argument has been advanced as to why and how this may occur. Cases illustrating its occurrence in the form of consumer boycotts have been presented. The argument rests on an understanding of how markets work (Chapter 1), the problem of the social control of business (Chapters 2 and 3), and the role and tactics of pressure groups (Chapters 4, 5, and 6). The focus of the study is on consumer boycotts as the way in which consumer sovereignty may ensure social responsibility in business. Their role in this respect is examined here before looking at less manifest and deliberate forms of ethical purchase behaviour and how they may affect social responsibility in business.

Importantly, it was recognised that the term social responsibility in business has come to be debased. It is, at least, subject to different interpretations according to the position of the user on the priorities of social issues. It is probably best restricted to descriptions of managerial attempts to be socially responsible, a self-regulation doctrine. Hence social control of business is a better term for describing the use to which consumer sovereignty is put in ethical purchase behaviour. The concept of the social control of business also emphasises the concern with the exercise of power by business. Couched in these terms, it can be seen that ethical purchase behaviour involves the consumer exercising the power that arises from being a buyer in the market-place in an effort to control business. Put otherwise, consumer sovereignty is used in the social control of business. This is most apparent in consumer boycotts.

The method by which consumer boycotts can operate as a social control mechanism was first considered in Chapters 5 and 7, included in which was a model of pressure group influenced ethical purchase behaviour. It was suggested that the pressure group plays an important role in providing the information on a social responsibility in business issue which is necessary for ethical purchase behaviour to take place. The pressure group may go so far as to organise ethical purchase behaviour, in an attempt to tackle the issue, in the form of a consumer boycott. The case studies in Chapter 8 illustrate this. All the consumer boycotts reported, including those in Appendix B, are most definitely about social responsibility in business. Many consumer boycotts are promoted using this term or implying it. Tarmac, for example, was asked whether it would have tendered for and built Hitler's gas chambers. This highlighted the weakness in the company's claim that it had to be guided by market demand or, at least, requests from the government; a claim suggesting that the company is unable to, or should not define for itself, what is socially responsible. (A not entirely worthless claim even if it is impracticable, as earlier discussed.) So social responsibility in business was at issue in the consumer boycott case studies.

279

In some consumer boycotts, the idea as proposed here, that consumer sovereignty in the market-place is being used in the social control of business, is made explicit. Cesar Chavez, for example, referred to the grape boycott as 'capitalism in reverse'. CND's use of the consumer boycott at least had this intention. Consumers were asked not to support those businesses whose practices they deplored – be it nuclear arms manufacture or the exploitation of labour – in an attempt to end them. This idea is well expressed in the editorial from the *Financial Times* which followed the conclusion of the Barclays boycott (see Chapter 8). So consumer boycotts confirm the argument advanced on ethical purchase behaviour. It is a method, which seems to work in the way proposed, for the social control of business. Hence the second concern subsumed by the question given above has been addressed, though some comment needs to be made on how the method differs in symbolic boycotts. But before turning to this, it is necessary to consider the third concern in the research question, that of the success or potential of consumer boycotts in the social control of business. Whereas consumer boycotts have the intention of the social control of business, they do not necessarily achieve it.

The review of pressure group use of the consumer boycott in Chapter 9 shows that there are a number of factors which may militate against this use of the market in the social control of business. Indeed, this conclusion specifically identifies strategies and tactics which business may use to avoid being called to account in this way. It is not necessary to reiterate the weaknesses from a pressure group perspective of the consumer boycott tactic. Suffice to note that it has drawbacks as a social control mechanism. In particular, the vulnerability of firms will vary. Some firms will be more susceptible to consumer boycotts than others, regardless of their 'guilt' on a social responsibility issue. There may be a fear of the wrong people getting hurt (the firm's employees). Cultural factors, such as the level of education, may be important. There may need to be a tradition of boycotting. In other words, there are necessary and sufficient conditions for consumer boycotts to be successful. There has to be support on the issue and consumer sovereignty as here defined; consumers must be concerned, willing, and able to act on the issue for the social control of business to be realised. The prevalence of this sort of activity has not been assessed in this study. It may be that of the many calls for consumer boycotts, only an exceptional few are successful.

As Chapter 9 emphasised, the boycott should not be seen in isolation from other tactics. The aggregate of the pressure on the firm for social responsibility achieves success, not the boycott alone. In any case, there is the frequency of boycotts to consider; one cannot boycott everything. Even in the grape boycott, while the consumer boycott was the most important pressure on the growers, there were other tactics employed, including the strike, which forced capitulation. Boycotts may be inadequate in themselves or only a minor contributor to success. Of course, causality can rarely be asserted with any certainty. Was it, for example, the boycott that 'caused' Nestlé to agree to the pressure group demands? While there is little evidence to suggest the boycott was effective and coerced management, the boycott can be said to have been the cause in so far as it symbolised opposition to Nestlé. This leads neatly into the distinction between symbolic and effective boycotts. For this distinction has a bearing on the success or potential of boycotts as well as the method concern noted above.

Consumer boycotts may be successful in the social control of business without being effective. Boycotts can be symbolic or effective and successful in either case. Whether successful or not, consumer boycotts are still important as statements about social responsibility in business. Indeed, this would have been the main conclusion on consumer boycotts if it had not been realised that, contrary to the literature, boycotts may be successful, in achieving compliance with demands made, without being effective. So mass support, or more specifically, mass refusals to purchase a firm's products, need not be necessary for a consumer boycott to achieve corporate social responsibility. Moral pressure rather than economic pressure may be sufficient. This does, however, raise two important issues and weaknesses to the thesis advanced. First, what is the form of social control at work? Is it, as argued, the market, or is it moral obligation? Second, if it is not the market, then in symbolic boycotts the idea of purchase votes and political participation via the market-place is questioned. The latter issue is addressed later. The former is the concern of the remainder of this section.

A model was proposed in Chapter 3 which identified three forms of social control of business: legislation, the market, and moral obligation, corresponding to the three types of power found in society. The vulnerability of a firm to consumer boycotts reflects its susceptibility to moral as well as economic pressure. Symbolic boycotts are successful because of their impact on corporate image, morale, and in distracting corporate attention, rather than their economic impact. This amounts to moral obligation working in combination with markets in the social control of business. Of course, as in the earlier discussion of the problems with the moral obligation form of control, this may be leaving too much to management discretion; though again it can be commented that discretion is less than it might appear when the social conditioning impact on human choice behaviour is taken into account. Yet even if the form of control is moral obligation working through the market, the market is still playing an important role in providing an outlet for the expression of grievances. Hence accountability may not be directly to the market, but it is achieved through the market. Finally, it should be emphasised that the threat of ethical purchase behaviour – and not necessarily only in the deliberate form of consumer boycotts – may be more important than its practice; in which case, this is the market more clearly ensuring the social control of business. This is considered in the next section.

So, in sum, consumer sovereignty has ensured social responsibility in business. It may do so in symbolic as well as effective consumer boycotts. But its success or potential as a mechanism for the social control of business is limited by a number of drawbacks to the boycott tactic. It may simply not be sufficient, or appropriate, or possible on many issues of social responsibility. Yet the threat of ethical purchase behaviour should not be underestimated. Ethical purchase behaviour, and particularly in consumer boycotts, may be successful in the social control of business in its absence.

In ethical purchase behaviour

The study has not specifically looked at the method and the success of ethical purchase behaviour in the social control of business other than in the consumer boycott. At least, it has not done so empirically. Yet it can be observed that one would expect less organised forms of ethical purchase behaviour to have an impact, even though they may be more haphazard. More importantly, it is probably the threat rather than the actuality of ethical purchase behaviour that constitutes the greater social control of business in this way.

The method by which less organised forms of ethical purchase behaviour operate is no different to that in consumer boycotts, except that the pressure group role may be less pronounced or entirely absent. The importance of the pressure group role lies in its provision of information. In consumer boycotts, a pressure group is deliberately setting out to use ethical purchase behaviour as a tactic against a firm. Yet ethical purchase behaviour may result without this, by the pressure group not calling for a boycott but still providing the necessary information. In both cases, it is serving as an important countervailing power to business. Alternatively, the information may come from other sources, especially the media. But this is more haphazard because it depends on consumers thinking of and doing 'the right thing'. So a concerted action is less likely.

Vogel has noted that corporate accountability *per se* is too abstract a concept to capture the public's imagination.[1] But a sense of moral outrage, the right issue at the right time, might provoke a response in the market-place reflecting consumer concern on an issue. This is apparent in consumerist issues – those that affect the consumer in the consumption of the product. So why not wider issues? Japan Air Lines, for example, reported a 22 per cent drop in domestic passenger volume following its 1985 disastrous 747 crash.[2] The Campaign for Real Ale (CAMRA) obliged the brewers to restructure their business to account for consumer preferences expressed in the market-place that contradicted the designs of a production-oriented industry.[3] The argument then is that if consumer sovereignty can express disapproval on these consumerist issues, it can also do so on less parochial issues. In other words, consumer preferences on issues of social responsibility can also be found in the market-place.

Examples of this have already been given, such as on animal issues or buying British. But it is this possibility of a spontaneous consumer reaction in the market-place that makes the threat of ethical purchase behaviour important in the social control of business. It is another consideration, alongside other social control mechanisms, that business must take account of in its decision-making. Accordingly, from the public policy perspective, ethical purchase behaviour may be a viable alternative to legislation; though it depends on the right mechanisms to provide the necessary information, namely pressure groups and the media. Ethical purchase behaviour could then act as a deterrent, encouraging corporate social responsibility, or to curb corporate excesses. Importantly, given the arguments about political participation, social responsibility would be defined in this alternative to legislation by the consumer. However, this argument is less valid where only some consumers are enfranchised; that is, in the market for the company's products.

This is not to suggest that the market will answer all things. It merely reflects the recognition that legislation as a form of social control of business is overloaded and limited. As moral obligation also has its limitations, public policy might usefully seek to make greater use of the market and ethical purchase behaviour to control business. Governments are unlikely to do this directly because of potential conflicts of interest. Witness, for example, the reluctance of the British Ministry of Agriculture to release the report it commissioned on healthy eating which criticised processed foods. But greater cooperation with and encouragement for concerned pressure groups, in the pluralistic mode, could enhance the usefulness of the market in the social control of business. Consumer expressions of concern could at least be a forerunner to legislation on the issue.

It is important not to overstate the potential of the market for the social control of business. The role of politics, even Mises counsels, should not be forgotten. Many issues are particular to government and legislative action. Many issues could not be resolved by ethical purchase behaviour because the firms involved are not susceptible to it. Indeed, some issues should not be resolved by ethical purchase behaviour because of franchise restrictions, as discussed above. Yet, this said, the potential and actual role of the market in the social control of business has probably been overlooked by business and society writers and others. There is a role for consumer sovereignty in the social control of business, through consumers actually or potentially expressing their preferences on social issues. This is ethical purchase behaviour and consumer pressure for corporate accountability.

The role of the market in the social control of business may have been understated because of the failure to recognise ethical purchase behaviour. For it to take place, consumers have to be concerned, willing, and able to act in the market-place on a social issue. This involves a novel interpretation of consumer sovereignty, suggesting that it has domain as well as degree. Of course the whole argument here hinges on consumer sovereignty. So consumer sovereignty can ensure social responsibility in business through ethical purchase behaviour but this will depend on the degree and particularly the domain of consumer sovereignty.

Ethical purchase behaviour and the limits to consumer sovereignty

The concern here is with the question: How far does consumer sovereignty extend? The study suggests that the domain of consumer sovereignty is *only* limited by information and choice. This is the essential answer to this question, but it is important to distinguish between a theoretical notion and consumer behaviour. It can at least be asserted that, as the consumer boycott cases clearly show, consumer sovereignty in practice extends well beyond the physical product. The study has suggested a fairly radical perspective on consumer sovereignty. It has proposed two dimensions. Conventionally, consumer sovereignty is conceived as having degrees, according to how competitive the market is. So writers refer to the amount of consumer authority in a market when using the term consumer sovereignty. Here it is proposed that one can also refer to the domain of consumer sovereignty. This refers to the jurisdiction of consumer authority in a market. The identification of this second dimension stems from economic and marketing theory and consumer practice. First, consumer practice: reference to the domain of consumer sovereignty in this way is simply in the acknowledgement of a consumer interest in purchase beyond the more immediate characteristics of the product. This is exemplified in the case studies. It would not be claimed that in these cases the consumer had a great amount of authority, but certainly the jurisdiction of that authority was more than over the immediate product. The consumer was able to express a preference on far wider issues. This is in keeping with marketing thought on the nature of products, particularly the augmented product concept. It is merely observed here that the product as a package can contain costs as well as benefits for the consumer. Included in these costs may be a social practice of the firm or some other issue that the consumer associates with the product. However unintended, there can be negative product augmentation.

Political economy indicates that consumer sovereignty is the rationale for capitalism. Decisions on the allocation of resources under capitalism are said to be made by consumers in markets. Critics of this, such as Galbraith, are sceptical about the authority of consumers relative to producers. They ask *whether* decisions are made by consumers in markets. Their interest lies with the degree dimension of consumer sovereignty and, accordingly, whether markets are competitive. This is important here, in so far as competition, by providing choice, permits ethical purchase behaviour (though it could be argued that this was not necessary in the grape boycott). However, the study focuses on the domain of consumer sovereignty. It asks the important question: *What* decisions do consumers make in markets? It cannot, of course, entirely answer such a big question, but it does serve to show that these decisions may involve social issues and demonstrates the significance of asking the question.

The answer to the question bears on the legitimacy of capitalism; for if consumer sovereignty has domain as well as degree, then it is important to know what decisions are made in markets and whether they are made by consumers. Hence, the argument for ethical purchase behaviour is an argument for capitalism. In its absence, consumer sovereignty, the rationale for capitalism, may be questioned. So Cesar Chavez's claim that the grape boycott was 'capitalism in reverse', while sounding attractive, is ill-founded. Similarly, it would be wrong to suggest that ethical purchase behaviour is marketing inverted. In its basis in consumer sovereignty, it is the ultimate expression of the marketing concept. It will be recalled that a definition of the consumer boycott earlier given was 'responding to an unsatisfactory product as perfect competition says one should'.

One weakness to all this is that consumer sovereignty can be very limited in real markets. However, the extent of consumer sovereignty may be enhanced, as proposed here, by pressure groups providing the necessary information. This then creates negative product augmentation. The legitimacy of the product is questioned by the pressure group drawing attention to the firm's provision of unintended and unattractive product attributes. In so doing, another weakness of economic systems, more readily acknowledged by free market economists, is addressed. For the externalities of social costs can become private costs through the role of legitimacy in the marketing mix and negative product augmentation. The firm has to pay if the consumer practises ethical purchase behaviour and rejects its offering.

It was earlier noted that Vogel distinguishes between ecologically concerned consumption and politically or ideologically motivated purchasing. It was suggested that both could be described as ethical purchase behaviour. Some comment can be usefully made at this point to make explicit the preference for 'ethical' to other terms such as 'political' or 'ideological'. The distinction Vogel makes is based on the relationship between the purchase behaviour and the social problem. With ecologically responsible consumption the relationship between what is consumed and the social problem is more direct than in a consumer boycott. Yet it can now be observed that this merely reflects the connection factor, the connection between the product and the grievance. So he need not have differentiated because the two are the same type of behaviour, both reflecting the domain of consumer sovereignty dimension. The question then arises as to what this behaviour should be called. Why ethical purchase behaviour?

One might suggest that there is ecologically concerned or socially responsible consumption when consumers choose to buy a low pollutant petrol or prefer goods in biodegradable packaging. Similarly, consumers preferring to buy the products of a unionised firm to a non-unionised firm constitutes ideologically motivated purchase behaviour; refusal to buy from a firm that funds a political party is political purchase behaviour; and the purchase of halal meat or the avoidance of pork is religious purchase behaviour. Yet in all such cases the behaviour may be described as ethical purchase behaviour. There are three reasons for this.

First, it is useful to have a 'catch-all' term. Ethical investment may similarly reflect a variety of interests, but the term used is not political or religious investment because the behaviour is principally the same in each case. Second, ethical is appropriate as the all-embracing term because it reflects the absence of self-interest or, at least, the enlightened self-interest in the motivation for the behaviour. Political purchase behaviour, given a broad definition of politics, was at one time thought by the author to be adequately descriptive of the behaviour to be described. It could, conceivably, apply to purchase behaviour influenced by issues as diverse as vivisection and South Africa. Yet ethical was preferred because of the element of enlightened self-interest in this form of purchase behaviour. Finally, and this is again a reason for rejecting the term political purchase behaviour, the concern is with a moral act. On many occasions, moral outrage is very important and so it is 'more' than a political act. Thus, an all-embracing term, reflecting the ethical motivation to consumers exploiting the domain dimension of consumer sovereignty, was preferred: ethical purchase behaviour. Although this is contentious, even religious influence on purchase behaviour, such as the examples above, is ethical purchase behaviour. It is based in a code of ethics.

Some might dispute the role of ethics in consumer boycotts and other forms of so-called ethical purchase behaviour. It might be argued that an ethical reason is merely masking self-interest. Vegetarians, for example, may simply not like the taste of meat and post-rationalise their rejection of it with the ethical reason of not wishing to eat dead animals. Yet while this may be the case for some vegetarians, and perhaps for others the ethical reason is not that strong, the complexities of human decision-making should not obscure the role of ethics in their purchase behaviour. After all, the term ethical purchase behaviour is merely a long-overdue acknowledgement of some role for ethics. As noted at the outset, ethical purchase behaviour includes ethical considerations as one influence in purchase behaviour, as well as outright refusals to buy or a deliberate restriction of choice (see Introduction).

It should be emphasised that ethical purchase behaviour is always about social responsibility in business in some way. This may not be explicit or deliberate but it is invariably so. The consumer is saying 'I will not support this business practice (of which I disapprove) by buying your product.' Of course, it is social responsibility in business as defined by the individual. A vegetarian, for example, would argue that a butcher could never be socially responsible in a business which by definition involves the killing of animals. A similar argument could be applied to nuclear arms manufacturers. Ethical purchase behaviour involves the consumer making a statement about and trying to influence what, to he or she, is an issue of social responsibility in business.

Finally, ethical purchase behaviour is probably more likely in an affluent society. This was argued when examining the Arab boycott. But affluence, although permitting greater flexibility to the consumer, is not essential. The consumer need only be concerned, willing, and able to practise ethical purchase behaviour. The extent of consumer sovereignty is only limited by information and choice.

Pluralism, political participation, and countervailing power: the role of pressure groups and the market

Political participation and ethical purchase behaviour

The study may be seen as the outcome of an improbable marriage of conservative and liberal thought: conservative because of its market emphasis, liberal because of the issues for which the market is or could be employed. It is presented within the framework or ideology of the competitive model of capitalism, with the market working as conservative thinkers say it 'should'. Yet in so doing it has the market employed on issues which these thinkers would probably ascribe a low priority. The free market economist might baulk at the impact on market efficiency of ethical purchase behaviour. But it could not be denied that the argument proposed is well within, if not lauding, the competitive model of capitalism. Some of the argument is conjecture: ethical purchase behaviour may, as yet, be more celebrated than practised. But given the caveats expressed, the argument is plausible. Attention should now be turned to how ethical purchase behaviour produces political participation and the role of pressure groups in this. It should be emphasised that although largely speculative, such an idea is nothing more than a literal interpretation of the free market economist's notion of purchase votes in the market-place. As Mises writes:

> With every penny spent the consumers determine the direction of all production processes and the minutest details of the organization of all business activities. This state of affairs has been described by calling the market a democracy in which every penny gives a right to cast a ballot.[4]

Just as consumer sovereignty has been more literally interpreted here than most economists grant, so has the notion of 'votes' in product markets. Such an interpretation is grounded in the reality of consumer purchase behaviour which attempts to deal with social issues.

Ethical purchase behaviour is political participation in so far as it allows the consumer to make a statement about and try to influence a particular issue. That statement is more likely to be heard and acted upon if other consumers do likewise. In an organised action, a consumer boycott, the chances of this are greater. It is, in particular, spelled out to the firm why consumers are choosing not to buy its products. A consumer boycott, it was noted in Chapter 4, provides for political participation in three ways: by stopping a firm committing a grievance, using the firm's insider status with government (to lobby for appropriate government action on the issue), and by mobilising public opinion against the grievance and putting it on the political agenda. Ethical purchase behaviour that is not organised in the form of a consumer boycott probably works likewise but less effectively.

So it is suggested that ethical purchase behaviour increases political participation and, it might be added, as it involves social responsibility in business, on issues less accessible to government. This is held to be desirable because of the role ascribed to the market under capitalism and the virtue of people being 'free to choose' therein. Yet ignoring the franchise restrictions consequent on whether people are in the market for firms' products (though as firms get larger and more diverse this is increasingly less of a problem), is such a view tenable and to be approved?

One weakness to the notion of a substantial degree of political participation from ethical purchase behaviour is that, in controlling business, it operates largely as a possibility rather than an actuality. So if this is political participation then it is very indirect. Of course, how much ethical purchase behaviour there is, and its impact, are unknown. But given that symbolic boycotts seem more prevalent than effective boycotts, mass support in the boycott form of ethical purchase behaviour seems rare in Western society. So although ethical purchase behaviour may have an impact on issues, this is hardly much greater political participation if it is a consequence of only a few purchase votes. Indeed, can one refer to 'social' control of business via the market if it results from the activities of a small minority of consumers? There must certainly be doubts about ethical purchase behaviour providing political participation if it is only used by the educated middle class.

Yet taking an élitist and liberal perspective this may be desirable. Chapter 4 commented on the conservative tendency of public opinion and the dangers of right-wing radicalism exploiting this. Consider this scenario. An increase in racial tension accompanied by substantial unemployment could lead to greater public support for immigrant repatriation. It is conceivable that a consumer boycott of ethnic minority shops or businesses employing ethnic minorities could then be organised. So although this study has referred to the use of ethical purchase behaviour on liberal issues this need not be the case. As David Vogel has commented (in a letter to this author), boycotts can come from the right and the left. This, at least, is the US experience and there is no reason why it should not be repeated in the UK. There is, indeed, every reason why it should be repeated here. Ethical purchase behaviour, as the exercise of consumer sovereignty, lets the consumer decide how to 'vote'. This is the pluralism of the market-place. The harnessing of the power of consumer sovereignty is up for grabs. It may be easier to recruit mass support for a boycott on right-wing rather than liberal issues. So, many might question the desirability of the type of populist democracy that might be achieved through large numbers of consumers practising ethical purchase behaviour.

These are muddy waters indeed. Suffice to note that it is likely that organised ethical purchase behaviour in consumer boycotts is liable to have a greater impact. Given that this is organised by pressure groups and that, as Chapter 4 noted, they are for the most part of a liberal disposition, then these doubts to this 'vision' are somewhat expelled. Moreover, of course, it does contain a certain element of conjecture. Symbolic boycotts may continue to be the norm and ethical purchase behaviour in general may only command mass support in the most extreme circumstances and where moral outrage is so great that it constitutes a clear and universally accepted breach of what society deems acceptable.

Lindblom has suggested that decision-making is more generally of an incremental nature, with policy evolving in accord with the successive limited comparisons (or branch) method.[5] This is in contrast to what is assumed – the rational comprehensive (or root) method. In the latter, the decision-maker would attempt to analyse comprehensively every known facet of the decision and make a rational judgement on which is the appropriate means for the desired ends. The former, however, is 'muddling through': 'both praised as a highly sophisticated form of problem-solving and denounced as no method at all.' Yet it can be systematic and effective and, in any case, the comprehensiveness of the root method is often impossible. The importance of this here is Lindblom's recognition that 'the incremental pattern of policy-making fits with the multiple pressure pattern'. A policy evolves through a process of mutual adjustment involving the various parties to the decision. This, then, is the way pressure groups within the pluralistic model contribute to policy decisions. Accordingly, ethical purchase behaviour when affecting decision-makers will be one input to the policy outcome. So given that outcomes are the result of this muddy process of 'muddling through', concern about the undue influence of one contributor is misplaced.

Taking this analysis right back to the individual consumer, it can be seen that his or her preferences on social issues expressed in the market-place will ultimately contribute, in however small a way, to a policy outcome. As Thomas has observed and was noted, understanding policy outcomes as a result of this process of disjointed incrementalism means that each individual consumer's 'vote' can contribute to some change in the socio-economic system. Even if ethical purchase behaviour is quite rare, it can overall, and for each consumer practising it, have some impact. Because each individual is making a contribution to the outcome, power is therefore decentralised. NVDA involves an effort to gain a decentralisation of power. Sharp's analysis of NVDA is permeated by the political ideal of the redistribution of power. It can be seen that the idea of purchase votes speculated on here is in keeping with this ideal. Power becomes diluted as it falls into the hands of each individual consumer practising ethical purchase behaviour. This, of course, is only what classical or neoclassical economists would claim for the market anyway.

The realisation of this vision, if such a term may be excused, hangs on the degree and domain of consumer sovereignty. At a more down-to-earth level, recognising the likely greater impact of organised ethical purchase behaviour points to the role for pressure groups. The idea of consumer preferences on social issues expressed in purchase having an impact on firms' and governments' decisions and their outcomes is most likely to be realised through pressure groups. Their role in this respect is considered next.

To conclude, the study and argument advanced is in keeping with the competitive model of capitalism. It proposes, in ethical purchase behaviour, some evidence for the free-market economists' notions of consumer sovereignty and purchase votes. It is argued that if the consumer has votes in the market-place then he or she thereby has political participation. The votes cast, however, may be used on extreme issues and for many it may be reassuring that ethical purchase behaviour can probably only rarely command mass support. It is also likely to be more effective when organised in consumer boycotts by pressure groups, which tend to be of a liberal disposition. Yet the 'vision' of each individual's ethical purchase behaviour contributing to changes in society is in keeping with Lindblom's disjointed incrementalism view of the realisation of policy outcomes. Indeed, it is a highly refined form of pluralism. There may be a preference for a more élitist form of decision-making than this populist vision involves, but it does involve a dilution of power. Recalling the question in the Preview to Chapter 7, the masses would be powerful through consumer sovereignty if such a vision were realised. Accepting the idea that ethical purchase behaviour is more effective in its absence, as a threat, and that it is unlikely to be practised by large numbers on other than exceptional issues, this vision is nearest to being realised in consumer boycotts.

Pressure groups in the marketing system

If ethical purchase behaviour provides the potential for greater political participation, this is more likely to be through pressure group inspired consumer boycotts. Pressure groups, after all, are in need of more effective tactics and increasingly for use against business. Pressure groups are assuming a growing and important role in politics, and business is inevitably involved in this. Where they cannot attain or do not want insider status they use direct action, particularly NVDA. One tragic indication of the current significance of pressure groups and this type of action is the recent blowing-up of the Greenpeace ship Rainbow Warrior by the French government, prior to its attempts to prevent French nuclear tests. Authorities can only respond in this way for so long before the moral jiu-jitsu of NVDA obliges a change or their downfall. Faced with intransigent authorities, pressure groups will turn more often to direct action. That, where business is concerned, is likely to mean more consumer boycotts.

Pressure groups are a feature of grassroots politics. Demassification, a decline in interest in party politics, and all the factors in the rise of promotional pressure groups, contribute to grassroots politics involving consumer action if effective tactics are sought. Particularly where the firm is responsible for the grievance, solutions may be sought in consumer boycotts. If the trend continues, consumer boycotts may become more effective than symbolic.

Disclosure is a precondition for political participation. Pressure groups may make the disclosures other parties would rather conceal. When these parties are companies, then pressure groups are providing information which consumers can act on directly in ethical purchase behaviour. Pressure groups provide the information and, in consumer boycotts, the method for political participation. They thereby redress, as in the Nestlé case, a societal power equation often seen as greatly in favour of business. So the pressure group role in the marketing system is as a countervailing power to business. This means it provides consumers with the information on business practices that dilutes business power, by allowing the exercise of the power in consumer sovereignty to call business to account.

Much of this study has assumed that pressure groups are 'right'. Whether they are or not is largely irrelevant. Under pluralism, as earlier discussed, it is very much a case of 'might is right'. Accordingly, a pressure group's influence would depend on the support it commanded. But some brief, final comment needs to be made on the coerciveness involved in ethical purchase behaviour, the use of dubious tactics by pressure groups, and their impact on market efficiency.

Market efficiency may be impaired by boycotts and other forms of ethical purchase behaviour. Yet it should be recalled that efficiency is not the sole criterion by which market systems are assessed. Consider, for example, Coca-Cola's reversal of its decision to close its Guatemalan plant following the threatened consumer boycott. Let it be assumed that solely economic factors prompted the decision, in which case, efficiency has been lost. However, given the social implications of the unemployment that would have been created, the market system has gained on the criteria of equity and altruism (see Chapter 1 for a discussion of these criteria). Coca-Cola may have lost out but there may be a net social gain. Coca-Cola has, after all, only been socially responsible, even if it was under duress. Regardless of this, nothing can be done about it anyway. Coca-Cola could have employed some of the strategies and tactics discussed earlier, but they were perhaps too vulnerable. In any case, if this is market inefficiency, it is as a result of a market judgement. The market, effectively, prompted the reversal of the decision. Ethical purchase behaviour can only be with great difficulty accused of impairing market efficiency when it involves decisions made in the market.

A more worrying aspect is the intimidation by picket lines used to promote consumer boycotts. Do they amount to an enforced restriction on consumer choice? Picketing was discussed in Chapter 7 and it was noted that Harper claims that the right to peaceful picketing should be defended because of its effectiveness. The legal issue is less important here than the implications for consumer choice. On balance, picketing can be defended. This is because of its importance in boycott effectiveness, and because it is likely to be non-violent, as NVDA. Etzioni's arguments about demonstration democracy and the need for forms of political expression may also be used here.

Where stores are persuaded not to stock a boycotted item then consumer choice may be involuntarily restricted. Consumers can always walk past picket lines. The pressure group is unlikely to gain consumer support if its pickets are hostile, and it may attract police attention. Yet if the product is not on the shelves then the consumer is unable to make a choice. In this case, it must be assumed that either other stores have the product, to which the consumer could go, or the cause is so well-supported that consumers do not mind. Otherwise, there is cause for concern from a consumerist perspective, from management's perspective, and in terms of the argument of purchase votes. But the likelihood of an entirely effective consumer boycott without over-whelming consumer support seems so remote as to be discounted. Even the grape boycott was not more than 50 per cent effective. The suggestion that management is unfairly coerced may also be largely dismissed. Symbolic and effective boycotts depend on support for their success. Where this is forthcoming, any coercion of management can be defended as the social control of business.

Finally, on pressure group use of dubious tactics, it can only be argued that this is unlikely to produce success should such tactics be used. Pressure groups, for all the reasons discussed, are volatile as organisations. Their credibility and support are even more so. They could ill afford to risk losing this; though it is worth noting that Wootton, in reference to all types of pressure groups, comments on the importance of disclosure and training for critical awareness, to ensure the public is not misled.[6]

A summary of the key findings

The study of ethical purchase behaviour reported here has produced a number of interesting conclusions, within which there are five key findings:

(1) *The recognition of ethical purchase behaviour.* Consumers may be influenced in purchase by what may be broadly described as ethical concerns. This behaviour seeks social responsibility in business as defined by the consumer.

(2) *Consumer boycotts should be judged as symbolic acts as well as on their effectiveness; the former may be more important in their success.* There is a distinction between boycott effectiveness and success; the two do not necessarily go hand in hand. Boycotts also have expressive functions as well as instrumental functions. Accordingly, there are two types of boycott: the symbolic and the effective. The former achieves compliance with demands made through moral pressure, the latter through economic pressure. Factors in boycott effectiveness and success can be identified according to the choice of target, pressure group organisation and strategy, and response to the boycott, but conditional factors vary. It is only possible to refer to necessary and sufficient conditions for a successful consumer boycott at a generalised level. They are: support on the issue and consumer sovereignty. Put otherwise, consumers must be concerned, willing, and able to act. However, boycotts should not be judged in isolation from other tactics likely to be employed by pressure groups alongside the boycott.

(3) *Management response strategies to consumer boycotts are: ignore, fight, fudge/explain, comply; although a proactive strategy, in anticipation of increasing pressure group activity, has most to recommend it.* The proactive strategy involves management cooperating with pressure groups. Within an identification of those market segments containing consumers concerned about particular ethical issues, it attempts to enhance the legitimacy element in the firm's marketing mix and thereby avoid negative product augmentation.

(4) *There is a role for pressure groups in the marketing system in the social control of business.* Pressure groups act as a countervailing power to business. In the marketing system they enhance consumer sovereignty by providing the necessary information for ethical purchase behaviour. They may organise ethical purchase behaviour in the form of consumer boycotts. There are three forms of social control of business according to the type of power involved: legislation (force), market forces (inducement), and moral obligation (manipulation). Pressure groups, in using the consumer boycott, are attempting to employ the market form of control. In symbolic boycotts, however, control is more a result of moral obligation working through the market.

(5) *The domain of consumer sovereignty is only limited by information and choice.* Ethical purchase behaviour suggests that consumer sovereignty may have two dimensions: degree and domain. Domain refers to the jurisdiction of consumer sovereignty. It depends on choice through competition and, especially, information. The importance of pressure groups in the marketing

system stems from their provision of information on social issues. Where consumers act on this information in purchase then there is political participation or purchase votes in the market-place. Yet the possibility or threat of ethical purchase behaviour, acting as a constraint on firms, is important in itself for the social control of business.

Consumer sovereignty can ensure, and has ensured, social responsibility in business. This is achieved through ethical purchase behaviour; though, as indicated above, there are important caveats. Most important of all is the extent of consumer sovereignty.

Appendix A:
Markets and marketing

This study is indicative of a wider domain for marketing than the narrow concerns of producers. It observes that consumers and their interests, as they relate to markets, are appropriate to a discipline studying markets. This is more than saying marketing should take an interest in consumer behaviour – because it will affect the firm's performance in the market-place. That is focusing on producers' interests. Consumers may have interests that conflict with those of producers. Marketing should address the interests of both parties in markets. It is interesting that the only marketing literature on a form of ethical purchase behaviour is about socially responsible consumption. Of all the social issues marketing writers choose to study where purchase behaviour can have an impact, they choose a social issue where the consumer may be blamed. Socially responsible consumption involves a rejection of those products which create social problems in their consumption. Producers marketing such products are largely absolved from blame because they are, after all, merely responding to consumer demand. The bias may not be deliberate, but it is a further indication of the partisan character of the discipline.

If marketing is to become a social science, then it must at least become less partisan. It must address the interests of consumers, the other major party in markets. It should get back to its economics roots and reorient its emphasis to the study of markets. Unlike Hunt,[1] it is argued that micromarketing as well as macromarketing can be scientific – or, at least, as scientific as economics and other social sciences – but only if the interests of both parties or the process involved are attended to. Macromarketing can be scientific by looking at the marketing system. In micromarketing there could be a greater concern with the interests of consumers, to redress a partisan imbalance. A neutral position is largely unobtainable. Social science cannot avoid the act of interpretation and unconscious bias is difficult to control. Being partisan is easier to control if the researcher is aware of it. For example, while family background may be a factor beyond the researcher's control, whether one writes for pressure groups or management is not. One may, as here, write for both. A neutral position is also unobtainable because of the requirement for a perspective. This may be a managerial, consumer, or even a public policy perspective. But it is necessary if the researcher is to have a vantage point from which the research problem may be surveyed. The closest the researcher can come to having a neutral position is by acting as a sociologist and studying social processes. This can be envisaged under macromarketing and, though this is less obvious, micromarketing.

So, to conclude. If marketing is (or wants) to become more scientific and less ideological as a discipline, then it must be concerned with the study of markets. In so doing, it must address the interests of consumers as well as producers. This is possible under macromarketing and micromarketing. Bias in social science can only be minimised, not avoided. But the researcher may be less partisan by attempting, as here (though with limited success perhaps), to address the interests of consumers and producers. Perspective is important, though less so if the concern is with social processes. It is just that the perspective is too often that of management for a discipline about the study of markets to advance.

Appendix B :
Other instances of consumer boycotts

This is a list of some of the consumer boycotts identified during the study other than those in the case studies. It is not intended to reflect the prevalence of the tactic or report the most important boycotts of recent years. It is merely some indication of the uses of the boycott and shows that the tactic has been used quite widely. These instances are drawn from a number of sources. The variety in consumer boycotts means that they cannot all be categorised in the same way. There might, for example, be a boycott of an entire country's products (such as South Africa), or a boycott of an industry (Californian grapes), or a boycott of one firm (Nestlé). So blanks in the table indicate inappropriate categories. A dash (–) indicates not known. On effectiveness and success:

E   is effective (significantly reduced sales)

I   is ineffective

S   is successful (achieved stated demands)

N   is not successful

(S)   is success achieved, but not primarily as a result of the boycott

Other boycotts are also referred to in Chapters 5 and 7.

No.	Place	Year	Product	Business	Group	Issue and Comments	Effect-iveness	Success
1	Britain	1984	Petrol	Esso	Automobile Association	Drivers urged to boycott Esso over price rise.	–	–
2	Britain	1983	Holiday accommodation	Algarve (Portugal)	Association of British Travel Agents (*Sunday Times*)	*Sunday Times* call for ABTA to organise boycott of Algarve following tourist poisonings by faulty gas appliances.	–	–
3	Saudi Arabia	1983		Dunlop		Arab boycott threat over offensive advertising unless agency (Saatchi and Saatchi) dismissed.	–	S
4	South Africa (SA)	1983		All white business	Black consumers	Black consumer boycott threatened by Buthelezi over changes to the constitution excluding blacks.	–	–
5	Britain	1984	Fireworks	Brock	British Society for Social Responsibility in Science	Local authorities urged to break contracts for fireworks with Brock over firm's manufacture of rubber bullets. Injunction sought and granted against group.	–	–
6	Britain	1984	Paint (with lead)		CLEAR	Paintmakers Association announced phasing out of lead in paint (by 1988) following boycott threat.	–	S
7	USA	Late 1960s		White business	Black consumers	Black boycott of the business community in Cairo, Illinois, over civil rights.	E	–

							E	N
8	South Africa	1983	Bus service	Ciskei Transport Corporation	Black consumers	Boycott of bus service, nominally over 10% rise in fares. Authorities tried to force people to use the buses with resultant clashes claiming at least seven lives.	E	N
9	USA	–	Soft drinks	Coca Cola	Black consumers	Jesse Jackson used threat of boycott to increase black employment.	–	S
10	International	1984	Soft drinks	Coca Cola	International Union of Foodworkers	Boycott threatened over proposed closure of Guatemala plant.	–	S
11	South Africa	1981		Colgate (SA)	–	Although signatories to Sullivan, Colgate refused union recognition.	–	–
12	USA	–	Beer	Coors	–	Anti-union stance and conservative politics of owners.	–	–
13	USA	Late 1960s	Saran Wrap Handi Wrap	Dow Chemical	Anti-war protesters	Consumer boycott over Dow's manufacture of napalm used in Vietnam. Dow stopped manufacture because it lost the contract when it came up for renewal. Its bid was said to be deliberately uncompetitive.	E	S
14	USA	1973–1974	Clothing	Farah Manufacturing Company	Amalgamated Clothing Workers Union	Nationwide consumer boycott over union recognition.	E	S
15	Switzerland	1977	Food products		Swiss Federation	Swiss consumer body organised boycott of products not listing ingredients resulting in more listing and speeding-up of legislation.	–	S

	Country	Year	Product	Company	Organization	Description		
16	Britain	1982	Amusement park	Clacton Pier	Greenpeace	Call for boycott over capture and imprisonment of whales and dolphins.	–	–
17	USA	1971	Petrol	Gulf	Gulf Boycott Coalition and others	Over Gulf's policies in Angola during war of independence. Some effectiveness recorded but Vogel describes it as 'minimal'. No conclusion to the boycott as independence achieved and MPLA happy to keep Gulf in Angola.	E	S
18	France	1980	Veal			Use of hormones in fattening calves. Sales fell by 50% in one week. Policy changed.	E	S
19	Japan	–	Television sets		Japanese equivalent of Women's Institute	Boycott of colour TV sets until manufacturers agreed to lower the price by £25.	–	S
20	Japan	–	Cosmetics		Ditto and others	Following success over TV set turned to world's third largest cosmetics company.	–	–
21	Japan	1984	–	Sony and others	Japanese farmers	Boycott of 3 Japanese companies following their criticism of farmers' protection by high tariff barriers.	–	–
22	USA	1966-1967		Kodak	FIGHT	Kodak's failure to provide adequate employment for blacks in Rochester, New York. Call for national boycott.	I	(S)

23 Britain	1980		Lloyds Bank	Young Liberals	Account closure over loans to Chile.	N	–
24 USA	1983		Lucky Supermarkets	United Farm Workers (UFW)	UFW asked shoppers to boycott Lucky because it is the largest purchaser from the Bruce Church lettuce growing company, a non-union firm in conflict with UFW for over a decade.	–	–
25 USA	1971–1972		White business in Marianna, Arkansas	Black consumers	Black unemployment and civil rights demands led to a highly effective boycott of white businesses. Some gains were made but the action was said not to be entirely successful.	E	–
26 Britain	1983		Barker and Dobson, Bowyers, Britvic, Lyons Maid	Liverpool City Council	Campaign to boycott 4 firms which had closed plants on Merseyside, support by Labour and Liberal councillors. Cadbury Schweppes, United Biscuits, and Huntley and Palmer were threatened with boycott should closure plans go ahead. 83% of Merseyside school leavers were said to face the dole or training schemes at the time.	–	–
27 USA	1955–1956	Bus services	Montgomery City Line	Black consumers (organised by Rev. Martin Luther King, Jr.)	Black boycott over civil rights. The bus company was nearly bankrupt 4 months after the action started and ended segregation. Similar actions proved successful in many other Southern cities.	E	S

No.	Country	Year	Product/Industry	Company	Organisation	Details		
28	Britain	1983	Fireworks	—	National Campaign for Firework Reform	NCFR call for local authorities to cancel orders for firework displays because of manufacturers' 'callous disregard' for the many injured at back garden firework parties.	—	—
29	USA	1983	Rail services	—	Consumers organised by Morty Batler	Boycott of commuter rail line from Long Island to New York over poor service.	E	
30	Britain	1982	—	Norwegian products/services	International Fund for Animal Welfare (IFAW)	Call for consumer boycott over Norway's sealing industry.	—	—
31	Britain	1983		Plessey		£2-m order for telephone equipment cancelled by Tower Hamlets council because firm near the top of UN blacklist of firms with links with South Africa. Possibly reprieved on grounds that Plessey in SA pay more than minimum wage and allow unionisation, and were the last all-British company in the industry.		
32	International	1970-1971	Photographic	Polaroid	Polaroid Revolutionary Workers Movement	Boycott organised over firm's supply of equipment for SA identity card system. Gave rise to the slogan 'Polaroid imprisons blacks in just 60 seconds'. Polaroid made changes, including end to sale of its equipment to SA	—	S

					government. Ultimately it ended all economic involvement in SA, the first US firm to do so because of citizen pressures.		
33 South Africa	1982		Rowntree-Mackintosh	Black trade unions	Boycott of Wilson Rowntree in SA over refusal to recognise trade union. TGWU and Anti-Apartheid involved in activist shareholder action against Rowntrees but did not extend the boycott to Britain.	–	–
34 Britain	Early 1970s	Soft drinks	Schweppes	Friends of the Earth	Over non-returnable bottles. Described by Smith 'as the nearest UK consumer and allied organisations have come to organising an outright consumer boycott'.	E	N
35 International	1983-1984	Fish	Canadian fish products (in Britain: John West, Ross, Birds Eye, & others)	IFAW	Well-organised international boycott of Canadian fish products over seal hunting by Canadian fishermen. In Britain Tesco received over 10,000 protest letters from consumers and stopped stocking Canadian fish products. IFAW published adverts, saying thank you to Tesco. Other stores followed suit but Sainsbury said it was for the consumer to decide. Findus stopped using Canadian cod. Issue largely resolved by legislation.	E	(S)

	Country	Year	Product	Target	Organisation	Description	
36	France	1976	Oil products	Shell	Union Fédérale de la Consommation (UFC)	UFC boycott of Shell over Amoco Cadiz oil spillage cut sales by 10% until injunction to desist granted.	E
37	Britain	–	Petrol	Shell	–	Petrol boycott by town after unfavourable mention in Shell guide.	–
38	Britain/USA	1983	Planes	Short Bros	–	US Republican sympathisers lobbied Congress to stop an order for 18 transport planes for USAF because of Short's alleged discrimination against Catholics in recruitment (only 10% of employees were Catholic).	–
39	Japan	–	Various		Shufuren (the Japanese consumer association)	National boycotts used on 'everyone from rice growers charging excessive prices to canned food manufacturers whose labels conceal the truth'. Shufuren said to have 6m members.	–
40	West Germany	1930–1945		Jewish business	Nazi party	Anti-Semitic boycotts were commonplace throughout this period and others – see Chapter 5 (and also for Pan-Arab Israeli boycott).	–
41	Britain	1983		South Korean products	IFAW	Treatment of dogs and cats in South Korea.	–
42	USA	1960s		Supermarkets	–	Truth-in-packaging.	–

	Product	Supermarkets	Housewife pressure groups			
43 USA 1966				Price increases.	–	S
44 Sweden 1976–1980	Pharmaceutical	Ciba-Geigy	–	Doctors and vets boycott over Ciba-Geigy marketing of dangerous drugs to the Third World. Estimated $12m loss of sales and market share down from 4.3% to 3.2%.	E	–
45 Switzerland 1967	Butter		Fédération Romande des Consommateurs (FRC)	Price increases. Prices were reduced and 4 years later were still lower than in 1967.	–	S
46 Switzerland 1971	–		FRC	Inflation. Described as 'less successful' (than nos. 15 and 45).	–	–
47 Switzerland 1972	Cooked meats		FRC	Polyphosphates. Described as 'less successful' (than nos. 15 and 45).	–	–
48 Switzerland 1975	Meat		FRC	High prices. Described as 'less successful' (than nos. 15 and 45).	–	–
49 USA –		White business	Black consumers	Boycott of business community in Tuskegee, Alabama.	–	–
50 France 1976	Food products	–	UFC	Boycott of foods with colouring led to introduction of colourant-free alternatives.	–	S
51 France 1976	Wine	–	UFC	Boycott of red wine contaminated with asbestos fibres from filtration processes. UFC sued for £400,000 by 4 firms. They lost and had to promise not to use asbestos.	–	S

No.	Country	Year	Product	Organizer/Target	Details		
52	France	1976	Aerosols	UFC	Hazards, damage to the environment, and waste of aerosols led to boycott. Sales down by 10%.	E	–
53	France	1976	Tyres	UFC	Boycott of one brand of tyres as 4 times more liable to blow-outs. Subject to legal action.	–	–
54	Britain	–	Veal	–	Factory farming.	–	–
55	Britain	1983	Security Services	Group 4	Group 4 had a contract to cover the Warrington printing works of Eddie Shah, then in dispute with NGA. Liverpool City Council, supporters of the NGA, advised Group 4 that they were not happy with their involvement. Group 4 withdrew security cover, without notice, from the works. The firm had a £215,000 contract with Liverpool, half the city's local security business; the remainder was held by Securicor. The Shah contract was worth about £1,000 a week.	–	S
56	Britain	1983	Campus facilities	National Union of Students	Boycott organised of Warwick University bars and bookshops in response to £30,000 'fine' imposed by the university, following the rough treatment of Sir Keith Joseph when visiting Warwick. The 'fine' was returned.	–	(S)

No.	Country	Year	Company	Organising group	Description		
57	Britain	1983	Icelandic fish products	Greenpeace	Threatened boycott over declining whale stocks.	–	–
58	USA		Wonder Bread	–	Threatened boycott of its products in minority areas over employment practices.	–	–
59	USA	1960 on	Woolworths (& others)	Congress of Racial Equality (CORE)	Over segregated lunch counters. Segregation ended 1962. In March 1960 Woolworths reported turnover 8.9% down, attributed to the boycott. CORE subsequently organised many other successful boycotts to secure black employment (including Tip Top bread, Borden's milk, Montgomery Ward).	E	S
60	USA	1959–1962	Various	Church group organised by Leon Sullivan	Selective use of black consumer boycott against 30 companies produced 5,000 jobs for blacks. Boycotts of Pepsi Cola, Gulf, Sun Oil, and Tastee Baking Company described by Vogel as 'particularly effective'. Gave rise to 'Operation Breadbasket'.	E	S
61	USA	1966 on	A. & P. (& others)	People United to Save Humanity (PUSH) and Operation Breadbasket	Various successes by these groups under Jesse Jackson (see quotation in Chapter 7 Preview) in securing greater black employment. A. & P. boycott is described as 'the most intensive and exhaustive boycott of a major	E	S

	Country	Date	Product	Company	Opposition	Description		
62	USA	1968–1973	Heating systems and computers	Honeywell	Honeywell Project, Clergy and Laity Concerned (CALC), and others	food chain in recent history'. A. & P significantly improved its black employment record. Manufacturer of particularly abusive anti-personnel weapons for the Vietnam war. Many actions against the company, including activist shareholder actions and 'Corporate Crimes Hearings', with Honeywell accused of war crimes. One organiser commented 'We didn't know what our definition of success was. We began with simple moral outrage and came to understand power.' The firm ceased manufacture of all but one anti-personnel weapon.	—	(S)
63	USA	1972	Hostess Twinkies, Wonder Bread, other ITT products	ITT	Women's Strike for Peace	Vietnam war, because ITT 'makes bread which everyone sees as well as sophisticated weaponry which hardly any of us see'.	—	—
64	Germany	Early 1970s	—	Siemens		Over participation in the Cabora Bassa dam project in Mozambique, considered likely to strengthen white Africa.	—	—
65	South Africa	1984 on		White business		Black consumer boycotts in protest at apartheid, causing many stores to close.	E	—

Notes and references

Introduction

1. 'A Gallup poll for a food firm earlier this year found that a million Britons are vegetarian and a further million do not eat red meat, mainly for health reasons' (Ezard, John, 'Getting meat's image off hook', *The Guardian*, 30 November 1984).
2. 'Hard bargains', *New Society*, 14 August 1980.
3. Embree writes, 'The mass media molds everyone into non-passive roles, into roles of more frantic consuming, into human beings with fragmented views of society. But what it does to everyone, it does to women even more. The traditional societal role for women is already a passive one, already one of a consumer, already one of an emotional non-intellectual who isn't supposed to think or act beyond the confines of her home. The mass media reinforces all these traits' (Embree, Alice, 'Media images 1: Madison Avenue brainwashing – the facts', in Morgan, Robin (ed.), *Sisterhood is Powerful,* New York, Random House, 1970). For further examples of polemics in criticism of sex-role stereotypes in the media, see Florika, 'Media images 2: body odor and social order', in *idem*; or Kinzer, Nora Scott, 'Soapy sin in the afternoon', *Psychology Today*, August 1973.
4. See, for example, the observations of: Coote, Anna and Beatrix Campbell, *Sweet Freedom: The Struggle for Women's Liberation*, London, Picador, 1982, pp. 198-200; Naughton, John, 'The ad man's women', *The Observer*, 22 November 1981; Cooper, Ann, 'Why sexism will no longer sell', *Marketing*, 28 October 1981; Wolk, Susan, 'Women gain new ad image', *Marketing*, 25 June 1980. Rosemary Scott offers many more sources on sex-role stereotypes in the media and in advertising in particular. She identifies two consistent themes in the portrayal of women in the media. First, a woman's goal in life is to attract and attain a man, which subsumes: (a) women are always attractive – they are sexual objects; (b) women operate alone – they do not relate with other women, only to men; (c) men are intelligent, women are not – men do not like intelligent women (who are 'unfeminine'), women have inferior ability. Second, women are ultimately and naturally housewives/wives and mothers, which

subsumes: (a) women do not work outside the home; (b) when women work outside the home they are not successful, they do not do 'male' jobs; (c) women are happy doing housework, it is satisfying; (d) men and women have strictly delineated sex roles and household duties; (e) little girls grow up to be housewives, wives, and mothers. See Scott, Rosemary, *The Female Consumer*, London, Associated Business Programmes, 1976, p. 224 ff. So commenting on the status of women in society, Yvette Roudy (Minister for Women's Rights, France) suggests, 'Women are still seen as the virgin, the mother, or the whore, and not as a human being' (*The Observer*, 10 March 1985).

5. See Katz, Phyllis A., 'The development of female identity', *Sex Roles*, Vol. 5, No. 2 (1979); or Oakley, Ann, 'What makes girls differ from boys?', *New Society*, 21 December 1978.

6. So as Jennings *et al.* explain: 'Television commercials telescope and exaggerate the same stereotypes that girls and women have been exposed to throughout their lives, not only at home and at school but from all mass media. Although men are sometimes portrayed in an unflattering way, they are nevertheless presented as the "important ones" whose needs and preferences take priority ... Women, however, have been taught by commercials and live models to be subservient helpers who conform to the wishes of those around them, rather than to be initiatory and resourceful on their own behalf', Jennings [Walstedt], Joyce, Florence L. Geis, and Virginia Brown, 'Influence of television commercials on women's self-confidence and independent judgement', *Journal of Personality and Social Psychology*, Vol. 38, No. 2 (1980).

7. Such as: Winship, Janis, 'Advertising in women's magazines: 1954-1974', Stencilled Occasional Paper, Centre for Contemporary Cultural Studies, University of Birmingham, 1980; Schneider, Kenneth C. and Sharon B. Schneider, 'Trends in sex roles in television commercials', *Journal of Marketing*, Vol. 43 (Summer 1979); Scott, Rosemary, *Sex-Role Stereotypes in Women's Magazine Advertisements*, PhD thesis, Applied Psychology Department, University of Aston, June 1979; Scheibe, Cyndy, 'Sex roles in TV commercials', *Journal of Advertising Research*, Vol. 19, No. 1 (February 1979); Williamson, Judith, *Decoding Advertisements: Ideology and Meaning in Advertising*, London, Marion Boyers, 1978; National Advertising Review Board (NARB), *Advertising and Women: A Report on Advertising Portraying or Directed to Women*, New York, NARB, 1975; Millum, Trevor, *Images of Woman*, London, Chatto and Windus, 1974; Wagner, Louis C. and Janis B. Banos, 'A woman's place: a follow-up analysis of the roles portrayed by women in magazine advertisements', *Journal of Marketing Research*, Vol. X (May 1973); Courtney, Alice E. and Sarah W. Lockeretz, 'A woman's place: an analysis of the roles portrayed by women in magazine advertisements', *Journal of Marketing Research*, Vol. VIII (February 1971); Bardwick, Judith M. and Suzanne I. Schumann, 'Portrait of American men and women in TV commercials', *Psychology*, Vol. 4 (1967). For many others and articles about other research on sex-role stereotypes in advertising,

see Courtney, Alice E. and Thomas W. Whipple, *Sex Stereotyping in Advertising: An Annotated Bibliography*, Cambridge, Marketing Science Institute, Report No. 80-100, February 1980.

8. See, for example, Oakley, Ann, *Subject Women*, Oxford, Martin Robertson, 1981; Jennings *et al.*, op. cit. (n. 6); Hartnett, Oonagh, Gill Boden, and Mary Fuller (eds), *Sex-Role Stereotyping: Collected Papers*, London, Tavistock, 1979; Katz, op. cit. (n. 5); Oakley, Ann, *Sex, Gender and Society*, London, Maurice Temple Smith, 1972.

9. Judie Lannon, Research Director at the J. Walter Thompson advertising agency, in interview 21 April 1982.

10. As Lannon (and White) write: 'Ads have to portray life in a form in which the people for whom they are written will recognise it. An ad is not a thesis on what society might be like under different or changed conditions: it is simply a tool for selling products to people as they are now. And since active, articulate agreement with, and understanding of, women's lib attitudes is very much a minority phenomenon, the vast majority of ads, which are directed to the mass market, have no business to be running counter to majority attitudes ... it is not the role of advertising to change society. Nor could it do so if it tried' (White, Roderick and Judie Lannon, 'Advertising and society', in J. Walter Thompson Company, *The Case for Advertising*, London, J. Walter Thompson Company, 1976, p. 10).

11. Gallagher, Margaret, *Unequal Opportunities: The Case of Women and the Media*, Paris, The UNESCO Press, 1981, p. 30. She writes 'The mass media role is primarily to reinforce definitions and identities set in a framework constructed for and by men. When that framework expands to admit women, the media can be seen to reflect this expansion. This interrelationship between mass media and politico-economic systems highlights the very limited sense in which the media can be described, much less used as independent change agents' (ibid.).

12. Reed, Jane, 'Is Adman being awful to Eve?', *Marketing*, 29 April 1982. Lowry similarly comments, 'Many advertisers have cottoned on to women's resistance to being portrayed as stew-stirring, all purpose housewives and many have stopped doing it, for the only reason that cuts ice: it no longer sells' (Lowry, Suzanne, 'The ads you love to hate', *The Sunday Times*, 23 May 1982).

13. Beasley, Maurice and Sheila Silver, *Women in Media: A Documentary Source Book*, Washington, Women's Institute for Freedom of the Press, 1977, p. 163.

14. Hamilton, Robert, Brian Haworth, and Nazli Sardar, *Adman and Eve: An Empirical Study of the Relative Marketing Effectiveness of Traditional and Modern Portrayals of Women in Certain Mass-Media Advertisements*, Report by the Marketing Consultancy and Research Services of the Department of Marketing in the Lancaster University School of Management and Organisational Sciences, for the Equal Opportunities Commission, Manchester, April 1982, p. ii.

15. Some advertising may still carry traditional stereotypes to appeal to minority, traditional market segments. Moreover, if the changes in

advertising simply reflect increases in female employment outside the home, that is more diverse roles for women in society rather than a wider adoption of feminist thinking, some objectionable stereotypes may remain. Women may continue to be portrayed as sex objects, especially in advertising directed at men. By this argument, society gets the advertising it deserves. As, and if, society's ideas about the sexes evolve, then so will advertising.

16. In Silk, Leonard and David Vogel, *Ethics and Profits: The Crisis of Confidence in American Business,* New York, Simon and Schuster, 1976, p. 91.
17. Gist, Ronald R., *Marketing and Society: A Conceptual Introduction,* New York, Holt, Rinehart and Winston, 1971, p. 33.
18. Wight, Robin, *The Day the Pigs Refused to be Driven to Market: Advertising and the Consumer Revolution,* London, Hart Davis MacGibbon, 1972, p. 237.
19. See Frankel, David S., *A Behavioural Analysis of the Advertising Agency: Behavioural Determinants of Effectiveness in Advertising Agency Account Groups,* PhD thesis, University of London, 1975.
20. The distinction between economic and non-economic considerations can only be arbitrary. Is a consumer decision on a product based on its South African origin any less economic – or more non-economic – than one based on its packaging? What matters are consumers' perceptions of appropriate considerations, not economists', if only because this reflects what happens in practice.

Chapter 1: Capitalism and consumer sovereignty

1. Honour, T. F. and R. M. Mainwaring, *Business and Sociology*, London, Croom Helm, 1982, p. 36. Also, but slightly modified, Samuelson, Paul A., *Economics*, Tokyo, McGraw-Hill Kogakusha, 1980, p. 798.
2. Smith, Adam, *The Wealth of Nations*, Everyman, 1971 (first published 1776), Vol. 1, p. 400.
3. Lindblom, Charles E., *Politics and Markets: The World's Political-Economic Systems*, New York, Basic Books, 1977, p. ix.
4. See, for example, Lipsey, Richard G., *An Introduction to Positive Economics*, London, Weidenfeld and Nicolson, 1983, pp. 72-3.
5. Mills, C. Wright, *The Sociological Imagination*, New York, Oxford University Press, 1959, p. 40.
6. Of course, in a free-market society, not all decisions will be made in the market. However, although Adam Smith was no anarchist, he did advocate a minimal role for government, restricting its activities to defence, policing, and public works. So in a free-market society the citizen may also have power in addition to that as a consumer, such as in voting for representatives in government. The matter is one of degree, however, for the point is that in a free-market society, the arrangements under which men live would be predominantly determined in the market as the role of government would be extremely limited.

7. Galbraith, J. K., *American Capitalism: The Concept of Counter-vailing Power*, Harmondsworth, Penguin, 1963 (first published 1952), p. 38.
8. Mises, Ludwig von, *Human Action: A Treatise on Economics*, London, William Hodge, 1949, p. 265.
9. Ibid., p. 279.
10. Ibid., p. 280.
11. Friedman, Milton and Rose Friedman, *Free to Choose: A Personal Statement*, London, Secker and Warburg, 1980, pp. 2-3.
12. Mises, op. cit. (n. 8), p. 283.
13. Ibid.
14. Ibid.
15. Hayek, F. A., *The Road to Serfdom*, London, Routledge & Kegan Paul, 1944, p. 19.
16. Ibid., p. 75.
17. Heilbroner, Robert L. and Lester C. Thurow, *Economics Explained*, Englewood Cliffs, NJ, Prentice-Hall, 1982, pp. 3-16.
18. Polanyi, Karl, *The Great Transformation*, New York, Octagon Books, 1944. Also, Steiner, G. A. and J. F. Steiner, *Business, Government and Society: A Managerial Perspective*, New York, Random House, 1980, pp. 39-53.
19. Heilbroner and Thurow, op. cit. (n. 17), p. 4.
20. Ibid., p. 9.
21. Ibid., p. 15.
22. Ibid., p. 16.
23. Kamarck, Andrew M., *Economics and the Real World*, Oxford, Basil Blackwell, 1983.
24. Gill, Richard T., *Economics: A Text with Included Readings*, Pacific Palisades, Goodyear, 1973.
25. Samuelson, op. cit. (n. 1).
26. Honour and Mainwaring, op. cit. (n. 1), pp. 36-65.
27. Samuelson, op. cit. (n. 1), p. 784.
28. Honour and Mainwaring, op. cit. (n. 1), p. 37.
29. Ibid., p. 43.
30. Ibid., p. 44.
31. Ibid., p. 51.
32. Ibid.
33. Ibid., p. 52.
34. Ibid., p. 53.
35. Ibid., p. 56.
36. Schmitter, Philippe C., 'Interest intermediation and regime governability in contemporary Western Europe and North America', in Berger, Suzanne, Albert Hirschman, and Charles Maier (eds), *Organising Interests in Western Europe: Pluralism, Corporatism and the Transformation of Politics*, Cambridge, Cambridge University Press, 1981.
37. Hernes, Gudmund and Arne Selvik, 'Local corporatism', in Berger *et al.* (eds), ibid., p. 104.

38. Friedman, Milton, *Capitalism and Freedom*, Chicago, University of Chicago Press, 1962; Friedman and Friedman, op. cit. (n. 11); Hayek, op. cit. (n. 15).
39. Hayek, op. cit. (n. 15), p. 11.
40. Schumpeter, Joseph A., *History of Economic Analysis*, London, George Allen and Unwin, 1954, pp. 888-9.
41. Hayek, op. cit. (n. 15), p. 44.
42. Ibid., p. 10.
43. Steiner and Steiner, op. cit. (n. 18), p. 50.
44. Robbins, Lionel, *The Theory of Economic Policy*, Macmillan, 1978 (first published 1952), pp. 192-3.
45. Lindblom, op. cit. (n. 3), p. 264.
46. Ibid., p. 265.
47. Friedman and Friedman, op. cit. (n. 11), p. 2.
48. Hekman, Christine R. and John S. Hekman, 'Review of *Free to Choose*', *Harvard Business Review*, September-October 1980.
49. Steiner and Steiner, op. cit. (n. 18), p. 51.
50. Friedman and Friedman, op. cit. (n. 11), pp. 1-2.
51. Steiner and Steiner, op. cit. (n. 18), pp. 175-8.
52. Silk, Leonard and David Vogel, *Ethics and Profits: The Crisis of Confidence in American Business*, New York, Simon and Schuster, 1976, p. 91.
53. Meredith, Mark and Peter Riddell, 'Thatcher tells voters to banish Marxism', *Financial Times*, 14 May 1983.
54. Thatcher, Margaret and Brian Connell, 'Report from the Prime Minister: Margaret Thatcher defends her government to date and looks forward towards a third term in office', *Time and Tide*, Summer 1984. Mrs Thatcher's proclaimed and often ridiculed cry for 'a return to Victorian values' is more accurately described as an argument for individualism, as this quotation indicates.
55. Smith, op. cit. (n. 2), Vol. 1, p. 13.
56. Le Grand, Julian and Ray Robinson, *The Economics of Social Problems: The Market versus the State*, London, Macmillan, 1984.
57. Galbraith, op. cit. (n. 7).
58. Berle, Adolf A., Jr., *The Twentieth Century Capitalist Revolution*, New York, Harcourt Brace, 1954.
59. See Lipsey, op. cit. (n. 4), pp. 459-75; Heilbroner and Thurow, op. cit. (n. 17), pp. 169-78; Gill, op. cit. (n. 24).
60. Heilbroner and Thurow, op. cit. (n. 17), pp. 165-7.
61. Friedman, op. cit. (n. 38), p. 201.
62. Spencer, Herbert, *Essays*, Macmillan, 1891, Vol. iii, p. 354.
63. Hayek, op. cit. (n. 15), p. 10.
64. Honour and Mainwaring, op. cit. (n. 1), p. 38.
65. See, for example, Friedman, op. cit. (n. 38), Chapter 10. This view gives rise to the argument, frequently expressed in America, for black capitalism as a solution to inner-city problems (as discussed in Hay, R. D., E. R. Gray, and J. E. Gates, *Business and Society*, Cincinnati, South-Western Publishing, 1976, pp. 195-7).

315

66. Friedman and Friedman, op. cit. (n. 11), pp. 136-7.
67. Honour and Mainwaring, op. cit. (n. 1), p. 38.
68. Lindblom, op. cit. (n. 3), pp. 39-40.
69. Gill, op. cit. (n. 24), p. 719.
70. Lipsey, op. cit. (n. 4), p. 474 and p. 483.
71. Honour and Mainwaring, op. cit. (n. 1), p. 39.
72. Steiner and Steiner, op. cit. (n. 18), p. 178.
73. Mises, op. cit. (n. 8), p. 270.
74. Baumol, William J., and Alan S. Blinder, *Economics: Principles and Policy*, New York, Harcourt Brace Jovanovich, 1982, p. 786.
75. Galbraith, J. K., *The New Industrial State*, Harmondsworth, Penguin, 1974 (first published 1967), pp. 216-7.
76. Kirzner, Israel M., *Competition and Entrepreneurship*, Chicago, University of Chicago Press, 1973, p. 179.
77. There is not the space here to do justice to Kirzner's argument: see ibid., particularly pp. 169-80.
78. Galbraith, op. cit. (n. 75), p. 18.
79. Fulop, Christina, *Consumers in the Market: A Study in Choice, Competition and Sovereignty*, London, The Institute of Economic Affairs, 1967, p. 11.
80. Ibid., p. 86.
81. Ibid., p. 85.
82. Lindblom, op. cit. (n. 3), p. 97.
83. Heilbroner, Robert L. and Lester C. Thurow, *Understanding Micro-economics*, Englewood Cliffs, NJ, Prentice-Hall, 1978, p. 167.
84. Drucker, in Boyd, Harper W., Jr., and William F. Massy, *Marketing Management*, New York, Harcourt Brace Jovanovich, 1972, p. 3.
85. McCarthy, E. Jerome, *Basic Marketing: A Managerial Approach*, Homewood Ala., Richard D. Irwin, 1975, p. 19.
86. Christopher, Martin, Sherril H. Kennedy, Malcolm McDonald, and Gordon Wills, *Effective Marketing Management*, Farnborough, Gower, 1980, p. 3.
87. Kotler, Philip, *Marketing Management: Analysis, Planning and Control*, Englewood Cliffs, NJ, Prentice-Hall, 1984, pp. 22-3.
88. Baker, Michael J., *Marketing: An Introductory Text*, London, Macmillan, 1974, pp. 21-2.
89. Ibid., p. 22.
90. Ibid., p. 26.
91. 'Marketing orientation is itself no more than an appropriate response to a given market structure' (Foxall, Gordon, 'Marketing's Domain', University of Birmingham Faculty of Commerce and Social Science, Discussion Paper, Series B, No. 75, p. 13). Also, Bartels, Robert, *The History of Marketing Thought*, Columbus, Grid, 1976, pp. 1-8.
92. Baker, Michael J. (and others), *Marketing: Theory and Practice*, London, Macmillan, 1983, p. vii.
93. Ibid., pp. 3-11.
94. Bartels, op. cit. (n. 91).

95. Andreski, Stanislav, *Social Sciences as Sorcery*, London, Andre Deutsch, 1972. Andreski also notes that it is uncommon for those within a discipline to criticise that discipline, despite the hypocrisy of this in the claim that academic work is in some sense a pursuit of truth. He writes 'Every craft, every occupation – no matter whether shady or even downright criminal – gravitates towards the principle that "dog does not eat dog"' (p. 13). But in answer to the question 'Why foul one's nest?' he concludes that some at least will question and seek the truth.
96. Baker, op. cit. (n. 88), pp. 281-2.
97. Ibid., p. 280.
98. Ibid., pp. 283-4; Christopher *et al.*, op. cit. (n. 86), pp. 50-4; Kotler, op. cit. (n. 87), pp. 85-6.
99. Jefkins, Frank, *Dictionary of Marketing and Communication*, Aylesbury, International Textbook, 1973, p. 20. A number of sources suggest that company responses to consumerism have been in the form of token gestures rather than affirmative action, as in Webster, Frederick E., Jr., 'Does business misunderstand consumerism?' *Harvard Business Review*, September-October 1973.
100. Hughes, John, *The Philosophy of Social Research*, London, Longman, 1980, p. 127.
101. Lindblom, op. cit. (n. 3), pp. 4-5.
102. Ibid., pp. 38-9.
103. Fisk, George, *Marketing Systems: An Introductory Analysis*, London, Harper International, 1966, p. 681.
104. Fulop, op. cit. (n. 79), p. 84.
105. As discussed, for example, in Wight, Robin, *The Day the Pigs Refused to be Driven to Market: Advertising and the Consumer Revolution*, London, Hart Davis MacGibbon, 1972, pp. 10-11.

Chapter 2: Social control of business: corporate social responsibility

1. Quoted in Galbraith, J. K., *The New Industrial State*, Harmondsworth, Penguin, 1974 (first published 1967), p. 216.
2. Jones, Thomas M., 'An integrating framework for research in business and society: a step toward the elusive paradigm', *Academy of Management Review*, Vol. 8, No. 4 (1983), pp. 559-64.
3. Honour, T.F. and R. M. Mainwaring, *Business and Sociology*, London, Croom Helm, 1982.
4. Sethi, S. Prakash, *Up Against the Corporate Wall: Modern Corporations and Social Issues of the Seventies*, Englewood Cliffs, NJ, Prentice-Hall, 1974 (second edition).
5. Silk, Leonard and David Vogel, *Ethics and Profits: The Crisis of Confidence in American Business*, New York, Simon and Schuster, 1976, p. 120.
6. Heilbroner, Robert L., 'Controlling the corporation', in Heilbroner *et al.*, *In the Name of Profit*, New York, Doubleday, 1972, p. 237.

7. Quoted in Weidenbaum, Murray L., *The Future of Business Regulation: Private Action and Public Demand*, New York, AMACOM, 1979, p. 8.
8. Sadler, Philip, 'The socially responsible organisation', *Professional Printer*, Vol. 19, No. 5.
9. Ackerman, Robert W., *The Social Challenge to Business*, Cambridge, Harvard University Press, 1975.
10. Sturdivant, Frederick D., *Business and Society: A Managerial Approach*, Homewood, Ala., Richard D. Irwin, 1981 (first published 1977).
11. Bell, Daniel, *The Coming of Post-Industrial Society: A Venture in Social Forecasting*, Harmondsworth, Penguin, 1973, p. 287.
12. Steiner, George A. and John F. Steiner, *Business, Government and Society: A Managerial Perspective*, New York, Random House, 1980.
13. Jones, op. cit. (n. 2).
14. Beesley, Michael and Tom Evans, *Corporate Social Responsibility: A Reassessment*, London, Croom Helm, 1978, p. 33.
15. Nader, Ralph (ed.), *The Consumer and Corporate Accountability*, New York, Harcourt Brace Jovanovich, 1973.
16. Vogel, David, *Lobbying the Corporation: Citizen Challenges to Business Authority*, New York, Basic Books, 1978, p. 46.
17. Simon, John G., Charles W. Powers, and Jon P. Gunnemann, *The Ethical Investor: Universities and Corporate Responsibility*, New Haven, Conn., Yale University Press, 1972, p. 1.
18. Heilbroner, op. cit. (n. 6), p. 225.
19. Hay, Robert D., Edmund R. Gray, and James E. Gates (eds), *Business and Society*, Cincinnati, South-Western Publishing, 1976, p. 299.
20. Heilbroner, op. cit. (n. 6), pp. 223-4.
21. Ibid., pp. 224-5.
22. Sethi, S. Prakash (ed.), *The Unstable Ground: Corporate Social Policy in a Dynamic Society*, Los Angeles, Melville Publishing, 1974, p. 2.
23. Bell, op. cit. (n. 11), p. 270.
24. Heilbroner, op. cit. (n. 6), p. 233.
25. Ibid., p. 236.
26. British Institute of Management, *The British Public Company: Its Role, Responsibilities and Accountability*, Occasional Paper – New Series, OPN 12, London, British Institute of Management, 1974, p. 33.
27. Vogel, David, 'The corporation as government: challenges and dilemmas', *Polity*, Vol. 8, No. 1 (1975), pp. 5-37.
28. Berger, Peter L., 'New attack on the legitimacy of business', *Harvard Business Review*, September-October 1981, pp. 82-9.
29. Chinoy, Ely, *Society: An Introduction to Sociology*, New York, Random House, 1967 (second edition), p. 325.
30. Silk and Vogel, op. cit. (n. 5), p. 128.
31. Berger, op. cit. (n. 28).
32. Heilbroner, op. cit. (n. 6), p. 235.
33. Berle, A. A and G. C. Means, *The Modern Corporation and Private Property*, New York, Macmillan, 1932.

34. Silk and Vogel, op. cit. (n. 5), p. 142.
35. Berle, Adolf A., Jr.,*The Twentieth Century Capitalist Revolution*, New York, Harcourt Brace, 1954.
36. Blumberg, Phillip I., *The Megacorporation in American Society: The Scope of Corporate Power*, Englewood Cliffs, NJ, Prentice-Hall, 1975, p. 177.
37. Medawar, Charles, *The Social Audit Consumer Handbook*, London, Macmillan, 1978, p. 15.
38. Ibid., p. 4.
39. Quoted in Beesley and Evans, op. cit. (n. 14), p. 187.
40. Sethi, op. cit. (n. 22), p. 6.
41. Silk and Vogel, op. cit. (n. 5), p. 197.
42. See, for example, Orr, Sir David, 'Unilever's responsibilities as an international business', advertisement in *The Guardian*, 20 May 1982; and, in more detail, Orr, Sir David and H. F. van den Hoven, *Unilever's Responsibilities as an International Business*, London, Unilever PLC, 1982.
43. Medawar, op. cit. (n. 37), p. 3.
44. Beesley and Evans, op. cit. (n. 14), p. 13.
45. Farmer, Richard N. and W. Dickerson Hogue, *Corporate Social Responsibility*, Chicago, Science Research Associates, 1973, p. 6.
46. Hoskins, W. Lee, 'An economic solution to pollution', in Hay *et al.* (eds), op. cit. (n. 19), pp. 364-5.
47. Ibid., and Marlin, Alice Tepper, 'Corporate social performance: a comparative perspective', in Bradshaw, Thornton F. and David Vogel (eds), *Corporations and Their Critics: Issues and Answers to the Problems of Corporate Social Responsibility*, New York, McGraw-Hill, 1981.
48. Klein, Thomas A., *The Social Costs and Benefits of Business*, Englewood Cliffs, NJ, Prentice-Hall, 1977, p. 4.
49. European Societal Strategy Project, *Facing Realities: The Report of the European Societal Strategy Project*, Brussels, European Institute for Advanced Studies in Management, and the European Foundation for Management Development, 1981, p. 43.
50. Sturdivant, op. cit. (n. 10), p. 11. Also, for a UK perspective, see Thomas, R. E., *Business Policy*, Deddington, Philip Allan, 1983 (second edition; first published 1977), pp. 73-9.
51. Andres, William A., 'Creative corporate philanthropy', in Bradshaw and Vogel, op. cit. (n. 47). Andres was writing as Chairman, Dayton Hudson Corporation. It is worth noting here that, in a similar way, IBM identifies within its corporate '3, 4, 5 culture', five stakeholders: shareholders, employees, customers, suppliers, and the community.
52. Jones, Thomas M., 'Corporate social responsibility revisited, redefined', *California Management Review*, Vol. XXII, No. 2 (Spring 1980), pp. 59-67.
53. Beesley and Evans, op. cit. (n. 14), p. 38.
54. Shepherd, Harry, 'The moral of St Michael', *Marketing*, December 1975.

55. Quoted in Sethi, op. cit. (n. 22), p. vii.
56. Farmer and Hogue, op. cit. (n. 45), p. 7.
57. Heilbroner, op. cit. (n. 6), p. 228.
58. Simon *et al.*, op. cit. (n. 17), p. 18.
59. Ibid., p. 22.
60. Consideration must, however, be given to the issue of purity versus effectiveness. Is it better not to invest at all in companies who have links with South Africa, or to invest and work for change from within? Simon *et al.* prefer the latter (ibid., pp. 25-6 and p. 53); though this is an issue of ethical philosophy for which there is no solution, each individual needs to adopt a personal position. It is a question of whether the ends justify the means.
61. Ibid., p. 27.
62. See British Institute of Management, op. cit. (n. 26), for example.
63. Vogel, in Bradshaw and Vogel, op. cit. (n. 47); Beesley and Evans, op. cit. (n. 14); Chamberlain, Neil W., *The Limits of Corporate Responsibility*, New York, Basic Books, 1973.
64. Vogel, op. cit. (n. 63), p. ix.
65. Silk and Vogel, op. cit. (n. 5), p. 228.
66. Drucker, Peter F., 'The new meaning of corporate social responsibility', *California Management Review*, Vol. XXVI, No. 2 (Winter 1984).
67. For example: Marlin, op. cit. (n. 47); Briscoe, Robert, 'Utopians in the marketplace', *Harvard Business Review*, September-October 1971; Hay *et al.*, op. cit. (n. 19); Sethi, op. cit. (n. 22).
68. Quoted in Ackerman, op. cit. (n. 9), p. 7.
69. Marlin, op. cit. (n. 47), p. 167.
70. Sethi, op. cit. (n. 22), p. 1.
71. Haas, Walter A., Jr., 'Corporate social responsibility: a new term for an old concept with new significance', in Bradshaw and Vogel (eds), op. cit. (n. 47).
72. British Institute of Management, op. cit. (n. 26), p. 59.
73. Ibid.
74. Hayek, F. A., 'The corporation in a democratic society: in whose interest ought it and will it be run?', in Ansoff, H. Igor (ed.), *Business Strategy*, Harmondsworth, Penguin, 1969, p. 225.
75. Friedman, Milton, *Capitalism and Freedom*, Chicago, University of Chicago Press, 1962, p. 133.
76. Ibid.
77. Heilbroner, op. cit. (n. 6), pp. 237-8.
78. Bell, op. cit. (n. 11), pp. 293-5.
79. Banks, Louis, 'Taking on the hostile media', *Harvard Business Review*, March-April 1978.
80. Jacoby, Neil H., *Corporate Power and Social Responsibility*, New York, Macmillan, 1973, pp. 195-8.
81. Johnson, Harold L., *Disclosure of Corporate Social Performance: Survey, Evaluation and Prospects*, New York, Praeger, 1979, p. 5.
82. Hay *et al.*, op. cit. (n. 19), p. 4.

83. Blumberg, op. cit. (n. 36), p. 4.
84. Hay *et al.*, op. cit. (n. 19), p. 5.
85. Ibid., p. 13.
86. Cited in Bell, op. cit. (n. 11), p. 293 and Silk and Vogel, op. cit. (n. 5), p. 241.
87. Blumberg, op. cit. (n. 36), p. 5.
88. Hay *et al.*, op. cit. (n. 19), p. 6.
89. Ibid., p. 11.
90. Ibid., p. 13.
91. Steiner and Steiner, op. cit. (n. 12), p. 173 ff.
92. Heilbroner in ibid., p. 186.
93. Ibid., p. 190.
94. Silk and Vogel, op. cit. (n. 5), p. 136.
95. Vogel, op. cit. (n. 27).
96. Silk and Vogel, op. cit. (n. 5), p. 136.
97. Ibid., p. 137.
98. Friedman, op. cit. (n. 75), p. 133.
99. Simon *et al.*, op. cit. (n. 17), p. 30.
100. Silk and Vogel, op. cit. (n. 5), p. 138.
101. Simon *et al.*, op. cit. (n. 17), p. 35.
102. Ibid., p. 36.
103. Ackerman, op. cit. (n. 9), p. 39.
104. Mintz, Morton and Jerry S. Cohen, 'Crime in the suites', in Nader (ed.), op. cit. (n. 15), pp. 76-9.
105. Green, Mark, 'When corporations become consumer lobbyists: on conscience and profits', in Bradshaw and Vogel (eds), op. cit. (n. 47), p. 21.
106. Simon *et al.*, op. cit. (n. 17), p. 37.
107. Ackerman, op. cit. (n. 9), pp. 39-40.
108. Simon *et al.*, op. cit. (n. 17), p. 38.
109. Bradshaw, T. F., 'Corporate social reform: an executive's viewpoint', in Sethi (ed.), op. cit. (n. 22), p. 24.
110. Silk and Vogel, op. cit. (n. 5), p. 139.
111. Vogel, op. cit. (n. 63), p. xiii.
112. Quoted in Sethi, op. cit. (n. 22), p. viii.
113. Friedman, op. cit. (n. 75), p. 134.
114. Davis, Keith and Robert L. Blomstrom, *Business and Society: Environment and Responsibility*, New York, McGraw-Hill, 1975 (third edition), p. 34.
115. Quoted in Steiner and Steiner, op. cit. (n. 12), p. 196.
116. Simon *et al.*, op. cit. (n. 17), p. 42.
117. Silk and Vogel, op. cit. (n. 5), p. 140.
118. Simon *et al.*, op. cit. (n. 17), p. 46.
119. Davis and Blomstrom, op. cit. (n. 114), pp. 30-5.
120. Beesley and Evans, op. cit. (n. 14), p. 16.
121. For an alternative summary see Davis and Blomstrom, op. cit. (n. 114), pp. 24-30; or Steiner and Steiner, op. cit. (n. 12), pp. 197-200.
122. Steiner and Steiner, op. cit. (n. 12), p. 203.

Chapter 3: Social control of business: from responsibility and philanthropy to accountability

1. Samuelson, Paul A., *Economics*, Tokyo, McGraw-Hill Kogakusha, 1980 (eleventh edition), p. 784.
2. Steiner, George A. and John F. Steiner, *Business, Government and Society: A Managerial Perspective*, New York, Random House, 1980, p. 141.
3. Medawar, Charles, *The Social Audit Consumer Handbook*, London, Macmillan, 1978, p. ix.
4. Silk, Leonard and David Vogel, *Ethics and Profits: The Crisis of Confidence in American Business*, New York, Simon and Schuster, 1976, pp. 136-7.
5. Heilbroner, Robert L., 'Controlling the corporation', in Heilbroner *et al., In the Name of Profit*, New York, Doubleday, 1972, p. 231.
6. Jacoby, Neil H., *Corporate Power and Social Responsibility*, New York, Macmillan, 1973, pp. 7-10.
7. Ibid., pp. 10-15.
8. Heilbroner, Robert L. and Lester C. Thurow, *Economics Explained*, Englewood Cliffs, NJ, Prentice-Hall, 1982, p. 183.
9. Heilbroner, op. cit. (n. 5), p. 245.
10. Beesley, Michael and Tom Evans, *Corporate Social Responsibility: A Reassessment*, London, Croom Helm, 1978, p. 41.
11. Galbraith, J. K., *The New Industrial State*, Harmondsworth, Penguin, 1974 (first published 1967), p. 116.
12. Heilbroner, op. cit. (n. 5), p. 248.
13. Beesley and Evans, op. cit. (n. 10), p. 103.
14. Heilbroner, op. cit. (n. 5), pp. 248-9.
15. Lindblom, Charles E., *Politics and Markets: The World's Political-Economic Systems*, New York, Basic Books, 1977, pp. 95-6.
16. Heilbroner, op. cit. (n. 5), p. 261.
17. See, for example, British Institute of Management, *The British Public Company: Its Role, Responsibilities and Accountability*, Occasional Paper – New Series, OPN 12, London, British Institute of Management, 1974.
18. See, for example, Leibowitz, Arleen, 'Are corporations undemocratic, private minigovernments?' in Johnson, M. Bruce (ed.), *The Attack on Corporate America: The Corporate Issues Sourcebook*, New York, McGraw-Hill, 1978, pp. 23-4; Sturdivant, Frederick D., *Business and Society: A Managerial Approach*, Homewood, Ala., Richard D. Irwin, 1981 (first published 1977), p. 388 ff; Steiner and Steiner, op. cit. (n. 2), pp. 546-8.
19. Beesley and Evans, op. cit. (n. 10), p. 43.
20. Brookes, Christopher, *Boards of Directors in British Industry*, Department of Employment Research Paper No. 7, 1979.
21. Nader, Ralph, 'The case for federal chartering', in Nader (ed.), *The Consumer and Corporate Accountability*, New York, Harcourt Brace Jovanovich, 1973, p. 351 ff.

22. Bauer, Raymond A. and Dan H. Fenn, Jr., 'What is a corporate social audit?', *Harvard Business Review*, January-February 1973.
23. Medawar, op. cit. (n. 3), pp. ix-x.
24. As noted by Steiner and Steiner, op. cit. (n. 2), pp. 227-37, and others.
25. Sturdivant, op. cit. (n. 18), p. 166.
26. Silk and Vogel, op. cit. (n. 4), p. 139.
27. Nader, op. cit. (n. 21), pp. 291-2.
28. Sturdivant, op. cit. (n. 18), p. 365.
29. Such as the prosecutions in the UK of the civil servants Sarah Tisdall and Clive Ponting. Also, in the corporate area, the case of Stanley Adams, who revealed the illegal trading activities of the Swiss drugs combine Hoffmann La Roche. His wife committed suicide after she was told he would be imprisoned for twenty years for industrial espionage.
30. Commenting on material leaked to the Sizewell Inquiry, the inquiry inspector, Sir Frank Layfield, said he was reluctant to place much weight on material produced other than by proper disclosure ('Anger at leaked Sizewell papers', *The Guardian*, 20 July 1984, p. 4). The Adams–La Roche case referred to above is another example of reluctance on the part of the authorities to listen to ethical whistle-blowing (see, for example, Erlichman, James, 'Long wait for justice for the man who took on Roche', *The Guardian*, 15 February 1984, p. 19; or Adams, Stanley, *Roche Versus Adams*, Jonathan Cape, 1984).
31. Beesley and Evans, op. cit. (n. 10), pp. 46-7.
32. Ibid., p. 45.
33. Lydenberg, Steven D., *Minding the Corporation Conscience 1980: Annual Meetings Round-Up*, New York, Council on Economic Priorities, 1980.
34. Beesley and Evans, op. cit. (n. 10), p. 254.
35. Simon, John G., Charles W. Powers, and Jon P. Gunnemann, *The Ethical Investor: Universities and Corporate Responsibility*, New Haven, Conn., Yale University Press, 1972.
36. Marlin, John Tepper, 'Pollution control: let's stop waiting for government', in Sethi, S. Prakash (ed.), *The Unstable Ground: Corporate Social Policy in a Dynamic Society*, Los Angeles, Melville Publishing, 1974.
37. Jones, Thomas M., 'An integrating framework for research in business and society: a step toward the elusive paradigm', *Academy of Management Review*, Vol. 8, No. 4 (1983), pp. 559-64.
38. Russell, Bertrand, *Power: A New Social Analysis*, London, Unwin, 1960 (first published 1938), p. 25.
39. In Worsley, Peter *et al.*, *Introducing Sociology*, Harmondsworth, Penguin, 1970, p. 232.
40. Galbraith, John Kenneth, *The Anatomy of Power*, London, Hamish Hamilton, 1984, p. 4.
41. Ibid., p. 12.
42. Beesley and Evans, op. cit. (n. 10), p. 39.

43. Ibid.
44. Silk and Vogel, op. cit. (n. 4), p. 52.
45. Weidenbaum, Murray L., *The Future of Business Regulation: Private Action and Public Demand*, New York, AMACOM, 1979, pp. 6-7.
46. Ibid., p. 172.
47. Foxall, Gordon, 'Towards a balanced view of consumerism', *Cranfield Management Review*, Vol. 2, No. 2 (1978).
48. Medawar, op. cit. (n. 3), p. 13.
49. Ibid., p. 12.
50. See, for example, Macarthur, Brian, 'Newspaper folly', *The Sunday Times*, 3 July 1983; or Robertson, Geoffrey, *People Against the Press: An Inquiry into the Press Council*, Quartet Books, 1983.
51. Medawar, op. cit. (n. 3), p. 14.
52. Cited by various American sources including Vogel, David, *Lobbying the Corporation: Citizen Challenges to Business Authority*, New York, Basic Books, 1978, pp. 5, 9, 232; Drucker, Peter F., 'The new meaning of corporate social responsibility', *California Management Review*, Vol. XXVI, No. 2 (Winter 1984); Silk and Vogel, op. cit. (n. 4), p. 153. Professor Ralf Dahrendorf has similarly commented on the UK in his *On Britain* (BBC, 1982), as have other observers of the UK scene.
53. Beesley and Evans, op. cit. (n. 10), p. 31.
54. British Institute of Management, op. cit. (n. 17), p. 8.
55. Ibid., p. 41.
56. Marlin, op. cit. (n. 36), p. 348.
57. Heilbroner, op. cit. (n. 5), p. 228.
58. Stone, C. D., in *Where the Law Ends*, New York, Harper and Row, 1975, identifies the limits to legal control.
59. Gist, Ronald R., *Marketing and Society: A Conceptual Introduction*, New York, Holt, Rinehart and Winston, 1971, p. 33.
60. Silk and Vogel, op. cit. (n. 4), p. 131.
61. Weidenbaum, op. cit. (n. 45), p. 145.
62. Steiner and Steiner, loc. cit. (n. 2), as quoted in the Preview to this chapter.
63. Berle, Adolf A., Jr., *The Twentieth Century Capitalist Revolution*, New York, Harcourt Brace and Company, 1954, p. 188.
64. Ackerman, Robert W., *The Social Challenge to Business*, Cambridge, Harvard University Press, 1975.
65. Quoted in Brookes, op. cit. (n. 20).
66. Corfield, Kenneth G., *Business Responsibilities*, London, Foundation for Business Responsibilities, 1972.
67. Silk and Vogel, op. cit. (n. 4), p. 146.
68. Heilbroner, op. cit. (n. 5), p. 242.

Chapter 4: Pressure groups and pluralism

1. Latham, Earl, 'The group basis of politics: notes for a theory', in Zisk, Betty H. (ed.), *American Political Interest Groups: Readings in Theory and Research*, Belmont, Wadsworth Publishing, 1969, pp. 17-18.

2. Wilson, Des, *Pressure: The A to Z of Campaigning in Britain*, London, Heinemann, 1984, p. 21.
3. Kimber, Richard and J. J. Richardson, *Pressure Groups in Britain: A Reader*, London, Dent, 1974, pp. 3-10.
4. Willetts, Peter (ed.), *Pressure Groups in the Global System*, London, Frances Pinter, 1982, Preface.
5. Kimber and Richardson, loc. cit. (n. 3).
6. Wootton, Graham, *Pressure Politics in Contemporary Britain*, Lexington, Lexington Books, 1978, pp. ix-x.
7. Shipley, Peter (ed.), *Directory of Pressure Groups and Representative Associations*, Epping, Bowker, 1979 (second edition).
8. Coxall, W. N., *Parties and Pressure Groups*, Harlow, Longman, 1981, pp. 108-9.
9. Ibid., p. 109.
10. Quoted in 'Pressure groups', *New Society*, 26 April 1979, p. iv.
11. Wallace, William, 'The pressure group phenomenon', in Frost, Brian (ed.), *The Tactics of Pressure: A Critical Review of Six British Pressure Groups*, London, Galliard, 1975, pp. 92-5.
12. Marsh, David (ed.), *Pressure Politics: Interest Groups in Britain*, London, Junction Books, 1983, p. 4.
13. Pym, Bridget, *Pressure Groups and the Permissive Society*, Newton Abbot, David and Charles, 1974.
14. Wallace, op. cit. (n. 11), p. 108.
15. Kotler, Milton, 'New life for American politics', *The Nation*, 30 October 1976, pp. 429-31.
16. Berry, Jeffrey M., *Lobbying for the People: The Political Behaviour of Public Interest Groups*, Princeton, NJ, Princeton University Press, 1977, pp. 288-9.
17. Sadler, Philip, 'Management and the social environment', *Long Range Planning*, August 1975.
18. European Societal Strategy Project, *Facing Realities: The Report of the European Societal Strategy Project*, Brussels, European Institute for Advanced Studies in Management, and the European Foundation for Management Development, 1981.
19. Kenny, Ivor, 'Business, politics and society', in Kakabadse, Andrew and Suresh Mukhi (eds), *The Future of Management Education*, Aldershot, Gower, 1984.
20. Wilson, op. cit. (n. 2).
21. Wootton, op. cit. (n. 6), p. 22.
22. Roberts, Geoffrey K., *Political Parties and Pressure Groups in Britain*, London, Weidenfeld and Nicolson, 1970, p. 78.
23. Rose, Richard (ed.), *Studies in British Politics: A Reader in Political Sociology*, London, Macmillan, 1976 (third edition), pp. 340-1.
24. Kimber and Richardson, op. cit. (n. 3), pp. 1-2.
25. Vogel makes a similar point about American political scientists. He quotes March: 'Political scientists have generally defined their field in a relatively modest way, limiting their attention to phenomena that occur in, or in close conjunction with, explicitly governmental

institutions ... By any reasonably descriptive definition of political science, the business firm is outside the domain.' This seems equally true in Britain. See Vogel, David, 'The corporation as government: challenges and dilemmas', *Polity*, Vol. 8, No. 1 (1975), pp. 5-37.

26. Wootton, op. cit. (n. 6), p. 13.
27. Mackenzie, W. J. H., 'Pressure groups in British government', in Rose, op. cit. (n. 23), p. 344 ff.
28. Coxall, op. cit. (n. 8), pp. 10-11.
29. Kimber and Richardson, op. cit. (n. 3), p. 3.
30. Wallace, loc. cit. (n. 11).
31. Marsh, op. cit. (n. 12), pp. 3-4.
32. McKensie, R. T., 'Parties, pressure groups and the British political process', in Kimber and Richardson, op. cit. (n. 3), pp. 281-2.
33. Willetts, Peter, 'Pressure groups as transnational actors', in Willetts, op. cit. (n. 4), pp. 2-9.
34. Ibid., p. 8.
35. Wootton, op. cit. (n. 6), p. 18.
36. Ibid., pp. 19-22.
37. Wilson, op. cit. (n. 2).
38. Mackenzie, op. cit. (n. 27), p. 346.
39. Wilson, op. cit. (n. 2), p. 2.
40. Mackenzie, loc. cit. (n. 38).
41. Wilson, op. cit. (n. 2), p. 7. Interestingly, Berry, in referring to the American situation, uses the same terms (op. cit. (n. 16)).
42. Roberts, op. cit. (n. 22), p. 96.
43. Pym, op. cit. (n. 13), p. 19.
44. Wilson, op. cit. (n. 2), pp. 2-3.
45. Coxall, op. cit. (n. 8), pp. 86-7.
46. Kimber and Richardson, op. cit. (n. 3), p. 13. Willetts (op. cit. (n. 4), p. 182), comes to a similar conclusion.
47. Coxall, op. cit. (n. 8), p. 84.
48. Marsh and Locksley describe the influence of business interest groups over government (not, however, business power elsewhere in society), remarking their surprise at the little previous work done in the area. Although, given the observations above about the limited domain of politics, this omission does not seem greatly surprising. They note, in reference to Lindblom, that capital (a term they use in preference to business for semantic reasons) is different from other interests because it exercises power or influence in two ways: directly, through interest groups, and structurally, as a constraint, because of its position in control of production, investment, and employment decisions which shape the economic and political environment within which government makes policy. See Marsh, D. and G. Locksley, 'Capital: the neglected face of power?' in Marsh (ed.), op. cit. (n. 12). Also see Ward, H., 'The anti-nuclear lobby: an unequal struggle' (in ibid.), for a case study illustrating business power in society at large and over government, and especially p. 194 and p. 207.

49. There are other avenues such as local government, particularly important for pressure groups addressing a local issue, and EEC or United Nations' bodies.
50. Marsh, op. cit. (n. 12), pp. 5-6.
51. Christoph, James B., 'Capital punishment and British politics: the role of pressure groups', in Kimber and Richardson (eds) op. cit. (n. 3). Grey, Anthony, 'Homosexual law reform', in Frost (ed.), op. cit. (n. 11).
52. Wootton, op. cit. (n. 6), pp. 40-50.
53. Rose, Richard, *Politics in England: An Interpretation for the 1980s*, London, Faber and Faber, 1980 (third edition), pp. 229-32.
54. Wilson, op. cit. (n. 2).
55. Ward (op. cit. (n. 48), pp. 191-2) notes that Friends of the Earth Ltd. had a total budget of £250,000 in 1980, whereas the Nuclear Power Information Group (set up by the nuclear industry in 1979 to promote nuclear energy and funded, in the last resort, from public money) spent £5 million on pro-nuclear information in the same year.
56. Marsh, D. and J. Chambers, 'The abortion lobby: pluralism at work?', in Marsh (ed.), op. cit. (n. 12).
57. Olson, Mancur, *The Logic of Collective Action: Public Goods and the Theory of Groups*, Cambridge, Mass., Harvard University Press, 1965, p. 2. Also see Berry, op. cit. (n. 16), p. 21 and p. 37 ff
58. Olson, op. cit. (n. 57), p. 132.
59. Ibid., p. 165.
60. Forbes, J. D., 'Are consumer advocacy groups political pressure groups?' in *Proceedings of the Tenth International Research Seminar in Marketing, June 7-10 1983*, Aix-en-Provence; Institut d'Administration des Enterprises, Université d'Aix-Marseille III; 1983.
61. Colby, Peter W., 'The organisation of public interest groups', *Policy Studies Journal*, Vol. 11, No. 4 (1983), pp. 699-708.
62. Rose, op. cit. (n. 53), p. 233.
63. Shipley, Peter (ed.), *The Guardian Directory of Pressure Groups and Representative Associations*, London, Wilton House, 1976.
64. Roberts, op. cit. (n. 22), p. 97.
65. Ward, op. cit. (n. 48).
66. Wallace, op. cit. (n. 11), p. 104.
67. Wilson, op. cit. (n. 2).
68. Coxall, op. cit. (n. 8), pp. 91-2.
69. Ibid.
70. Klein, Rudolf, 'The case for elitism: public opinion and public policy', in Rose (ed.), op. cit. (n. 23), p. 334.
71. Colman, Andrew, 'The psychology of influence', in Frost (ed.), op. cit. (n. 11), p. 11.
72. Willetts, Peter, 'The impact of promotional pressure groups on global politics', in Willetts (ed.), op. cit. (n. 4), pp. 181 and 195.
73. Wilson, op. cit. (n. 2), p. 116.
74. Mackenzie, op. cit. (n. 27), pp. 352-4.
75. Shipley, op. cit. (n. 63), p. 14.
76. Willetts, op. cit. (n. 72), pp. 192-3.

77. Wilson, op. cit. (n. 2), p. 18.
78. Shipley, op. cit. (n. 63), p. 19; and others.
79. Marsh, op. cit. (n. 12), p. 7.
80. Berry, op. cit. (n. 16), p. 212.
81. Ibid., p. 214.
82. Ibid., p. 285.
83. Ibid., p. 263.
84. Willetts, op. cit. (n. 72), p. 182.
85. Berry, op. cit. (n. 16), p. 276.
86. Vogel's work is an exception, especially *Lobbying the Corporation*, but he makes the same observation.
87. Some groups see 'the establishment' as their target, included in which are the corporations.
88. Wootton, op. cit. (n. 6), p. 35.
89. Berry, op. cit. (n. 16), p. 233.
90. Etzioni, Amitai, *Demonstration Democracy*, New York, Gordon and Breach, 1970, p. 45.
91. Berry, op. cit. (n. 16), pp. 232-3.
92. Lipsky, Michael, 'Protest as a political resource', in Zisk (ed.), op. cit. (n. 1), p. 270.
93. Bailey, Robert, *Radicals in Urban Politics: The Alinsky Approach*, Chicago, University of Chicago Press, 1974, pp. 83-4.
94. Hain, Peter, 'Direct action and the Springbok tours', in Benewick, Robert and Trevor Smith (eds), *Direct Action and Democratic Politics*, London, George Allen and Unwin, 1972, p. 194.
95. Ward, op. cit. (n. 48).
96. Brown, Paul and Colin Brown, 'Government blames Sellafield chiefs for leak', *The Guardian*, 15 February 1984.
97. Marsh, op. cit. (n. 12), pp. 7-8.
98. Turner, Louis, 'There's no love lost between multinational companies and the Third World', in Heilbroner, Robert L. and Paul London (eds), *Corporate Social Policy*, Reading, Addison-Wesley, 1975.
99. Hearst, David, '"Spiked" sweet eaters unscathed', *The Guardian*, 19 November 1984.

Chapter 5: The boycott tactic

1. Quoted in Bondurant, Joan V., 'Ahimsa', in Hare, A. Paul and Herbert H. Blumberg (eds), *Nonviolent Direct Action: American Cases: Social-Psychological Analyses*, Washington, Corpus Books, 1968, p. 315.
2. Quoted in Laidler, Harry W., *Boycotts and the Labor Struggle: Economic and Legal Aspects*, New York, Russell and Russell, 1963 (reissued, first published 1913), pp. 25-6.
3. Etzioni's principal point in *Demonstration Democracy* is that (peaceful) demonstrations are 'an integral part of democratic politics'. See Etzioni, Amitai, *Demonstration Democracy*, New York, Gordon and Breach, 1970, p. 38.

4. Gregg, Richard, 'Moral jiu-jitsu', in Hare and Blumberg (eds), op. cit. (n. 1), pp. 330-1.
5. King, Martin Luther, Jr., 'The Montgomery bus boycott', in Hare and Blumberg (eds), op. cit. (n. 1), p. 77.
6. Bondurant, Joan V., *The Conquest of Violence: The Gandhian Philosophy of Conflict*, Berkeley, University of California Press, 1965 (first published 1958).
7. Sharp, Gene, *The Politics of Nonviolent Action*, Boston, Porter Sargent, 1973, p. v.
8. Ibid., p. 67.
9. Ibid., p. xx.
10. Ibid., p. 6.
11. Ibid., pp. 12-26.
12. Ibid., pp. 31-2.
13. Boyle, Ed, 'The politics of protest: guerrilla tactics to keep Dallas out of Dorking', *The Listener*, 11 October 1984.
14. Sharp, op. cit. (n. 7), p. 219.
15. Lakey, George, 'Mechanisms of nonviolent action', in Hare and Blumberg (eds), op. cit. (n. 1), p. 388.
16. *The Times*, 10 December 1984.
17. Some might argue that the mass actions which have taken place at the Greenham Common airbase contradict this claim.
18. Wilson, Des, *Pressure: The A to Z of Campaigning in Britain*, London, Heinemann, 1984, p. 33.
19. See, for a typical example, Linton, Martin, 'Warbler heath escapes bulldozer', *The Guardian*, 23 October 1984.
20. Wilson, op. cit. (n. 18), p. 34. His discussion of the case for and against law-breaking by pressure groups is well reasoned (pp. 33-6).
21. Laidler, op. cit. (n. 2).
22. Etzioni, op. cit. (n. 3), p. 27.
23. Laidler, op. cit. (n. 2), pp. 23-7; Nelson, Walter Henry and Terence C. F. Prittie, *The Economic War Against the Jews*, New York, Random House, 1977, p. 25.
24. Wootton, Graham, *Pressure Politics in Contemporary Britain*, Lexington, Lexington Books, 1978, pp. 168-71.
25. Laidler, op. cit. (n. 2), p. 7.
26. Ibid., p. 27.
27. Wolman, Leo, *The Boycott in American Trade Unions*, Baltimore, The Johns Hopkins Press, 1916, pp. 10-13. Yet as will be seen even Wolman goes beyond the limited meaning of boycott as employed in this study, by including restrictions on employers' purchases of goods. This is where employees refuse to handle or use certain goods, referred to then as a 'materials boycott' (as opposed to the 'consumption boycott') and known today as 'blacking'. The intention of the action is to put pressure on the supplier, but as any refusal to purchase that may result is largely involuntary on the employer's part and as those taking the action are not directly exercising their consumer sovereignty, it would not be classed here as a consumer boycott.

28. Laidler, op. cit. (n. 2), p. 64.
29. Wolman, op. cit. (n. 27), p. 13.
30. Laidler, op. cit. (n. 2), p. 64.
31. Wolman, op. cit. (n. 27), p. 14.
32. Ibid., p. 14.
33. Laidler, op. cit. (n. 2), pp. 60-3.
34. Hotaling, Edward, *The Arab Blacklist Unveiled*, Landia Publishing, 1977.
35. Wolman, op. cit. (n. 27), p. 24.
36. Laidler, op. cit. (n. 2), p. 7.
37. Wolman, op. cit. (n. 27), p. 18.
38. Ibid., p. 79.
39. Ibid., p. 135.
40. Laidler, op. cit. (n. 2), p. 127.
41. Ibid., p. 132.
42. Grant, A. J. and Harold Temperley, *Europe in the Nineteenth and Twentieth Centuries*, London, Longman, 1927 (sixth edition, revised and edited by Lillian M. Penson, 1952), p. 428.
43. Quoted in Sharp, op. cit. (n. 7), pp. 247-8.
44. Ibid., p. 247.
45. Ibid., p. 248.
46. Remer, C. E., *A Study of Chinese Boycotts: With Special Reference to Their Economic Effectiveness*, Baltimore, The Johns Hopkins Press, 1933, p. 9. Sharp writes, 'China is often regarded as the classic home of the national consumers' boycott', (op. cit. (n. 7), p. 229).
47. Ibid., p. 2.
48. Ibid., pp. 10-20.
49. Ibid., p. 35.
50. Ibid., p. 246.
51. Ibid.
52. Roberts, Adam, 'Do economic boycotts ever work?', *New Society*, 11 September 1975. Sethi writes, 'It is estimated that approximately ninety countries are boycotting at least one other country in the world at the present time' (Sethi, S. Prakash with Carl Swanson, 'United States versus Bechtel Corporation', in Sethi, S. Prakash, *Up Against the Corporate Wall: Modern Corporations and Social Issues of the Eighties*, Englewood Cliffs, NJ, Prentice-Hall, 1982, p. 49).
53. Dekker, P.G., 'Economische oorlogvoering: enige opmerkingen over boycot en embargo' (Economic warfare: a note on boycott and embargo), *De Economist (The Economist*, Netherlands), Vol. 121, No. 4 (1973), (with summary in English).
54. Losman, Donald L., 'The effects of economic boycotts', *Lloyds Bank Review*, No. 106 (October 1972).
55. Galtung, Johan, 'On the effects of international economic sanctions: with examples from the case of Rhodesia', *World Politics*, Vol. XIX, No. 3 (1967).
56. Nelson and Prittie, op. cit. (n. 23), p. 4.
57. Hotaling, op. cit. (n. 34), p. 3.

58. Ibid., p. 4.
59. Ibid., pp. 4-7.
60. Winchester, Simon, 'How Britain gives in to pressures from Arab boycott', *The Sunday Times*, 2 September 1984; *The Guardian*, editorial, 'What price a boycott?', 31 October 1984.
61. Winchester, op. cit. (n. 60).
62. Nelson and Prittie, op. cit. (n. 23), p. 47.
63. Ibid., pp. 6-11.
64. Winchester, op. cit. (n. 60).
65. Ibid. and *The Guardian*, op. cit. (n. 60).
66. Nelson and Prittie, op. cit. (n. 23), p. 26.
67. Ibid., pp. 173-4.
68. Vogel, David, *Lobbying the Corporation: Citizen Challenges to Business Authority*, New York, Basic Books, 1978, pp. 192-6.
69. Nelson and Prittie, op. cit. (n. 23), p. 57.
70. Ibid., p. 135.
71. Ibid., p. 163.
72. Ibid., p. 191.
73. Ibid., p. 211 ff.
74. Ibid., p. 27.
75. Ibid., p. 223.
76. Ibid., pp. 227-8.

Chapter 6: Pressure groups in the marketing system

1. Quoted in Levitt, Theodore, 'The augmented product concept', in Rothberg, Robert R. (ed.), *Corporate Strategy and Product Innovation*, New York, The Free Press, 1976, p. 149.
2. Thomas, R. E., 'Marketing a new capitalism', *CBI Review*, Autumn 1974.
3. Fisk, George, *Marketing Systems: An Introductory Analysis*, London, Harper International, 1966, p. 506.
4. Bartels, Robert, *The History of Marketing Thought*, Columbus, Grid, 1976 (second edition, first published 1962).
5. Hughes, G. David, *Marketing Management: A Planning Approach*, Reading, Addison-Wesley, 1978, p. 278.
6. Foxall, Gordon R., *Strategic Marketing Management*, London, Croom Helm, 1981, p. 71.
7. Foxall, Gordon R., *Consumer Behaviour: A Practical Guide*, London, Croom Helm, 1980, p. 33.
8. The version used here is Levitt, op. cit. (n. 1).
9. Vogel, David, *Lobbying the Corporation: Citizen Challenges to Business Authority*, New York, Basic Books, 1978, p. 45.
10. Smith, Craig, 'The legitimacy concept – a fifth element in the marketing mix?', in Christopher, Martin, Malcolm McDonald, and Angela Rushton (eds), *Back to Basics: The 4 P's Revisited*, Proceedings of the Marketing Education Group 16th Annual Conference at Cranfield School of Management, July 1983.

11. Kotler, Philip, *Principles of Marketing*, Englewood Cliffs, NJ, Prentice-Hall, 1983, p. 655.
12. Marks and Spencer is enhancing the legitimacy of its offering by telling the customer that over 90 per cent of its goods are British made.
13. Fisk, op. cit. (n. 3). Bartels (op. cit. (n. 4), pp. 202-6) examines the contributions to marketing of marketing systems approaches. He suggests that 'through systems analysis, marketing thought has been infused with a wider dimension of management strategy, better understanding of influences shaping marketing structure as a whole, and keener appreciation of the countervailing forces playing within and around the marketing systems' (p. 206).
14. Fisk, op. cit. (n. 3), p. 12.
15. Such as King, William R. and David I. Cleland, 'Environmental information systems for strategic marketing planning', *Journal of Marketing*, Vol. 38 (October 1974), pp. 35-40; and others in the tradition of Aguilar.
16. For example, Purcell, Theodore V., 'Reprise of the "ethical investors"', *Harvard Business Review*, March-April 1980; *idem*, 'Management and the "ethical" investors', *Harvard Business Review*, September-October 1979; Henderson, Hazel, 'Toward managing social conflict', *Harvard Business Review*, May-June 1971.
17. Such as Nolan, Joseph, 'Protect your public image with performance', *Harvard Business Review*, March-April 1975.
18. Rapoport, Carla, 'Why executives must learn to live with pressure groups', *Financial Times*, 4 February 1983, p. 12.
19. Ackerman, Robert W., 'How companies respond to social demands', *Harvard Business Review*, July-August 1973.
20. *Idem, The Social Challenge to Business*, Cambridge, Mass., Harvard University Press, 1975.
21. Ford, D. and B. Vezeridis, 'Ecological pressures on the firm: cases and conclusions', *Cranfield Management Review*, Vol. 2, No. 2 (1978).
22. Simon, John G., Charles W. Powers, and Jon P. Gunnemann, *The Ethical Investor: Universities and Corporate Responsibility*, New Haven, Yale University Press, 1972, p. vii.
23. Vogel, David, 'Trends in shareholder activism – 1970-1982', *California Management Review*, Vol. XXV, No. 3 (Spring 1983); also Vogel, op. cit. (n. 9); the annual reports of the Council on Economic Priorities, *Minding the Corporate Conscience*; Purcell, op. cit. (n. 16); Simon *et al.*, op. cit. (n. 22); and others.
24. Vogel, op. cit. (n. 23). Legislation has been passed by some states in America restricting state pension funds investments in companies doing business in South Africa. See 'US pension funds hit out at apartheid', *The Guardian*, 24 April 1984; and Omond, Roger, 'Investment ban is blow to Pretoria', *The Guardian*, 10 January 1983. Vogel, op. cit. (n. 9), reports the classic ethical investment actions of Campaign GM, along with many other sources.
25. Hencke, David, 'Charities selling tobacco shares', *The Guardian*, 15 January 1985; also see *idem*, 'Cancer charities in BMA list of

shareholders in tobacco firms', *The Guardian*, 14 January 1985.

26. *Idem*, 'BMA votes to sever investment links with tobacco companies', *The Guardian*, 3 July 1984.

27. See Macintyre, Donald, 'Row brews on pit pensions', *The Sunday Times*, 13 November 1983; also Rodgers, Peter, 'The pension funds have done as Scargill wanted, even though he lost in court', *The Guardian*, 27 April 1984, p. 16 (reports the disinvestment in overseas shares but attributes this to feelings that the US stock market seemed to be nearing a peak); Wainwright, Martin, 'Scargill proves court jester with a cause', *The Guardian*, 27 March 1984, pp. 1 and 2; 'Worker trustees on the board', *The Guardian*, 14 September 1983, p. 25.

28. Pagano, Margareta, 'TUC presses for ban on South Africa', *The Guardian*, 16 May 1983.

29. Halsall, Martyn, 'Church pulls out of firm over pay in South Africa', *The Guardian*, 19 November 1984, p. 3.

30. 'Working assets – a money market fund for people who want to put their savings to good use' (advertisement in *Business and Society Review*, No. 48 (Winter 1984)).

31. Ward, Sue, 'How ethics can be taken into account', *The Guardian*, 18 July 1984. She reports on the activities of Robert Schwartz, a vice-president of Shearson/American Express, and responsible for placing over $1bn in ethical investments. Research he has undertaken found that over a period of ten years a theoretical ethical portfolio performed considerably better than the average. He suggests, 'if you are a poor manager who does not care about your workforce or your environment, the chances are that it will spill over into your business practices as well'.

32. Lloyd, Stephen, 'A question of conscience money', *The Guardian*, 17 September 1983; also *The Observer*, 6 January 1985; Lever, Lawrence, 'Keeping it clean', *The Guardian*, 13 October 1984, p. 23.

33. Harper, Keith, 'Trade union bank has investment it needs to open', *The Guardian*, 10 April 1984; Rodgers, Peter, 'Thirty unions launch their own bank', *The Guardian*, 20 January 1984, p. 17; and others.

34. *EIRIS Newsletter*, No. 2 (November 1983); or see Ward, op. cit. (n. 31); Lever, op. cit. (n. 32); or Shearlock, Peter, 'Cream of the clean', *The Sunday Times*, 13 November 1983.

35. Such as the Council on Economic Priorities, mentioned above, or those listed in Marlin, John Tepper, 'Pollution control: let's stop waiting for government', in Sethi, S. Prakash (ed.), *The Unstable Ground: Corporate Social Policy in a Dynamic Society*, Los Angeles, Melville Publishing, 1974, p. 355.

36. Luthans, Fred, Richard M. Hodgetts, and Kenneth R. Thompson, *Social Issues in Business: Strategic and Public Policy Perspectives*, New York, Macmillan, 1984, p. 82. They are here quoting from De George, R. T., *Business Ethics*, New York, Macmillan, 1982, described by Hanson as 'the most scholarly approach to the subject', see Hanson, Kirk O., 'Book review: *Business Ethics*', *California Management Review*, Vol. XXVI, No. 1 (Fall 1983).

37. Steiner, George and John F. Steiner, *Business, Government and Society: A Managerial Perspective*, New York, Random House, 1980, pp. 383-9. Their concern here is with ethics for management practice.
38. Luthans *et al.*, op. cit. (n. 36), p. 84.
39. Purcell, Theodore V., op. cit. (n. 16).
40. Engel, James F. and Roger D. Blackwell, *Consumer Behavior*, New York, The Dryden Press, 1982, p. 610.
41. Webster, Frederick E., Jr., *Social Aspects of Marketing*, Englewood Cliffs, NJ, Prentice-Hall, 1974, pp. 107-9.
42. Kotler defines the societal marketing concept as 'a managerial orientation that holds that the key task of the organisation is to determine the needs and wants of target markets and to adapt the organisation to delivering the desired satisfactions more effectively and efficiently than its competitors in a way that preserves or enhances the consumers' and society's well being', see Kotler, Philip, *Marketing Management: Analysis, Planning and Control*, Englewood Cliffs, NJ, Prentice-Hall, 1980 (fourth edition), p. 35. Webster suggests that the managerial objective of his fourth phase in market development, where the revised concept of marketing is to be found, is 'Profit through true value creation and social responsibility', and writes of a desired end of 'a net improvement in the quality of life for all consumers and in the public welfare' (ibid., p. 108).
43. Anderson, W. Thomas, Jr., and William H. Cunningham, 'The socially conscious consumer', *Journal of Marketing*, Vol. 36 (July 1972).
44. On collinearity: is it surprising that the scale and the independent sociopsychological variables correlate when, for example, item 6 on the scale assesses agreement with 'People would be a lot better off if they could live far away from other people and never have to do anything for them', and there is an 'independent' variable of alienation: 'a feeling of isolation from one's community, society, and/or culture'? This in itself is sufficient to invalidate the use of discriminant analysis. Further technical criticisms could also be made, such as whether the data for the independent variables is interval, which it needs to be for discriminant analysis, or whether (and this seems more likely) it is nominal/categorical. The major criticism must be, however, that the finding that sociopsychological variables are better discriminators than demographic variables is probably largely to do with the problem that the dependent variable of the social responsibility scale and the so-called independent sociopsychological variables are measuring the same thing. So this empirical work on socially responsible consumption, if nothing else, falls down by the very rules established for positivistic quantitative research. Its principal value is in giving some credence to the notion of ethical purchase behaviour, even if the authors have not actually gone out and measured that.
45. Kassarjian, Harold H., 'Incorporating ecology into marketing strategy: the case of air pollution', *Journal of Marketing*, Vol. 35 (July 1971). He writes: 'the next hypothesis predicted that this group would claim to be more willing to pay a higher price for a pollution reducing gasoline

than might its less concerned neighbors. This hypothesis could perhaps be tested most accurately through the use of competitive sales figures ... However, these data were not available to the author. Further, he did not believe that consumers could be asked whether or not they would be willing to pay more and expect a correlation between the claimed responses and actual behavior patterns.'

46. Engel, James F., Roger D. Blackwell, and David T. Kollat, *Consumer Behavior*, Hinsdale, The Dryden Press, 1973, pp. 620-1.

47. Ibid., p. 640. They also note, 'consumers do not voluntarily purchase catalytic emission control devices for their automobiles (which are available) but are willing to support laws which require manufacturers to install them. Perhaps consumers realise that these indirect decisions are passed on to themselves as added costs or perhaps not.' Again this seems to illustrate a problem of the logic of collective action and how sanctions are required if people are to act 'voluntarily' for the collective good. If sanctions were applied for not purchasing catalytic converters then they would probably be fitted – even if the sanctions were less costly than the device. People may then need to be denied the choice as to whether to practise socially responsible consumption – once choice is denied they happily practise it.

48. Kinnear and Taylor examine the relationship between the amount of concern for the ecology that buyers indicate and their perceptions of detergent brands. Again, despite sophisticated analysis and a large sample size, actual behaviour was not examined, and there was also a likely correlation between dependent and 'independent' variables. They conclude that there is a relationship between ecological concern and brand perceptions: 'the higher the buyer's ecological concern the more salient is the ecological dimension in perception, and the greater is the perceived similarity of brands that are ecologically non-destructive.' They warn that as 'A large proportion of the sample is not motivated to perceive products on the basis of concern for the ecology ... it is unlikely that the purchasing pattern of consumers will shift enough to non-polluting products to force those products that do pollute off the market. Other methods such as legislation and moral pressure on producers and distributors will likely be necessary to assure the elimination of polluting products. Concern for the ecology is not a universally strong enough dimension to complete this task by itself.' See Kinnear, Thomas C. and James R. Taylor, 'The effect of ecological concern on brand perceptions', *Journal of Marketing Research*, Vol. X. (May 1973). Kinnear *et al.* in a later paper did intend 'to get closer to the marketplace than Anderson and Cunningham did'. In this paper, the research previously reported is again used, this time in conjunction with the socio-economic and personality characteristics of the respondents. They attempt to improve on the Social Responsibility Scale used by Anderson and Cunningham by developing a new scale incorporating behavioural and attitudinal measures. They continue to rely, however, on verbal statements of behavioural intention, not actual behaviour, which may be no different to attitudes (as the work of Fishbein and

others bears witness). Kinnear *et al.* conclude that 'Appeals to the ecologically concerned segment should take advantage of the psychological profile for that segment', for they suggest that ecological concern can be identified from personality characteristics. Yet again, however, this claim is weakened by the dubious independence of the 'independent' variables. Doubts are expressed on whether ecologically concerned consumption could end pollution; 'the preferences of consumers operating through market mechanisms will not eliminate pollution externalities in consumption.' See Kinnear, Thomas C., James R. Taylor, and Sadrudin A. Ahmed 'Ecologically concerned consumers: who are they?', *Journal of Marketing*, Vol. 38 (April 1974).

49. Such as Murphy, Patrick E., Norman Kangun, and William B. Locander, 'Environmentally concerned consumers – racial variations', *Journal of Marketing*, October 1978; or Webster, Frederick E., Jr., 'Determining the characteristics of the socially conscious consumer', *Journal of Consumer Research*, December 1975. In support of Engel, Kollat, and Blackwell's remark about belief in socially responsible consumption, consider Feldman's unsubstantiated claim: 'To date, societal satisfaction has had either a residual or a negligible influence on consumer purchasing behaviour. However, there are currently numerous indications that societal considerations will assume greater importance as consumers begin to understand the resource implications of product use.' The example given is of consumers switching from phosphate-based detergents to others containing less harmful chemicals. He suggests, 'If the trend continues, the ethic of conspicuous consumption that underlies much of contemporary middle-class consumption behaviour will be regarded with the same distaste in the future as today's generation regards the lavish displays of wealth exhibited by the nouveau riche at the turn of the century.' See Feldman, Laurence P., 'Societal adaptation: a new challenge for marketing', *Journal of Marketing*, Vol. 35 (July 1971). Laczniak *et al.*, in using expert opinion to predict likely features of the business environment in the future, found that consumerism and other social pressures on business would not go away and were likely to increase. They suggest, 'The consumer movement, however, may not take the form it has traditionally', and quote Louis Stern, commenting on consumer behaviour in much the same way as Feldman: 'I believe the consumer movement will be reflected by individual behavior rather than by collective actions. That is, more individuals will stand ready to confront alleged "wrongs" in the marketplace.' See Laczniak, Gene R., Robert F. Lusch, and Jon D. Udell, 'Marketing in 1985: a view from the ivory tower', *Journal of Marketing*, October 1977. In contrast, Fisk has called for producer initiated responsible consumption, in Fisk, George, 'Criteria for a theory of responsible consumption', *Journal of Marketing*, Vol. 37 (April 1983); while Kotler has advocated the case for 'countermarketing' to curb unwholesome demand and 'demarketing' where there are or may be shortages (see Kotler, op. cit. (n. 42), p. 26).

50. Thomas, R. E., 'Marketing a new capitalism', *CBI Review*, Autumn 1974. See chapter Preview for a quotation and ensuing discussion.
51. *Idem*, 'After Kotler: marketing "Consciousness Four"', *Advertising Quarterly*, Autumn 1974.
52. Brozen thus argues that the market can sustain an ethic, see Brozen, Yale, 'The ethical consequences of alternative incentive systems', in Brozen, Yale, Elmer W. Johnson, and Charles W. Powers, *Can the Market Sustain an Ethic?*, Chicago, University of Chicago, 1978, p. 13.
53. Schultze, Charles L., *The Public Use of Private Interest*, Washington, The Brookings Institution, 1977, p. 18.
54. Ibid.
55. Wight, Robin, *The Day the Pigs Refused to be Driven to Market: Advertising and the Consumer Revolution*, London, Hart Davis MacGibbon, 1972, p. 40.
56. Vogel, David, 'The corporation as government: challenges and dilemmas', *Polity*, Vol. 8, No. 1 (1975).
57. Kotler, op. cit. (n. 42), p. 16.
58. Ibid., pp. 33-6. Also see above (n. 42) for his definition of the societal marketing concept.

Chapter 7: Consumer boycotts of business

1. Mills, C. Wright, *The Power Elite*, London, Oxford University Press, 1956, p. 3.
2. Rev. Jesse Jackson, the first black American presidential candidate; quoted in Vogel, David, *Lobbying the Corporation: Citizen Challenges to Business Authority*, New York, Basic Books, 1978, p. 39.
3. Ibid., p. 4.
4. 'Black (lists) and white', *New Republic*, 26 October 1968, pp. 7-8.
5. Laidler, Harry W., *Boycotts and the Labor Struggle: Economic and Legal Aspects*, New York, Russell and Russell, 1968 (reissued, first published 1913), p. 27.
6. Ibid., pp. 27-30.
7. Wolman, Leo, *The Boycott in American Trade Unions*, Baltimore, The Johns Hopkins Press, 1916, p. 23.
8. Nelson, Walter Henry and Terence C. F. Prittie, *The Economic War Against the Jews*, New York, Random House, 1977, pp. 9-10.
9. Sharp, Gene, *The Politics of Nonviolent Action*, Boston, Porter Sargent, 1973, p. 221 ff.
10. Vogel, op. cit. (n. 2), p. 5.
11. The computer databases BLAISE and SSCI (Social Science Citation Index) proved to be the most useful of the secondary sources' abstracts available. Even these sources, although at least including boycott as a topic, provided few references. The BLAISE search for listings under consumer, customer, and economic boycotts identified 41 references. Most of these were about the Arab boycott. Only those about the use of the boycott by the American labour unions were about consumer boycotts. SSCI identified 11 articles on boycotts (again consumer,

customer, and economic); three of these were about consumer boycotts, two on boycott legality, and one on the economics of boycotts referred to later.

12. Even Des Wilson's *Pressure: The A to Z of Campaigning in Britain*, London, Heinemann, 1984, has little to say about boycotts. When questioned on this following the success of a threatened boycott, to be organised by the group CLEAR against paint manufacturers' use of lead in paint, Mr Wilson replied 'I've had little experience of the consumer boycott, although the mere threat of it seemed to achieve our objective in the paint area. I agree with you that consumer boycotts are activities with very considerable potential' (letter to this author, 3 December 1984).

13. There is a British business and society text but it is dated and out of print: Kempner, Thomas, Keith Macmillan, and Kevin Hawkins, *Business and Society: Tradition and Change*, London, Allen Lane, 1974. Michael Beesley and Tom Evans's *Corporate Social Responsibility: A Reassessment*, London, Croom Helm, 1978, is more useful if one takes – as suggested in Chapter 2 – the social control of business as the central issue in business and society.

14. Hay, Robert D., Edmund R. Gray, and James E. Gates (eds), *Business and Society*, Cincinnati, South-Western Publishing, 1976.

15. Luthans, Fred, Richard M. Hodgetts, and Kenneth R. Thompson, *Social Issues in Business: Strategic and Public Policy Perspectives*, New York, Macmillan, 1984 (fourth edition), p. 400.

16. Nadel, Mark V., *The Politics of Consumer Protection*, Indianapolis, Bobbs-Merril Company, 1971.

17. Stern, Louis L., 'Consumer protection via self-regulation', *Journal of Marketing*, Vol. 35 (July 1971), pp. 47-53.

18. Box, Jo M. F., 'Consumerism in an area of decline: does it still have a future?' Paper presented at the Tenth International Research Seminar in Marketing, June 7-10 1983, Aix-en-Provence. Organised by Institut d'Administration des Enterprises and Université d'Aix-Marseille III.

19. Smith, George, *The Consumer Interest*, London, John Martin, 1982, pp. 297-8.

20. Ibid., p. 290.

21. Ibid., p. 301.

22. Ibid., p. 290.

23. MP Jack Ashley suggested a selective boycott of Merrell by the government using NHS purchasing powers, as although £92m compensation had been paid to American families, it had not been offered to British families. See *The Guardian*, 17 July 1984.

24. Wight, Robin, *The Day the Pigs Refused to be Driven to Market: Advertising and the Consumer Revolution*, London, Hart Davis MacGibbon, 1972, p. 81.

25. Ibid., pp. 21-2.

26. Mises, Ludwig von, *Human Action: A Treatise on Economics*, London, William Hodge, 1949, p. 280.

27. Rea, Samuel A., Jr., 'The economics of a consumer boycott', *Journal of Economics and Business*, Vol. 27, No. 1 (1974).
28. Krieger, David M., 'The "another mother for peace"' consumer campaign – a campaign that failed', *Journal of Peace Research*, Vol. 8 (1971).
29. Berry, Jeffrey M., *Lobbying for the People: The Political Behaviour of Public Interest Groups*, Princeton, Princeton University Press, 1977.
30. Vogel, op. cit. (n. 2), p. 229. Furthermore, an SSCI search for articles citing Vogel failed to unearth anything specifically about boycotts, even though nearly 100 citations were generated. Some referred to the other tactic prominent in *Lobbying the Corporation*, activist shareholder actions, but most were about the social control of business in general rather than specific methods for the achievement of this.
31. Nelson and Prittie, op. cit. (n. 8), p. 28.
32. Dolores Huerta, UFWOC (United Farm Workers of California) Vice-President and Chief Negotiator. Quoted in Brown, Jerald Barry, *The United Farm Workers Grape Strike and Boycott, 1965-1970: An Evaluation of the Culture of Poverty Theory*, PhD thesis, August 1972, p. 205.
33. John Bank, California grape boycott organiser, in interview, 6 December 1983.
34. Aaron, Benjamin, 'Methods of industrial action: courts, administrative agencies, and legislatures', in Aaron, Benjamin and K. W. Wedderburn (eds), *Industrial Conflict: A Comparative Legal Survey*, London, Longman, 1972, p. 102.
35. Ibid., p. 103. The UFW could employ the materials boycott tactic without being liable to prosecution under the NLRA (National Labor Relations Act) as they were not covered by it. As Aaron observes, 'It is somewhat ironic that farm workers, who, for the most part, are not "employees" covered by the NLRA and have been deprived of its guarantees of the right to organise and to bargain collectively, have recently profited by their freedom to engage in boycotts, which are illegal if conducted by employees covered by the Act.'
36. Ibid., pp. 103-6.
37. Inevitably, this is merely a tentative observation. No legislation in Britain appears to cover consumer boycotts specifically and there do not seem to be any precedents established in case law. Further, no sources seem prepared to hazard an opinion or even give the matter consideration. This probably reflects the limited use of the boycott in Britain and the unwillingness of a boycotted firm to resort to the law in any case. In a Monopolies and Restrictive Practices Commission report, collective discrimination by buyers, referred to as a buyers' boycott, is viewed as against the public interest. The concern however is with exclusive-buying agreements within trades, such as those encouraged by the National Union of Retail Tobacconists against manufacturers, rather than consumer boycotts, but a similar view might be taken with consumer boycotts and particularly secondary boycotts (The Monopolies and Restrictive Practices Commission, *Collective*

Discrimination: A Report on Exclusive Dealing, Collective Boycotts, Aggregated Rebates and Other Discriminatory Trade Practices, Cmnd. 9504, London, HMSO, 1955, pp. 64-8).

38. Harper, Michael C., 'The consumer's emerging right to boycott: NAACP vs. Claiborne Hardware and its implications for American labor law', *The Yale Law Journal*, Vol. 93, No. 3 (January 1984).
39. Harris, Margaret A., 'Political, social and economic boycotts by consumers: do they violate the Sherman Act?' *Houston Law Review*, Vol. 17, No. 4 (1980).
40. Harper, op. cit. (n. 38).
41. Blodgett, Timothy B., 'Review of *Lobbying the Corporation*', *Harvard Business Review*, July-August 1979.
42. Vogel, op. cit. (n. 2), Preface.
43. Ibid., p. 6.
44. Ibid., p. 23.
45. Ibid., p. 41.
46. Ibid., p. 42.
47. Ibid.
48. Ibid., p. 61.
49. Ibid., p. 73.
50. Ibid., p. 5.
51. Ibid., p. 212.
52. Ibid., p. 215.
53. Ibid., p. 216.
54. Wolman, op. cit. (n. 7), p. 100.
55. Ibid., p. 128.
56. Ibid., p. 110.
57. Ibid., pp. 119-20.
58. Ibid., pp. 112-13.
59. Laidler, op. cit. (n. 5), pp. 67-8.
60. Wolman, op. cit. (n. 7), p. 134.
61. Ibid., p. 93.
62. Ibid., pp. 95-7.
63. Ibid., p. 84.
64. Ibid., p. 90.
65. Reed, Christopher, 'Computer in battle against supermarket', *The Guardian*, 27 July 1983.
66. Harper, op. cit. (n. 38).
67. Harris, op. cit. (n. 39).
68. Laidler, op. cit. (n. 5), Chapter X.
69. Wolman, op. cit. (n. 7), p. 86.
70. Ibid., p. 78.
71. Ibid., pp. 86-7.
72. Ibid., p. 92.
73. Ibid., p. 83.
74. Ibid., pp. 76 and 123.
75. Ibid., p. 142.
76. Ibid., p. 35. Also time and place considerations, p. 125.

77. Ibid., pp. 26-32, and pp. 34-5.
78. Ibid., pp. 106-7, and see pp. 106-12.
79. Laidler, op. cit. (n. 5), p. 86.
80. Remer, C. E., *A Study of Chinese Boycotts: With Special Reference to Their Economic Effectiveness*, Baltimore, The Johns Hopkins Press, 1933, p. 238.
81. Ibid., p. 243.
82. Luthans *et al.*, loc. cit. (n. 15).
83. Rea, op. cit. (n. 27).
84. *New Republic*, op. cit. (n. 4).
85. Kinnear, Thomas C., James R. Taylor, and Sadrudin A. Ahmed, 'Ecologically concerned consumers: who are they?' *Journal of Marketing*, Vol. 38 (April 1974).
86. Harper, op. cit. (n. 38), note 115.
87. Krieger, op. cit. (n. 28).
88. Smith, op. cit. (n. 19), pp. 298-9.

Chapter 8: Consumer boycott case studies

1. The survey research undertaken provided evidence of actual and potential support for consumer boycotts. It also assisted in identifying suitable case studies and the development of the ethical purchase behaviour concept. A survey of Cranfield MBAs sought information on previous boycotts and whether there was potential support for boycotts. As both consumers and managers the sample chosen was considered particularly appropriate. It was also easily accessible and had known characteristics. In essence, an answer was sought to the question: Will people boycott? The response rate was high (64 per cent, 105 responses) and the quality of the response reasonable. There was substantial awareness of the Barclays and Nestlé boycotts (reported here) and, more surprisingly, 10 per cent claimed to have boycotted Barclays. The most prominent issues identified by the respondents as prompting ethical purchase behaviour were: South Africa, animal cruelty and conservation, the Arab–Israeli conflict, and the Falklands campaign; though many other issues were also identified. A question specifically asking about potential support for boycotts over major current issues indicated substantial support, with, for example, 66 per cent claiming they would be willing to boycott businesses that contribute to pollution. This question was identically phrased to one in a much larger survey. The similarity in the response on pollution and also the similarity of the response on South Africa to a South African embassy survey, gives tentative support to the claim that the survey had validity and that the findings are generalisable beyond its small and specific sample.

   It was thought that asking about potential support for a boycott would be influenced by a 'willingness to boycott' factor as well as the issue. Although a few respondents showed a marked antipathy towards boycotts, in this sample support for a boycott seems likely to have more to do with the issue than the appropriateness of boycott action. The findings indicated considerable – or, at least, greater than anticipated – actual or potential support for boycotts, particularly on issues such as pollution, South Africa, animal cruelty and conservation, racial discrimination, and nuclear arms. More than a quarter of the sample described some boycotts as having been substantial and 46 per cent claimed to have boycotted a product for some reason. Thus a pressure group calling for a boycott might be able to command a significant level of support. So the survey provided an affirmative answer to the question: Will people boycott? It did not alert the researcher to many British boycotts not previously identified, but it did contribute to the case study research. It guided the choice of case studies and provided useful material for discussion in the case study interviews. The survey also contributed to the conceptualisation of ethical purchase behaviour. It prompted the realisation that boycotting was simply the most manifest and deliberate form of a much wider type of behaviour.

2. Discussed in Glaser, Barney G. and Anselm L. Strauss, *The Discovery of Grounded Theory: Strategies for Qualitative Research*, New York, Aldine, 1967. Saturation means 'no additional data can be found whereby the sociologist can develop properties of the category' (p. 61).

3. Mitchell, J. Clyde, 'Case and situation analysis', *The Sociological Review*, Vol. 31 (1983).

4. Case studies are often incorrectly criticised on the basis of their lack of representativeness; such critics ask: How do you know your cases are typical? Representativeness is not necessarily relevant to the case study method. Concern with it is then epistemologically erroneous and reflects a failure to recognise the interrelationship between epistemology and research methods. Some sources suggest representativeness can be viewed as temporarily irrelevant, that cases may be exploratory or can be developed to include supposedly necessary, quantitative, and statistical procedures, to provide representativeness. Although these sources are useful in acknowledging the value of case studies, they still make the inaccurate positivist assumption that inference can only take place where there is statistical analysis. Representativeness can be irrelevant because the cases are intended to have an entirely descriptive theoretical purpose or, as here, because inferences are to be made which are theory dependent rather than correlations which are based on representativeness. The validity of explanations or theory derived from the case studies depends on the logic of the analysis and acknowledgement of *ceteris paribus* conditions, not on how typical the cases may be. There is an important distinction between logical inference and statistical inference. See ibid. for a detailed exposition of the logic of case study analysis.

5. The cases draw on interviews with representatives of the various interested parties as well as many secondary sources. The author is grateful to the many people who gave up their time to discuss these cases with him. The cases are described in more detail, with the acknowledgement of principal sources, in Smith, N. Craig, *Ethical Purchase Behaviour and Social Responsibility in Business*, PhD thesis,

Cranfield School of Management, Cranfield Institute of Technology, 1985. For the Barclays case, also see *idem*, 'A strategy for corporate social responsibility: the case of the withdrawal from South Africa by Barclays Bank', paper presented to the Seventh Annual Conference of the Strategic Management Society, Boston, 14-17 October 1987.

6. Her Majesty's Government, *Code of Conduct for Companies with Interests in South Africa*, Cmnd. 9860, London, HMSO, 1986.
7. Longford, Charles, *South Africa: Black Blood on British Hands*, London, Junius, 1985, p. 12.
8. Lipton, Merle, *Capitalism and Apartheid: South Africa 1910-1986*, Aldershot, Wildwood House, 1986, p. 365.
9. First, Ruth, Jonathan Steele, and Christabel Gurney, *The South African Connection: Western Investment in Apartheid*, London, Temple Smith, 1972.
10. *Financial Times*, 25 November 1986.
11. Ball explained that the withdrawal was principally attributable to a drop in market share to 6 per cent in the student market compared with a 25 per cent share overall and US pressure (in response to a question by this author at the White Plains International Conference on South Africa in Transition, October 1987).
12. Sampson, Anthony, *Black and Gold*, Sevenoaks, Coronet Books, 1987.
13. 'CND's next 25 years', *New Statesman*, 18 February 1983.
14. The *Daily Telegraph* reported: 'Tarmac Construction, "blacklisted" by Peterborough City Council after winning contracts for the proposed cruise missile base at RAF Molesworth, Cambs., is closing its regional office in the city with the loss of 20 jobs.' ('20 jobs go at banned firm', *Daily Telegraph*, 1 August 1985).
15. Andrews, Geoff, 'Ridley aims to prevent political conditions in council contracts', *The Guardian*, 22 October 1986.
16. The text of the statement read: 'MAN has supplied over the last 10 years a number of truck tractor units to the West German Army. One of these, a cross country all wheel drive unit, has been supplied for some eight years. More recently MAN won a contract to supply 450 of these truck tractors to the US Army. The Army is in turn using them to pull cruise missile transporters. Volkswagen is not involved in any way. The only link between the two companies is a joint production and marketing agreement involving the MT 6-9 tonne truck range – a purely civilian vehicle. Neither Volkswagen nor MAN make any missiles, missile transporters or missile launchers. Both companies are commercial enterprises engaged in the pursuit of their normal business — making and selling trucks, buses and cars. We believe the CND action against MAN is misguided. Action against Volkswagen and against Volkswagen owners and dealerships really is stretching the point beyond credibility. We do not believe that reasonable people will support CND in this action and do not expect it to have any effect on our business.'
17. The sole data source for this case is Professor Geert Hofstede, Dean at Semafor, Arnhem. He kindly supplied materials and answered

questions on the case that went beyond his published version: 'Angola coffee – or the confrontation of an organisation with changing values in its environment', *Organisation Studies*, Vol. 1, No. 1 (1980).

18. This case has been widely documented. See, for example: Post, James E., 'Assessing the Nestlé boycott: corporate accountability and human rights', *California Management Review*, Vol. XXVII, No. 2 (Winter 1985); Chetley, Andrew, *The Politics of Baby Foods: Successful Challenges to an International Marketing Strategy*, London, Frances Pinter, 1986.

19. Ibid.

20. Clarkson, Fred, 'The taming of Nestlé: a boycott success story', *Multinational Monitor*, Vol. 5, No. 4 (April 1984).

21. An important data source for this case, which addresses these issues, is: Brown, Jerald Barry, *The United Farm Workers Grape Strike and Boycott, 1965-1970: An Evaluation of the Culture of Poverty Theory*, PhD thesis, Cornell University, 1972.

22. See Chapter 4.

Chapter 9: Effectiveness in the use of boycotts and management responses

1. His advice to writers. It might also be good advice for firms, as indicated here.

2. Churchill, Charles, *Night* I.311. From the *Oxford Dictionary of Quotations*, Oxford, Oxford University Press, 1979 (third edition).

3. BTR did not report for the period 1 July 1981 to 30 June 1982 (the 1983 report), but did report the following year.

4. The author showed an organiser of National CND a possible strategic planning procedure for pressure groups incorporating the consumer boycott tactic. While the respondent considered it appropriate, he explained that it was not likely to be realised within CND.

5. Body Shop newsletter.

6. The poster showed a woman carrying a bleeding fur coat and carried the copy: 'It takes 40 dumb animals to make a fur coat. But only one to wear it. If you don't want animals to be gassed, electrocuted, trapped or strangled, don't buy a fur coat.'

7. See for example, Bougeois, Jacques C. and James G. Barnes, 'Viability and profile of the consumerist segment', *Journal of Consumer Research*, Vol. 5, No. 4 (March 1979), pp. 217-28. They found, in their Canadian study, that 15 per cent of consumers are 'consumerist'.

Conclusions

1. Vogel, David, *Lobbying the Corporation: Citizen Challenges to Business Authority*, New York, Basic Books, 1978, p. 215.

2. Reported in *The Guardian*, business news section, 14 October 1985.

3. See Pharoah, Neale, 'Corporate image research in the brewing industry or From red revolution to country goodness in ten years', *Journal of the Market Research Society*, Vol. 24, No. 3.

4. Mises, Ludwig von, *Human Action: A Treatise on Economics*, London, William Hodge, 1949, p. 271.
5. Lindblom, C. E., 'The science of "muddling through"', in Ansoff, H. Igor (ed.), *Business Strategy*, Harmondsworth, Penguin, 1969.
6. Wootton, Graham, *Pressure Politics in Contemporary Britain*, Lexington, Lexington Books, 1978, p. 171.

Appendix A: Markets and marketing

1. Hunt, Shelby D., 'The nature and scope of marketing', *Journal of Marketing*, Vol. 40 (July 1976).

Author index

Subject index

349